Paul Elmer More

Paul Elmer More

BY ARTHUR HAZARD DAKIN

PRINCETON, NEW JERSEY

PRINCETON UNIVERSITY PRESS

1960

✧

Publication of this book has been aided by the Ford Foundation
program to support publication, through university presses,
of works in the humanities and social sciences.

✧

Printed in the United States of America
by Princeton University Press, Princeton, N.J.

PREFACE

A LEADING American man of letters in the first third of the twentieth century, Paul Elmer More has been praised, disparaged, and disinterestedly discussed as an editor, a classicist, a critic of literature and society, a teacher, a humanist, a Platonist, and a Christian theologian, not to mention his minor activities as poet, novelist, biographer, and orientalist. Though in private life he was an admirable relation, friend, and colleague, even those closest to him, acquainted with the outline of his career and with the facets of his character discernible in their association, had little means of obtaining a reasonably full and intimate account of his personality.

Apart from other causes this was due to his reserve and independence and to the complexity of his nature. Though honored by those who appreciated his abilities, he came nearest to general notice in 1930, when he was mentioned as a possible recipient of a Nobel Prize in literature and when he was drawn into the flurry caused by the publication of *Humanism and America*. For decades he had fought against naturalism for distinctively human values and had prompted others to do so, but a few years before he was hailed as a leader of humanism he had, while endorsing it as far as it went, moved on to theism. When his early Calvinistic piety succumbed to rationalism and romanticism, he came under the influence of medieval and Vedantic mysticism and passed through a phase of vague religiosity before ending in a blend of Anglicanism, Buddhism, and Platonism. He has been called the finest English-speaking critic of ideas, literature, and religion since Coleridge, Matthew Arnold, and Newman. In religion he could, on account of his reverence for spiritual realities as he apprehended them, subscribe without reservation to no prevailing creed; despite the catholicity of learning and taste in his *Shelburne Essays*, he was more a moralist than a literary critic in the narrower meaning of the words; and that traditional moralism made him less a

Preface

detached and widely piercing than a sincere and frequently sound thinker. Tradition, however, did not shackle his individualism; his Platonism, for example, was as uniquely his own as were his approaches to literature and religion. In short, when anything deeply concerned him, disregarding the usual labels and categories he courageously followed his feelings and convictions. His distinction came from within rather than from any occupation or position that he adorned.

This volume would chart the main course of his inner life against a rough chronicle of his daily doings, in the hope that the data thus assembled may serve those inclined to interpret them. When practicable, his own words have been used in preference to others for their generally greater authority, grace, and immediacy, and as a means of offering a selection of extracts from his correspondence.

It has been infeasible to do equal justice to his books, few of which are now in print. Unfortunately far more quotation from them than could here be indulged in would be necessary to convey their substance to a generation that has been unable to obtain and read them. Apart from a clue to their contents, most of the material in the *Shelburne Essays* and *The Greek Tradition* has had to be ignored in favor of scattered passages showing the thread of his noetic life as distinguished from his wide-ranging erudition. Nevertheless his works, which first made him partially known, may themselves be better understood as expressions (as the more important of them were) of a character memorable for a high degree of frankness, wisdom, and integrity. The record of such a man in grappling with serious artistic, ethical, philosophical, and religious subjects, in trying to strike a balance between the constructive and the destructive forces in his nature, may provoke and reward thought even in those least congenial to his temperament, methods, and conclusions.

Because attention to the development of his inner life makes that topic loom larger in his consciousness than it did among

Preface

his varied interests and warm sympathies, as far as compatible with that central theme many of his traits great and small are here included, in order to present him in the round and at his average or better. The conflicting responses that he evoked proves how difficult it is to write about him without intrusive subjectivity; but the duty to weigh as well as to depict him has in this book been largely performed by Mr. More himself, whose introspection—often keener than criticism from without —in the course of time tended to reveal to him the strengths and weaknesses of his personality that others would observe.

Childhood and youth having languages of their own, what he wrote has been copied as exactly as possible in the first chapter. Thereafter in heretofore unprinted matter hasty abbreviations and obvious errors have been silently corrected to conform to the rather flexible standards he adopted in preparing his manuscripts for publication.

Brevity and avoidance of confusion or of repetition account for most of the deletions. Now and then a phrase likely to offend someone as an individual rather than as a representative of a group or of a point of view has been dropped without substantial distortion; for sharp as Mr. More's words could be and severe his judgement, he was notably free of personal ill will. Also, very rarely, it has seemed right to prevent the identification of certain people, though this necessitated the omission of episodes unusual but indicative of the quality of his heart and mind. A slight acquaintance of his, for instance, on going insane sought asylum in Mr. More's house. His host, after persuading him to see a doctor, instead of hurrying the intruder to a hospital with humiliating publicity for his guest, treated him like an unhappy member of his family, until relatives came for him a few days later.

As scarcely a fact or idea or expression follows for which someone has not already been thanked (though none can be blamed for the use to which his or her gift has been put), the omission of the sources of several quotations and paraphrases

Preface

is due not to negligence, ingratitude, or plagiarism, but to the informants' stated or presumed desire for privacy. As a rule they were willing that whatever they said or wrote should be published, provided attention was not attracted to themselves. For this reason they usually asked that the comments with which Mr. More continually encouraged his friends in their undertakings be left out; and this has ordinarily been done, with the result of presenting a slightly better picture of his discrimination than of his affection. Eventually most of the material on which this book is based and much more not currently known or available will probably find its way from its present possessors into libraries (that of Princeton University being particularly appropriate), where whatever is now dark will then be light.

You could not read these pages without the gracious permission of Mr. More's daughters, Mrs. Harry B. Fine and Mrs. E. Gilbert Dymond, to publish letters under their control; without the recollections and information they unstintingly provided; and without their kindness in supplying, among masses of other papers, the letters he received from Dean Louis Trenchard More, who furnished the other half of the fraternal correspondence and reminiscences of great value, enriched by those of his daughter, Miss Catherine Elmer More, now Mrs. Douglas W. Olcott. Mrs. Edward Anson More was among the few people then living who remembered her brother in his infancy, childhood, and youth; she assisted also, with her son Mr. Lucius Elmer More, as an enthusiastic and expert guide to houses, schools, and other places in St. Louis, where Paul Elmer More passed most of his first twenty-eight years.

Others (several no longer with us) to whom thanks are due for hitherto unpublished material by, to, or concerning Mr. More and printed in this volume are *The Atlantic Monthly*, Mrs. Irving Babbitt, Professor Maurice Baum, Reverend Bernard Iddings Bell, Mrs. Joseph Colt Bloodgood, Mrs. Archibald A. Bowman, Reverend Richard W. Boynton, the Trustees of Bryn Mawr

Preface

College, Professor P. R. Coleman-Norton, Mr. Seward B. Collins, Columbia University, Miss Mary Gates Cone, Mr. Samuel P. Cowardin, Jr., Mr. S. E. Dubbel, Mr. T. S. Eliot, Professor George Roy Elliott, Professor Norman Foerster, Mrs. Prosser Hall Frye, Reverend George E. Ganss, S. J., Miss Marie R. Garesché, Dean Christian Gauss, Professor Marcus Selden Goldman, Professor James L. Hagerty, Harvard University, Henry Holt and Company, Miss Sylvia Holt, Dean Lynn Harold Hough, Houghton Mifflin Company, Professor Percy H. Houston, University of Illinois, Dr. Thomas H. Lanman, Dr. Folke Leander, University of Leeds, Professor C. S. Lewis, Professor Frank Jewett Mather, Jr., Reverend Cyril N. McKinnon, S. J., Mr. Robert Elmer More, Reverend Hugh H.F.O. Morton, Professor Edward DeLos Myers, Miss Erna Obermeier, Oxford University Press, Professor William Lyon Phelps, Mr. Lawrence E. Philbrook, Mr. Carr W. Pritchett, Mr. Philip S. Richards, Professor Robert Shafer, Mrs. Stuart Pratt Sherman, Professor Norman Kemp Smith, Professor William Mode Spackman, Professor Alan Reynolds Thompson, Professor Willard Thorp, Professor William P. Trent, Mr. Paul F. Vaka, Professor Austin Warren, and Mr. John Frederick Wolfenden.

Though many others have supplied indispensable but either not directly or lengthily quoted information, some among them, not listed above, for their special pains deserve more than a private expression of appreciation: Professor David F. Bowers, Reverend Rockwell S. Brank, Mr. James M. Breckenridge, Mr. James A. Carr, Professor Edward F. D'Arms, Mr. Vest Davis, Reverend William G. Eliot, Jr., Professor Warner Fite, Professor Theodore M. Greene, Mr. J. Hugo Grimm, Mrs. W. A. Hawkins, Professor Asher E. Hinds, Mrs. Hamilton Holt, Mr. William E. Mills, Mr. Hoffman Nickerson, Professor Robert Scoon, Professor J. Duncan Spaeth, Reverend John Martin Thomas, and Mr. William C. Vandewater.

Grateful mention should be made of the kind help of Mr.

Preface

and Mrs. Harry B. Fine, Mrs. Alfred Brooks Merriam, and the Princeton University Press in suggesting ways to improve this book while it was in manuscript; of the courtesy of Mr. More's daughters and the Press in permitting the use of many pages under their copyrights; and of the permission of Houghton Mifflin Company, G. P. Putnam's Sons, and the Society for Promoting Christian Knowledge to quote from their publications.

CONTENTS

ILLUSTRATIONS

Following page 62

ABBREVIATIONS

A   *Anglicanism*: The Thought and Practice of the Church of England, Illustrated from the Religious Literature of the Seventeenth Century, compiled and edited by Paul Elmer More and Frank Leslie Cross, London (Society for Promoting Christian Knowledge), 1935

BF   *Benjamin Franklin*, by Paul Elmer More, Boston, New York, and Chicago (Houghton Mifflin Company), 1900

CF   *The Catholic Faith*, by Paul Elmer More, Princeton (Princeton University Press), 1931

CIE   *A Century of Indian Epigrams, Chiefly from the Sanskrit of Bhartrihari*, by Paul Elmer More, Boston and New York (Houghton Mifflin Company), 1898, reprinted after 1919

CNT   *The Christ of the New Testament*, by Paul Elmer More, Princeton (Princeton University Press), 1924

CW   *Christ the Word*, by Paul Elmer More, Princeton (Princeton University Press), 1927

DA   *The Demon of the Absolute*, by Paul Elmer More, New Shelburne Essays, vol. I, Princeton (Princeton University Press), 1928

EP   *The Evening Post* (New York)

GR   *The Great Refusal: Being Letters of a Dreamer in Gotham*, edited by Paul Elmer More, Boston and New York (Houghton Mifflin Company), 1894

HOP   *Helena and Occasional Poems*, by Paul Elmer More, New York and London (G. P. Putnam's Sons), 1890

HP   *Hellenistic Philosophies*, by Paul Elmer More, Princeton (Princeton University Press) and Lon-

Abbreviations

don (Humphrey Milford, Oxford University Press), 1923

IND   *The Independent* (New York)

JL   *The Jessica Letters, An Editor's Romance*, New York and London (G. P. Putnam's Sons), 1904

M   "Marginalia," Part I, by Paul Elmer More, *The American Review* (New York), Nov. 1936, vol. 8, no. 1, pp. 1-30

N   *The Nation* (New York)

OBH   *On Being Human*, by Paul Elmer More, New Shelburne Essays, vol. III, Princeton (Princeton University Press) and London (Humphrey Milford, Oxford University Press), 1936

P   *Platonism*, by Paul Elmer More, second edition, revised, Princeton (Princeton University Press), 1926

PB   *The Prometheus Bound of Æschylus*, translated with introduction and notes by Paul Elmer More, Boston and New York (Houghton Mifflin Company), 1899

POD   *Pages from an Oxford Diary*, by Paul Elmer More, Princeton (Princeton University Press) and London (Humphrey Milford, Oxford University Press), 1937

RP   *The Religion of Plato*, by Paul Elmer More, Princeton (Princeton University Press) and London (Humphrey Milford, Oxford University Press), 1921

SAR   *The Sceptical Approach to Religion*, by Paul Elmer More, New Shelburne Essays, vol. II, Princeton (Princeton University Press), 1934

SE I   *Shelburne Essays*, First Series, by Paul Elmer More, Boston and New York (Houghton Mifflin Company), new edition, no date, copyright 1904

SE II   *Shelburne Essays*, Second Series, by Paul Elmer

Abbreviations

More, Boston and New York (Houghton Mifflin Company), reprint of Aug. 1930, copyright 1905

SE III   *Shelburne Essays,* Third Series, by Paul Elmer More, New York and London (G. P. Putnam's Sons), 1906

SE IV   *Shelburne Essays,* Fourth Series, by Paul Elmer More, Boston and New York (Houghton Mifflin Company), reprint of Dec. 1922, copyright 1906

SE V   *Shelburne Essays,* Fifth Series, by Paul Elmer More, Boston and New York (Houghton Mifflin Company), new edition, no date, copyright 1908

SE VI   *Shelburne Essays,* Sixth Series, Studies of Religious Dualism, by Paul Elmer More, Boston and New York (Houghton Mifflin Company), new edition, no date, copyright 1909

SE VII   *Shelburne Essays,* Seventh Series, by Paul Elmer More, New York and London (G. P. Putnam's Sons), 1910

SE VIII   *The Drift of Romanticism,* Shelburne Essays, Eighth Series, by Paul Elmer More, London (Constable and Company) and Boston and New York (Houghton Mifflin Company), 1913

SE IX   *Aristocracy and Justice,* Shelburne Essays, Ninth Series, by Paul Elmer More, Boston and New York (Houghton Mifflin Company), Oct. 1915

SE X   *With the Wits,* Shelburne Essays, Tenth Series, by Paul Elmer More, Boston and New York (Houghton Mifflin Company), 1919

SE XI   *A New England Group and Others,* Shelburne Essays, Eleventh Series, by Paul Elmer More, Boston and New York (Houghton Mifflin Company), 1921

SL   *Student Life* (Washington University, St. Louis, Mo.)

Paul Elmer More

1

ST. LOUIS (1864-1888)

EDWARD ELMER (believed to be a grandson of John Aylmer, or Elmer, consecrated bishop of London in 1568) helped his minister, Thomas Hooker, to found Hartford, Connecticut. Edward's grandson, Daniel Elmer, taught and preached in New England and New Jersey. Daniel's son, another Daniel, renouncing his father's Congregationalism or Presbyterianism and becoming a Baptist, disinherited any of his children who might aid or abet Presbyterianism—an invitation to defiance that, with typical Elmer independence or self-will, most of them accepted. One of these, Ebenezer Elmer, of Cedarville and Bridgeton, New Jersey, who served seven years in the Revolution, practised medicine, was speaker in the state legislature, a member of the House of Representatives, a brigadier-general in the New Jersey militia, and for several years a judge, remarked in his old age: "However much, amidst the alluring vanities of the world, I deviated from Christian integrity, the Bible was ever precious to me, and I can heartily recommend it to others as containing all things necessary to make us wise unto salvation, and to lead us safely through life."[1] His only son, Lucius Quintius Cincinnatus Elmer, an officer in the War of 1812, a member of the twenty-eighth Congress, and attorney general and justice of the Supreme Court of New Jersey, saw with some dismay the third of his four daughters—Katharine Hay Elmer, a short, dark, sensitive, retiring girl with well cut features—married in 1846 to Enoch Anson More.

This blond, blue-eyed man of muscular medium build with a

---

[1] *Genealogy of the Elmer and the More Families*, compiled by L.Q.C. Elmer, with additions by Brookes More, Boston (Cornhill Publishing Co.), 1930, p. 60. *History of the Early Settlement and Progress of Cumberland County, New Jersey; and of the Currency of This and the Adjoining Colonies*, by L.Q.C. Elmer, Bridgeton, N.J. (George F. Nixon, publisher), 1869, also provides information about the Elmers.

gift for drawing and mathematics, an appreciation of painting, sculpture, music, and poetry, and a longing to be an architect, which was thwarted by the necessity of doing something more practical, had little apart from his personal qualities to commend him to the Elmers. His father, Enoch Hudson More, of Bridgeton, a Presbyterian elder, owner of a woolen mill, and a member of the New Jersey state senate in 1844, never saw his own father, Enoch Moore (as it was then spelt), who died of black fever in a camp of the Continental Army near Philadelphia.

The young couple, fervent Calvinists, in 1859 followed their minister, James H. Brookes, from Dayton, Ohio, where Enoch Anson More's business of buying, selling, and binding books had failed, to St. Louis, Missouri. There, as in Dayton, he became a Presbyterian elder, an office that he held until his death. He also superintended Sunday Schools in St. Louis, including the Biddle Market Mission with a membership of about a thousand pupils. During the Civil War he was enrolled in the Missouri state militia as a brigadier-general in the commissary department. In his rented, small, brick house on the south side of Papin Street west of Fourteenth Street on December 12, 1864, was born the seventh of his eight children, his fourth son, whom the Reverend Doctor Brookes on April 16, 1865, at the Sixteenth Street Presbyterian Church[2] christened *Paul Elmer*.

Bright, sensitive, conscientious, genial in talk, swift in laughter, with a pale white skin that easily blistered and bled profusely, sharp, small, weak, grayish blue eyes, and hair that darkened from gold to brown with auburn glints, throughout his childhood Paul remained undernourished, anaemic, and so frail that as he returned one day from his class in the Stoddard School[3] on the corner of Lucas Avenue and Twenty-Eighth Street he had to be carried into a saloon until a hail storm passed that had beat him to the pavement.

[2] Then commonly known as the "Walnut Street Church"; now called the Memorial Presbyterian Church of St. Louis.
[3] Since enlarged and renamed the Banneker School.

His emotional, reticent father, "almost a minister in bearing," respected in that border state by Northerners and Southerners alike and attractive on account of an irresistible gregariousness manifesting itself not in familiarity but in a natural suavity of manner, tried various businesses—hardware, wholesale grocery, and the purchase in bulk and sale in smaller lots of nails, tobacco, oil, starch, glass, and other things—with results ranging from years of moderate success to months of impoverishment. He saw that his children had morning and evening prayers, grace at meals, church on Sunday, and no dancing or gambling at home. In relaxed and companionable moods he took his youngest sons Paul and Louis[4] shooting and fishing, activities that never appealed to Paul, though he shared his father's liking for nature.

Free of the diffuse emotionalism that disquieted her husband and that with ill health and ill luck caused him to become irritable and morose in his later years; unable to share his leanings towards mathematics, fine arts, and field sports; cool, definite, and undemonstrative—Mrs. More concentrated on the toil of rearing their many children. Secretly proud of them but afraid of feeding their or her own vanity, she avoided praise and practised an understanding firmness. Not unaccustomed, since her marriage, to poverty, she warned them against the deceptions of life and impressed upon them the necessity of industry and thrift. About 1872 Brigadier-General More ordered built for his family a three-story brick house with a brownstone front and a mansard roof, in "a nice yard and a big garden,"[5] where Paul picked gooseberries, in the suburbs of St. Louis at 3113 Washington Avenue. Here in the room where her children played, Mrs. More rested after lunch, waking only to calm a quarrel or to soothe an injury. Her nap over, she read enough from the Old and the New Testaments to ensure her completing

[4] Louis Trenchard More, born 1870.
[5] Undated letter from P. E. More to his oldest surviving brother, Enoch Anson More, Jr., nicknamed "Ainsie," who was born in 1854. A yet older brother, Lucius Elmer More, born in 1851, died in 1854.

[5]

the Bible once a year. Whenever she could read at all, as while dressing a baby or knitting, she propped a book on a table or chair beside her; and Paul soon delved into books as insatiably as his mother.

Her daughters, Katharine ("Kate") and Alice, respectively about seventeen and fifteen years old at the time of Paul's birth, aided her—the former (brilliant, artistic, erratic, domineering) chiefly in housekeeping, the latter in looking after Paul and Louis. On Sunday afternoons, while their father slept, when the boys, not permitted to leave their yard or to welcome playmates there, tired of sitting on the fence and talking to their neighbors, Alice read aloud to her "babies," as she called her youngest brothers, from Milton, Shakespeare, Southey, Bunyan, or the Bible, so exquisitely that she held them spellbound, at times so movingly that little Louis burst into roars and tears.

"ther are 2 ways to do every thing," Paul affirmed in one of the sermons that, at about ten years of age, he used to write on odd bits of paper as he sprawled on the floor, "they are the right and the rong and ah there are two ways of being christian that is pretending to be a christian the ernest and the unernest or the right and the rong to be ernest we hafto love and try to be like Jesus we cant be perfect but we can be as near perfect as we can. and must not think we are the best people in the world because we pray 3 times a day and because we go to church and because we pray in the corners of the street. we must think that we are no better that any other person that is that god thinks more of us than any other person. we must pray 3 times a day but we must pray secretly as daniel did. . . . we must not talk to Jesus as we would to the winds and the waves but we must talk to him like we would to one of our friends and with the feeling that he hears us and that he cares for our prayers . . . some people believe in Jesus and some dont. some people are lost from god. But god sais. I will not forsake them that seek me. But these people wont seek god, and so loose him. and others seek and find him. The Lord sais in anothe place. Ye

[6]

shal seek me and find me, when ye shall search for me with all your heart. . . . (so there are two way to love) loving god and loving the devil. a sinner loves the devil and a christian loves god. a cat loves meat and a bird loves bread or crumbs. there are to ways to do every thing the GOOD and the EVIL."[6]

Religion, if his deepest interest, competed with the wanton wiles that make the young Adam father of the old. By suddenly applying the brake from the rear platform of a horse car, he used to jolt the passengers. After wedging pegs into the turn-table at the end of the line, he would, with suitable impatience or sympathy, watch the driver find and remove them in order to turn the car for its run back to the city. On a Fourth of July, having tossed a pack of lighted firecrackers into a car, Paul tied its only door shut so that no one could escape before the explosion.

Though catching barehandedly Jim's[7] relentless pitching disfigured some of his fingers and though he lost a front tooth playing "old sow," fighting and wrestling with Louis took no toll. Peritonitis and typhoid fever further taxing his fragile constitution, he passed much of his time indoors, enjoying the usual games of a large family, inventing others, and devising new languages each with its intricate grammar. Tearing from books and magazines their own definitions of words, he and his brothers pasted and sewed them together into vocabularies and dictionaries. The More boys could sleep Saturday mornings until ten or eleven, a privilege denied to their young neighbors, who used to call to them to come down and play. As Paul described

[6] Parts of three sermons are combined in this quotation. His first publication, written about this time, was printed under the caption "Little Paul's Hock Sermon" by a former pastor of his in *The Presbyterian*, vol. XLV, no. 23, June 5, 1875, p. 11. Cf. *JL*, 50-51, and *POD*, v.

[7] Until about 1918, after which he preferred to be called Brookes, Brigadier-General More's sixth child and third son, James Brookes More (born 1859), was known to his family as Jim. Cf. *Life and Poems of Brookes More*, by Wilmon Brewer, Boston (Marshall Jones Co.), 1940, which contains photographs of L.Q.C. Elmer, Brig.-Gen. and Mrs. Enoch Anson More, Brookes More, Enoch Anson More, Jr., Paul Elmer More, Louis Trenchard More, Mary Caroline More, and Alice More.

through his window the chores Mrs. More had assigned to her sons, the children beneath it would volunteer to do them while he dressed and breakfasted, provided he rewarded them afterwards, as he did hour after hour, with tales of adventure (like Jacob Abbott's Rollo stories) drawn from his imagination.

In the second-story back room where they slept, Paul insisted that, as the elder, he had the right, despite objections, to warm his cold feet on Louis's back. Ainsie, Jim, and Paul, stripping and painting their bodies with phosphorous matches, would steal around Louis's bed like ghosts, which so terrified the child that he used to flee for safety to the bathroom near his mother's door. These diversions, however, did not discourage Louis from singing when he woke. Paul, too, would sing now and then mockingly a different tune until Louis, losing his own, bawled with frustration. On investigating one of these outbreaks, Alice found Louis lying on the floor roaring in his characteristic way and Paul sitting in a corner with his face to the wall alleging that he was thinking. One of the strongest remembrances of his boyhood, Louis confessed, was of being so coolly tormented by Paul that only inability to devise a sufficiently torturous way of doing so prevented him from killing his tormentor.

A nightly paganism for many months accompanied their daily Presbyterianism. Paul, then about thirteen, produced a small shrine (the size of a shoe box) of the goddess Khâla, a spirit, like mana, imperfectly personified, who reigned from this tiny temple. Before going to bed in their dark room, Louis knelt in front of the shrine and prayed to Khâla, while Paul, austere in priestly night clothes, led the service. When Louis sought guidance from the goddess, she answered by flashing the word YES or NO into his dazzled eyes. Bowing before her in the morning, he would submit to her his conduct of the previous day. Paul, her hierophant, whirled in the air a short black rod, one end of which was red, the other blue. If the blue end first touched the floor, Louis's conduct pleased the goddess; his reward, a cheerful conscience. Had Louis, however, been saucy to his sacerdotal brother or otherwise offended Khâla, the invariable hitting of the floor first by the red end indicated the necessity of a sacrifice—a cent or an edible delicacy slipped through the slot in the top of the temple. Scientific experiment and mystic insight proved that the goddess responded most favorably to maple sugar. Once a month, their room sealed against betraying gleams of light, as the church bells struck midnight the devotees stealthily celebrated a sacred feast with Khâla. In addition to the pickles and candy they had secreted, Khâla herself fed them; for the bits of maple sugar formerly deposited in her temple miraculously emerged as new, whole cakes. But the zeal of her house ate them up. Into her mysteries they decided to initiate a friend who stayed with them over night. Having supped heartily on strawberries and cream, the neophyte found the ritual banquet so much beyond his capacity that adults had to be called in—with the usual blighting effect.

His first two years at high school (1880-82) Paul passed at Branch High School No. 1 on the corner of Seventh and Chestnut Streets, and his third (1882-83) at Central High School, Fifteenth and Olive Streets. He graduated June 15, 1883, with a grade of 90.2 for the complete course, which included three years of Latin and English, two of German and chemistry, and one each of arithmetic, algebra, geometry, geology, zoology, physiology, history, and natural philosophy. Though his grade surpassed the class average by about ten points and was unequalled by any of the boys who graduated with him, two of the girls in his class slightly excelled it.

Possibly the school's best public speaker and debater, at the thirteenth Annual Exhibition of the St. Louis High School Literary Society on May 26, 1882, he delivered an oration on "Our Country," and at his graduating exercises one on "The Fall of Constantinople." As president of the Literary Society, after beginning with a well delivered, soberly received address of welcome, he would conduct a meeting with a maturity beyond his years. The formality—which on official occasions or among strangers verged on pompousness—of this short, slender, erect, painstaking student with distant or downcast eyes drew ridicule from his companions. His long aquiline nose brought him the nickname "Paulus Hook." Not an easy mixer, he nevertheless bore teasing well, but if angered, pale to begin with, he became completely colorless, while retaining his iron control of speech and bearing. During the half hour recess at noon he was rarely seen in the narrow, brick-paved yard, where most of the huskier boys, dividing into sides and trying to keep a baseball flying from one to another within the same team, engaged in chaotic scrimmages. Anyone unable or unwilling to take his medicine there by catching a swift ball passed the rest of his life under the suspicion of being a butter-fingers. Where physical exertion and courage were indispensable, however, Paul showed, as when caught in a storm while rowing on the Mississippi, no lack of stamina and resolution.

He skated with the energetic, forthright, boisterously laughing Henrietta Beck, two years his junior, about five feet five, dark haired, with clear, high-colored complexion, hazel eyes, a negligible nose, and a sweet disposition, who, living but two doors from the Mores' and playing continually at their house, became almost one of their family. For her, Cary T. Hutchinson, and a few other friends he conducted a stenography class for about eight weeks in his father's dining-room. He could never talk enough with Bertha Obermeyer, a South Street Jewess, one of the two girls leading his class in scholarship, whom until almost his dying day he associated with poetry and music.

At a birthday party given for Nettie Beck early in January 1883 by her mother's sister, Mrs. Clifford Richardson, Paul met Clara Gardiner. The beautiful fifteen-year-old blonde instantly inspired his tongue and pen. After Sunday School at the Biddle Market Mission, where she and Nettie taught some of the younger children, he would pursue them as they walked home together, explaining breathlessly that he had been delayed by counting the collection, for which, as an assistant to his father, he regularly passed the plate. On his frequent calls he brought poems to "Agricola Clarissima," wrote acrostics about her, and discoursed vividly on his reading and studies, or else listened while she sang to him her favorite Scotch and Irish ballads. She revealed to him, so he claimed, the insignificance of reason and character in comparison with the surrender of self to feeling; she opened to him a new heaven and a new earth; his love for her, he vaunted, would enable him to do wonders. In ardent letters he discussed Bulwer-Lytton's *Zanoni* and the Cabbala and cited passages from Novalis as casually as he quoted Heine in conversation.

In the summer of 1884, while visiting his mother's relatives in Bridgeton, he joined a group of his contemporaries daily for tennis, boating, or picnics by a wooded lake. Their derision of him for taking himself and his intellectual ambitions seriously he met with ready repartee. Swimming and flirting with the girls did not prevent his mailing a proposal of marriage to his Agricola Clarissima in St. Louis. The missive first caught Mrs. Gardiner's eye. After steaming the envelope open and reading its contents, she told Clara she was too young to know her own mind. The determined mother dictated a polite note of rejection, which her obedient, miserable daughter wrote and mailed. Thereafter Paul received no answer to the letters he addressed to her and was turned away at her door. His last words to her reached her soon after they had been composed:

In Memory of an Autumn Day
(October 16, 1886.)

I.

There is a time ere winter comes amain,
Like peaceful twilight's calm that holds awhile,
When many things seem leaguers to beguile
The hours of labor from us, with the strain
And waste of getting; when the winds are fain

To cease their moil; and, like a sleeper's smile,
A misty veil is spread o'er sharp defile
And rugged top to smooth each line of pain.
I know not what the cause may be, I care
Not to inquire: yet with each dropping leaf,
And with each hushing of the drowsy air,
And muffling of each sound, some worldly grief
Is borne away, some thought we would not bear,
And gentle dreams steal in with sweet relief.

II.

Here will I lie beneath this spreading tree
And woo the sweetness of the day:—the stream
Of clouds o'er yonder boughs, moves in a dream
That through the bars of wakefulness I see;
The hidden brooklet murmuring stealthily,
Bears on its bosom mingled sounds that seem
As echoes borne from unknown lands; the scream
Of solitary crows that heavily
Move o'er the trees, is but the farewell cry
Of darker thoughts that leave me here alone;
The breeze that creepeth up the hill with sly
And wayward steps, whispers in trembling tone
Of hopes I dare not hope, of hopes so high
They flit like visions o'er me and are gone.[8]

In the meanwhile Brigadier-General More had been obliged
to sell his Washington Avenue real estate and to rent a modest
brick house on the east side of Lay (now Euclid) Avenue.[9]
There Kate's increasing nervous instability added to the family's anxieties. Distance and poverty reduced Paul's contacts

[8] *HOP*, 73-74.
[9] Variously numbered 1520 and 1742, the house was near that of his
third daughter, Mary Caroline ("May," born 1856), who after her marriage in 1879 to her cousin Edward Anson More ("Ned") had gone to
live on Côte Brilliante Avenue.

with former friends. At times eggs from their own chickens and the little milk they could afford to buy stood between the Mores and starvation. Without a legacy from Mrs. More's father, who died in March 1883, they might have foundered. By its aid Paul enrolled that autumn in the College of Liberal Arts at Washington University.

But for Alice's devotion he could not have continued; for during his first three years his eyes gave out so often that he had to bathe them in hot water, remain in a dark room, and for weeks at a stretch put books aside. On these occasions Alice read his assignments aloud to him in English, Latin, French, and, possibly, German, and studied enough Greek to help him learn that language. His periods of partial blindness and her keen and wholehearted tutoring strengthened his powers of concentration and memory.

Most of his amusements he sought at home. He played tennis fairly well; an occasional ride on one or the other of his father's two horses proved more than enough; delighting in natural scenery, he liked to walk; and during the sultry summers, whenever he was not working in a bank or a jewellery shop, he read contentedly in a hammock under the trees by the house. He used to play his wooden flute while Louis, a self-taught pianist, accompanied him on the Steinway salvaged from Washington Avenue.

"I snatch this time to write to you from a day devoted to poetizing," he began an undated letter to Alice in the spring of 1886. "To tell the truth I am writing rather extensively to a *new* one—'fair, kind, and true.' You see I am taking advantage of your absence to give my feelings or fancies, or whatever you may call them, a loose rein. In this case at least I am and shall be innocent. The weaker sex opened battle first and I only take the defensive. The yard is so beautiful now with the violets and lilacs that I can't help weaving a little web of their fragrances to snare another's favor—verstehen Sie? . . .[10]

[10] Cf. *HOP*, 6.

"I believe Jim misses you more than any one in the house, as he has now only one critic to refer to—Kate doesn't count in poetry—and that one not altogether satisfactory. It really seems pitiful to me, he is getting so dependent. Indeed he acts as if he could not rely on his own judgment in the matter at all; and almost invariably accepts my emendations. Sometimes I think he doesn't really know what he is writing. I tell him there is a contradiction here and generally he says 'that's so, I didn't notice that,' just as if he wrote pleasing words and read them over afterwards to note any absurdities. I have always considered him the obstinate one, but I believe I ought rather myself to bear the rebuke. Whenever you or he disapprove of my verses, I seem to like them the better for it. I don't know whether you have ruined me or whether it is the natural degeneracy of character but I have almost entirely lost that dependency on others' judgment. Now I form my own estimation of what I write, and favorable or adverse criticism doesn't affect it in the least. Nevertheless I have taken myself into hand concerning this matter of flattery. From the way it is fired at me broadside from certain quarters, I am beginning to fear I must be exceedingly gullable. I often wonder whether they—the girls especially—fire at every body as the[y] do at me. Really—you needn't laugh now—they embarrass me so sometimes that I suffer agonies. Sometimes I console myself by imagining from their discrimination that they must be in earnest; but then girls are fearfully cute in finding out one's weak points. . . ."

A few weeks later he sent Alice this report on a long poem called "Malchus," which he then hoped to publish but which, with most of his youthful writings, he apparently destroyed later. "Te Deum laudamus quum editum sit poema, non prius! In other words, don't crow before you're out of the woods. I was utterly astonished at my feelings when I wrote down the last word of Malchus—indeed I did not feel at all. I had expected to go fairly wild with pleasure & exultation; but it seemed in reality the [most] trivial of matters and my pulse did not even quicken.

I am now making the final copy—hence this violet ink—of the fourth canto and I do not feel as if it were finished until the completed manuscript has left me forever. I would feel a little flat if not *forever*. The new part consists of only ninety odd lines—I looked for 150—but I believe these are quite up to the standard—you know my estimation of the whole. On going over this canto I find that instead of adding I only abridge. The complete poem will not contain over 1750 verses, not one half as long as Endymion. I think there will be about an equal number of verses in the shorter poems."

When Alice's friend, Marie R. Garesché, was about to end a visit at the Mores' on October 20, 1886, he presented her with the following lines:

The loving Master blest whoso but gave
A cup of water in His name: and I,
A pilgrim of the world, beneath a sky
Parched by the climbing sun, would even crave
That blessing on thy head. How good to lave
In waters cool, to drink after the dry
And hot and beaten road! how sweet to buy
From hands whose sole reward is just their brave
And ready cheerfulness! And when this time
Of rest is o'er, the solitary day
Shall seem not quite so long; and like the chime
Of village bells that haunts us on our way,
This draught of thy soul's sweetness in my prime,
Shall be to calm, to strengthen and allay.

The same month there appeared in *Student Life*, the undergraduate publication of Washington University, another poem of his:

To Mrs. Grover Cleveland
(On Seeing Her Picture in Harper's Bazar)

Unconscious bride of Fortune! I, who dwell
Remote and buried in the simple crowd,

St. Louis

Would be a simple voice to cry aloud
Across the continent to thee, and tell
How queenly fair we deem thee, and how well
The crown becomes thy brow. O be thou proud
In tender grace, whilst gathering tempests shroud
The State's horizon and the murmurs swell
Of many fretful winds, to be a sign
Like as the gentle moon o'er storms above,—
An emblem to the world that peace and love
And beauty, in its infinite design
Of calm repose and sweet content, are strong
To bind our hearts and win them from the wrong.[11]

Like "The Haunted Tower," about a lady immured in marble walls and singing forevermore, or "Anacreontic," wherein the poet finds Cupid collecting rose thorns with which to tip his arrows, many of Paul's verses are simply exercises. Others unite a romantic feeling for the world without to a longing for a sort of holiness within, like that of the youthful Jonathan Edwards for "a sweet, pleasant, charming, serene, calm nature; which brought an inexpressible purity, brightness, peacefulness and ravishment to the soul."[12]

My heart shall be a paradise
   Begirt by varied mountain;
And there amid the trees shall rise
   Full many a balmy fountain.

And there shall be eternal spring
   And ever-blooming flowers;
And there the nightingale shall sing
   In unmolested bowers.

And there I'll walk upon the hills
   And in the vernal meadows;

[11] SL, Oct. 1886, vol. 10, p. 19.
[12] SE XI, 41, quoting Edwards.

Or dream beside the purling rills,
And watch the flitting shadows.

And thou shall be the angel sent
To guard the gleaming portal,
That never sin may enter in,
Or hateful thought and mortal.[13]

Besides writing poetry he read and discussed with a brilliant girl, Clara Sherwood, some of the works of Spinoza, Kant, and Hume. In his earnest ignorance he identified "the spirit of Christianity" with the "particular formulation of theism" in which he had been bred. The personal religious faith of the Bible on its way to him through Calvin's *Institutions* had become predominantly rationalistic, a development of the logical consequences of conceiving God "as the absolute unconditioned Cause of all things." As such in his uncritical childhood and for his ancestors in their pioneering and active lives it had maintained an impressive "authority over the conscience" and had provided intellectual "consistency to the fluctuating world of the spirit." But also it had "ruthlessly evicted," in its "form of belief" and "practice of worship," "the office of the imagination and of the aesthetic emotions."[14] Depending too much on logic alone, it collapsed rather than righted itself when its limitations became obvious to more searching and disinterested thought.

"I began to question the very notion of a God so constructed; and I can remember the hour when these doubts reached a climax and forced me to make a final and so far as Calvinism was concerned, irrevocable decision. It was a Sunday morning service, and the minister, a powerful and eloquent expositor of the creed, was preaching on that terrible text: 'And this is the condemnation, that light is come into the world, and men loved darkness rather than light, because their deeds were evil.' He

[13] *SL*, May 1886, vol. 9, no. 9, opening contribution (page unnumbered).
[14] The quotations in this paragraph are from *M*, 23-25.

[17]

spared not, and I knew that, properly applied, the words of the text were true; but did they apply to that theological system the preacher was urging me to accept? Here was a question of reason, not of the choice between good and evil."[15] "The doctrine was bred into my bones; I saw the folly of it intellectually, but the emotional comfort of it was the very quintessence of my life. . . . Was I too deliberately turning my back on the light? I hid my face and cried. That was the end. I came out of the church free, but I had suffered too much." Perfect faith, "which nothing can replace," "passed from my life."[16] ". . . with belief in the inherited dogmas of a sect went the whole inheritance of Christianity. . . . I left the church that forenoon as one goes out of a spiritual home to wander in the bleak ways of an alien world."[17]

On returning from his business, doubtless expecting merely to read his paper and then sit silently as usual all evening while Alice, Paul, and Louis carried on their exclusive and lofty conversation, Brigadier-General More in amazement found Paul in tears. He could not, he told his father, any longer take communion;[18] Calvinism was not only unscientific but a substitution of metaphysical absurdities for the facts of religious experience; though it meant breaking with his family in what they most cherished, there was no other way out. His mother, as distressed as himself, thought her boy "lost"—a conviction that remained, softened by love and time, a sad rift between them. But his father, to Paul's gratitude, understood; he seems to have shown nothing but respectful sympathy as from then on his son groped along his own religious way.

"Quasi Deus," an anonymous[19] article in the December 1886 issue of *Student Life*, preserves a contemporary if faint reflection

---

15 *M*, 24-25.   16 *JL*, 51-52.   17 *M*, 25.
18 Paul had joined the Second Presbyterian Church in St. Louis in 1876.
19 The reference in that article to Jacob's wrestling with the Lord appears again in a similar context in *GR*, 97. Also the article displays lines of thought about religion that continued the rest of Paul's life.

of the "unspeakable agony"[20] Paul then endured. "There is but one alternative," the article asserts, "pantheism or religion, a mere first cause . . . or a finite God of goodness. . . . Philosophy must conceive God as infinite, and hence without attributes, an unknowable force informing a creation not distinguishable from the creator. Thus it inevitably falls into pantheism, avowed or unavowed. . . . Religion must worship Him as hating iniquity and loving righteousness, a finite father and ruler. . . . Surely the Bible does not teach an infinite God in that verse which contains the whole gospel, 'God so loved the world, that he gave his only begotten Son,' etc. We know the stickler may quote an abundance of texts, such as I Cor. xv. 28, to prove that God is all in all. We can only retort that these, too, are reachings out into the darkness, philosophical gropings not religious; that the very existence of every religion demands the estrangement of man from God and the reality of sin, hence a finite God. And this is not irrational; it is as logical as any philosophy, only starting from a different premise. . . .

"Here, indeed, is a hard matter; impersonal or finite, which shall it be? Ay, like Jacob, we have wrestled with the Almighty until the breaking of day, and cried, Tell me, I pray thee, thy name. And He has touched the hollow of our thigh that we are lame; but has He blessed us? Rather have we gone out under the stars, baffled, halting and crying in bitterness, What is truth? away with it! Beauty and feeling shall be our gods."

At Washington University Paul for four years took exercises in English composition and courses in mathematics, physics, and American and European history (with emphasis on government and international law). Latin, French, and English literature he studied for three years; botany, for two; ethics, elocution, German literature, chemistry, mineralogy, geology, astronomy, physiology, logic, Hamilton's metaphysics, and political economy, for one year each. With Greek, which was required of him for the freshman year and the first semester

[20] *JL*, 51.

of the sophomore year, he might have continued longer had it been taught better. But apparently deeming the enjoyment of Greek literature beyond the capacities of youth, his instructor used the language primarily as a means of disciplining the mind. For him this consisted less in cultivating taste, imagination, and judgement through intimacy with a great civilization than in overloading memory with rules of Greek accent set forth, with all variations and exceptions, on eleven pages of an obsolete grammar, which, with archaic forms of words, his pupils had to learn by heart and rattle off with precision. Nevertheless compared with the "mental grip" needed to master physics, mathematics, Latin, and Greek, the effect of training provided by the "non-mathematical sciences on the immature mind," Paul concluded, is "almost negligible."[21]

In addition to his college courses he steeped himself in German romanticism—Tieck, the Schlegels, Novalis, Heine, and Goethe, his "god for years."[22] Only one student ranked ahead of him in chess, several games of which Paul could play at a time blindfolded. His steady contributions of prose and verse to the undergraduate magazine led to his election in May 1886 to the presidency of the *Student Life* Association. His shyness and gentleness combined with his recognized intelligence and integrity made him less popular than respected. But his indifference to sports and to many of the ordinary concerns of undergraduates caused him to appear, in the eyes of at least two of his contemporaries, critical, self-centered, unsociable, and aloof. "He felt his superiority," one of them complained, "and was at no pains to hide it."

With a four years' average of 83.81 he graduated on June 9, 1887, the only one of his seventeen classmates to receive the Bachelor of Arts degree *cum laude*. As part of the commencement ceremonies he recited "in an easy conversational manner, his oratory on 'astrology.' The subject matter was good and his delivery excellent."[23]

[21] *SE* IX, 47.   [22] To Erna Obermeier, Jan. 28, 1935.
[23] *SL*, June 1887, vol. 10, pp. 158-59.

1864-1888

At Smith Academy—then a department of Washington University, housed in a large, ugly, brick building (and a small annex) on the corner of Nineteenth Street and Washington Avenue, which had an annual attendance of about three hundred boys preparing for "college, polytechnic school and business"—Paul worked as an Assistant in 1887-88 and 1889-90, as teacher of the Fifth Class in 1890-91, and as teacher in charge of the First Year Class in 1891-92. With faculty and learners he seems to have got on well—almost too well with a woman instructor whose pursuit he had some difficulty in eluding. His natural dignity alone maintained order. "You would have thought of jumping out of the window," one of his pupils stated, "as soon as doing anything mischievous in his classroom."

He seems to have taught arithmetic, beginning Latin, and English. His clarity, methodical ways, and intellectual keenness stimulated the boys, no matter how sadly elementary instruction failed to satisfy his own capacities. In order to interest his pupils in books, he gave them ample opportunity to read them aloud and discuss them. "I had a class of young boys in a subject which seemed to me and to them little better than a waste of time," he wrote later about one of his courses; "so I used to take that hour to talk with them about all sorts of extraneous matters. . . . Well, it is like enough the information they got from me was more curious than useful; but I at least learned a truth I shall never forget. I learned the capacity of the boy's intellect, his eagerness to think, his willingness to search . . . for knowledge if his taste is once fairly whetted."[24]

[24] "Children's Books," by "P.E.M.," *N*, Dec. 2, 1915, vol. 101, no. 2631, p. 651.

2

EUROPE (1888-1889)

LONELY, bored, and disgusted to tears, the first night on the S. S. *Nebraska* More retreated to the hurricane deck, where he watched "the water and the moonlight streaming across it, and the sailors at work in the rigging of the foremast. I do not know a more romantic scene than this spreading of the canvas, the peculiar shrill whistle of the boatswain and the 'Heave ho, haul away,' of the hands."[1] The next day he began making acquaintances rapidly; with every wave his buoyancy increased; and on July 1st the "sail up the Firth of Clyde" impressed him as "lovely beyond description—hills and mountains rising precipitously from the water, or sloping down with sides fresh and green."[2]

Quickly leaving Glasgow he "tramped over Edinburgh from one end to the other," where the "guides and keepers" reminded him of "Edison's patent phonographs."[3] After glimpses of Melrose Abbey and Abbotsford, he sailed for Hamburg. Cologne cathedral passed into his "very life as a symbol of wonderful beauty."[4] But a feather bed at Coblenz—"a most ingenious instrument of torture worthy of the German intellect"—caused him to dream he was "at a prayer meeting. The audience was large and there were a number of ministers on the platform. Silent prayer was called for and we prayed and prayed for an hour or two. Finally somebody said amen and we raised our heads. Then one of the ministers held up an enormous boot and said, 'Here is a boot-full [of prayer] for the Lord!' "[5]

[1] To Alice More, June 23, 1888.
[2] To the same, July 1, 1888. Cf. *RP*, 310.
[3] To Brig.-Gen. Enoch Anson More, July 3, 1888.
[4] To Alice More, July 21, 1888.
[5] From a fragment of a letter by P. E. More attached to his letter of July 17, 1888, to Mrs. Edward Anson More. The interpolation in square brackets is More's.

1888-1889

He met Mrs. Richardson, her niece, Nettie Beck, and others of their group at Frankfurt am Main and, again, after he had tramped in Heidelberg, at Baden-Baden, where "beauty comes down to the very doors of the houses and is not far off as in most places."[6] Music, walks, theatre, wine, and poetry sped the days like a dream. At a booth by the entrance to the Garden— "the foreign biblical society planted in the very gate of Vanity Fair"[7]—he bought a Latin testament and psalter, and memorized the first two psalms. "Whenever I return to Latin after an interval of other tongues, I am struck again with its majestic rhythm and its grand harmonies. There is no doubt of it: Latin is the language of my heart. Others I appreciate but Latin I love."[8]

At the end of July and the beginning of August as he wandered alone among the Alps[9] he became so distraught by meditation on sin and separateness, a "mood in which Satan and his angels have taken possession of me,"[10] that he could not write home what was in his mind. This summer seems to have belonged to that period when "thoughts of God were supplanted by a morbid introspection and the practice of worship gave way to indulgence in a self-commiserating egotism. Naturally I was lonely and unhappy; but the more wretched I grew, the more assured I became that my isolation was the sign of a grand mission; somehow my very despair was to be the saviour of myself and of mankind. Under that malign spell I composed lyrics and tragedies and, at the last, a huge epic[11] . . . which should portray the long conflict of humanity, the war between the personal will and impersonal law, the contest of doubt with faith, the opposition of centrifugal inert matter and central force. As champion in this struggle[12] . . . I myself figured as the Wandering Jew, whose curse began with Cain's murder of Abel and was renewed at his contemptuous rejection of Christ on the

---

[6] To Alice More, July 21, 1888.   [7] *Ibid.*
[8] *Ibid.*   [9] Cf. *SE* III, 166, 172.
[10] To Alice More, Sept. 1, 1888. Cf. *SE* I, 24-26, 40.
[11] *POD*, v.   [12] *GR*, 146.

[23]

way to the cross[13] . . . until at last reconciliation came in submission to all-controlling, all-embracing Fate. . . .[14] Fortunately those ebullitions of a frenzied imagination went into the flames."[15]

Fortunately, too, at Gletsch he chanced upon Mrs. Richardson and her companions on their way to Rigi-Kulm. When they left for Munich, he went down to Rigi-Klösterli, "a most detestable place," to a *pension* "full of women in various stages of homeliness. I shut myself in my room except for eating and walking and never spoke to anybody. My hair was hideously long and I think they took me for some sort of bedlamite. Two English damosels sat next to me who would converse until one evening at supper when one of them asked me something I turned to her and said, 'Did you hear the noise this afternoon?' —'What noise?'—'When I was fighting with Satan!'—I don't know what she thought, but I know it shut her up."[16]

On the way to Munich a few days later, "I found myself in a 'Nicht Rauchen' compartment with a party of French people consisting of father, mother, two young children, and maid. Such a spoiled child as the younger I never saw in my life—and such an incompetent useless mother I never saw. I wanted to give them both a good shaking. The nurse and mother spoke English and likewise the children when they would. At last late in the evening I asked the little boy if he would like to hear a story. He sat on my lap for a while but soon grew tired as he did not know enough English to understand. But the girl two or three

---

[13] *POD*, v.   [14] *GR*, 146.

[15] *POD*, v. How factual this report is no one can say on account of the fictional elements in *GR* and *POD*. Apparently no contemporary evidence remains of More's "project of a New Philosophy which should prove once for all that the world and men are the product of a fatalistic Law of Chance and Probability." [*POD*, v.] He knew, however, the fascination of mathematics and "felt that exaltation when the mind opens to the thought of illimitable dynamic law. . . . There is the imagination of science as of religion. Some minds may dwell in one and the other of these alternately, or even confuse them together. . . ." [*SE* VI, 168-69. Cf. *M*, 25.]

[16] To Louis T. More, Aug. 26, 1888.

years older was interested and I kept her quiet for some time. Such an idea as trying to amuse the poor little wretches did not seem to have [entered] the head of any of the party."[17]

At Munich besides inspecting churches, museums, and royal stables, he went with Mrs. Richardson, Nettie, and some of their friends "to a garden exhibition—lights, music, emperor of Austria. . . . One thing I never [saw] before was illuminated fountains which looked like streams of colored light. These with gay society, champagne, and music made things enjoyable."[18]

From late August to late September at the house of Frau Hofrath Sauter, Augusten Strasse 17, Stuttgart, but for his "strict vows," bad German, and the constant presence of her mother, Paul felt he might have made "desperate love"[19] to his landlady's younger daughter. In addition to attending the theatre and feeding the fish in the Schloss Garten ("the noise of their sucking sounds like a whole regiment of cows walking through the mud"[20]), his "chief amusement" was to explore "the Hasenberg, a hill just outside of town heavily wooded. Here one can have the 'Waldeinsamkeit' to his heart's content. Two days ago while walking in the woods in rather a desperate mood, it suddenly occurred to me to write a tragedy on Edwy, king of England. . . . Today I wrote most of the first scene—rather a long one—in prose. Part of it I expect to write in poetry. I was astonished to find I wrote it so readily. . . . I believe I shall be able to do my best work in the drama—comedy and tragedy. But then I confess I am totally unable to judge what I have written in this case. Likely enough I shall never finish it."[21]

Some three weeks later: "I am laid up again blind from too steady application. Here I sit like a dumb thing with my books scattered about me and my tragedy all completed save the last two scenes. I can not read or write a word for weeks. Even this letter is a breach of discipline. . . . Most of the day I spend

[17] *Ibid.*   [18] *Ibid.*
[19] To Brig.-Gen. Enoch Anson More, Sept. 12, 1888.
[20] *Ibid.*   [21] To Alice More, Sept. 1, 1888.

walking up and down the room or lying flat on my back on the lounge. I have created a new world in my fancy since I have been here and were it not for that I don't know what I'd do. In the evening I walk for an hour or two. Twice now I have [met] the Fräuleins without speaking to them I was so absorbed in this 'new created world'. . . ."[22]

To be settled before the University of Berlin opened on October 16th, he expected to go to that city about September 28th. But, changing his mind, he went instead to France, having first made a pilgrimage to several places associated with Goethe and having "climbed the spire of Strassburg (a feat of real danger), not because I was fond of such things, but because my hero had done so to cure himself of giddiness."[23]

In Paris on October 14, 1888, More was introduced by Henry Otis Chapman, a student of architecture staying in the same *pension* at 86 Boulevard de Port Royal, to three American girls, Clara Thacher, Harriet Murphy, and Mary Gates Cone, who, with their chaperone and a maid, were touring Europe. The next day, when the five of them inspected the Luxembourg, Mary Gates Cone—"a rather quiet girl, but full of mischief, having a glance from the eye and a curl of the lip, sarcastic enough to raise seven devils in one so susceptible as myself"[24]—and Paul drifted away from the others and went about by themselves, as they continued to do the rest of her fortnight in Paris, talking, laughing, walking without end.

He was then a short, slight, well-proportioned young man weighing about one hundred forty pounds, of poised but not nervous movements, with fine features and a pensive, colorless, pleasant expression free of anxiety or dissatisfaction, smiling easily and breaking into hearty and quick response. From his college days onwards, as his friends observed, his clothes, except in hours of physical recreation, were notably neat—"a matter

[22] To Alice More, Sept. 24, 1888.
[23] To Erna Obermeier, Jan. 28, 1935.
[24] To Louis T. More, Nov. 29, 1888.

of significance to him," as he later remarked about John Ingle-sant and George Herbert.[25]

Miss Cone questioned her new acquaintance about his future plans. Despite their indefiniteness, he showed only a quiet confidence without conceit. He discussed religion, not to convince her apparently, but in order better to formulate his own thoughts. If they sounded agnostic and irreligious to the other girls, to Miss Cone their form mattered less than the honesty behind them. What charmed her most in him was an ardent search for truth, a beauty of character, an exquisite inner grace.

After they had explored the catacombs, attended "Aïda," strolled through the Madeleine and St. Augustin, climbed to the tops of Notre Dame and Tour St. Jacques, passed hours at Cluny and days in the Louvre, and roamed the Champs Elysées and the Bois de Boulogne, he proposed to her. Informed, however, that another suitor awaited her at home, he urged her to postpone her answer until, after her imminent trip to Italy, she had returned to the United States.

During her Italian tour he wrote to her frequently in prose and verse. Against the near and doleful day when she should cross the Atlantic on the S. S. *La Champagne*, he produced a series of poems for her,[26] composed, "like almost all the verses of any merit I write, . . . during the night while lying awake from strong passions."[27]

". . . if you once get your imagination aroused over mathematics," Paul encouraged Louis, then a freshman at Washington University, "you will find them interesting and absorbing. I felt something toward them as you do until I got deeper into them, and then it was only my regret that I could not devote my life

---

[25] *SE* IV, 81-82.

[26] Cf. *HOP*, 31 ff. Robert Shafer reprinted a few of these stanzas on pp. 297-98 of his *Paul Elmer More and American Criticism*, New Haven (Yale University Press), 1935. Other poems addressed to Miss Cone in *HOP* are "After the Opera" (p. 66), "To a Photograph" (p. 72), and "Reflections" (p. 77).

[27] To Louis T. More, Feb. 4 [mistakenly dated "Jan. 4"], 1889. Cf. *SE* II, 3.

to the study. . . . As for shop-work, my advice is to *cut it to the utmost limit*. . . . time is too precious to be wasted planing boards. But do not neglect drawing. A man who cannot draw—especially I refer to free-hand sketching—is only half educated. I never appreciated this until I came abroad. For one thing a man can not see a thing with precision till he can reproduce it. This you will find true in every branch of life. Only a poet knows poetry, and only a musician knows music. Indeed I am beginning to feel that with all my superficial knowledge, I am cut off by lack of education from the greater part of the world. Drawing I must renounce forever, but I hope to do a little more music when I come home. I can't tell you how much I miss your playing, and how often after the day's work I long to hear one of Mozart's or Beethoven's sonatas. We will study thorough bass this summer as you say. And I will learn much from your playing."[28]

On his twenty-fourth birthday, December 12, 1888, More and Chapman, having met the girls at the station on their return from Italy, took them to "Le Prophète." Two days afterwards Paul and Miss Cone looked for the last time in the Louvre at her favorite pictures and the Venus of Milo. ". . . I bade Miss Cone good-bye and walked home not exactly happy but congratulating myself that it was all over. I purposely made arrangements so as not to go with them to the train in the evening. But Mr. Chapman while alone with Miss Thacher made an engagement for himself and me of such a nature that I could not escape. Miss Cone and I rode together to the station. My strength of mind ebbed away and we are to correspond. This only means that the bitter struggle is put off for another time. Have no fear on one point," he declared to Alice. "I at least have acted and will act honorably; and I will come out without any stain so far as having done her any wrong. I do not care to say more—indeed I am still in no condition to think calmly. Her kiss has burned into my very heart. I have had my last lesson and learned

28 To Louis T. More, Nov. 29, 1888.

the whole matter of love. So help me memory and experience I will not love again till I wed. Would to God I could say I never had. When the passion comes over me I am scarcely master of myself, there is a devil in me. . . . It is terrible as it is ruthless. . . .

"One matter I must speak of. You have all joined the new church.[29] Mother asked me if I wished to take out my letter with the rest, or to let it lapse. I am sorry, more than sorry, I can not go with you. But I know mother would not wish me to belie myself. I do not believe as a Christian should and so far as I can judge myself never shall. I have found God and have learned some peace from this knowledge—but this is not to be a Christian. I am sorry, I say, more than sorry that I can add no more; because I know what pleasure that more might give. Let me work out what faith and charity—perhaps even hope—there are in me in my own way, but do not ask a creed."[30]

He and Chapman grew to be "the best of friends. His character is most admirable in many respects, and well suited to counterbalance some of my weaknesses. He *knows* architecture and has taught me a great deal. He is quite ignorant in all literary and general matters, and in these I have taught him a great deal. Just at present he is reading Byron aloud to me. To keep him agoing I had to perjure myself by flattering his reading, but that is not much. His sense of rhythm seems to be strong and I think he will learn to read poetry with an agreeable singsong. You know I like the rhythm strongly marked in verse."[31]

Two new boarders arrived at the *pension*, an English teacher, "entertaining although . . . a little dyed by his trade," and his daughter, Miss Comfort, "just seventeen . . . a sweet-looking girl who has the most charming naïve manners. I love to talk

[29] When Brig.-Gen. More and his family moved in the autumn of 1888 to the new house built for him at 5889 Plymouth Avenue, St. Louis, they joined the near-by Presbyterian church on Cabanne Place.

[30] To Alice More, Dec. 16, 1888. Cf. *SE* III, 43-44.

[31] To James Brookes More, Oct. [mistakenly dated Nov.] 30, 1888. Cf. *SE* I, 120-21, and *SE* III, 86, 157.

with her just to hear the tones of her voice. Her laughter is as
sweet as the warble of a bird. Oh, it makes me sick to think of
the rasping, nasal, squeaking, unoiled voices of our American
girls. The English have much pleasanter voices and speak English, which is what we Americans do not speak. Really I am
almost ashamed to talk with an Englishman, and am conscious
all the time of the words and accent I use. . . . she sings in the
sweetest, freshest, innocentest manner in the world. . . . You
don't know what an addition it is to my happiness to hear her
at her music. I can think better, work better; and as for dream-
ing—but you know I can do that without any stimulus."[32]

Soon after Miss Comfort's brief pause in Paris, Miss Cone's
postponed answer arrived in the negative. "I am free—free once
more, and there is no one to domineer over my mind and say,
Think thus. She has passed out of my life forever. I followed
the shadow to the very borders of the dusky land, where so
many have gone before. I introduced her to the shades of the
former fair, and departed sorrowing on my way. Now don't
laugh at all this for I speak seriously enough."[33]

"It is now ten o'clock in the evening. I am just home from
the depot to see Chap off. It's the old 'Farewell—a word that
has been and must be.' A shake of the hand, a smile, a wave of
the hat, and the best part of our life is gone. The mocking shriek
of the locomotive was ringing in my ears as I left the station;
and I am not ashamed to say my eyes were wet more than once
before I reached home. The room seems desolate, the very fire
is fluttering in the grate. For three months now we have been
constantly together, for the last few weeks have even slept in
the same room and have been separated scarcely half an hour
in the day. So warm a friendship I never had before and shall
never find again in all human probability, and it is not a little
thing to lose this of an evening—for God only knows when or
how I shall ever see him again. I can not tell you how congenial

[32] To Mrs. Edward Anson More, Dec. 25, 1888.
[33] To Alice More, Jan. 20, 1889.

our intercourse has been. Twice we had a gentle falling out, so to speak, but this only added to our future stock of amusement. His character is quite different from mine but has one point in common, the love of the beautiful in all forms and a mighty desire for something better than this world can give."[34]

". . . one can not begin to appreciate the supreme beauty of those pictures," after about his thirtieth trip to the Louvre Paul asserted to Alice, then a student in Washington University's St. Louis School of Fine Arts, "until he has looked and looked, and a new heart has been created in him. . . . There is a picture by da Vinci called the 'Mona Lisa' which is beautiful beyond belief. The colors are badly faded, but the expression remains; and the smile of the eyes and mouth will haunt me forever I think.[35] I am ashamed to say that when I first saw it I turned away with surprise that it should be so famous and made some silly remark about her catlike smile. . . . I expect to bring home three or four dozen photographs of the old Italian and Spanish masters. . . . Others may admire the Dutch painters, but to me everything, old and modern, looks very tame after the Spanish and Italian works."[36]

Fired by his study of Italian painting and by Longfellow's translation of Dante, Paul bought an Italian grammar. A fortnight later he was "reading Dante in the original; the poem is very absorbing. Without rival I think the conception of it is the most sublime and original ever given to human intellect. The power of expression is at times startling. Read the fifth canto of *The Inferno*. Read it again and then again, and the force of it will fairly master you. That wind which never rests, that cry of love from the very heart of hell, has nothing like it in all literature."[37]

At the Sorbonne and the Collège de France he listened to three or four lectures daily "on all sorts of subjects, art, literature, science, and religion. It is no little thing to hear such men

---

[34] To Alice More, Jan. 28, 1889. [35] Cf. *HOP*, 75.
[36] To Alice More, Jan. 20, 1889.
[37] To Louis T. More, Feb. 4 [mistakenly dated "Jan. 4"], 1889.

as Guizot and Ernest Renan talk. Yesterday was the first time
I had heard the latter. His subject was a critical study of the
Hebrew prophets. The subject was anything but popular (he
studied them in the original) and only a score or more were
there in a small room to attend. I awaited the entrance of the
great scholar with no little interest. Never was I more surprised
than at his appearance. He is quite short and stout and walks
with a hobble. His neck is wanting and his head rises directly
out of his breast. He is clean shaven and his cheeks are fat and
puffy, very broad at the angle of the jaw, and actually hang
down on his shoulders. His forehead is large enough and finely
formed, broader across the brow than above, and only a little
wrinkled despite his age. His gray hair is long and falls down on
either side over his ears. His eyes are rather small, light blue,
slightly asquint I believe, and much inflamed from poring over
crabbed eastern characters. He has a trick of looking sidewise
with them, often half closing the lids. At times he shuts them
entirely as if they hurt him and so goes on talking. You will
judge he is not exactly handsome from this description; but
whether it is from a knowledge of his great learning or from
some quality actually in his countenance, I could not take my
eyes from him; he fairly fascinated me. I understood only a
little of his discourse, because he talks quite indistinctly, at times
impelling his words with difficulty from his half closed lips, and
again letting his voice descend to a mere growl or grumble.

"Have you ever read his 'Vie de Jésus'? To me this was one
of the grandest books I ever read, and expressed almost precisely what I believed. Whether you agree with him or not, his
description of the life of Jesus as a man is beautiful and interesting in the highest degree. At times the sentiment rises almost
to the sublime. I was astonished at the total absence of anything
like mockery, but on the contrary the great feeling of reverence
which pervades the book. . . . The language is pure and exquisitely beautiful."[38]

[38] To Enoch Anson More, Jr., Feb. 7, 1889.

As his stay in Paris drew to an end and as no position awaited him except the one he had held in Smith Academy, he began to "read and think in order to write a Latin commentary on Spinoza for an M. A. . . ."[39] ". . . when I return," he confessed, "I shall not be able to talk either German or French."[40] "However, I have learnt what is of most importance to me, that is to read French with a tolerable accent, and to be able to scan poetry. I shall never attempt to teach spoken French. And I can now pronounce it better than anybody in our university."[41]

Despite his failure as a linguist, he insisted to his mother that "what I have learned in other respects can hardly be calculated. And my character has changed wonderfully. I do not know whether you will see any difference in me, probably very little; but I assure you it is there, and it is treasure inestimable."[42] What rejoiced him most was to have breathed, especially in Paris, "the very art-atmosphere of life," to have been introduced to the "higher life" of the spirit, to a realm endless in its exactions and satisfactions, where he felt himself "a better and a stronger man."[43]

"As I look back over my travels it seems to me that in many ways they were unsuccessful. Many things I did not see which I should have seen. . . . In fact most of the time I was so occupied with certain wanderings of the spirit that the things about me seemed unworthy of notice. To travel from the land of despair to the Kingdom of Content is a long journey, and there is very much to see on the way—ruins, cathedrals, palaces, triumphal arches, which cast a shadow over those one reads of in Baedeker. That journey I have made—O little sister, it was a long, long way. And many a time as I sped in the cars, or tramped through the great cities, or wandered among the silent

[39] To Mrs. Enoch Anson More, Dec. 23, 1888. Cf. *POD*, ix. Washington University awarded More a Master of Arts degree on June 11, 1891 (not 1892 as has been often misstated).
[40] To Louis T. More, Nov. 29, 1888.
[41] To Brig.-Gen. Enoch Anson More, Jan. 5, 1889.
[42] To Mrs. Enoch Anson More, Dec. 23, 1888.
[43] To Alice More, Jan. 28, 1889.

mountains—many a time it all seemed to me only an emblem of the real journey I was making in the spirit realm. Now don't suppose I am coming home gay and lighthearted—such a disposition I never cared to win—but I am coming home contented. I am satisfied to go on with my work doing what I can. My work is more to me than success. Other men may accomplish more, but I am proud to say no man ever aspired higher."[44]

[44] To Alice More, Jan. 20, 1889. Leaving Paris on February 14th for London via Dieppe, he planned to stay a week in England before sailing from Glasgow February 22nd on the S. S. *Indiana*, with the expectation of reaching St. Louis about March 6th.

3

THE GREAT REFUSAL, HARVARD, AND BRYN MAWR (1890-1897)

ON THE front flyleaf of Alice's copy of his first book, *Helena and Occasional Poems*, Paul inscribed on August 12, 1890:

> Sister! nearest of humankind to me,
>   Who in the time of sorrow camest with cheer,
>   And in the days of labor still wast near
> To lend thy larger hope, not as a fee
> For valued time I bring this book to thee,
>   The first-fruits of my life: ah, never fear
>   But that I hold thy priceless love too dear
> For purchasing; I make my offering free
> As thou hast given thy care. And yet I hold
>   It altogether right that men should know
> How not alone my heart has dreamed its dream;
> And how thy fearless love hath made me bold
>   To sing through years of sorrow, and to go
> In dark ways where it gave the only beam.

The volume of seventy-eight pages begins with twenty-five hendecasyllabic, somewhat Theocritean stanzas, all but two of which refer to Helen or, where the metre requires it, Helena. More appears in them as her lover named Mallon, under which pseudonym he had intended until February 1890 to publish the book. They are verses of dalliance in garden and country-side from spring to autumn, when another courter wins "snow-white" Helena's fickle heart. The rest of the book contains poems to Mary Gates Cone and Clara Gardiner,[1] verses reprinted from

---

[1] Louis T. More, according to Robert Shafer ["Paul Elmer More: A Note on his Verse and Prose Written in Youth, with Two Unpublished Poems," *American Literature*, March 1948, vol. 20, p. 50], believed, rightly or wrongly, Helena to be Clara Gardiner. In 1941, however, she

Student Life, and stanzas written while he travelled in Europe and on other occasions.

Before its publication, however, *Helena* was ancient history. The Reverend Doctor Robert Garland Brank, pastor of the Central Presbyterian Church in St. Louis, had two children: Rockwell S. Brank, about thirteen, whose "beauty and grace" unconsciously rendered bearable Paul's "barren year"[2] at Smith Academy after his return from France, and Sarah Warfield Brank, about twenty-one, tall, lean, vigorous, "radiant beyond telling,"[3] whom Paul first met probably in the spring of 1890. Vivacious, kindly eyes, which admirers compared to topazes, animated with gentle humor her cameo-like head, whose rich brown hair heightened the fresh and china-white transparency of her skin. In general appearance she was frequently compared to Queen Louise of Prussia as shown on the stairs in Gustav Richter's painting. With her wit and her appreciation of it in others, her wide interests and versatility, she excelled as a talker. On account of her soft, full voice, so perfect of its kind as to require no cultivation, and her naturally gracious presence, she was a much commended member of the St. Louis Choral Society. As a student in the St. Louis School of Fine Arts she painted exquisite water colors. Her unselfish, sympathetic attention focused on those around her, in whom she found and praised talents they sometimes scarcely recognized. She cherished

---

thought only one poem in the book, "In Memory of an Autumn Day," concerned herself. If, without her knowledge, she inspired certain passages in the Helena poems (those, perhaps, about Helen's hiding in the garden, mocking Mallon when he asked for a kiss on parting, pouting when she thought she should be angry with him, and laughing at him from the window whence she tossed him a rosebud and vanished), other scenes and actions in those poems, when compared with the facts known about his courtship of her, appear either to be imaginary or to concern someone else, possibly the "*new* one—'fair, kind, and true,'" mentioned on page 13 above.

[2] *GR*. 18; cf. *ibid.*, p. 130. This is the boy affectionately referred to in the poem called "The Pedagogue," influenced by James Thomson's exercise in "the geometry of delirium," "The City of Dreadful Night." Cf. *GR*, 19-36, and *SE* V, 170, 184, 187.

[3] *GR*, 131.

many friends, who generally considered her the most charming person they had ever met. In picnics and concerts she delighted but, as a pastor's daughter, in her youth never danced or went to the theatre. Instead she enjoyed the generous hospitality of the manse, where few evenings passed without callers, including suitors enough for Penelope.

The principal record of Paul's most overwhelming love—*The Great Refusal, Being Letters of a Dreamer in Gotham*, "edited," with an introduction, by Paul Elmer More, who would thus cloak his authorship of it—contains letters and poems he wrote to Sadie, as she was usually called. Before its publication in 1894, however, shrinking from any "indecent exposure of personal emotion,"[4] he revised the correspondence to conceal her identity and his; added new material throughout, especially in the preface and at the end; and blended the whole into a strained, melancholy tale. As a result the tone seems to have become more distant than it may have originally been. The young man who could gravely address his sweetheart with, "You have never, I suppose, read the Latin works of Giordano Bruno,"[5] seems, despite a few amorous touches,[6] to have preferred to present Esther (for so Sadie is named in this book) oftener as impalpably fair, a star, a moon, or some other symbol of metaphysical beauty, than as a particular girl of flesh and blood.

In a fictitious love letter written a few years later he tried to explain such a situation. "You complain of my letter because I argue a philosophical proposition in it while pleading for love. Do you not know that this is man's way? And I would not try to deceive you: this philosophical proposition, which seems to you almost a matter of indifference, is more to me than everything else in the world. For it I could surrender all my heart's hope; for it I could sacrifice my own person; even, if the choice were necessary, which cannot be, I might sacrifice you. There is this duality in man's nature. The ambition of his intellect, the passion it may be, to force upon the world some vision of his im-

[4] *SE* II, 84.   [5] *GR*, 50.   [6] *GR*, 102-05, 113.

agination or some theorem of his brain, works in him side by side with his personal being, and the two are never quite fused. . . . That is . . . the eternal dualism in masculine nature which a woman can never comprehend. . . . For a woman is not so. There exists no such gap in her between her heart and brain, between her outer and inner life. . . . She calls the man selfish and is bitter against him at times, but her accusation is wrong. It is not selfishness which leads a man if needs be to cut off his own personal desires while sacrificing another; it is the power in him which impels the world into new courses. A man's virtues are aggressive and turned toward outer conquest and may have little relation to his own heart. But a woman's virtues are bound up with every impulse of her personal being; they work out in her a loveliness and unity of character which make the man appear beside her coarse and unmoral. . . .

"And because of this harmony, this unconsciousness in woman's virtue, a man's love of woman takes on a form of idealisation which a woman never understands and indeed often resents. What in him is something removed from himself, something which he analyses and governs and manipulates, is in the woman beloved an integral part of her character. Virtue seems in her to become personified and he calls her by strange names. For this reason . . . a man's love of woman assumes such form of worship as Dante paid to Beatrice or Petrarch to Laura. It would be grotesque for a woman to love in this way, for virtue is not a man's character, but a faculty of his character. And so is it strange that I should approach you asking for love that my soul may have peace? It cannot enter into my comprehension that such a cry should come from you to me. All that I strive to accomplish in the world, all that I gird myself to battle for, the ideals that I would lay down my life that men might behold and cherish,—is it not now all gathered up in the beauty and serenity of your own person?"[7]

For a while after his repudiation of what he supposed was

[7] *JL*, 162-65. Cf. *SE* II, 171.

Christian dogma Paul tried to retain Christianity's "imaginative beauty." "If religion is a fraud, at least the intricacies of this catholic faith have grown up from the long yearning of the human heart, and possess this inner reality corresponding with our spiritual needs." In the emotional labyrinth of *The Great Refusal* may be traced a fusion of his "Christian symbolism"[8] with his worship of Lady Esther and a subsequent fission of love human and divine.

"At one time in my life I was ready to give up liberty and ambition of thought in order to become a disciple of the faith that promised peace in this world and resurrection in the next; but, thank God, the pride of my intellect revolted from such a betrayal of its nobler, if yet austerer, aspirations. Let me bear my bitterest doubts with me to the end rather than succumb through lassitude to an easy belief promising repose. It is possible to submit with the heart when the intellect rebels: it is the abnegation of all that is divine within us, a moral cowardice not to be countenanced. There are many who believe without reflection, a few who are led captive by honest but shallow reasoning; there are others who surrender to a creed that offers hope, because they are not strong enough to endure the conflict of doubt unto the end. Ah, if I could bow to this Jesus and serve him, not with the serenity of the disciple whom he loved; but if at least the bitterness and isolation of my soul could somehow be brought into his service, transforming the marks of sorrow into the stigmata of victory! If they could be the signs of witness-bearing to a great truth instead of the stigmata of a despair that I am almost ashamed to uncover before you. But alas! alas! *quid est veritas*? we must ask again, and again surrender the Lord to the scoffers of this world.

"And then I thought of that other Master unto whom I am willingly bounden; and of the saying, God is love; and of that other saying, Now abideth faith, hope, and love, but the greatest of these is love. It came to me as a new gospel of deliverance.

[8] The last three quotations are from *JL*, 52.

For if I serve faithfully this Lord of love, and to follow after him cast away all sordid impulses and unclean fancies and unworthy desires and mean affections, shall I not have done what that other Lord Jesus commanded? And if amid the temptations which offer fruition in place of devotion, I hold fast to the true love, deeming its bondage better than the liberty of others, shall I not have taken up my cross and left all and followed him?"[9]

"You ask me if there is nothing better in the world to love and worship than a woman. There is not.[10] I am not a follower of Jesus. I do not know his God, cannot find him, do not hear his voice. The great self-abnegation and passion of Jesus seem to me often a greater mistake; for what blessing has he brought to the world? To miseries which he cannot alleviate he has added only the further miseries of sympathy. I am not a disciple of Dante. His vision of heaven and hell has passed away forever. His faith is a thing outworn. The new vision must somehow be a justification and glorification of the life that is bounded by the narrow walls of time. My eyes are too dim to discern this glory; there is too much of darkness within me. And yet, at times when the thought of you is most vivid, when love comes to me as something from without and above, I do catch glimpses of this vision which make the heart within me leap up for delight. It is the transfiguration of love. It is the image of a beautiful body so strongly imprinted on the eye that all objects are tinged and made radiant by it, and come in some way to strange relationship and similarity thereto, acquiring transcendent loveliness. It is the belief in a moral beauty so firmly implanted in our mind that all the relations of life are colored by it, and the motions of the spiritual world fall into harmony as if circling about this mighty central idea. Such a love may in these days be the revelation we have so long sought in vain."[11]

In 1891 and 1892 Paul read the Latin not only of Giordano Bruno but of Scotus Erigena, Albertus Magnus, and other medieval religious thinkers. His "mighty desire for something

[9] *GR*, 107-08.   [10] Cf. *SE* VI, 350.   [11] *GR*, 122-23.

better than this world can give," his fundamental "obsession of a mystery beyond the senses,"[12] an obsession strengthened by a critical view of phenomena derived from his scientific and philosophic studies, impelled him to investigate whether the "ancient eastern dreamers and pantheists found, in their contemplation of the deceitful Mâyâ and ineffable Brahma, that peace of heart which we of the west so vainly seek."[13] What drew him to "Oriental faith, whether Vedanta or Buddhism, was just this, that it was in fact and efficacy a faith, yet demanded belief in none of the things I had discarded. Here was a creed, if so it might be called, which in its final formulation included no omnipotent God as Creator and Ruler, nor had any apparatus of Platonic Ideas or of an eternal heaven and hell; its appeal (I speak of it always in its most expurgated form) was to what might be called pure spirituality, to something deeper than what we ordinarily think of as 'soul', to that in us which has no attachment or relation to the phenomenal world or to concrete experience. And I saw that by that creedless faith peace was attained and a peculiar kind of saintliness produced."[14]

To further his exploration of Oriental thought he notified Professor Charles R. Lanman on May 24, 1892, of his intention "to study at Harvard next year, with the degree of Doctor of Philosophy in view. My work will be in Sanskrit, Greek, and Latin. My aim is to make Sanskrit my chief study and subordinate my other work to it. To this end I wish to start in next year as well prepared as possible, and expect to devote the summer months to acquiring the elements of the language."

In his thanks to Professor Lanman on June 9th for his advice and for his pamphlet on Hindu pantheism, he added: ". . . it is the philosophic and religious side which attracts me most to Sanskrit." By July 5th, having plunged into a Sanskrit reader and grammar and having questioned Professor Lanman on pronunciation and accent, he reported: "I am putting the best of

[12] *M*, 25.   [13] *GR*, 70.   [14] *M*, 26.

the day's work on Sanskrit but must spare part of my strength for Greek and Hebrew."[15]

In *The Great Refusal* the pretended author concludes that the pursuit of beauty, physical and moral, succeeds up to a certain point at which it becomes "above all things the most dangerous illusion."[16] At that point love of an individual, or even universal Christian charity, attaches us too much to the false realm of selfhood and desire to permit our mystical "readmission into God."[17] Led by the Indian concepts of Brahma and Paramatman he seeks to transcend the dualism between the infinite, eternal, and unchangeable, and the finite, temporal, and changing, by renouncing the latter for the sake of realizing, through abstraction and meditation, the identity of his inner self with the greater and higher Self behind the clouds of illusion. "This conception of the inner and the outer Self, and their essential unity, is undoubtedly the ultimate achievement of thought. And this is clearly to be distinguished from a philosophy that would exalt the individual *Ego* of a man. For the *Ego* says within us, *this is I! this is mine!* and is but a fiction of the brain, rising and perishing with the body: but the Self is precisely that within us which is least individual, which suffers not nor enjoys, which knows neither birth nor death, which is not a portion or emanation of the Eternal, but is that eternal Self."[18]

In the story he first saw Lady Esther as she passed a graveyard. Towards the end of the book, pausing at the same cemetery, he announced to her: "The consummation of my hope is near; my heart has found the mystic haven of rest. Some prophetic import lay in the finding of love here where all the passions of men are quieted, a premonition that love should lead me, not into the fullness of joyful possession, but into the more abiding fullness of renunciation. For love is crucified within me,

[15] More's letters to Professor Lanman in the Harvard University Library were made available by its and Dr. Thomas H. Lanman's courtesy
[16] *GR*, 7.   [17] *GR*, 8.   [18] *GR*, 134.

and henceforth I listen only to the divine voice speaking from the infinite calm of the heart."[19]

"And I think now, Lady Esther, you know what I wish to say, and the harshness of my message is softened. . . . Perhaps mine has been the most unfortunate of human temperaments. A mind that always doubts, united with an imagination that continually reaches after the infinite and finds no abiding place among transient things,—such a union must form a most unhappy disposition. . . . I have boasted that through the intensity and breadth of my love for you I would build up a faith in beauty able to bind the physical with the moral world, and to content my heart. But you have understood my words expressed more an ideal than a reality, and have wisely held my love as a thing fair but insubstantial. The completeness of your life will not be endangered if this is withdrawn from it. The beauty of your life will suffer no real detriment if you do not see me again."[20]

On his way to Harvard late in the summer of 1892, while he and his ailing sister Kate visited a maiden aunt in the garden-encircled house on East Commerce Street, Bridgeton, which had belonged to their grandfather, Lucius Q. C. Elmer, Paul somewhat embarrassed his staid, practical Eastern relatives by frittering his time away on Sanskrit and poetry, smoking cigarettes under the trees, and flirting with young Sadie Westcott, who also happened to be visiting relatives in Bridgeton. He felt some compunction, after he had left, lest his sentimental philandering had shocked her by ending as abruptly as it had begun.

[19] *GR*, 129.
[20] *GR*, 137-38. One acquainted with Paul More at that time and intimately acquainted then, as well as before and afterwards, with Miss Brank and her family, believed that though she requited More's love she rejected him because she felt she could not measure up intellectually to being his wife, because she feared his strange imaginations, and because she sensed beneath his infatuation with her a greater love of things of the mind. So questionable, however, is even the best guess about the causes of another's actions that how and why the courting ended may and need never be known. On her engagement soon afterwards to a Presbyterian clergyman, she returned to Paul the letters he had written to her.

The Great Refusal, Harvard, Bryn Mawr

At Harvard, lonely and green, one of those

> "who veil their worth,
> And offer to the careless glance
> The clouding grey of circumstance,"[21]

he found the university as dismal as his attic room at 32 Wendell Street, Cambridge. Under the supervision of Professor Lanman, who sympathized with his desire to push beyond linguistics to an understanding of the spirit of the Vedas and of the sacred writings of Buddhism, and moved by a book that inducted him "into the reading of Saint Augustine and into the comparative study of religions,"[22] More published his first "learned" article, "The Influences of Hindu Thought on Manichaeism," in the April 1893 issue of the *Proceedings of the American Oriental Society*. "Having dropped away from allegiance to the creed of Calvin, I had for a number of years sought a substitute for faith in the increase of knowledge; like many another I thought to conceal from myself the want of intellectual purpose in miscellaneous curiosity. And then, just as the vanity of this pursuit began to grow too insistent, came the unexpected index pointing to the new way,—no slender oracle, but the ponderous and right German utterance of Baur's *Manichäische Religionssystem*.[23] It would be impossible to convey to others . . . the excitement amounting almost to a physical perturbation caused by this first glimpse into the mysteries of independent faith. It was not . . . that I failed . . . to see the extravagance and materialistic tendencies of the Manichaean superstition; but its highly elaborate form, not without elements of real sublimity, acted as a powerful stimulus to the imagination. Here, sym-

[21] Whittier as quoted in *SE* III, 41.

[22] *SE* VI, 65.

[23] Whether he read this book after reaching Harvard, as might be inferred from his mention of it in a report (in the Harvard University Library) to Professor Lanman of the works he consulted for his article on "The Influences of Hindu Thought on Manichaeism," or shortly before in 1891, the year given in his letter of Oct. 22, 1931, to Professor Robert Shafer, may be open to question, if in that letter he relied on his good but fallible memory.

bolised by the cosmic conflict of light and darkness, was found as in a great epic poem the eternal problem of good and evil, of the thirst for happiness and the reality of suffering, which I knew to lie at the bottom of religious thought and emotion."[24]

Receiving his M.A. from Harvard in June 1893, Paul joined Louis (then a graduate student of physics at Johns Hopkins) for several weeks at a boardinghouse in Biddeford Pool, Maine. Almost daily for swimming, sailing, tennis, walking, or picnics, the brothers called on Nettie Beck at "Stonecliffe," Mrs. Richardson's summer cottage, with its private landing and its great veranda overlooking Saco Bay.

"I have been thinking a good deal in my leisure about my work next winter," More wrote in August to Professor Lanman, "and have come to a conclusion which may surprise you, at least it surprised me. It seems to me I shall do better not to try at all for the Ph.D. and not to write any elaborate thesis to that end. Such a thesis would, it seems to me, occupy too large a portion of my time, and keep me harassed just when I ought to be free for wide and general reading. I shall probably never have such another opportunity for thorough study, and feel it would be foolish to sacrifice the advantage in any way. This will cut me off, I suppose, from whatever chance I had of a fellowship and travel in India; but for some reasons it will be best for me perhaps to make up my mind to look for a position after next year and do what work I can in the best place offered to me. I shall not be able it may be to advance myself as an orientalist, but possibly I may find a position where I can combine teaching Sanskrit with Greek or Latin."[25]

Throughout the next academic year at Harvard he studied Sanskrit and Pali and, for a while, Emerson. Trying to "see why amidst all the confusion and inconsistency of" Emerson's "words he always leaves a definite impression on the mind," Paul concluded: "I believe the secret . . . is laid bare in his essay on Compensation more than anywhere else. . . . He has a wonderful

[24] *SE* VI, 65-66. Cf. *SE* VIII, 149.
[25] Aug. 19, 1893; courtesy of Harvard University Library and Dr. Thomas H. Lanman.

eye to see the two sides of every question. In one page he tells you that the features are the mirror of the soul, and that a beautiful face is index of a beautiful heart: on the next page he sees the reverse and his saints are homely with no loveliness to be seen in them. And so on every subject. It is the observation we all make, though few of us ever stop to wonder at it, or to ask for the reconciliation. In Emerson the reconciliation comes through his perception of the higher ideal beauty of which the lower is only the type. We must watch his words to see whether they deal with things of this world or of the other. Always there are two faces to Nature, always there is one view that is above and about them both. Let me quote a paragraph from his chapter on 'Fate.' There is nothing better in his books.

" 'One key, one solution to the mysteries of human condition, one solution to the old knots of fate, freedom, and foreknowledge, exists, the propounding, namely, of the double consciousness. A man must ride alternately on the horses of his private and his public nature, as the equestrians in the circus throw themselves nimbly from horse to horse, or plant one foot on the back of one, and the other on the back of the other. So when a man is the victim of his fate, has sciatica in his loins, and cramp in his mind; a club-foot and a club in his wit; a sour face and a selfish temper; a strut in his gait and a conceit in his affection; or is ground to powder by the vice of his race; he is to rally on his relation to the Universe, which his ruin benefits. Leaving the demon who suffers, he is to take sides with the Deity who secures universal benefit by his pain.' "

One who "understands the meaning of this double consciousness . . . has no need to study Sanskrit to get at the wisdom of the east."[26]

Early in 1894 word reached him of Kate's death in St. Louis. Death, he observed to Alice, who devoted herself to the care of their parents and worked as an instructor in the St. Louis School of Fine Arts, compels us "to look through the miserable

[26] To Alice More, March 12, 1894. Cf. *SE* I, 75, 252-53.

shadows about us into the spirit-world that is above and about and within. Do you remember how the Athenians went every year from the city along the 'Sacred Way' to the quiet town of Eleusis where the mysteries were celebrated that showed them in symbols the emptiness of life and the meaning of death, the burial, the resurrection, and the new existence?[27] We think it strange that the great poets and statesmen of Athens held to the solemnity of this performance with such childlike reverence. Yet I think every funeral in our days is much the same thing. We go out from the city to celebrate the great mystery in our own fashion. And what a poor, sordid, utterly insignificant matter this life would be if there were no sorrow for the death of those we love and no fear for our own. If the money-getting and the reading of books meant nothing more than the passing of the day. Love too would shrivel up but for death. It is the infinite within us, breathing through us as the wind passes through a forest, that binds us one to another in a mystical sympathy and union. It is in death we see the petty soul that for a time had seemed so important to itself sink into the infinite life, return to its God we say. And those who remain are broken, as if the walls of their individual strength fell at the sound of the trumpet. They too merge their lives into that infinite life where there are no differences. In that union lies the deepest love.

"Am I plain, or do my words mean nothing?"[28]

Except for the professors whose courses he took—like William Watson Goodwin, Lanman, Edward Stevens Sheldon, and Ephraim Emerton, who by their own and their families' hospitality did much to relieve his loneliness—he saw as little of the Harvard faculty as of their students; for "it is hard for me to establish any sufficient bond between my intellectual life and my personal relationships. . . ."[29]

[27] Cf. *PB*, 18-19.
[28] To Alice More, postmarked Feb. 1894, the day of the month being illegible.
[29] *JL*, 36.

The Great Refusal, Harvard, Bryn Mawr

". . . I have made a new tripartite classification of scholars. Mark it well:

"1st. Commercial students, who are working only for their future salary. Many of them are respectable men but naturally the finer results are not to be expected from them. . . .

"2nd. Those penetrated by German influences. I call them after Darwin the *verdammte dutch* with a good strong accent to the first word. They are quite different from the first class and would scorn to be joined with those. They are our hardest workers. Their labors are immense. They publish most of our learned works. Their search for knowledge is sincere and indefatigable. But they exalt the work above the man. They do not know that figs are not to be gathered from a thorn tree, and that the finer results of scholarship come not from study but from living sympathy. They are learned but not cultured. They are strong specialists and sometimes even more than this. Above all they have never learned the difference between knowledge and truth, or wisdom. . . . All knowledge is equally good to them, they do not discriminate. . . .

"3rd. The *Children of Light*, who are briefly what the others are not. These are the *pii vates* who speak things worthy of Apollo. Their light is from within and their happiness only is known by men. They worship the truth and count very much of human knowledge as no better than a burden. I see so many men toiling in science and erudition, and only one or two have I seen who wore his learning with grace. Babbitt is one [of] these few, Norton is another. . . . I wish I could call myself one of this third class, but a sort of intellectual inertia must place me outside the pale of all three classes I fear."[30]

He regarded as providential—as "the fairest and most enduring part" of his college education[31]—his contact, at this critical moment, with one who, by altering "the whole current" of his being, kept him from succumbing to "the most unwhole-

[30] To Alice More, April 14, 1894.
[31] *SE* VII, 67.

some traits" of his temperament.[32] His acquaintance with Irving Babbitt, then twenty-six or -seven years old—"ce grand garçon au teint frais, aux joues roses, au corps massif, la tête engagée dans les épaules, toujours campé dans une attitude de lutte"[33]— began in the autumn of 1892, when they formed the whole of one of Professor Lanman's classes. Besides frequently walking together, the young men met often in More's "narrow quarters. . . . I can see, almost hear . . . [Babbitt] now as he used to pace back and forth the few steps from wall to wall, arguing vehemently on whatever question might be broached, or recounting the adventures of his youth (a strange and mixed experience), pausing at every fourth or fifth turn to take huge draughts from the water jug on my washstand, and pretty well emptying it in the course of an evening."[34]

Although by the time he reached Harvard More was "in a state of transition" and had begun to question the validity of his adolescent surrender to feeling and temperament, nevertheless his religious cravings and "the romantic virus not yet expelled from" his "system" gave him "a predilection for the Sanskrit literature of the *Upanishads*, the *Bhagavad Gîta*, and the Vedantic theosophy."[35] Babbitt's views, on the other hand, moulded by Greek and Latin classics, especially by Horace, "were already formed and fixed."[36] The Buddhistic side of Hinduism and the Pali language, "in which the most authentic record of Buddha's teaching is preserved," appealed to him. With Buddha he challenged "the lazy yielding to the impulses of temperament" and championed "the constant exercise of the active will."[37] ". . . it is easy to see that here was a situation to call out all Babbitt's fighting powers in debate; and nobly did

[32] *POD*, XXXI.
[33] Sylvain Lévi, *Irving Babbitt, Man and Teacher*, New York (G. P. Putnam's Sons), 1941, edited by Frederick Manchester and Odell Shepard, pp. 34-35.
[34] *OBH*, 27-28.   [35] *OBH*, 28, 33.   [36] *OBH*, 28.
[37] *OBH*, 32. Cf. *New England Saints*, by Austin Warren, Ann Arbor (University of Michigan Press), 1956, p. 159.

he respond to the summons. I would never acknowledge defeat, but I was often left prostrate on the field of battle."[38]

His summer at home in 1894 More called "a grand loaf."[39] His brother, Ainsie, married and living in Colorado, sent him for criticism the manuscript of a novel called *Out of the Past*. After recommending that it be entirely rewritten, Paul continued:

"Tell more simply what happens, dwell less on the accompanying sensations. If your narrative is clear, orderly, clean, direct, the reader will himself supply the sensations, just as he would if undergoing the actual experience. . . . Read your work and note the frequent use of such expressions as:—shivers, pantings, shrieks, sickening sensations, shame, terror, prayers, tears, thrilled, pangs, shock, shrinking, fascination, guilt, stifled, loss of manhood, etc., etc.—why, man, is all the world hysterical? The best of it is that this is an error readily rectified; it is chiefly to be remedied by omission, though occasionally softening down will accomplish the result. . . ."[40]

"In conversation, too, you have considerable study before you reach a style at once 'conversational' and dignified. This is a matter, I recognize, of extreme difficulty, but none the less to be sought after. It is much easier to a man who has been brought up in cultivated society; but to us who have seen very little really good society, it must be acquired by labor and study of good models."[41]

Since that spring Paul had been translating the *Bhagavad Gita*, with the thought of publishing it and an introduction to it that he planned to write later, either separately or as a contribution to the Harvard Oriental Series. He reread "carefully and somewhat critically" the *Divina Commedia*, finding it "more wonderful than ever before."[42] Reflections of these occupations appear

[38] *OBH*, 33.
[39] Undated (early summer, 1894) letter to Enoch Anson More, Jr.
[40] Cf. *SE* II, 167-68.
[41] To Enoch Anson More, Jr., Nov. 26, 1894.
[42] To the same, undated (early summer, 1894).

in *The Great Refusal*,[43] which he prepared for publication that autumn. Expecting nothing from sales, he hoped the mere existence of the book might help him a little at Cambridge, where, for the academic year 1894-95, as assistant to Professor Lanman in Indo-Iranian languages, he was to teach Sanskrit three hours a week at a salary of five hundred dollars and to have the rest of his time free for his studies.

Supported by his Harvard professors More negotiated in the spring of 1895 with Martha Carey Thomas for a teaching position at Bryn Mawr. Professor Lanman described him as "remarkably well read, especially on the early patristic literature. As for his not having taken a Ph.D.,—I think you would do wrong to be too careful about what Mrs. Grundy might say."[44] Professor Goodwin, who had "formed a very high idea of the general soundness" of More's "scholarship and of his promise for the future," predicted that "More will grow."[45] President Thomas accordingly offered More, who promptly accepted it, the position of Associate in Sanskrit and Classical Literature for a period of two years, beginning September 1, 1895, at a salary of $1,400 the first year and $1,500 the second.

In the summer of 1896 and possibly in that of 1895 he visited the Ephraim Emertons at their hilltop cottage above the Philbrook farm at Shelburne, New Hampshire—a village in an intervale of the Androscoggin River between Bald Cap (about thirty-one hundred feet high) and the rest of the Mahoosuc Range on the north and Mount Moriah (about four thousand feet high) and its fellows to the south. Across this peaceful valley edged by spruces, firs, and pines—among which canoe birches gleam like nymphs or, on sullen days, streak the woods with white

[43] For example, in *GR*, 117, 118, 119, and 121 appear poems translated from various Sanskrit sources and reproduced (occasionally with a revision) in *CIE*, 63 and 102, 78, 39 and 89 and 122, and 123, respectively.
[44] Charles R. Lanman to Martha Carey Thomas, March 23, 1895; courtesy of the Trustees of Bryn Mawr College.
[45] William W. Goodwin to Martha Carey Thomas, March 31, 1895; courtesy of the Trustees of Bryn Mawr College.

hairs—he could look through a break in the southern range to the peaks of Madison and Adams and to the north sides, mighty, grim, and oppressive, of Jefferson, Clay, and Washington.

He proposed again, for at least the fourth time, in the autumn of 1895. ". . . there is no especial mystery about it," he informed Alice from Bryn Mawr. "You know I always told you Nettie was my fate, and that if should only fall in love with I would ask her to marry me.[46] Well, the condition became rather suddenly fulfilled. I asked her and you see the result. Was I unwise? It must have been rather startling news to you having left us together so recently with apparently no suspicion. Indeed you had little need to suspect then. But more of this when we meet. I think you would rather I should marry her than anyone else you know, wouldn't you? It must make no difference in our relations, yours and mine. Any change there would be for me at least too great a sacrifice to brook. One thing which encouraged me to enter into this new engagement was the fact that you and Nettie were in a way so fond of one another. Does this sound like apologising for what I have done? I don't mean exactly that, and yet I do mean that you must continue to love me just as you always have and that you must be confident that your place in my heart is not usurped by another."[47]

Poverty postponing their marriage, he and Nettie continued their separate ways. At Bryn Mawr he taught a greater variety of subjects than had been borne jointly by several of his predecessors. Each of his undergraduate courses—three in Greek (one on Homer, another on Plato's *Republic*, and the third on Greek literature, particularly Homer, the chief lyric poets, the dramatists, Aristotle, and Plato) and two in Latin (one on Horace and the other on Latin literature, particularly Lucretius, Catullus, Cicero, and Virgil)—ran for two hours a week throughout the year. His graduate course in beginners' Sanskrit, meeting one

[46] More wrote just that—and probably did so on purpose.
[47] To Alice More, Oct. 3, 1895.

[52]

hour weekly during the year, used Lanman's *Reader*. "How is this for regular diet on Wednesdays?" he asked its author. "Write up a lecture on Greek Literature which I dispose of at 12:15. In the afternoon study up Plato for a reading course at 8 p.m. Come home at nine only to sit down to prepare a lecture on Latin Literature to be delivered at nine the next morning."[48]

Students expecting, from Miss Thomas's reputation for bringing brilliant young men to Bryn Mawr, an eloquent lecturer and an irresistible teacher were rather disappointed in him. The range of his knowledge and the sharpness and strength of his mind awed them. He treated them with the greatest courtesy, with inexhaustible patience, responding to an absurd translation with an apt correction, a whimsical smile, or an ironic remark soft enough to check the first trembling tear (the mere sight of which would floor him). When he quietly bade them, "Notice the anacoluthon," a girl might gasp as though expecting to see a snake glide under her chair. In classifying their instructors

"1. a gentleman and a scholar
2. a gentleman but—
3. a scholar but—
4. but—but—"

none would have denied him who conformed so rigorously to the highest personal and intellectual standards a place in the first category. Though he did full justice to his topics, however, most of the girls felt he did less justice to himself and to them. The more attractive they were, the more scrupulously he avoided looking at them. Lecturing with his eyes fixed either on his papers or on the wall behind his audience, he seemed fascinatingly detached and exasperatingly bored. Yet now and then, as in the study of *The Republic* (which he considered the greatest prose work ever written[49]) or of *The Nicomachean Ethics*, his

[48] To Charles R. Lanman, March 6, 1896; courtesy of Harvard University Library and Dr. Thomas H. Lanman.
[49] Cf. *SE* VI, 248.

The Great Refusal, Harvard, Bryn Mawr

enthusiasm for some metaphysical or moral principle would open up to his students horizons beyond horizons, only to be as suddenly closed by a return to routine recitation. If he lacked an actor's adaptation to his audience and if immature girls—"kittle cattle" he used to call them—increased his shyness, he nevertheless enjoyed talking with them after class; and his few graduate students, who met him in small groups, found him companionable and stimulating. In casual conversation on the campus, though he shunned discussion of his personal concerns, he was invariably interesting, easy, and friendly.

"This is a frightful treadmill I have got into," he grumbled to Professor Lanman, "and any word from without is more than welcome. . . . The place has its advantages to be sure. There is good solid work done here—I mean among the faculty—but the life is depressing. We are quite shut off from the world, and ten men could scarcely be more isolated in a convent than are we of Kuserlof and Yarrow cottages. And then with all these women swarming and swirling about I feel like Ulysses tossed about in the μέγα λαῖτμα θαλάσσης. The chief amusement of the men in our few moments of freedom is scandal-mongering. Such tittle tattle I never heard in my life—and ye gods, what tales are told of the poor girls! . . . I went in to the Oriental Club last night and heard enough rubbish talked to addle my brain, and smoked and ate enough to sour my liver, which may account for my gloomy temper today. Talcott Williams read us a paper on 'Was primitive man a modern savage?' Heaven preserve us;—was he? Williams says he wasn't and drew a fine Jean Jacques picture of primitive felicity, a true Saturnian age. Brinton says he was a most disagreeable cannabalistic savage. . . . After the feast of reason came a true Turkish repast prepared for our special indigestion by an Arabian woman, funny little cakes, and preserves, and cucumbers stuffed with spiced hash et cetera, and everything served in inverse order beginning with the sweets."[50]

[50] To Charles R. Lanman, Jan. 19, 1896; courtesy of Harvard University Library and Dr. Thomas H. Lanman.

Fortunately generations of Elmer starch sustained him. "To-day I have been casting up in mind the many things for which I owe gratitude to you," he wrote to his parents with his "best wishes and deepest love" on their fiftieth wedding anniversary, "and this seemed to me the greatest boon, that I inherited a pride of family and a pride of self which enable me to pass through life without overmuch regarding the ways and people of the world, nor coveting overmuch its honors and riches. Per-haps this is not far removed from the religious spirit in which you trained me. May it not be called a form of that faith which makes the invisible world more real than the visible, which my eponymous saint called the substance of things hoped for, the evidence of things unseen? This I count the richest inheritance in life. And if sometimes it seems to you that the pure faith of tradition has become obscured in me, this has been no idle vagrancy of my own mind but a result of the new times. We upon whom the ends of the world are come, must seek out a new form of faith as everything changes around us, a new form, let us say, but still the old faith that God is within us and that we are children of the Father."[51]

He dreamed of being married in the spring of 1897 and of renting a house in Bryn Mawr until one could be built for Nettie and him. As much as his crowded routine allowed, he increased his college activities. To counteract an aesthetic tendency among the girls, he added to his course on Plato a lecture on Pater and Paterism. He spoke to the Philosophical Club on ancient Brahmanism. Having, in answer to the "prayer" of a Calcutta scholar, permitted *The Oriental Miscellany* to be dedicated to him, he was blandly informed that, as its patron, he should contribute at least a hundred dollars towards its publication. Yet on the whole, though his colleagues liked and admired him, he felt himself so much adrift, so superficially engaged in life, that when his contract with the college expired in 1897 and Miss

[51] To Brig.-Gen. and Mrs. Enoch Anson More, April 29, 1896.

The Great Refusal, Harvard, Bryn Mawr

Thomas, who offered to renew it without change, rejected his ultimatum for more pay and less work, he resigned and, with Nettie's understanding acquiescence, went "out into the solitudes to meditate on the paths of ambition."[52]

[52] *SE* I, 204.

4

SHELBURNE (1897-1899)

"THERE'S nothing like that on earth," Augustus Eugene Philbrook replied to More's inquiry in the summer of 1897 for a place where he could work in solitude. Mr. Philbrook's father, however, rather than see Shelburne disgraced by a town pauper, had provided the lumber, and Manson Green, who lived near him to the west, the land, for the three-room cottage the neighbors built a mile down the gravel road from the Philbrook farm for Manson's brother, shiftless old Darius Green. In More's visionary eyes the weathered, red, clapboarded cabin, long abandoned after Darius's death to wandering sheep and barnyard fowls—with a well and a pump near the front door, a clear view to the south, over a rolling pasture, of Mount Moriah, and to the north a sheltering hill of towering pines—seemed idyllic. Once it had been shovelled out, scraped, scrubbed, repaired, and painted, with shelves installed from floor to ceiling in the living room and a Franklin stove set up there and a cooking stove in the kitchen, Diogenes could not have been more pleased with his tub than More was with his hermitage.

"If you ever think of me at all in the midst of your manifold occupations," he addressed Professor Lanman, "you must wonder how I feel now that I have had a taste of real hermit life. My summer was broken up by a thousand different interruptions —many of them pleasant indeed—so that work suffered a good deal. My sister [Alice] and brother [Louis] were here at different times; other friends came, Mr. Babbitt spent a week with me—and in fact I have been alone only for the last two weeks. So you see I am only a very young hermit and not yet hardened to solitude. My house is quite comfortable and cozy, indeed I have never been so pleasantly fixed since I left home. You may be amused to hear how the day passes—and one day is as like

Shelburne

another as are two peas in a pod. I get up about eight, start a wood fire, dress, and make breakfast. This last consists of a cup of good Java coffee and toast—a good enough breakfast for an emperor you see. Then there is a little dish washing and straightening up to do, and about half past nine I am at my desk. I read and write until one when I go to Philbrook's for dinner. The afternoons are a bit dreary. Somehow I don't feel like doing very much, and a long walk with my dog is really the most serious work of that part of the day. Supper I make myself —eggs, wheat, beans, bacon and the like give sufficient variety, and so far I have enjoyed the meal very much. Then at seven I am ready for work again. Two or three pipes sprinkled through the day lend a little zest to life—and altogether the world spins merrily and my heart is light as a feather. I wrote very little during the summer, but have begun in good earnest now, and hope to have something to show for my winter of leisure. I ought to mention my dog and cat which are my companions all day. I told you about the dog, Râj I call him, short for Dharmarâja you know.[1] He has turned out a noble fellow, perfectly docile and a choice comrade. All the ladies this summer admired him so much that I feared the rascal's head would be quite turned. He overcame the temptation however and shows no signs of excessive vanity. If I had to characterize him in a single word, I think it would be Aristotle's μεγαλοψυχία. The cat is only a kitten, but a canny little wretch and a terrible torment to poor Râj. She is thoroughly convinced that Râj ought to supply the place of mother or wet nurse at least. You might suppose he was constructed like the famous statue of Ephesus from the way she roots all over him. His manly soul rebels at this, and when he has stood it as long as possible he shakes her off with a look of ineffable disgust."[2]

"Every afternoon now for about an hour I saw wood for

[1] Cf. *SE* II, 213.
[2] To Charles R. Lanman, Oct. 26, 1897; courtesy of Harvard University Library and Dr. Thomas H. Lanman.

exercise and find it admirable for health and pleasure. It is hard enough work to bring the sweat out, and then you don't know how delightful it is to see the pile of sawed sticks gradually grow larger. It has shown me too how wide the perversity of nature extends. My logs you understand are of regular cordwood length, that is four feet. These are to be cut into three pieces of sixteen inches. Now you would hardly believe it, but it is a solemn fact that each and every one of these sticks has just two knots and these knots are invariably just where I must saw. This makes the work harder, but it also gives me a good lesson in philosophy. Sawing wood is better sport and perhaps an honester employment on the whole than writing, but I can't saw all day, and so for change must exercise the pen a few hours. Just now Houghton Mifflin have my book of Indian Epigrams[3] which they are to publish next fall, also an article on the Arthurian Epos to appear in the February *Atlantic*.[4] *The New World*, a sort of religious-ethical quarterly, has accepted my first paper on Greek Ethics;[5] so you see I am not idle."[6]

The three hermits went for food to the Philbrook farm— Sinha, the kitten, digging her claws into the back of the short-haired St. Bernard puppy, to hold on, and More, the pale, clear complexion of his hatchet face reddened by the winter wind, wading through the snow with in one hand his staff (which Râj chewed like a pencil) and in the other a basket for provisions, or a small milk can, or a pail into which the hospitable Philbrooks poured corn meal mush for the dog's delight. Neither too obvious nor too distant, he seemed to them "always just right, as nice a fellow as you could ask for." With their elder daughter he spoke German; when a younger, kept out of school by illness,

---

[3] *A Century of Indian Epigrams, Chiefly from the Sanskrit of Bhartri-hari.*

[4] Anonymous review of *King Arthur and the Table Round* . . . , by William Wells Newell, *The Atlantic Monthly*, Feb. 1898, vol. 81, pp. 278-84.

[5] "Two Famous Maxims of Greece," *The New World*, March 1898, vol. 7, pp. 18-35.

[6] To Mrs. Edward Anson More, Nov. 30, 1897.

fell behind in her French, he helped her with her lessons. If the children surreptitiously pinned up the sleeves of his overcoat, he would obligingly exaggerate the difficulties of getting into it again. When deep snow prevented the daily walk that kept him, except for occasional colds, in constant health, he skated with them on the Androscoggin, while Râj, wary of the ice, ran barking up and down the bank.

He saw hardly anyone in winter except these neighbors. Once, lonely and "hungry for emotion," he started on "a complete set of Dickens" from the village library. Overlooking the lack of style and the strain of vulgarity that later distressed him, he "read them through—read them as only a starved man can read, without pause and without reflection, with the smallest intermissions for sleep. It was an orgy of tears and laughter, almost immoral in its excess, a joy never to be forgotten. . . . For there is a right and a wrong way to read, or at least to enjoy, Dickens. . . . he who opens his Dickens must be ready to surrender himself unreservedly to the magician's spell. And then, what a place is this into which he is carried!"[7]

Having arranged with the Philbrooks for the care of Râj during his absence, after a visit to Cambridge in February 1898 he stayed, until his brother's return for the summer vacation from the University of Nebraska (where Louis then taught physics), at home in St. Louis, looking after his father, now in painful decline, while Alice, gradually becoming the invalid she was to be for the rest of her life, went to Europe.

"Last night as I was reading to you my paper on Nemesis," he recalled in a farewell letter to his sister, "I kept thinking to myself all the time of the family Até that seems to have pursued us with the malignant envy of the gods. Who is responsible for the ill luck that has followed us all, what guilty ancestor brought the curse upon us, I don't know. Doubtless the cause lies nearer to home in our own character—and yet when I think of all [the]

[7] *SE* V, 42-43.

1897-1899

trouble and disappointment you have gone through[8] I am inclined again to take refuge in the old belief in the divine
envy. . . .[9] At least there is one lesson we may learn from it all
and this is plain. We must take our comfort in ourselves and in
one another. The world at large seems to be only a great instrument ready to the hand of the jealous Nemesis. . . .

"I wonder whether at night the lookout on the forward deck
calls out at every bell tap, 'All's well,' and the lights are brightly
shining, and then the curt reply of the officer on duty, 'All right.'
That used to be the most romantic incident of the voyage to
me."[10]

While in St. Louis, More constantly saw Nettie, who gave
much of her time to her dying grandmother. After recording for
Alice the "rather funereal" meals at home and the latest "hospital news"[11] from Nettie's family, it was doubtless with relief
that he exclaimed: "How I should like to be with you in old
Paris; and what memories would come back to me as I walked
the streets. The two happiest weeks of my life, I suppose, were
passed in that city. They were almost the only fortnight of my
life when I had not a minute to think of myself."[12]

In March *The New World* published his essay on the "Two
Famous Maxims of Greece"—"Nothing too much," the principle
of moderation, restraint, balance, and measure, and "Know thyself," which expresses "the inner spiritual phase of Greek life,
just as the 'golden mean' gives the model of outward practical
conduct."[13]

[8] Early in 1895 Alice had asked Paul to send her "a list of the best
translations from the classics" for a Swedish nobleman who, having married beneath him, came as a painter with his wife and children to America, where Alice met him at the St. Louis School of Fine Arts. Within
the next two years their regard for one another so increased that Paul
declared: "Some of your troubles have been such as I too have gone
through and I know their sting and the desolation of them." [To Alice
More, Jan. 17, 1897.] She turned to travel and silence; the Swede and his
family left St. Louis.
[9] Cf. *PB*, 44.   [10] To Alice More, March 15, 1898.
[11] To the same, April 7, 1898.   [12] To the same, June 3, 1898.
[13] *SE* II, 199.

[61]

Shelburne

"It seems to me," More replied to Charles Eliot Norton's comments on the article, "that in the study of ethics we must make a distinction between two kinds of doctrines,—those which attempt merely to utter the common belief of the time and people, and those which profess a higher authority and aim at reform. These two classes may be more or less merged together, but it seems to me that in Greek literature as a whole we have a clear example of the first, whereas the Christian teachers are plainly of the second type. One might go a step further and call this the difference between philosophy and religion, and say that the Greeks were eminently philosophical whereas the Christians are religious. . . . The μηδὲν ἄγαν is not a religious dogma imposed on the people from above, but the simple expression of the popular consciousness. No one would claim that we even approach the golden rule in our conduct; but is it not true that the Greeks for a time did really as a people live up to the Delphic maxim? Does not that peculiar poise and rest universally recognized in Greek art and literature result from this very harmony of belief and action? Accordingly then the decay of the Greeks springs from an inner cause of which this maxim is only the outward expression. Perhaps my own balance of mind has been marred by too much attention to the Orient and our own Middle Age; deeply as I admire the great works of Greece, still I am always haunted by a feeling that such earthly perfection can only be bought at the price of some higher celestial virtue,— which yet the poor deluded soul can never attain.

"As for the γνῶθι σαυτόν certainly you are right in claiming for it all the wisdom the world has discovered. However, in the deeper sense, as you understand it, it came to the Greeks only after their decay was begun. Indeed can it ever come to a people except at such a time? It requires the fullness of self-consciousness. Now this complete self-consciousness means that the individual has learned to distinguish clearly his own interest from the general good, and this, as I take it, is the inevitable and infallible sign of over-ripeness, the beginning of ruin. And in this

Barclay Bros.

Paul Elmer More

Rösch

P. E. More, Washington University, 1887

House occupied by More, Shelburne, N.H., 1897-1899

More and Râj, Philbrook Farm, Shelburne, N.H., 1897

Paul Elmer More, 1928

Paul Elmer More

More at The Cedars, Essex, N.Y.

fatal course the human race seems to revolve from doom to doom. There is a higher sense in which self-knowledge sees, and consciously now, that the individual is but part of the whole, and may recognize this higher oneness so thoroughly as to find in self-sacrifice its highest joy. So Plato understood the γνῶθι σαυτόν and this is the real meaning of his dialectical climbing to the skies. But is it possible to expect such wisdom in the mass of people? There, I think, the real discrepancy comes in. Self-knowledge has a higher and a lower meaning—it is a two-edged sword."[14]

For Houghton, Mifflin and Company "tediously but surely"[15] Paul prepared an edition of Byron's complete poetical works. In the introductory biographical sketch, scrutinized by Babbitt before it was printed and praised by Charles Dudley Warner after its appearance in the December 1898 *Atlantic Monthly*, More passed from his former "insidious relaxing sentimentality"[16] to a more realistic attitude towards life and letters.

"Love"—to cite a topic then of much interest to him—"in Byron is commonly the beast that enslaves and degrades, or it it the instinctive attraction of youth uncorrupted by the world, that simple self-surrender, unquestioning and unpolluted, which to the aged sight of the wise Goethe and the subtle Renan seemed, after all was said, the best and truest thing in life. Other poets in search of love's mystic shadow have philosophized with Plato or scaled the empyrean with Dante; but rarely in these excursions have they avoided the perils of unreality or self-deception, of inanity or morbidness. There is at least a certain safety in seeing in love the simple animal passion, pure or perverted as the case may be."[17]

While recognizing that classicism and romanticism contribute

---

[14] To Charles Eliot Norton, May 6, 1898; courtesy of Houghton Library, Harvard University. Cf. *SE* VI, 116.

[15] To Alice More, June 3, 1898.

[16] *The Complete Poetical Works of Lord Byron*, Cambridge Edition, Boston and New York (Houghton, Mifflin and Company), 1905, p. xvii.

[17] *Ibid.*, p. xviii.

to "the true classics, Homer as well as Shakespeare,"[18] now, influenced by Babbitt, More accentuates the "classical," meaning by that "a certain predominance of the intellect over the emotions, and a reliance on broad effects rather than on subtle impressions; these two characteristics working harmoniously together and being subservient to human interest."[19] "Classical art should result in self-restraint and harmony of form, but to this Byron never attained except spasmodically, almost by accident it should seem." His very qualities, his "superabundant physical vigor" and "mental impetuosity," lacking wisdom and control, led to his destruction. "In the end this solitary pride and isolation, this morbid exaltation of our personal existence, become a creation of Frankenstein, from whose oppression we long for deliverance. To the Spirits who offer him dominion and all the joys of the senses the smitten and defiant soul can only cry out for forgetfulness:—

> 'Oblivion, self-oblivion—
> Can ye not wring from out the hidden realms
> Ye offer so profusely what I ask?'

It is the perfect and ever memorable tragedy of the spirit of revolution, of individual isolation, of unrestraint, of limitless desires, which found in Byron side by side with his classic intelligence its most authentic utterance."[20]

On his way back from St. Louis More stopped, in July 1898, to see Babbitt in Cambridge and to arrange with Houghton, Mifflin and Company to translate and edit for them, by which means, together with contributions to their magazine, *The Atlantic Monthly*, he hoped to earn enough to marry within a year. He promptly began an article on Meredith; translated Plato's *Apology, Crito*, and the closing scene of the *Phaedo*, which, with an introduction, was published in December by Houghton, Mifflin as *The Judgment of Socrates*; and translated Aeschylus's

[18] *Ibid.*, p. xiii. Cf. *SE* VIII, ix-xi, and *SE* X, 17.
[19] *The Complete Poetical Works of Lord Byron*, p. xii.
[20] *Ibid.*, pp. xix-xxi.

Prometheus Bound, which the same firm published the next spring.

When he returned to Shelburne he found that pendent toes had so twisted Râj's hind legs that nothing short of amputation could prevent him from being continually lame. Dr. Marble, Mr. Philbrook, his son Howard, and More "muzzled the poor beast with straps and tied his legs with rope; Philbrook sat with one leg thrown over the dog's neck while I held his head and soothed him. Howard assisted the doctor as he cut. It was a nasty bloody business. Râj struggled at first, but soon succumbed and only moaned at times. His legs are now bandaged and pretty sore but I hope he will be all right in a few days. It is absurdly hard for me to pain or thwart the beast in any way. To leave him behind when I go for a walk, takes away all my pleasure."[21]

In summer several Harvard professors—Emerton, Grandgent, Greenough, Goodale, Sheldon, Williston, and Wright— either occupied Philbrook cottages or roomed as well as boarded at the farm. Mrs. Scudder, her daughter Vida, and the latter's friend, Florence Converse, also stayed there regularly, lunching at the same table with More. In the afternoon he often joined others for a walk. To fulfil one of the farm's traditions, a night on Cabot, a group of guests loaded with blankets and food would trudge up the woodland trail to the bare top of the little mountain, where a few straggling trees provided balsam boughs for bedding. An open shelter of stones, laboriously constructed by Professors Allen and Greenough, had its roof of branches renewed on each such visit. Beneath this fragrant canopy the more delicate members of the party rested, while the hardier reclined on a stony ledge where altruistic insomniacs kept a fire burning throughout the night. If More dismissed his first climb as scarcely worth the effort, later he led an expedition with due enthusiasm.

A favorite walk took him through the ancient white pines behind his cabin to Mill Brook,[22] four hundred yards or so away,

[21] To Alice More, July 30, 1898.
[22] Since renamed Austin Brook or Burbank Brook.

and up it about a mile to the Bowls and Pitchers, where the stream falls some thirty feet, roaring over five or six rocky steps or terraces into a bowl carved by the swirling waters out of a ledge of stone. In this chilly hollow children love to splash and then slide down a slippery groove in the boulders to a still pool, or swimming hole, below. But for More it was enough to lie there "on a warm sunny rock for a long time wrapt in a kind of dreamy delight,"[23] or to watch "the flies weaving a pattern over the surface of the quiet water," or, "in that charmed and lonely spot," to read *Walden* and nourish his soul on him who said: "To be a philosopher is not merely to have subtle thoughts, nor even to found a school, but so to love wisdom as to live according to its dictates, a life of simplicity, independence, magnanimity, and trust."[24]

"For the baked bean," he used to say, he supped Saturdays at the farm. Often invited out, he reciprocated, as well as his cobwebby purse permitted, with tea. One evening when several of his summer acquaintances gave him a surprise "pound party," each bearing a pound of coffee, jam, sugar, or crackers, he gaily transformed his hosts into their own as well as his guests. But on mornings jealously consecrated to work, as he "sat by a window with his lean greyhound face dipped down into a book,"[25] if walkers or a carriage full of strangers asked him the meaning of the inscription he had painted in Devanagari on the lintel of his front door, he did not hesitate to translate the words, "For the sake of solitude,"[26] into, as the occasion required, "Avoid women, whence all troubles come," "Let no woman enter here," or "Keep out."

On Sunday nights at the Scudders', after supping on wild

---

[23] To Alice More, May 8, 1899.

[24] *SE* I, 8, 11, 20; cf. *SE* V, 109-10.

[25] In her description of Tristram Lawrence's appearance in *The Children of Light*, Boston (Houghton, Mifflin and Company), 1912, Florence Converse had More in mind, but she used him only as a point of departure; for in no other respect is Lawrence intended to represent him.

[26] Cf. *On Journey*, by Vida Dutton Scudder, New York (E. P. Dutton & Co.), third printing, Oct. 1937, p. 207.

strawberries, he used to read aloud in "a low, resonant voice," the words "coming from his lips delicately cadenced, like a strange music," his translation of Bhartrihari's epigrams, enriched with scholarly comment, or *The Odyssey*, either in Greek when someone else was present who enjoyed the language, or in Professor Palmer's English version.

With Vida Scudder and Florence Converse he engaged in frequent discussions, which flowed over Râj's head as he lay on their living room floor. Immersed in ancient Indian theologies and Greek philosophy More, though he esteemed the young women's philanthropic intentions, detested "their views as formulated into a dogma."[27] With persistent, cold intensity he assailed their "Christian socialism," which struck him as a form of "vaunting materialism, undisciplined feminism, everything that denotes moral deliquescence."[28] "Thou shalt love God with all thy heart and thy neighbour as thyself, was the law of Christianity. We have forgotten God and the responsibility of the individual soul to its own divinity; we have made a fetish of our neighbour's earthly welfare. We are not Christians but humanitarians, followers of a maimed and materialistic faith. . . ."[29] am I not justified in saying that true religion would at least change the order of ideas and declare that to serve mankind is, first of all, to give one's self to the service of God? . . ."[30] Surely the whole tenor of Christ's teaching is the strongest rebuke to this lowering of the spirit's demand. He spent his life to bring men into communion with God, not to modify their worldly surroundings. . . . He taught poverty and not material progress. Those he praised were the poor and the meek and the unresisting and the persecuted—those who were cut off from the hopes of the world."[31]

Though matters like the Trinity and the atonement did not concern him—"my faith has passed out of them—beyond them, I trust; and at least I do not call myself a Christian"[32]—More

[27] *JL*, 124.   [28] *JL*, 63. Cf. *SE* VII, 4.   [29] *JL*, 54-55; cf. *RP*, 299-301.
[30] *JL*, 126.   [31] *JL*, 127-28.   [32] *JL*, 125.

knew what a very present help in time of trouble God is to the believer. Humanitarianism, he complained, "has bartered away the one valid consolation of mankind for an impossible hope that begets only discontent and mutual hatred among men."[33]

"Consciousness, I hold, is the supremely valuable thing, and progress, evolution, civilization, etc., are only significant in so far as they afford nourishment to it. . . .[34]

"Mankind . . . are divided into two . . . classes: those to whom the visible world is real and the invisible world unreal or at best a shadow of the visible, and those to whom this visible realm with all its life is mere illusion whereas the spirit alone is the eternal reality. Faith is just this perception of the illusion enwrapping these phenomena that to those without faith seem so real; faith is the voluntary turning away of the spirit from this illusion toward the infinite reality. It is because I find among the men of to-day no perception of this illusion that I deny the existence of faith in the world. It is because men have utterly lost the sense of this illusion that religion has descended into this Simony of the humanitarians. . . .[35] the only true service to mankind in this hour is to rid one's self once for all of the canting unreason of 'equality and brotherhood,' to rise above the coils of material getting, and to make noble and beautiful and free one's own life."[36]

His principal literary event of the year was the appearance in September 1898 of *A Century of Indian Epigrams, Chiefly from the Sanskrit of Bhartrihari*. Bhartrihari and the ancient Hindu moralists, More recalled in his letter of dedication to Babbitt, "speak of the three paths, pleasure, worldly wisdom, and renunciation; but in reality they recognize only two ideals, between which they could conceive no substantial ground of mediation. Our poet states the contrast sharply in one of his epigrams: 'There are in the world but two things that men may cherish,— either the youth of fair girls who yearn ever for the renewal

[33] *JL*, 104.   [34] *JL*, 33.   [35] *JL*, 190.
[36] *JL*, 299.

of love's dallying, or else the forest-life.' "[37] Bhartrihari chose the latter not for asceticism but for "the deeper tranquility of isolation."[38]

"We read constantly of the monism of the Hindus, of their attempts to reduce all things to one substance. But this statement must be accepted with a reservation. In fact their intellectual attitude is the result of a keen perception of the dual nature of man and the world at large; and this holds true even in the Vedânta, commonly cited as the most radical of monistic systems. Furthermore, it would hardly be too much to aver that the spirituality of any philosophy or religion is measured by its recognition of this contrast. . . . Plato, speaking for Greece and transcending its old philosophy, traces the discord of existence to the opposition of spirit and matter; and this, likewise, is the theory of the Hindus. They proclaim the irreconcilable enmity of the soul and the body. Salvation with them, as with the Greek, is a system of purgation, a dying to the flesh, until the soul is made free to enjoy its own unalloyed perfection. Plato affirms that we can have knowledge only of the soul and of essences similar to the soul; touching the body and material things, there is only ignorance, or at best uncertain opinion. He is fond of identifying knowledge and virtue, ignorance and vice, and of avowing that by knowledge the wise man liberates himself from the world,—but knowledge of what? Hardly in Plato will you find an adequate answer to this simple and inevitable question. Now the Vedânta teaches the same doctrine of knowledge and ignorance; but it goes a step further, and herein lies its clearness and originality. Regarding the world without, we have only ignorance or false opinion. It therefore exists for us only in these, and for us ignorance is the cause of the world. With the acquisition of knowledge ignorance is destroyed, and the world of which it is the cause ceases for us to exist. We win deliverance by knowledge,—and knowledge of what? By apprehension of this definite truth, that the soul has real existence, and that the

[37] *CIE*, 5.   [38] *CIE*, 8.

Shelburne

world has only a phantom existence in illusion. Knowledge, it may be added, is not a verbal conviction merely, but something akin to faith, a realization of truth that touches the whole character of man, springing up of itself by some strange incommunicable force."[39]

"As you will understand from the great freedom I have taken," More explained to Professor Lanman, "I meant the Epigrams to stand . . . as English verse primarily, and yet I have tried not to traduce while translating but to preserve the spirit of the original so far as was possible. I fear I can expect but scant appreciation from the critics in this respect; they will know nothing either of Sanskrit or of English as the case may be."[40]

Of the epigrams Babbitt's and Lanman's first choice was LXIV:

> Here nothing is, and nothing there,
> And nothing fronts me wheresoe'er;
> And reckoning all I find the whole
> Mere nothing, nothing—save the reckoning soul.

"For my own part," More declared, "considering the difficulty and other matters, I should place no. XCIII (Dear Heart, I go a journey) at the head. It cost me a pretty tussle to boil down the long-winded passage of the *Upaniṣad* into anything like lyric form."[41]

> Dear Heart, I go a journey, yet before
> Would speak this counsel, for I come no more:
> One love our life had, yet a greater still
> The Spirit must fulfil.

> Not now the wife is dear for love of wife,
> But for the Self; and this our golden life
> For life no more we treasure, it is dear
> For that the Self dwells here.

[39] *CIE*, 13-15. Cf. *SE* VI, 1-42.
[40] To Charles R. Lanman, Sept. 26, 1898; courtesy of Houghton Library, Harvard University.
[41] *Ibid.*

And this beguiling world, the starry dome
Of purple and the gods who call it home,
Man, beast, and flowers that blow and blowing perish,
    Not for themselves we cherish,

But for the Self. And this is love, and they
Who look for other on the lonely way
Are still forsaken.—Tremble not, dear Heart!
    Love stays though I depart.[42]

Brigadier-General More, who had been confined to his bed in late November 1898, died January 28, 1899. On his return to Shelburne after attending his father's funeral in St. Louis, visiting Nettie in Buffalo, and calling on Babbitt in Cambridge, Paul remarked to Professor Lanman, whose "benign influence" he sought to set him "rolling again": ". . . I must by hook or crook get a position to teach next year or go to the state poorhouse as an incurable imbecile. I trust that institution is not so hard to get into as our colleges. . . . I hardly think my two years outing have injured me *in esse*, as it has been a season of pretty steady reading and study in the classics, although I fear the visible output may not seem very alluring to the college president. The difficulty in my writing is that there is only a single well-paying magazine in the country that publishes the kind of work I do and hence there is no living in it. I don't want to sink to the sort of trash printed—and well paid—in the cheaper magazines."[43]

"My reading lately has been largely in Spanish which interests but does not satisfy—except Don Quijote which I am going through now and which leaves nothing to desire. Even *La Vida es Sueño* was lacking in some last touch of self-restraint or conscious thought which went far to lessen its peculiar charm. It seemed as if Calderón had never sounded the depth of his own

[42] *CIE*, 116-17.
[43] To Charles R. Lanman, April 12, 1899; courtesy of Harvard University Library and Dr. Thomas H. Lanman.

intuition.[44] *Quevedós Sueños* are immensely clever but the Spanish is too hard to make them agreeable reading for me as yet. While in St. Louis I went through a lot of novels chiefly by Galdós. They are powerful but not agreeable. Perhaps the brutality of Spanish provincial life is the cause of this. *Gloria* is certainly one of the greatest tragedies I ever read in prose—a much greater book I think than *Doña Perfecta* which is about the most revolting of all I have read of his."[45]

More's mother and his brother Louis went to Shelburne in August 1899. Prosser Hall Frye, an instructor at the University of Nebraska, stopped there two weeks with his bride, talking, walking, and playing "hearts" with the More brothers. And Irving Babbitt ran up for a while, vigorous and argumentative. As summer waned there came an invasion of trunks, then a maid, and finally a New York family, whose vivacious, brunette, débutante daughter, Beatrice de Trobriand Post, enchanted the hermit. So marked was his attention to her that everyone expected a match; everyone, that is, except his family and the Posts; for at the beginning of their acquaintance he told her of his engagement to Nettie. While Louis escorted her sister, Paul read aloud to them under the trees, *The Rubáiyát* or passages from Indian literature. From morn to night he talked to her of Babbitt. Absorbed in Hinduism he heaped scorn on Christianity's coddling of the individual soul, on the absurdity of churches, and on the deceptions of New Thought and Christian Science.[46] He directed her attention to reflective literature and philosophy, revealing to her by his talk and reading how alive the subjects of her heretofore rather perfunctory liberal education could be. But when he protested that "we shouldn't emphasize our emotional nature," or made some shallow remark on

---

[44] Cf. *PB*, 14.
[45] To Irving Babbitt, April 26, 1899.
[46] Cf. *SE* I, 79-84; "The Miracle of the Stone and of the Mountain," *IND*, May 9, 1901, vol. 53, pp. 1079-80; and "Old Superstitions and New" and "Christian Science Triumphant," *EP*, Feb. 3, 1906, p. 4, and June 9, 1906, p. 4, respectively.

music, instead of arguing with a bluestocking's irritating earnestness, she wafted away his misty theories with laughing flippancy and "purely feminine wit, bright, unreasonable and unanswerable."[47]

Meanwhile Professor Lanman approached various universities on More's behalf, but against serious odds. Was the candidate, as an official of Washington University insisted, conceited, impractical, tactless, and lacking in "team play"? If, as word came from Bryn Mawr, he balked at the routine of elementary classes but did exceptionally well with mature students, where was the customary Ph.D.? Not until autumn could he assure his mother: "Lanman wishes me to translate a Sanskrit text he is having edited for the Oriental Series. . . . I shall almost certainly accept the proposal—both for the present income and so as to be on the spot to obtain a position next year. He cannot tell me how much it will pay me until he has consulted with President Eliot, but assures me it will be enough to live on."[48]

[47] Alice More's words about the play, "Good gracious, Annabelle," but not inapplicable here. [Alice More to Marie R. Garesché, Jan. 30, 1917.]

[48] To Mrs. Enoch Anson More, postmarked Oct. 1, 1899.

5

MARRIAGE (1899-1901)

"MY WORK," Paul advised Alice from his former address at 32 Wendell Street, Cambridge (where he felt "a thousand times more" "lonely and isolated" "than in the solitude of Shelburne"[1]), "is to make a translation of *The Pancatantra* for the Oriental Series, the text being edited by a German scholar. This ought not to take more than a couple of hours in the morning and the rest of the day will be my own. I have a couple of articles engaged for *The Atlantic*[2] and shall probably edit Pope (or some other poet) in the Cambridge Series.[3] I get $600 from Harvard, and altogether I calculate my income will be eleven or twelve hundred this winter with next summer free for further work. This ought to enable me to pay off all my debts, replete my wardrobe, and get married comfortably in the spring provided next winter is settled. My living is very cheap. The Sheldons . . . are moving into a larger house,[4] and have insisted on my coming to live with them. I am to have a large room in the third story, otherwise unoccupied, private bathroom on the same floor. Mrs. Sheldon is an excellent housekeeper and sets a good table. I am asked to pay only $6 a week. The temptation was very great and I have accepted their offer. Of course I should for some reasons prefer to live as I am, as I am freer here. On the other hand my room is shoddy, and there is a stove to feed; my

[1] To Mrs. Enoch Anson More, postmarked Oct. 1, 1899.

[2] These were " 'The Seven Seas' and 'The Rubáiyát' " and "The Ancient Feud between Philosophy and Art" published, respectively, in the Dec. 1899, and the Sept. 1900, issues of *The Atlantic Monthly*, which in Oct. 1899 had printed his essay, "The Novels of George Meredith."

[3] Although his edition of Byron's poetry was his only contribution to Houghton, Mifflin and Company's Cambridge Edition of the Poets, the same firm engaged him for $350 to write a brief life of Benjamin Franklin.

[4] At 11 Francis Avenue, Cambridge.

[74]

board is horrible in a stinking room with a crowd of gobbling country louts."[5]

After a visit to Bayport, Long Island, to see Beatrice Post and Râj (whom she had adopted when his master left Shelburne) and "partly to help Mr. Post with his astronomical observations during the meteor showers,"[6] More received "a letter from Seymour Eaton, editor of the Home Study Circle of the *Chicago Record*," asking for "five or six papers of 800 to 1200 words each on Egyptian and Persian and Assyrian literature—all for the huge sum of forty dollars! And bless my soul, as he promised advance pay, I have accepted. The work will be quite easy for the simple, though paradoxical, reason that I know nothing whatever about any of the subjects. My ignorance is [so] complete that I shall merely run through one or two encyclopaedias and books of reference and throw together the proper number of words without any attempt at originality. As Dowden and men of that ilk are writing for the series it won't disgrace me in the public eye. . . . I am getting to be nothing but a cheap hack writer, but I don't mean to keep at it long. This year it is anything for money."[7]

He and his fiancée passed "a very bookish Christmas"[8] in Buffalo with Nettie's sister Kate and her husband, Augustine A. Heard. Prompted by Lou's gift of a copy of Boswell, More called on a Mr. Adam, a collector of Johnsoniana, "a white-haired Scotsman, rather a fine looking old fellow who was evidently pleased to exhibit his treasures—and such treasures. His extra-illustrations for Boswell will make forty great volumes,—autographs of Henry VIII, Elizabeth, and royalty galore, letters of innumerable famous authors, scholars, actors, soldiers, etc., a host of rare engravings, water colors and all manner of illustrations. Besides Johnson, he has an extraordinary collection of

[5] To Alice More, Oct. 9, 1899.
[6] To the same, Nov. 5, 1899.
[7] To the same, Dec. 20, 1899.
[8] To Louis T. More, Dec. 28, 1899.

material relating to Burns,—rare first editions, autograph poems, etc.—and also relating to Byron and Ruskin. Such a treat I never had. I longed to be shut up in the house for a week with nobody to restrain me and enjoy the treasures at my leisure."[9]

By February 1900, after discussing the matter with Nettie, whom he considered "rather foolishly sensitive"[10] about their prolonged engagement, More determined to be wedded in June. "I cannot but feel a little anxious about my approaching marriage," he admitted to Alice. "I have no doubt I shall be happy, and it is probably the best thing for me from every point of view; but on the other hand I have done so little and want to do so much, that I dread any curtailment of my liberty and choice in working. At any moment I may feel a terrible impulse to throw up everything and follow some new impulse, and the struggle against such a desire may be a most disagreeable one. There is some chance of my teaching next year, and that would simplify matters in some respects but hardly in others. The future looks a little blank to me at the best, but I have chosen and must abide my choice. I am writing to you simply to unburden my mind a bit, and also to assure you that neither marriage nor anything else can ever alter or diminish my love for you. That came too early and wrought too deeply in my life ever to be supplanted."[11]

Besides his Sanskrit and his essays for *The Atlantic Monthly* More toiled in vain over his tragedy about Edwy and, as one contemplating matrimony might do, delved into the genealogy of his family. With his sister May's son, Lucius Elmer More, then a freshman at Harvard, he often walked in the afternoons. Through Babbitt he became acquainted with Eleanor Cook, "one of the Cambridge belles, a very pretty girl indeed. She gave me a wretched *quart d'heure*. Last Wednesday I went in to Boston to order a pair of trousers and took my frock coat with me to be altered. As it was too large to go conveniently in my valise

[9] To Mrs. Enoch Anson More, postmarked Jan. 9, 1900.
[10] To Alice More, undated (probably late March 1900).
[11] To the same, April 19, 1900.

I wore it and carried my short coat in the valise to wear home. Of course I wore only my derby hat, that with a colored shirt, a valise in my hands, and a shabby old pair of trousers on my legs, made a curious combination with a frock coat, but as I never meet anybody on the cars I know, I felt pretty safe. But I had no sooner stationed myself on the back platform of the car than I saw Miss Cook sitting inside only a few seats from the door. It may have been foolish, but I felt silly and avoided her eye. Said I to myself, ten to one she gets off at Boylston Street where I have my destination. So sure was I of this that as we approached the station in the subway I got on the step ready to alight at once and escape. And sure enough as the car stopped I saw her rise from her seat. I just skipped into the crowd and up the steps as fast as I could, my coattails flapping wildly as only a frock coat can flap when you run up stairs."[12]

On another trip to Boston, at a reception for Mary Eleanor Wilkins, later Mrs. Charles M. Freeman, he "found the lioness rather shy and dull to meet, but am informed she is much more interesting when she thaws out. I could it seemed to me see in her face all the traits which she draws so skillfully in the New England character."[13]

As usual he did "a prodigious amount of reading . . . in French and Spanish, but chiefly in English filling up the lacunae there that have long worried me. I contrive to get through ten or twelve volumes a week, which is a good deal considering my other work. Babbitt looks at me aghast, and I think envies my absorbtive powers a bit."[14]

Nettie in the meanwhile had been looking for living quarters in East Orange, New Jersey, where the Heards had settled at 172 Arlington Avenue. She chose a house renting for thirty dollars a month at 265 Springdale Avenue, in "the best part" of East

[12] To Mrs. Enoch Anson More, Feb. 21, 1900.
[13] *Ibid.* Cf. *SE* II, 180, 184-85; "A Writer of New England," *N*, Oct. 27, 1910, vol. 91, pp. 386-87; and *EP*, Oct. 28, 1910, p. 8.
[14] To Alice More, undated (probably late March 1900).

Marriage

Orange, "just around the corner from Kate's."[15] With drawing-room, library, dining-room, pantry, and kitchen downstairs, four bedrooms, a dressing-room, and a bathroom on the second floor, and several more rooms on the third, the house lacked nothing but a fireplace.

Invitations now went forth for the seven o'clock wedding at the Heards' on June 12th. "I may not write to you again until after the 12th," the bridegroom apprised his mother, "but you need not fear that I shall now or ever forget the old home in the new or let another family take the place of my own. I think if I make any success at all as a husband—and I hope not to fail utterly—it will [be] due chiefly to your teaching."[16]

Professor Lanman again sought a position for his pupil. Enclosing copies of More's articles and books, he wrote of him, probably to Jacob Gould Schurman, president of Cornell: "If you want a man who can interest students in Greek or Latin primarily *as literature*, I think it would be worth your while carefully to consider his qualifications.

"He is a man of about 30,[17] of good physique, dignified bearing and manner, and of distinctively prepossessing personality. In Classical literature, his reading is far & away beyond that of the ordinary classical teacher not only in respect of its breadth and scope but also as regards the spirit in which he has approached the geniuses of antiquity. . . . He is at home with the writers of the strictly classical period and also with the Church

---

[15] To the same, May 19, 1900.

[16] To Mrs. Enoch Anson More, May 31, 1900.

[17] To have underestimated his age by nearly five years would then have been natural. A young friend of Babbitt's who called on More in East Orange in 1900 described him as "strikingly handsome, looking many years younger than he was, reserved rather than expansive, a quietly self-contained personality, nowise controversial or argumentative like Babbitt. He was at the time giving some attention to Spanish, and spoke with much admiration of the criticism of Juan Valera. . . . He impressed me as a very systematic worker, keen on utilizing time." For More, as for Goethe, work was "a kind of glorified prudential means of attaining happiness and self-development" and, as for Carlyle, a way of creating one's destiny. [*SE* I, 93-94. In regard to Valera see *SE* II, 164, 166.]

Fathers like St. Augustine and Irenaeus. His familiarity with modern literature has given opportunity for the development of the literary critical faculty to a very considerable degree, as is evidenced by his papers on Byron, Meredith, Kipling,—Omar Khayyám. Of his literary touch and sense, you may yourself judge by casual inspection of his translations of Plato & Aeschylus. . . ."[18]

Although, as More later learned, no suitable position at Cornell was then vacant, he accepted Schurman's invitation to deliver a lecture there, for fifty dollars, "on some Greek subject."[19]

"Your dear letter," Nettie acknowledged to Alice shortly before the wedding day, "and gift came this morning and I can hardly tell you how touched I was with both. You have done so much for Paul, and through helping him, for me that I expected nothing from you, and so there was surprise with my pleasure. I know how you love him and I hope when I am his wife that the love you have had for Nettie Beck may increase, not grow less. If devotion to him can do it, then you will take me more into your heart. I think the next happiest day after my wedding day will be the day when we welcome you and your mother to our house. May the day come soon is what I shall long for!"[20]

Her aunt, Mary Darrah (the widowed Mrs. Clifford Richardson), who had just returned from Europe, was having the ground floor of their house repapered for them, had given them their flat silver, and had sent for her piano and for some of her rugs, curtains, tables, chairs, and other things they needed. "I fear our furniture will not reach here in time," Nettie went on, "but, as I was feeling very broken up about it, Augustine told me a secret which he was going to divulge Sunday when Paul came. He has arranged a wedding trip for us to Taughannock Falls, a place beyond Ithaca, and while we are gone they propose to settle the house. Isn't that sweet of them? Paul knows nothing

[18] Undated letter; courtesy of Harvard University Library and Dr. Thomas H. Lanman.
[19] To Alice More, May 19, 1900.
[20] Henrietta Beck to Alice More, June 6, 1900.

of this gift and as the place is very beautiful and very quiet I feel sure he will be pleased. . . .

"I am glad Paul did not go to Cornell, as I feel sure the life he is now leading will be best in the end. Of course I realize we shall have many anxious days and sometimes our living will seem very precarious, but these long years of waiting have not been in vain and we have learned patience and our love is deeper, I think, than that of many people before they are married.

"I pray often that I may be as good a wife as you have been sister to him and then I know he will be happy."[21]

"Taughannock Falls, N. Y.
14 June, 1900.

"My dear Mother,

"You will be surprised to get a letter from this place and I will tell you how it comes to happen. When I came down to Orange I found that the furniture had not arrived and that the house was far from being in order. I had anticipated this and expected to go off to some place on the Jersey coast for three or four days. To my surprise I found that Augustine had made arrangements for us to come up here, providing passes[22]—railroad and Pullman—and even hotel bills, and so here we are in a very pretty place in the pine woods looking over Lake Ithaca. The wedding ceremony went off without anything particular to relate. Dr. Hollifield made the service very simple. When I came to put the ring on Nettie's finger the blame thing refused to go on as her hand was moist and I thought there would be trouble. However with her help it went on; but by that time I was rattled so that when I should make the responses I forgot what I was doing until Dr. Hollifield punched me in the belly and waked me to this world. There were some twenty-five or thirty people there. Cary[23] was my only friend and behaved in the nicest way. . . .

[21] *Ibid.*

[22] Augustine Heard was a General Passenger Agent of the Delaware and Hudson Railroad.

[23] Cary T. Hutchinson had moved to New York.

About 8:30 we started off in a coupé for Newark, where we took the Lehigh express for Tanghannock, getting here at 7:35 yesterday morning. Since then we have been walking about a little and taking things easy. Nettie is a good sweet girl, a woman I should call her now, and I think I shall never repent making her my wife. I trust she can say the same thing. I feel in glorious good condition today, quite like a fighting cock.

"Saturday night we leave for New York. I hope and expect the house will be in order when we arrive as Mrs. Beck is to see to having the furniture placed. . . . I am very happy today, dear Mother, and don't yet realize the sterner fight before me. But I am far from desponding about that. I am looking forward to the time when I shall be able to welcome you to the new home.

Affectionately your Son,
Paul E. More.

P. S. Nettie wishes to send her love to you all—and will have me say she is glad you had me for a son—which I take as a pretty compliment to myself.

P. E. M."

"I wish you and Alice could see how neatly I am housed," he wrote to his mother from "the locomotive," as he and Louis, who stayed there July and August, called the frame house at 265 Springdale Avenue (because it had a "mansard tower and stuck out on the sides" over a veranda), "and you will be astonished to learn that I have developed a vein of orderliness, so much so that there are no signs of work ever in the library. Nettie has taken down most of my Franklin on the typewriter to my dictation. She seems really to enjoy helping me, and I find I am learning to dictate with considerable fluency."[24]

After Louis came other guests—Frank Jewett Mather, Jr., who had taught with Babbitt at Williams College in 1893-94

[24] To Mrs. Enoch Anson More, Aug. 29, 1900.

Marriage

and who now wrote for the New York *Evening Post* and *The Nation*; Paul's sister May and her husband Ned; and occasionally students of Babbitt's, whom he had already begun to send to More as to a sage. Nettie's Aunt Mary, midway as usual between doctors and Europe, passed a week or two with them, thoughtfully paying her board. The Heards entertained the newlyweds at Christmas, when Paul received from Alice a book-plate she had designed, showing him reading in his chair at Shelburne with Râj on the floor beside him—"a memento to me of my two years in the wilderness—but, if the imagination is handmaid of heaven, a 'wilderness where sing the servants of God.' "[25] For a week in mid-April 1901 Babbitt and his wife visited the Mores. But the most longed-for guests were Paul's mother, now about seventy-five, and his sister Alice, just past fifty, who wished to relinquish their housekeeping in St. Louis for something simpler and more sociable. As the warm-hearted Nettie, knowing how much her husband loved his mother and sister and reciprocating their affection for her, urged them to live with Paul and herself, the older relatives, after much hesitation lest they be in the way, agreed to move into the third floor of "the locomotive" in June 1901.

Fortunately for Paul the details of daily existence, so boring to him, fascinated his wife. She devoted herself as intensely to housekeeping as he did to intellectual work. This, from a writer's point of view, being an ideal division of labor, he left everything, except the ordering of the coal, which he claimed was a man's job, to her, aided by such occasional cleaning women and maids as they could afford. When he closed the library door, she saw to it that no uninvited caller or other annoyance obliged him to open it. "And always by kindly service, by goodness and modesty and meekness, by her pliant ways, she gladdened her new friends, pleasing her new mother with a handmaid's care, and . . . by piety towards the gods and by humble speech. And all

[25] To Alice More, Dec. 27, 1900. Cf. *GR*, 138.

the time with loving words, serenity of heart, and secret services
she made her new lord happy."²⁶

His work while he sought employment was necessarily miscellaneous. He reviewed Santayana's *Interpretations of Poetry and
Religion* for *The Harvard Graduates' Magazine.*²⁷ On hot summer nights he toiled at *The Pancatantra.*²⁸ He revised his "Nature
in American Literature" from "A Hermit's Notes upon a Hermit" to "A Hermit's Notes on Thoreau," wherein he concluded
as the result of his Shelburne sojourn "that the attempt to criticise and not to create literature was to be his labour in this
world."²⁹ A second essay, "The Weird in American Literature,"
gradually grew into "The Origins of Hawthorne and Poe."³⁰ He

²⁶ *DA*, 171. The words (from More's translation of the *Mahâbhârata*)
originally applied to Sâvitrî.

²⁷ Though he found the book "full of wisdom and beauty," Santayana's
point of view seemed to him in the end "rather that of the cultured
aesthete than of the real thinker." [To William Roscoe Thayer, July 5,
1900; courtesy of Harvard University Library.]

Having dismissed his own Christian symbolism as "a sham, a pretty
make-believe"—"better the blindness of true religion than this illusion
of the imagination"—he could not accept Santayana's ultimate subjectiv-
ism. "No great religion was ever founded unless the prophet believed
that the visions he proclaimed were real, and existed outside his own
imagination as absolutely as does a stock or a stone to popular perception. And in so far as poetry is related to religion, no great poem was ever
composed whose author did not have equal faith in the reality of the ideal
world. And the greatest of philosophers has been a living force in the
world largely for the very reason that ideas existed for him objectively
and with a reality which the world of phenomena does not possess. When
religion 'surrenders its illusions,' when faith ceases to be 'the substance
of things unseen,' they cease equally to be vital and to be the source of
true art." ["Santayana's 'Poetry and Religion,'" *The Harvard Graduates'
Magazine*, Sept. 1900, vol. 9, no. 33, p. 21. Cf. More's review of Santayana's *Three Philosophical Poets: Lucretius, Dante, and Goethe, N,*
Nov. 3, 1910, vol. 91, no. 2366, pp. 418-19. The quotations in the first
sentence of this paragraph come from *JL*, 53.]

²⁸ In 1905 the Harvard Oriental Series announced that More's translation of *The Pancatantra* from the manuscript copy made by Professor
Richard Schmidt, of the University of Halle, had yet to be brought into
conformity with the revised Sanskrit text of Pūrnabhadra's recension.
Although in 1908 More had made an English translation of Pūrnabhadra's
text, the Series finally published Hertel's translation of the tales.

²⁹ *SE* I, 2.

³⁰ On the most distant of his youthful fishing trips with his father—

criticized in detail a paper by Frye on George Sand; meticulously
helped Ainsie prepare another novel; and rewrote and enlarged
"a screed of Lou's on the Doctrine of Motion in which I am
gathering together a whole Jeremiad of complaints against
modern civilization. It is preaching with a vengeance. I doubt no
editor will accept it."[31]

"In his shrewdness, versatility, self-reliance, wit," More observed in his short, discerning, graceful life of "the most alert
and most capacious intellect that ever concerned itself entirely
with the present,"[32] "as also in his lack of the deeper reverence
and imagination," Benjamin Franklin "more than any other man
who has yet lived, represents the full American character. . . ."[33]
Certainly his . . . lack of deep root in the past and his impres-
sionability, though limitations to his genius, make him the more
typical of American intelligence. . . ."[34] There was in him none
of the emotional nature and little of the spirituality that go to
make the complete Christian. His strength lay in his temperance,
prudence, justice, and courage,—eminently the pagan virtues. . . ."[35] If Franklin may in some ways be called the typical
American, yet the lonely, introverted, God-intoxicated soul of
Edwards stands as a solemn witness to depths of understanding
in his countrymen which Dr. Franklin's keen wit had no means
of fathoming."[36]

---

to Lake Minnetonka, near Minneapolis—Paul alone in a boat at night
heard in the lapping waves what he recorded as "a sibilant call to plunge
into [the] water." This ghostly apprehension and similar feelings of the
weird as he walked in the dark woods of Shelburne helped him to understand Hawthorne's writings, Thoreau's wondering awe towards nature,
and the loneliness and terror of his own Puritan forebears in their
strange new land.

In a notebook entry dated Oct. 4, 1933, and reprinted, slightly revised,
in *M*, 9, he mentions having several times heard loud metallic raps or
the calling of his first name while he was asleep or half asleep, in each
case so vividly that he awoke. But to these isolated experiences he attached no psychic importance.

[31] To Alice More, postmarked Oct. 17, 1900.
[32] *SE* IV, 152.   [33] *BF*, 2.   [34] *BF*, 6.
[35] *BF*, 39.   [36] *BF*, 63.

Benjamin Franklin[37] completed for Houghton, Mifflin's River-side Biographical Series, its author begged for "another of the volumes,—Washington or Hawthorne or Poe or Jonathan Edwards or old Cotton Mather. . . . At any rate I am hungry for work. . . ."[38]

He asked William Roscoe Thayer, the editor of *The Harvard Graduates' Magazine*, if he wanted a review of Barrett Wendell's *Literary History of America*. "Having looked at a good many works on American literature I almost always get the impression that the critic or historian has failed to see things in their true proportion. He has tried to make interesting (and so has exaggerated its importance) a subject which we must sorrowfully admit is for the greater part of trivial magnitude. Eight or ten names, none of which reaches the very first rank, do not make a literature. . . ."[39] Wendell has avoided this error at least—and in avoiding it has perhaps gone to the other extreme. By a process of perhaps over-discriminating selection he weeds out the uninteresting names. I think too he has kept the connection between literature and history very skillfully in view. I think his emphasis on our 'national inexperience' and on the fact that we have until the present always lagged behind England and Europe, as a reason for our lack of literature is quite just, and this, as I think could be shown, is not in opposition to Fiske's view that politically we have been in advance of England. Furthermore I found Wendell's constant reference to Boston society refreshing for its novelty, though undoubtedly the tone adopted proclaims the author a snob of the first water—a fact which needed no special proclamation. This historical sense however and this sense of the connection of literature and society seem to me to give the book a certain mark of maturity. That this maturity is

[37] Described by Allan Nevins as the best essay on Franklin written in the United States. [*New York Times* Book Review, Feb. 20, 1949, p. 3.]

[38] To Horace E. Scudder, Sept. 13, 1900; courtesy of Harvard University Library.

[39] In a letter of Oct. 31, 1932, to Nicholas Murray Butler, More named as his choice among American writers: Jonathan Edwards, Emerson, Hawthorne, Poe, Whitman, and Parkman.

untainted by that shallow worldly wisdom of which you complain, I am far from asserting. In a deeper sense, in spiritual values, Wendell is utterly lacking in historical insight. For this reason his chapters on the more worldly or less significant authors are more valuable than those which deal with such names as Emerson."[40]

"I had an interview yesterday with the editor, Dr. Ward, of *The Independent*," thanks to a letter of introduction from Thayer.[41] "I found him in the dirtiest little hole of an office you ever saw, himself still dirtier—a wizened little old man, with dusty bald head, near-sighted glass a quarter inch thick, queer watery eyes that wander helplessly and independently around the room, and puffy upper lids like a frog's throat—really an extraordinary individual, a scholar and a gentleman withal. I hope to get some reviewing for him, but cannot tell as yet."[42]

Another straw at which More clutched, in vain, was the five hundred dollar prize offered by the Paris *Herald* for the best translation of Jean Rameau's poem to Queen Wilhelmina. It occurred to him also to examine the Sunday editions of various leading Western newspapers to see whether they might have room for a weekly literary letter from New York. And his friend Cary T. Hutchinson introduced him to a publisher.

"The other day I took luncheon with Cary and Arthur Scribner, the latter taking us to the Aldine Association. Scribner is a pleasant and able fellow, who with his brother, Charles, manages the publishing house. Besides that he has just inherited a clean million (he expected ten millions) from a very wealthy uncle. Well, I got myself into trim for a luxurious luncheon, and I saw from the way Scribner was handling the bill of fare that he meant to treat us handsomely. At this my dyspeptic friend Cary chimes

[40] To William Roscoe Thayer, undated (probably early Dec. 1900); courtesy of Harvard University Library. Thayer decided to publish no review of the book.

[41] In May 1900 More had called in New York, with no results, on Wendell Phillips Garrison, editor of *The Nation*, to whom Thayer had written on his behalf.

[42] To Alice More, Dec. 14, 1900.

in with, 'Scribner, I don't know about Mr. More, but I always eat the simplest sort of a luncheon.' Scribner turns to me questioningly, and of course I repeat that I too always eat the simplest sort of a luncheon—which was true in the letter but false enough in spirit, heaven forgive me! 'Well,' says Scribner, 'if you gentlemen really mean it and are not putting up a big bluff, we'll have a simple luncheon.' And we ate mutton, boiled turnips, and boiled potatoes!"[43]

When things looked so black that More was ready to "apply to some teachers' agency,"[44] he announced jubilantly to Alice: ". . . I am about to pass from the despised position of one constantly having manuscripts rejected to the glorious class of those who do the rejecting. In other words I have been asked to join the staff of *The Independent.* . . . I am to have charge of the literary (review) department and shall probably also write the weekly 'Survey of the World.' Think of me conducting the political news of the world! I shall not begin until April 1st as the vacancy does not occur until then. I am however now writing reviews regularly as a paid contributor. My first article is in the issue of Jan. 31, a review of Brown's *Letters*[45] (they are capital, by the way; Mother ought to read them). Next week, probably, a review of an Irish anthology[46] will be printed; and I now have four other books on my desk to be written up. *The Independent*, perhaps you may not know, is the best weekly in the country to read if you wish to keep informed of what is going on. It is really a thoroughly respectable publication, and I am fortunate in starting so well. I was a good deal surprised when they approached me on the matter. I am to have only a temporary appointment, but feel little apprehension on that score. . . . I begin to believe a man generally gets in time what he wants if he only wants it persistently enough."[47]

[43] To Mrs. Enoch Anson More, Jan. 14, 1901.
[44] To Alice More, Jan. 30, 1901.
[45] *Letters of Thomas Edward Brown.*
[46] *A Treasury of Irish Poetry*, by Stopford A. Brooke and T. W. Rolleston.
[47] To Alice More, Jan. 30, 1901.

6

LITERARY EDITOR (1901-1909)

THERE was no question, after a few months, of the permanence of More's position on the staff of *The Independent*. He could remain in his "beastly little hole"[1] of an office at 130 Fulton Street, New York, sure of monotonous routine most of the week and of a mad rush on Mondays. "Monday morning the first thing I have to get my foreign survey in shape for the printer. Then about noon proofs begin to come in and these keep us pretty busy until late afternoon. About five all the editors (Holt, Ward, Root and myself) go down to the printers . . . to make up the paper,—i. e. get a last glance at proofs, arrange paragraphs, pages, etc. This we do in the compositors' room in consultation with the compositors. There is a certain excitement about it, at least at first."[2]

His colleagues, who relied much on his judgement, found him even tempered, cooperative, with a strong sense of humor and a steadily increasing range of ability. Each Saturday he lunched at a downtown Spanish restaurant with Holt and Root on heavy food and heady red wine. Others who joined them there included Mather; W. J. Ghent,[3] a Social Democrat; the muckraker, Gustavus Myers; a philanthropic millionaire, James Graham

---

[1] To Alice More, April 5, 1901.   [2] *Ibid.*

[3] On Ghent's *Our Benevolent Feudalism* More commented: "The book as a whole is brilliantly written and the argument is ably conducted, but its influence for good (and no sane mind can deny that there is much to challenge in the present state of society) is . . . largely impaired by . . . bitterness. . . . Beneath the insistent plea for humanity displayed in all this socialistic literature too often there rises the *amari aliquid*, the acrid cry of a spirit that hates because it is cut off from the wider sympathies of human nature." [*IND*, Dec. 4, 1902, vol. 54, p. 2894.] "My review of Ghent's book," More remarked to Prosser Hall Frye in a letter of Dec. 11, 1902, "has cut him to the quick, it seems, and he has avoided me ever since I published it. However, I vowed firmly when I came that no considerations of friendship or self-interest should influence me. If you write a book, look out for yourself."

Phelps Stokes; and Milo Maltbie, later a commissioner of public utilities. As several of these prided themselves on being advanced, their talk, inspirited by More's opposition, dwelt often on socialism.

"Some one will say that not wealth is the true ideal of the day, but humanitarianism, socialism, brotherly love, equal distribution of wealth. . . . Humanitarianism is in the end nothing else but the extension of the same ideal from the few to the many; a substitution at best of the ideal of comfort for the ideal of material power. I know that the socialist reformers look to the proper distribution of wealth as merely the first step which is to be followed by some greater spiritual reform. But as a matter of fact the spiritual ideal is at present a nebulous hypothesis; the creating of universal comfort is the actual aim and ideal held before the eyes. It is well in itself, but the present day exaggerated insistence on it arises from the absence of other ideals. . . . It is the flower of materialism, if you will; but it is still materialism, a mere dilution of the more concentrated ideal of wealth. The upholders of it look upon it as a propaganda against the ideal of wealth; they are in reality fostering what they seek to overthrow."[4]

Almost as close to him as his Saturday convives was a reviewer whom he had not yet met—Corra May Harris, then in her thirties, who, after the death in 1910 of her husband, Lundy Howard Harris, a Methodist minister in Georgia and Tennessee, became known as a writer of short stories and novels. When she had sent More scores of reviews and every few days for a year had deluged him with correspondence whose exhausting length, pronunciatory spelling, and unrestrained temperamentality accompanied an amusing, intelligent, and intense interest in fiction, he proposed they write a novel, the first at which she tried her hand. They decided on a love story in epistolary form between

[4] "Wealth and Culture," *IND*, May 1, 1902, vol. 54, p. 1061. Cf. "The Gospel of Wealth," anonymous editorial by More, *ibid.*, May 30, 1901, vol. 53, p. 1264.

an editor in New York and a young reviewer, Miss Jessica Doane, who discussed with him, among other things, books, religion, nature, and her life in Morningtown, Georgia. To roughen the course of true love, More suggested that the hero be married, which she found repulsive; or that there be some mystery attached to him, which she thought hackneyed; or that he be psychologically objectionable, which she almost adopted on account of her impression of More as "a disinterred intelligence";[5] or that he be heretical, which did not disturb her; or that she be a Christian Scientist, which, she retorted, she could no more be than he could be a Negro. She recommended, and he agreed, that her father be a preacher intolerant enough of the editor's heterodoxy to delay appropriately the happy ending. On this basis about once a month they exchanged and revised a letter, taking their cue from one another as to how their story should develop. To their anonymous product, *The Jessica Letters, An Editor's Romance*,[6] sweet, flimsy, and ephemeral as a valentine, she contributed the livelier writing and he his views on literary criticism, women, and, above all, humanitarianism.[7]

Besides his share in the "Survey of the World" and in the book reviews, he contributed to *The Independent* articles and editorials, some of them belonging to the crusade that lasted to the end of his life for a better understanding of the relation of the humanities, with their saving self-knowledge, to the sciences, with their increasing power of action.[8] He was one of the first

[5] *JL*, 26.

[6] In addition to royalties on the book, G. P. Putnam's Sons paid the co-authors for the right to publish the work as a serial in its monthly magazine, *The Critic*.

[7] Mrs. Harris wrote the letters signed by Jessica and by a minor character, Jack O'Meara. More attacked in particular the humanitarianism of Lyman Abbott, Jane Addams, and Florence Converse (referring to her not by name but by her book, *The Burden of Christopher*). Cf. *SE* IX, 193 ff.

[8] Cf. the following anonymous editorials in *The Independent*: "Classics and the Teachers of Them" (Jan. 1, 1903, vol. 55, pp. 47-48), "The Classics and the Historic Sense" (Jan. 8, 1903, vol. 55, pp. 104-05), "What Are Our Classical Men Doing?" (Jan. 22, 1903, vol. 55, pp. 216-

vigorously to attack the reigning "elective system" and the assumption that attention to the present and the practical is, or ever has been in anything other than vocational training, more essential to education than attention to the past. He thought it dangerous for a student to hop about at his Rousselian pleasure[9] or to confine himself to a specialty, before he had submitted his mind, emotions, imagination, and character to the discipline of human experience through history, the classics, and some of the modern languages and the more precise sciences.

As to the classics in particular, More opposed the predominance of the pseudo-scientific and the linguistic over the literary, the artistic, the historical, the religious, and the philosophical approaches to the study of Greek and Latin. He concluded that "nothing can reinstate them except a new perception of what they stand for in the history of Europe, that, in other words, the *method* of teaching them is not so much to blame (though much may be done in the way of reform here too) as the fact that teachers and pupils alike have fallen out of touch with what they stand for—hence they are meaningless and dead. We must reach something deeper than their aesthetic value, if we wish to make them live once more. And considerable reading of Pindar recently has led me to think that what we must rediscover and

---

18), "Pedantry and Dilettantism in the Classics" (Feb. 5, 1903, vol. 55, pp. 338-40), and "Classical Teachers and the Public" (Feb. 26, 1903, vol. 55, pp. 511-13); and the signed article, "The Teaching of the Classics" (*ibid.*, Aug. 6, 1908, vol. 65, pp. 327-29). See also "A New Intrusion of Pedantry" (*EP*, Dec. 19, 1903, p. 4, and *N*, Dec. 24, 1903, vol. 77, pp. 498-99); "The Value of Academic Degrees" (*The Bookman*, Aug. 1906, vol. 23, pp. 650-53); "The Historic Sense" (*EP*, Jan. 19, 1907, p. 4, and *N*, Jan. 24, 1907, vol. 84, pp. 74-75); "A Revolution in Greek" (*EP*, Dec. 20, 1910, p. 8, and *N*, Dec. 22, 1910, vol. 91, pp. 599-600); "The Opportunity of the Small College" (*EP*, Feb. 25, 1911, p. 6, and *N*, March 2, 1911, vol. 92, pp. 210-11); "Scholarship of Ideas" (*N*, May 11, 1911, vol. 92, pp. 462-63, and *EP*, May 13, 1911, p. 8); "The Loeb Classical Library" (*EP*, Nov. 4, 1911, p. 6, and *N*, Nov. 9, 1911, vol. 93, pp. 438-39); "An Apostle of Greek" (*EP*, April 6, 1912, p. 6, and *N*, April 11, 1912, vol. 94, pp. 354-55); *SE* IX, 36-38, 52, 89-100; "One of the Giants," *N*, May 7, 1914, vol. 98, pp. 535-36; and *SE* XI, 284-85.

[9] Cf. *SE* VI, 230-31; *SE* VII, 256; and *SE* VIII, 235-36.

again understand is the particular *aristocratic* principle that he and the other great Greeks stood for.[10] To analyse that principle, to show in what it differs from a false aristocracy, how it coincides with a true democracy and might correct our present tendency toward a false democracy—all this is a question not to be taken up lightly. But I believe that only in this direction lies the salvation of Greek. The issue is political, social, and aesthetic."[11]

After his marriage, without pretending to be a Christian, More regularly accompanied his family to the nearby Arlington Avenue Presbyterian Church.[12] Courtesy doubtless played a part in this, abetted by love of his wife, "a woman of natural, beautiful, intuitive piety,"[13] and of his devout, rigidly orthodox mother, whose strong mind and will he admired, though he believed a narrow view of the Bible had warped them. Behind these particular motives lay a disposition to purify and strengthen his religious life by respectful if critical exposure to tradition—to stay his "vague emotionalism," as Rousseau had recommended to deists, "on the more precise faith" of those who "believe energetically in the virtue of forms and creeds."[14]

The passengers of "the locomotive," who regarded themselves as transients in East Orange, took little part in local affairs, though Nettie joined a women's club and Alice gave some illustrated lectures on art. More's own roots in the place sank no deeper than those of the vegetables he tended in his back yard.

[10] Cf. *SE* V, 64-65, and *SE* IX, 60.

[11] To Charles R. Lanman, March 4, 1907; courtesy of Dr. Thomas H. Lanman and Harvard University Library.

[12] He persuaded John Martin Thomas, the pastor of this church, to review books for *The Independent*. Setting no policy but approving the formula (probably originated by Dr. Ward) to "tell the truth in a spirit of generous appreciation," More allowed his neighbor full freedom of expression, merely commending an occasional review by way of encouragement.

[13] Frank Jewett Mather, Jr., *Proceedings* of the American Academy of Arts and Sciences, 1938, vol. 72, no. 10, p. 371.

[14] *SE* VI, 233.

Except in 1902 he and Nettie passed several weeks each summer from 1901 through 1905 at Biddeford Pool, Maine, visiting May and Ned at "Eastmoreland" or staying either at "Stonecliffe" with Mrs. Richardson or in a cottage of hers called "The Casino." As his mother and Alice regularly summered at Biddeford Pool, as the Babbitts came there in 1904, and as that year and the next brought also Louis and his wife[15] and their little son, Paul could relax, as he greatly preferred, in the intimacy of his family and friends instead of adapting himself to strangers. He used to play golf and tennis; attend picnics on the rocks, where the elaborate outdoor cooking bored him; read a book of Homer a day "with the sound of his πολυσφλοίσβοιο θαλάσσης murmuring"[16] in his ears; and listen to Babbitt—"the same old man, still argumentative and contentious when, I confess, a little genialisch conversation would suit my mood better."[17] ". . . there isn't much to say about a summer resort, except that mankind is at its worst there. Babbitt avers that the initial sin of the modern world is the doctrine of Rousseau that men are essentially good and wise instead of evil and foolish, and I think a few weeks of vacation is enough to prove the theory."[18]

Because the birth of his daughter, Mary Darrah, in East Orange on February 24, 1902, greatly weakened his wife, that year More took a fortnight's furlough at home in September. Later "Net and I went up to Cambridge for a week and"—as guests of the Babbitts—"had a gay vacation."[19]

[15] In the autumn of 1902 Miss Eleanor Herron, a sister-in-law of William Howard Taft, governor of the Philippines, announced her engagement to Louis Trenchard More, then a professor of physics at the University of Cincinnati. The wedding, at which Paul was best man, took place in Cincinnati on March 17, 1903.

[16] To Prosser Hall Frye, July 26, 1903.
". . . I look on the reading of *The Odyssey* by the sea shore as the nearest earthy approach to what Crabbe calls 'the sober certainty of waking bliss.' . . ." [To the same, Dec. 6, 1901.]
During his vacations in 1903 and 1904 More let Professor and Mrs. Prosser Hall Frye occupy, rent free, his house in East Orange.
[17] To the same, Aug. 6, 1904.   [18] To the same, Aug. 18, 1904.
[19] To the same, Dec. 11, 1902.

Literary Editor

Rollo Ogden, editor of the New York *Evening Post*, telephoned More on October 23, 1903, "asking me to stay in and take dinner with him and Lamont, (Managing Editor of *The Evening Post*). Of course I did so. They intend to sever the literary department of *The Post* from *The Nation*[20] and put it in the control of a man who shall be entirely independent of Mr. Garrison. They asked me to take the place and after talking the matter over with them fully I agreed. . . . The place on *The Post* came to me entirely unsolicited and unexpected."[21]

"Have I never told you just what I am doing on *The Post*? In a word I write the Books and Reading column[22] and edit the Literary Department. Hitherto there has been no man to take charge of this latter task, but all the literary matter of *The Nation* has been emptied into *The Post* wherever and whenever there chanced to be a vacant column. Naturally this left the department of *The Post* in a state of haphazard and delay—especially delay since *The Nation* reviews to begin with are generally from a month to a year behindhand. Now I take what matter I choose from *The Nation* and provide also partly for myself. . . . The bulk of the literary matter comes out in the Saturday Supplement,[23] but by no means all. Thus there were three column of reviews in yesterday and again three columns today. I do less reviewing myself than I did on *The Independent*, in fact writing up only those books that I want to read and keep."[24]

Besides the editorial tasks that he was paid to do, about once

[20] In 1881 *The Nation* had merged in *The Evening Post*.
[21] To Prosser Hall Frye, Oct. 24, 1903. Frank Jewett Mather, Jr., had recommended More for this position to the editors of *The Evening Post*.
[22] Published almost daily.
[23] Usually covering two pages, this occasionally expanded into a "Book Section" of up to fourteen pages.
[24] To Prosser Hall Frye, Feb. 2, 1904. Before leaving *The Independent* by Dec. 1, 1903, More recommended Frye as his successor, who during summer vacations from the University of Nebraska, where he taught English, had worked for the magazine; but Edwin E. Slosson was chosen to fill the place.

a month he contributed gratis a long paper. *The Evening Post* benefited from "this magazine 'feature' ";[25] he benefited from the regular publicity it assured his essays. In September 1904 he published some of these papers—those on Carlyle, Yeats, and Lionel Johnson—together with previous ones from *The Atlantic Monthly* on Tolstoy, Thoreau, and Hawthorne, as well as one on English prosody from *The Sewanee Review*, another on Irish sagas from *The International Quarterly*, three from *The Independent* (on Emerson, Arthur Symons,[26] and "The Origins of Hawthorne and Poe"), and one, "The Religious Ground of Humanitarianism," which *The Independent* had rejected, in his first volume of *Shelburne Essays*. Eight months later came a second volume of *Shelburne Essays,* including his *Evening Post* articles on Elizabethan sonnets, Shakespeare's sonnets, Hazlitt, and Lamb, his papers in *The Atlantic Monthly* on Lafcadio Hearn,[27] Meredith, Crabbe, Kipling and FitzGerald, another on Hawthorne from *The Independent*, and two from *The New World*, one on Nemesis, the other on the "Two Famous Maxims

[25] To Prosser Hall Frye, Dec. 27, 1904.

[26] "As regards the Symons essay, I have . . . always felt that it was out of centre and *wrong*; the argument is too heavy for the man. And that is what always worries me on reading over my work, the sense that somewhere it is out of balance and does not report the fact exactly as I have seen it; does not convey the same emotion precisely which the book gave me. Yes, I believe that this worries me more than the concomitant, but really different, feeling that at every point some failure of my education or my native endowment prevents me from seeing the thing as it is and getting out of it the emotion which corresponds to that fact." [To Prosser Hall Frye, May 28, 1906.] Symons, however, in a letter to More of April 5, 1907, commended the essay as the most penetrating examination of his work as a whole that he had read.

[27] "Lafcadio Hearn had some row with Houghton Mifflin Co., as he did with most of his publishers. I wrote an essay on him for *The Atlantic*, knowing nothing of this. He saw the article and sent Bliss Perry, then the editor, a story, saying that he was so much pleased with the article that he hoped Perry would accept the story, with or without payment. Perry was kind enough to send me Hearn's letter and also the MS. of the story, the latter the most beautiful, faultless copper-plate writing I have ever seen. I naturally prize the letter." [To Robert Shafer, Jan. 30, 1926. Cf. Shafer's *Paul Elmer More and American Criticism*, New Haven (Yale University Press), 1935, p. 174 n.]

of Greece" now renamed "Delphi and Greek Literature." That
same spring or early in the summer appeared his edition, with
a biographical sketch, of *The Complete Poetical Works of Lord
Byron*. And on its heels, in the fall of 1905, sped the Third
Series of *Shelburne Essays*, reprinting his contribution on Sainte-
Beuve[28] and his delicately perceptive paper on Christina Rossetti
from *The Atlantic Monthly*, his *Evening Post* articles on Scott,
J. Henry Shorthouse, Sterne, Browning, Swinburne, Whittier,
and Cowper, and a hitherto unpublished essay, "The Quest of
a Century," which borrowed from Lou's screed on the doctrine of motion.[29]

William Roscoe Thayer considered the essays the best literary criticism printed in English since the death of Matthew
Arnold. He lauded their author for going beyond the classroom
rhetoric of Wendell, Mabie, and Van Dyke, which for a decade
had prevailed in America,[30] and for judging literature in its relation to life. Though never a disciple of Arnold to the extent,
for example, of William Crary Brownell,[31] More, who said "a
second time" some of the things that Matthew Arnold had "said
better the first time,"[32] belonged, as he wrote of Arnold, "to one

[28] Though the essay emphasizes the Frenchman's historic sense at the
cost of his psychological insight, it is sympathetic and full of passages
suggesting similarities to More: "the sense of disillusion, which was really
inherent in him from his youth, and the passion for truth hindered him
in his 'creative' work, while they increased his powers as a critic"—"his
life was a long endeavour to supplant the romantic elements of his
taste by the classical"—"what attracted him chiefly was that middle
ground where life and literature meet, where life becomes self-conscious
through expression, and literature retains the reality of association with
fact." [*SE* III, 69, 73, 78.]

[29] See p. 84 above.

[30] ". . . one of the chief obstacles in the way of good literary work
today is the lack of a sound and sharp critical atmosphere about one."
[To William Roscoe Thayer, May 20, 1905; courtesy of Harvard University Library. Cf. "More's Shelburne Essays," by George McLean
Harper, *The Atlantic Monthly*, Oct. 1906, p. 561.]

[31] Cf. *Matthew Arnold and American Culture*, by John Henry Raleigh,
University of California Publications, English Studies: 17, Berkeley and
Los Angeles (University of California Press), 1957.

[32] To Stuart P. Sherman, April 24, 1917; courtesy of the University of
Illinois Library.

of the great families of human intelligence, which begins with Cicero . . . and passes through Erasmus and Boileau and Shaftes-bury and Sainte-Beuve. These are the exemplars—not complete individually . . .—of what may be called the critical spirit: dis-criminators between the false and the true, the deformed and the normal; preachers of harmony and proportion and order, prophets of the religion of taste. If they deal much with the criticism of literature, this is because in literature more mani-festly than anywhere else life displays its infinitely varied mo-tives and results; and their practice is always to render litera-ture itself more consciously a criticism of life. The past is the field out of which they draw their examples of what is in con-formity with nature and of what departs from that norm. In that field they balance and weigh and measure; they are by intellect hesitators, but at heart very much in earnest."[33]

"Literary criticism is . . . only the specific exercise of a faculty which works in many directions. All scholars, whether they deal with history or sociology or philosophy or language or, in the narrower use of the word, literature, are servants of the critical spirit, in so far as they transmit and interpret and mould the sum of experience from man to man and from generation to generation."[34]

". . . the one desire that increases upon me," More disclosed to Frye, "is the wish to speak the truth. I do not mean by that to interpret life in conformity with any high generalization or idea. The surrender of such an aim is, I know, a confession of defeat in a way; a confession that we have not found ourselves, as does every great *artist*, strong enough to remould the world in accordance with our own nature. But there is a certain conso-lation in the effort to attain that lower truth which attempts merely to see each separate object and life as it is in itself. There is room enough here, too, for self-deception, God knows, but the purpose may remain constant. I should like my essay to be 'distinguished'; if I were sure it was 'right' I could be pretty

[33] *SE* VII, 218   [34] *Ibid.*, 244.

well content however if every other quality were lacking. To be more precise, I should say that rightness today, or any day, were a distinction rare enough to satisfy the most ambitious."[35]

On July 1, 1906, *The Nation*, which, until the first World War, possessed a general authority unsurpassed by any other American weekly, obtained More as its literary editor.[36]

"If I wrote what was really in my heart," he answered a "not entirely cheerful" letter from Alice about re-entering her treadmill that winter in the St. Louis School of Fine Arts,[37] "I should merely blacken paper with a long commentary on the emptiness of life—of my own life in particular. Here I have been toiling and renouncing and wrestling with heartache since I was a boy for fame, and now, when enough praise falls to me to show what fame would be, I find it adds not one jot to the meaning of life or to the pleasure in my work. This is a mystery the world has been trying to solve for a good many years, and apparently the solution is not to come from me. And withal I have a number of things which you have not. I do not wonder that you feel the bitterness of it. I beg of you, however, to keep one thing which I have lost—that is the power of sympathy. I won't say that, either. I have not lost it; in some ways it is quicker than it ever was; but continual absorption in study, and the endless necessity of writing, bury the simpler personal modes of expression and cut me off from more than you know. And above all don't grieve over having spoiled me! I have not yet found that anyone has been spoiled in this world by affection, have you? As for Darrah I feel sometimes that my own absorption produces a chilly at-

[35] To Prosser Hall Frye, May 28, 1906.

[36] "I am to be literary editor of both *The Post* and *The Nation* with a pretty comfortable increase of salary." [To the same, April 12, 1906.]

[37] Mary Darrah More being "the greatest rogue in Essex County" and taking "enough exercise in the course of the day to wear out a Sandow" [to the same, June 2, 1903], her grandmother and her invalid Aunt Alice moved from the strenuous atmosphere of 265 Springdale Avenue, East Orange, to the ancestral peace of Bridgeton, New Jersey. In 1906, after summering at Biddeford Pool, they went to St. Louis, where Alice resumed her former position as secretary and lecturer at the St. Louis School of Fine Arts.

mosphere about her, not altogether wholesome. She is well—
bloomingly well—and full of strange pranks and deep question-
ings. Just now she is alarmingly curious to know why her mother
is so big! . . . My evenings from half past eight are passed in
solitude and rather a saddened search for wisdom in books. I
begin to believe that peace cometh only from above—nay, perhaps, comes not, but awaits us there."[38]

Illness kept Nettie in bed much of the first half of 1906 or
left her barely enough strength to move about the house. Early
in April she had an appendectomy. In May kidney trouble appeared. And on June 28th at her house in East Orange she gave
birth to "a seven-pound girl, lusty and well-formed, and said to
be handsome . . . we are calling her Alice."[39] Although a few
weeks later More could inform his "dear big Alice" that the
mother "is doing excellently well, is sitting up, and begins to
walk tomorrow,"[40] from then on her health was permanently
undermined. For two years she dined on only two glasses of
milk, so good-naturedly and inconspicuously that others at the
table scarcely noticed it.

Her husband divided his vacation at home in halves that year:
a fortnight in July to be with her, and another in late September
and early October for reading. As the baby required Mrs. More's
attention, he used to put Darrah to bed, telling her a story be-
forehand and then, after tucking her in, singing to her until she
fell asleep. That autumn he swallowed "a dose of F. Schlegel,
Novalis, Schleiermacher, etc. . . . I am impressed by the fact
that we are for the most part simply chewing the cud of critical
ideas formulated then by F. Schlegel and his group. And nothing
is more bewildering than the apparent soundness of those ideas
with the fund of rottenness hidden in them. Take Schlegel's notion of Romantic Irony. How he has succeeded in involving a
profound thought with all sorts of false, slimy egotisms and

[38] To Alice More, May 23, 1906.
[39] To Mrs. Enoch Anson More, June 28, 1906.
[40] To Alice More, July 18, 1906.

nauseous morbidnesses! . . . I took up Euripides' *Iphigenia at Tauris*, and felt as if I had set my foot among realities again. And then my pleasure was suddenly checked by remembered [*sic*] that the Schlegels, others of the set, were just as enthusiastic over Greek as ever I could wish a man to be. The German Romantic School had that peculiar quality of transforming the best of life into its own likeness."[41]

During Mather's stay in Italy from about 1906 to 1909, More aided the understaffed *Evening Post* by writing occasional editorials in addition to his regular work. On receiving from his friend an "account of life in Florence with its mixture of *fare* and *far niente*—a composition that seems about impossible in this land of cheap strenuosity," More commented: "I have a wretched streak of puritanism in me. Beauty is suspect. Italy— I have never seen it—would I fear in a short time raise a kind of internal war within my members; I should either sink into dissipation or into futile disaccord with my surroundings. But to another Italy may be only a desirable and wholesome stimulus. And these things a man must determine from knowledge of himself. I am however inclined to think that *long* residence in Italy or anywhere else save where a man's roots are, brings at last a kind of paralysis of a man's higher faculties. A man's personal ambition needs to be interlocked with national ambition; he needs to feel that his work is, or at least aims to be, a part of the great and continuous intellectual life of his people. It is the great loss of America today that the heterogeneity of its population and culture weakens this feeling, but all the more we need to cling consciously and desperately to what associations of the sort we can discover. Of course, there is the opposite danger of narrowness and sterile isolation. . . . Certainly the machinery of the newspaper is depressing. I often wake up in the morning with a sense of despair at the endless repetition of routine. I would kick over the traces immediately if I could support myself as a free lance. But I am not magazinable, alas.

[41] To Prosser Hall Frye, Oct. 12, 1906. Cf. *SE* V, 125, 127, 130-31.

Perry, for instance, praises my work, has in fact just written to me in extravagant terms of my essays, but he would shy off mighty soon if I tried to place more than one of these same essays in *The Atlantic* in a year! And so I look forward to dying in the traces—and may God give me a season of rest in the end."[42]

"Babbitt came down for a couple of days" in December 1906 "and talked classicism versus romanticism till my soul was lame; but what a stream of eloquence the man has! He reminds me of the ancient days when men really talked."[43]

Shortly after the appearance of his Fourth Series of *Shelburne Essays*,[44] More, on learning that Norton had praised two articles signed "P. E. M." in *The Nation*[45] on "Thoreau and German Romanticism," begged him to "tell me where and how far you disagree with my judgment or with my tone. One of the hardest things a man has to contend against here and now is his isolation.[46] I hear so little criticism of my work that I respect, and nothing is more wholesome for a professional critic than to feel

[42] To Frank Jewett Mather, Jr., April 3, 1907.
[43] To Prosser Hall Frye, Jan. 3, 1907.
[44] On R. S. Hawker, Fanny Burney, George Herbert, Keats, Benjamin Franklin, Lamb, Whitman, Blake, "Paradise Lost," and Horace Walpole.
[45] Vol. 83, pp. 388-90, 411-12, Nov. 8 and 15, 1906, respectively.
[46] "The critic who is, so to speak, a greater critic than his age deserves, is isolated in a much more cruel way [than the artist]: for he remains in his own time ineffective." ["A Commentary," by T. S. Eliot, *The Criterion*, July 1937, vol. XVI, no. LXV, p. 666.] "More was a better critic than Pater; and I do not think it can be denied that he was of very much larger size than Arthur Symons." [*Ibid.*, p. 667.] "It would seem that the practical value of critical writing depends more immediately and obviously upon an element of journalism than does creative writing. This is not to say that creative writing also is not partly journalistic; it is only to suggest that effective criticism may demand a more conscious recognition of the contemporary situation. For Paul More, in America, there was, throughout the first part of his active life, no situation at all; and . . . his ineffectiveness in England was not essentially due to distance and to being unknown and out of touch: he would have been ineffective anyway because of having standards superior to those of the artists who were there to criticize. He had not the creative gift which alone could have given reality to his standards." [*Ibid.*, pp. 668-69.]

himself in contact with a certain body of readers who can hold him in check."[47]

". . . in one matter, the most fundamental of all," More replied to Norton's comments, "I am still in some doubt. You say: 'The rôle of the ideal critic is to express a judgment in which personal preferences, though they may have part, should make no appearance.' That, as I understand it, is unqualifiedly true of the *ideal*, or rather *classical*, critic—of Boileau, Matthew Arnold, Brunetière. But in this manner the critic must confine himself pretty closely to the few great names, or else indulge in satire. Is there not room for a perfectly legitimate criticism which deals with lesser names and tries to lend them interest by adventitious aids of various sorts? Sainte-Beuve's manner, for instance? In such work the judgment, while always in the background, may play a subordinate part. This need not be impressionistic writing in the bad sense of that word, but I conceive that it may take a personal color. My feeling is that the method to be employed if one designs to write a few essays on the great writers is different from that which is justifiable, almost necessary, if one looks forward to covering the byways as well as the highways. One must frankly adopt both the classic and the romantic models of criticism, while trying to suggest the proper perspective. Possibly such a method is self-destructive, but more probably I have simply shown lack of skill in fusing the elements. In reading over my essays I am, I admit, often pained to find that I have followed the bent of my personal taste too far. It is a constant temptation when one sees a point or feels a quality, to exaggerate."[48]

The daily grind—the routine that "settled down like a cloud of locusts, devouring every moment of time and leaving a devas-

[47] To Charles Eliot Norton, Dec. 21, 1906; courtesy of Houghton Library, Harvard University.

[48] To the same, May 2, 1907; courtesy of Houghton Library, Harvard University. Cf. *M*, 13.

tation"[49]—seemed to him a feverish dream from which he woke only at weekends devoted to

"The splendours of the intellect's advance,
The sweetness of the home with babes and wife."[50]

". . . you do not know what a terrible thing it is," he protested to Louis, who wondered why he did not hear from him oftener, "to have the presses calling to you all day and every day, for 'copy,' like a huge suction pump at your brain sucking the very juices out of you."[51]

As a momentary respite he spoke on February 27, 1907, to the Wednesday Club in St. Louis on "The Centenary of Long-fellow." About the same time he "debated with Miss Thomas," the president of Bryn Mawr, "against Brander Matthews and Lounsbury before the Contemporary Club of Philadelphia, and Miss Thomas treated me as if I were one of her long lost children. We never loved each other."[52]

Lamont, who in 1906 had succeeded Garrison as editor in chief of *The Nation*, did everything he could, by relieving More of general correspondence and office detail, to give him leisure for writing. After being on *The Nation's* staff for about a year and a half, he was freed from *The Evening Post's* column of "Books and Reading" in order to do more reviewing for *The Nation*—a change that increased his library at a pleasantly "alarming rate."[53] Early in May 1907, however, he had to "take off" his "coat and roll up" his "sleeves for real work,"[54] since Lamont left then for a trip to Europe. As the traveller underwent "a pretty severe operation"[55] on his return in July, More toiled

[49] To Prosser Hall Frye, Nov. 8, 1907.
[50] Quoted from Thomson's *City of Dreadful Night, SE* III, 140.
[51] To Louis T. More, March 9, 1908.
[52] To Charles Eliot Norton, Aug. 9, 1907; courtesy of Houghton Library, Harvard University.
[53] To Prosser Hall Frye, Feb. 6, 1908.
[54] To William Roscoe Thayer, May 2, 1907; courtesy of Houghton Library, Harvard University.
[55] To Charles Eliot Norton, Aug. 9, 1907; courtesy of Houghton Library, Harvard University.

in New York's "superheated hurly-burly"[56] after "Net, children, nurse, trunks, baby carriage, traveling ice-box, fifteen valises, one pasteboard box, bag of fruit, fans, alcohol stove, and God knows what else"[57] went off to Lakemont, New York, on August 1st, leaving a maid to look after him in East Orange.

Joining his family on August 17th as a boarder in a roomy farmhouse by Lake Seneca, he began an essay on Pascal. ". . . you will be surprised to hear that the people of the house here have in a way, and certainly without their own volition, helped me in this task. You see Pascal's faith was based on a contempt for human nature unrestored by Grace. Ordinarily the conventions of life so overlay the real instincts and acts of men that we see mankind in a kind of solid respectable gray. Now here I have been brought in contact with real unadulterated undisciplined human nature, and it has the effect of opening one's eyes to what we all at bottom are—a poor, restless, animal, evil thing. And as a moral I have before me the two opposite results of indulgence— a stupefied paralytic in whom the springs of action have been dried up, and an imbecile who has lost all power of inhibition so that there is no buffer of convention between fluttering impulse and action. . . . This morning I sat on the porch looking down on the lake and over to the long gradual slope on the other side.[58] A white mist was rolling up the lake, and through it the chequered farmland and vineyards of the opposite hills took on the romantic regularity of one of Maxfield Parrish's pictures. Out of the clouds came the continual cawing of the crows, and occasionally a small flock of them could be glimpsed as they swung from one cloud into another. These are things to see and to remember."[59]

After a month in "that home of bawdy, bedlam-and-babies," as he described the Lake Seneca farmhouse to Frye, he got back "in harness . . . half terrified by the work I see before me. However I have just had one grand joy—the reading for the first

[56] To Irving Babbitt, July 10, 1907.
[57] To Prosser Hall Frye, Aug. 2, 1907.
[58] Cf. *SE* VI, 112-13.
[59] To Louis T. More, Sept. 5, 1907. Cf. *JL*, 209.

time of Trollope's 'John Caldigate.' What a stunning story that is. When I get into Trollope's England I know that my home is there, and I have a kind of shuddering horror of days not so far in the future when we shall no longer be able to comprehend and enjoy the stability and character of the society he depicts— stability and character and magnificent stolidity. Balzac is infinitely greater than Trollope of course, yet how homeless and unsatisfied he leaves you in the end. . . . I am working to finish a fifth volume of essays for this spring, and a sixth next autumn. . . . Babbitt seems really to be getting on with his book on education, and, to judge from what of it he has sent me, I fancy it will make some talk in the academic frog pool."[60]

By the winter of 1907 Mrs. Richardson's health had so collapsed that Nettie, the only one of her family who went out of her way to look after her, found it exhausting to keep house in East Orange and to nurse her invalid aunt in New York. "After many delays and much doubting,"[61] on February 6, 1908, More signed "a lease for an apartment—or tenement, to be exact—at 260 West 99th. It is on the fourth floor of an old building, without elevator, the rooms, 9 (or 8½) and bath, fairly good size for New York and light. We go in the last of next month."[62]

Before settling in New York he was elected on February 10th

[60] To Prosser Hall Frye, Oct. 16, 1907. Babbitt sent More the manuscript of his *Literature and the American College: Essays in Defense of the Humanities*, and in return received from him many suggestions. After its publication Alice wrote to her brother: "I am just reading Babbitt's book and it gives me a curious sensation. I recognize so many of the ideas as common property of you both, and I understand what you mean by saying you owe him so much. I am not sure how much, as you were bound sooner or later to have reached your present point of view. The reason you got so much from I. B. was that it was your own. I can see that he has been a great stimulus to you, his book is scintillating, fairly reeling with ideas but his mind dwells in tents [;] he has little power of construction. His work makes me think of a kaleidoscope, his constant change of presentation, his bewildering superfluity of illustration so involve his theme that I hold on to it by force of will. However you may have started he might well now sit at your feet and learn not only to write but to think." [Alice More to P. E. More, May 18, 1909.]
[61] To Irving Babbitt, Feb. 8, 1908.
[62] To Prosser Hall Frye, Feb. 6, 1908.

to the National Institute of Arts and Letters. Apparently he could have soon entered the American Academy of Arts and Letters; for in September 1908, its secretary, Robert Underwood Johnson, wrote to him that he regretted More's refusal of election, since his gifts as a critic were much needed there. About this time he similarly shunned an honorary degree that a friend of his, a college president, wished to confer on him.[63] One of his close editorial associates believed he did this on account of modesty, which in him was as genuine as his desire to excel. On the other hand the college was then obscure and the Academy scarcely out of its growing pains.

Expecting Putnam's press to "proceed at its usual quiet pace I started the setting up of my fifth volume before the last essays were written. Now the machine has caught up with me, and is howling for copy."[64] But when the book rushed forth in April, it was scarcely noticed. The opening essay, "The Greek Anthology," may have demanded so much of readers that they rarely went on to the more familiar topics—Dickens, Gissing, Mrs. Gaskell, Philip Freneau, Thoreau, Longfellow, Donald G. Mitchell, James Thomson, Chesterfield, and Sir Henry Wotton.

It mattered little, however, to their busy author. Putting on a bright necktie sent to him by Babbitt's sister, he spoke at Bryn Mawr on May 1st about Sir Thomas Browne, "and felt in consequence like a young beau—all the girls were looking at me—or it."[65] Well on in his Sixth Series, he occupied himself with his family's summer plans and with his mother's stay at his apartment on her way with Alice to Biddeford Pool. As soon as their guest left, Nettie, the children, and two servants went to a cottage in Essex, New York, on Lake Champlain, which her sister, Mrs Heard, had found attractive the year before. The Crater Club "is a kind of private park, with a hotel and a number of small

[63] At the end of his life More had to decline, because of illness, honorary degrees from Duke University and Hobart College.
[64] To Louis T. More, Jan. 23, 1908.
[65] To Mrs. Irving Babbitt, May 6, 1908.

[106]

cottages, suitable if so desired for housekeeping. We shall do our own catering. The country from all I hear is lovely; not exactly mountainous, but hilly, and the lake of course beautiful. The town is some distance away. The people that go there are, I judge, very pleasant."[66]

During Lamont's vacation in July, More stayed in New York, getting his own breakfast, lunching downtown near *The Nation* offices, and dining at the Century "with other summer bachelors."[67] He put his apartment, when he went to the country, at the Fryes' disposal.

Louis and his family joined him in Essex for August—a month of reading, writing, outdoor work, walking, and cards. During a brief visit from Babbitt "the conversation was always good, because Babbitt would storm up and down the porch and Paul would sit quiet, and it was always an argument against Plato. Paul would often ask Babbitt a question and Babbitt would always stop and look puzzled and then would pour out words of scorn at him."[68] One cannot help remembering with a smile Socrates' belief that "the only occupation worthy of a free man" is "the earnest discussion of truth and virtue among friends."[69]

On the Nathaniel Ropes Foundation for the Comparative Study of Literature, at the University of Cincinnati, More delivered between January 6 and 16, 1909, lectures on Traherne, Pascal, Rousseau, Plato, and Tennyson, which last lecture he repeated on January 12th at Denison University, Granville, Ohio. "Such a welcome as I got from Darrah and Alice would almost reward one for traveling a thousand miles. Alice fairly screamed for delight on hearing me at the door."[70]

[66] To Louis T. More, March 17, 1908.
[67] To the same, July 6, 1908. More was elected to the Century Association on March 2, 1907.
[68] From Louis T. More's conversation as recorded, with his permission, by a stenographer.
[69] *SE* VI, 270.
[70] To Alice More, Jan. 20, 1909.

Soon after his return the Sixth Series of *Shelburne Essays*,[71] written, like so much of his work, as if addressed to "an audience of Coleridges, Johnsons, and Casaubons,"[72] "dropped into the puddle without making a splash. The book, I believe, is well calculated to miss every several class of readers—too academic for the literary, too literary for the academic; too sceptical for the religious, too religious for the sceptical; too human for the metaphysical and too metaphysical for the human. If it can't create its own readers, it will never get any."[73]

Far more disturbing, however, was the sense of uneasiness at *The Nation*. "Things here are in a state of suspense owing to the fact that Lamont is seriously considering a call to Williams College, and is in fact going up to Williamstown this afternoon in order to look over the field. Whatever happens, if he should accept, can scarcely be agreeable to me. I shouldn't submit to have a man from the outside put in over me, and on the other hand I dread having the responsibility of *The Nation* on my shoulders, fearing that it would interfere with my writing. However, nothing has happened yet."[74]

[71] These essays, except those on Pascal, Plato, and the *Bhagavad Gita*, had been previously published between 1893 and 1909. Despite the volume's subtitle, "Studies of Religious Dualism," only the three papers just named and those on "The Forest Philosophy of India" and Saint Augustine directly concern themselves much with religious dualism. The remaining chapters contain essays on Sir Thomas Browne, Bunyan, and Rousseau, and reprints of More's introduction to *The Judgment of Socrates* and of his translation of Plato's *Apology*.
[72] "Mr. P. E. More and The Wits," by Stuart P. Sherman, *The Review*, Jan. 17, 1920, vol. 2, no. 36, p. 55.
[73] To Prosser Hall Frye, April 2, 1909. Cf. *SE* VII, 29.
[74] To Louis T. More, April 21, 1909.

7

EDITOR OF *THE NATION* (1909-1912)

HAMMOND LAMONT died on May 6, 1909, "from the effect of a terrible operation; we are all pretty well broken up over the thing both for his loss as an editor and as a man."[1] ". . . he had those rarest of qualities—unweariable driving force and absolute integrity. Though our temperaments were in many respects different, we worked together without a rub and indeed he always treated me with extreme generosity. I had grown very fond of him. His absence leaves me editor of *The Nation* with a salary, beginning August 1, of $4500. I can't say that I dislike the honor, but I am fearful that the responsibility will make it harder for me to do my essay writing."[2]

Shortly before this, in April, Alice, discouraged by a change in the administration of the St. Louis School of Fine Arts had resigned from the school to become an instructor and lecturer in the St. Louis municipal art museum. Weakened by illness and depressed by the death of friends, she admitted to her brother, who prescribed a trip to Europe (where she went in the summer of 1910 while other members of the family looked after their aging mother), that for the first time she felt old, but shrugged it off as part of the common lot.

"I feel, as you do," Paul More conceded, "that the chief cause of your fatigue is the ornery lot of your family, in which category I humbly and sadly take my place.   . . . there seems to run a vein of uneasy egotism through most of our family. . . . I know how much of it I have and how often its upcropping mortifies me. The worst of it is the hard fight I have had to get my feet planted has intensified traits that might under other circumstances have been softened. I don't believe I would show

[1] To Irving Babbitt, May 7, 1909.
[2] To Louis T. More, May 14, 1909. More was appointed editor in chief of *The Nation* on May 11, 1909.

much of that clashing egotism if I lived with you alone or with our family. . . . I do feel that my marriage relations stand between us, and I grieve over it—but what can I do? They are kind to me and give me nothing to complain of, but there are reasons for that which do not hold good when it comes to the women of my family. Our family temperaments are utterly different. I merely laugh with them on the surface, and indeed find them in these relations very agreeable—but we only touch on the surface. Net is different from them in many respects as they know and resent—but they are her blood after all. I know her love for you and mother is very deep, but her interests are all —more than I could wish—with her own people. . . . My own life like yours—though not to so great a degree—is a crushing grind. I feel that cynicism and indifference creep every day closer to my heart; I read books by habit, and write for God knows what reason—not for money or fame, neither of which I could ever get. My letter is as comforting as the talk of Job's friends, but it is at least frank. I think we shall have good times yet before we die, and I am sure that my love for you is one of the few things that neither cynicism nor indifference has touched. That is rooted too deep and goes down to the sources of my life."[3]

That the conflicting needs of her severe, aggressive mother, her gently firm mother-in-law, and her unconsciously possessive sister-in-law, Alice, not to mention her lonely and helpless aunt, Mrs. Richardson, did not shatter Nettie's home life testifies to her charitable disposition, buoyant sense of humor, and strength of mind. Instead of severing herself and her husband from their relatives, she tried to create in her home a sphere of affection that embraced them all, an environment favorable to his happi-

[3] To Alice More, Oct. 7, 1909. "The dreadful truth is that the struggle for life has a sad disheartening effect on most of us. I feel it only too strongly in myself—feel a kind of hardening of the fibres, a disinclination to give myself out in sympathy, a shutting in within an ever narrowing circle. But the time has not come—I think it never will come—when I have no appreciation of the hard hills you have climbed. My grief is that I am powerless to help." [To Alice More, Aug. 6, 1910.]

ness and mental productivity. In the development and the maintenance of their family life she was the active and the stabilizing factor.

Notwithstanding the "crushing grind" of *The Nation*, More delivered a hastily written lecture on criticism in February 1910 to the Women's Club of St. Louis and, in a dull way, without any inflection in his voice, to a Yale group at the University Club in New Haven. As the same lecture served Columbia University on May 3rd, he made "a fair sum of money out of it."[4]

While visiting the Babbitts in Cambridge from March 17th to 20th, he arranged to have Harold de Wulf Fuller go a few months later to *The Nation* as an assistant editor. He also undertook to proofread Babbitt's *The New Laokoon*, which he described to Frye as "a pretty big thing."[5]

Fuller having proved to be dependable, the editor in chief passed the latter half of July and the last three weeks of August at his camp in Essex.[6] There he chopped down trees, carved through the stony soil with a pickaxe a path from his house to the road, completed the last essay of his Seventh Series,[7] and in an idle moment considered which authors had appealed to him most intimately: "Homer, Sophocles, Pindar, Plato, Virgil, Hor-

[4] To Irving Babbitt, Jan. 10, 1910.
[5] To Prosser Hall Frye, July 14, 1910.
[6] On Dec. 27, 1909, John B. Burnham and his wife conveyed by deed to Paul E. More the land and the cottage at the Crater Club in Essex known as "The Cedars." Mrs. Beck (and later the Heards) summered in a house about two hundred feet west of More's cottage. "Camp Barberry," which More had rented in 1908, which the Babbitts occupied in the summer of 1910, and which Louis T. More bought in 1912, stood about two hundred feet north of "The Cedars"—near enough for the brothers to call loudly back and forth about all sorts of intellectual and family matters.
[7] The book aroused so little comment that More felt, "as Babbitt says he feels, like a general without an army." [To Alice More, Nov. 3, 1910.] It had chapters on Shelley, Wordsworth (in whom More noted a "low physical vitality, which made him shrink from action, joined to a troubled moral sense, which sought ease of conscience in communion with a passive unmoral nature" [*SE* VII, 44]), Thomas Hood, Tennyson, William Morris, Louisa Shore, Thomas Bailey Aldrich, Francis Thompson, the socialism of G. Lowes Dickinson, the pragmatism of William James, criticism, and Victorian literature.

ace, Racine, Molière, Sainte-Beuve, Milton, Byron (the satire), Thackeray, and Matthew Arnold. You see that Shakespeare is out, and also all Spanish, Italian, and German authors."[8]

The sensible and affectionate companionship of matrimony had rid him of most traces of German romanticism. His *Shelburne Essays* turned from the reveries of *The Great Refusal* to the realities of "the simple passion of the flesh . . . the natural cry of a man of strong animal appetites and strong unperverted intellect."[9] Also they show, as in the sympathetic essays on Cowper, Whittier, and Longfellow, a devotion to the hearth, a prizing of "the homely associations of a love that is less a passion than a quiet haven from the vexations of life," as sung in "the gentle verses of Tibullus counting up the treasures of his love and pastoral content while the morning rain washes on the roof."[10]

". . . Mather came down from Lake Placid for three days, and he and Babbitt and I sat and walked, and talked until there seemed nothing more to say. . . . I find that sort of conversation at times very stimulating and very useful in orienting one's ideas. Too much of it may get to be a bit depressing, but then too much is not much of a danger, as we live in our scattered isolation."[11]

"What an outrageous scandal it is that a man like him" (More referred to Babbitt, who felt "bitterly the way in which Kittredge and one or two others" had "blocked his advancement"[12] at Harvard) "should be kept down while charlatans . . . are pushed up. . . . the feeling of revolt is very widespread against the particular form of philological teaching that Kittredge has imposed on the department, and . . . it is regularly eliminating the better sort of men. . . . A sober statement of the facts . . . sent to the Overseers would have an astonishing

[8] To Prosser Hall Frye, undated (probably Aug. 1910).
[9] *SE* I, 137; cf. *ibid.*, p. 200.
[10] *SE* I, 137. Cf. *SE* XI, 24, and "Herrick," *N*, Oct. 24, 1912, vol. 95, pp. 378-81, and *EP*, Oct. 26, 1912, Saturday Supplement, pp. 8-9.
[11] To Prosser Hall Frye, undated (probably Aug. 1910).
[12] To Stuart P. Sherman, Nov. 18, 1910; courtesy of the University of Illinois Library.

effect, for as a matter of fact the philological syndicate in the classics has already been panic-struck, and the same syndicate in the modern languages is already on the defensive. I call it a syndicate because it is true that a few men, at the head of whom stands Kittredge, really control to a very considerable measure, and consciously control, the English and modern language departments all over the country.[13] I hear this from many quarters. The great difficulty is that Kittredge and his band are in their own field strong men, whereas the so-called 'literary' men are likely to be weak-kneed dilettantes. . . . The great field of virile ideas is left deserted by the philologists on the one side and the semi-aesthetes on the other."[14]

Armed with an invitation to teach at the University of Illinois, obtained partly through the influence of Stuart Pratt Sherman,[15] a former student of his then on the faculty in Urbana, Babbitt sought from Abbott Lawrence Lowell assurance of promotion to a full professorship at Harvard a year later. More, writing on his friend's behalf to President Lowell, stated that in his opinion Babbitt was too great a teacher and scholar for Harvard to lose. Although he could not, in advance, assure Babbitt of promotion, Lowell answered, this did not imply that he would not be promoted. The year having passed, More congratulated Babbitt on the acquisition of the title, which would give him "a much stronger position for attack and defense."[16]

Mrs. Richardson died on January 3, 1911, and More with his wife, Mrs. Beck, and Augustine Heard, went to St. Louis for her burial. In appreciation of her niece's years of devoted

[13] Cf. "The Teaching of the Classics," by Paul Elmer More, *IND*, Aug. 6, 1908, vol. LXV, no. 3114, p. 329.

[14] To William Roscoe Thayer, Sept. 12, 1910; courtesy of Houghton Library, Harvard University.

[15] More and Sherman first met at Babbitt's house in Cambridge in 1905 or 1906. In 1908 More cultivated Sherman as a reviewer, and welcomed him that summer as a temporary addition to the staff of *The Evening Post* and *The Nation*. He urged him in vain, early in 1909, to join the staff permanently.

[16] To Irving Babbitt, Feb. 29, 1912.

care Mrs. Richardson left her an unexpectedly large part of her fortune, including real estate in Biddeford Pool and much of her tangible personal property.

Soon after their return to New York, the Mores moved into Mrs. Richardson's former house at 780 West End Avenue— "very grand, but too expensive . . . and it doesn't seem like my own, the ornaments don't fit me."[17] He longed for "a real house" in "some such place as Princeton" (where Mather had recently settled), with only three days a week at the office. But when he broached the matter to Oswald Garrison Villard, the editor and the president of the New York *Evening Post*, the latter "pulled a long face at the idea."[18]

While he thus chafed under city and editorial routine, Ernest Fox Nichols, president of Dartmouth, asked him whether he would teach English there. More had no intention, he replied, of relinquishing his present position and could be tempted only by an offer that would allow him an exceptional amount of time for writing. He seized the opportunity, however, to recommend Frye as a possible candidate.

Having, despite overwork, "tonsilitis, earache, and every other variety of cold,"[19] "jumbled together five essays on William Beckford, Newman, Pater, Nietzsche, and Fiona Macleod, under the convenient name of Types of Romanticism—blessed word!"[20] More read them aloud at the University of Wisconsin from March 16th to 23rd. Though they "passed off well enough," he found lecturing "certainly very distasteful."[21] Before Sherman met him at Champaign to pilot him to the University of Illinois, More spoke on March 24th and 25th in Milwaukee on Newman and Pater. From the 27th to the 31st he repeated at Urbana the five lectures he had given in Madison.

17 To Alice More, Feb. 13, 1911.
18 *Ibid.*
19 *Ibid.*
20 To Stuart P. Sherman, Feb. 11, 1911; courtesy of the University of Illinois Library.
21 To Irving Babbitt, March 16, 1911.

That August in Essex he polished his "aphorisms"[22] or "epigrams"[23] or "definitions"[24]—terse statements of his ultimate beliefs, which had long been burrowing about in his brain "like caged rats."[25] Then on September 9th he and his family moved from 780 West End Avenue to a three-story house, two rooms deep, with a winding staircase, at 159 West 92nd Street, on which he had obtained a three year lease for $1950. "It really looks like a bargain, though of course you can't tell what dreadful thing may happen in this Christian city. It is on a good block, between Amsterdam and Columbus, which contains St. Agnes' Chapel and another church."[26]

The nearness and congeniality of the chapel and his conviction that Protestantism tended to rationalism[27] and sentimental social service helped More to persuade his wife that, since the sermon, which he impassively endured "as a soporific to the senses which sets the fancy free to wander,"[28] generally proved to be disappointing, they might better go to a church the rest of whose service was redeemingly beautiful. They attended St. Agnes', therefore, and brought up their children as Episcopalians.

The Anglican Church had already attracted him much in *John Inglesant* and in Newman's preconversion writings. Indeed the Shelburne essay, "J. Henry Shorthouse," written in 1905, by the slant of its sympathies strikingly adumbrates More's own future course. The author of "the one great religious novel of the English language"[29] had been reared as a Quaker and steeped in Greek philosophy. That absolute confidence in faith,

[22] To the same, Oct. 13, 1910.
[23] To Alice More, "Saturday morning"; postmarked Aug. 26, 1911.
[24] To the same, Nov. 9, 1911.
[25] *Ibid.*
[26] To the same, July 17, 1911. Alice, then over sixty and ready to retire, also moved that year, building for her mother and herself a small house at 18 South Giles Street, Bridgeton, New Jersey.
[27] Cf. *SE* VIII, 56.
[28] To Stuart P. Sherman, May 5, 1918; courtesy of the University of Illinois Library.
[29] *SE* III, 227.

hope, and charity, and pragmatic willingness to give them such
content as experience from time to time prompts; that scepticism about creeds, and simple trust in God; that humble reverence for the Inner Voice—all those Quaker traits that caused
More to read Whittier "with ever fresh delight,"[30] Shorthouse
retained after entering the Church of England. "The step signi-
fied to him . . . a transition from the religion of conscience to
that of the imagination, from morality to spiritual vision"[31]—
to "the sense of the infinite as something that escapes the understanding and can be only grasped, if ever grasped, in types and
symbols. . . . 'Dangerous it were,' to quote Hooker . . . 'for the
feeble brain of man to wade far into the doings of the Most
High, whom although to know be life, and joy to make mention
of his name; yet our soundest knowledge is to know that we
know him not as indeed he is, neither can know him; and our
safest eloquence concerning him is our silence, when we confess without confession that his glory is inexplicable, his greatness above our capacity and reach.' "[32]

Shorthouse's position (like More's) "was akin to that of the
Low-Churchman in his hostility to the Romanising tendencies[33]
and his distrust of priestcraft, but he differed from them still
more essentially in his recognition of the imagination as equally
potent with the moral sense in the upbuilding of character. To
the Broad-Churchman he was united chiefly in his abhorrence
of dogmatic tests. . . . those troubled doubters who are held
aloof by the dogmas of Christianity, yet regret their lonely isolation from the religious aspirations of the community" may sympathize with what Shorthouse called the "one principle which
underlies all church worship . . . the sacramental principle. For
this is the great underlying principle of life, by which the com-
monest and dullest incidents . . . become instinct with a delicate

[30] *SE* III, 37.
[31] *SE* III, 229; cf. *SE* VII, 132.
[32] *SE* VI, 190-91.
[33] To the Papist argument John Inglesant replied, "Absolute truth is
not revealed." [*SE* III, 242.]

purity, a radiant beauty, become the 'outward and visible sign of an inward and spiritual grace.' Everything may be a sacrament to the pure in heart."[34]

The creator of *John Inglesant* "separated himself from the Broad Church in making religion a culture of individual holiness . . . in caring more for the guidance of the Inner Voice than for the brotherhood of charity or the association of men in good works. . . .[35] Platonism . . . made the bounds of the High Church too narrow for his faith. He did not hesitate at one time to say that Plato possessed a truer spiritual insight than St. Paul. . . .[36] Beauty was for him a kind of transfiguration in which the world, in its response to the indwelling Power, was lifted into something no longer worldly, but divine; and he could speak of our existence on this earth as lighted by 'the immeasurable glory of the drama of God in which we are actors.' It was not that he, like certain poets of the past century, attempted to give to the crude passions of men or the transient pomp of earth a power intrinsically equivalent to the spirit; but he believed that these might be made by faith to become as it were an illusory and transparent veil through which the visionary eye could penetrate to the mystic reality. . . .

[34] *SE* III, 230-31.

[35] "Unless the pulpit can give us something different from the exhortations of reformers, unless it can give us an individual religion, unless it can bring my soul, with no thought of any other man's soul, into immediate communication with God, I can see no reason why the Church should continue to exist as a separate institution. This is not to question the content of social reform—that is another matter. Nor is it to say (though I may seem to be falling into an inconsistency) that religion will be ineffective socially. The order of procedure is the important matter; which comes first. The only potent social sympathy is that which will come of itself from a common reverence of something above man—without that you will have endless talk about sympathy and a growing dissociation of men, ending in war and anarchy." [To Richard W. Boynton, June 18, 1918.]

[36] John Inglesant "showed—though this neither he nor Mr. Shorthouse, perhaps, would acknowledge—that at the bottom of his heart Plato and not Christ was his master, and that to him practical Christianity was only one of the many historic forms which the so-called Platonic insight assumes among men." [*SE* III, 240.]

"But if, intellectually, the vision of the Divine Light was vouchsafed to Plato more than to any other man, historically it had been presented to the gross, unpurged eyes of the world in the life and death of Jesus. . . . Somehow, in some way beyond the scope of logic, the idea which Plato had beheld, the divine ideal which all men know and doubt, became a personality that one time, and henceforth the sacraments that recalled the drama of that holy life were the surest means of obtaining the silence of the world through which the Inner Voice speaks and is heard.

"To some, of course, this will appear the one flaw in the author's logic—this step from the vague notion of the Platonic ideas dwelling in the world of matter, and shaping it to their own beautiful forms, to the belief in the actual Christian drama as the realisation of the Divine Nature in human life. Yet the step was easy, was almost necessary, for one who held at the same time the doctrines of the Friends and of Plato; their union might be called the wedding of pure religion and pure philosophy, wherein the more bigoted and inhuman character of the former was surrendered, while to the latter was added the power to touch the universal heart of man."[37]

Despite the attraction of Anglicanism, More at this time preferred, as his comments on Newman show as clearly as his rejection of Shorthouse's last step, a sort of "pure spirituality." "This, in the end, must be our reservation in the praise due to Newman's beautiful life, that he stopped short of the purest faith. He was born a man with deep religious needs and instincts, a man to whom the spiritual world was the absorbing reality, beside which the material world and its appearances were but as shadows gathered in a dream. But he was born also in an age when the old faith in an outer authority based on an exact and unequivocal revelation could be maintained only by doing violence to the integrity of the believer's mind. That was his dilemma, and there lay the tragedy of his choice. Two ways were open to him. On the one hand, he might have accepted man-

[37] *SE* III, 231-38.

fully the sceptical demolition of the Christian mythology and the whole fabric of external religion, and on the ruins of such creeds he might have risen to that supreme insight which demands no revelation and is dependent on no authority, but is content within itself. Doing this he might possibly, by the depth of his religious nature and the eloquence of his tongue, have made himself the leader of the elect out of the long spiritual death that is likely to follow the breaking-up of the creeds. Or, if that task seemed impossible or fraught with too great peril, he might have held to the national worship as a symbol of the religious experience of the people, and into that worship and that symbol he might have breathed the new fervour of his own faith, waiting reverently until by natural growth his people were prepared, if ever they should be prepared, to apprehend with him the invisible truth without the forms. It is written: 'Blessed are they that have not seen, and yet have believed.' But in the hour of need his heart failed him, and he demanded to see with his eyes and feel with his hands. He was not strong enough to hold fast to the actual discords of life and to discern his vision of peace apart from their illusory sphere, but found it necessary to warp the facts of spiritual experience so as to make them agree with a physical revelation."[38]

On reading in *The Nation* the lecture on Nietzsche that More had delivered six months before in the Middle West, Thayer suggested it be published as a book instead of being buried in the next volume of *Shelburne Essays*. Since More, unlike Sainte-Beuve,[39] had no following to appreciate his work, Thayer urged

[38] *SE* VIII, 73-75.

[39] "In point of methodical use of ample equipment, thoroughness of method, and courageous determination to tell the truth without fear or favor, Mr. More's essays are the best American parallels of those incomparable *Lundis* which for a quarter of a century every Tuesday morning sent Sainte-Beuve 'down to the bottom of a pit, not to reascend until Friday evening at some unknown hour'. . . ." [*The Outlook*, Nov. 18, 1905, vol. 81, p. 679.] Arthur Ransome, writing in England, also noted that More "occupies in America some such place as was held in France by Sainte-Beuve." [*The Bookman*, Sept. 1911, vol. 40, p. 262.]

him to write, like William James, for popular magazines and to let slip no decent aid to publicity.

"I need not tell you," More responded, "that I am very grateful for your generous praise of my Nietzsche. And so true is what you say of the difference between an American and English audience of to-day and the kind of audience that a Sainte-Beuve addressed, that I find myself excluding the general reader from my mind and writing with the expected judgment of yourself and two or three other men quite distinctly before me. This gives a man a high standard and also a very warm sense when occasionally he seems to reach such a standard. But it is equally true that there are very real dangers in thus narrowing one's range of intended appeal. I am going to take into consideration what you say about reprinting the Nietzsche. It is only too true, as you write, that an essay published in a series of volumes is in a way lost. Babbitt has told me most emphatically that he thought my sixth volume, for instance, would have made much more impression if it had been issued independently, with a title of its own; and I dare say he is right—at least looking at the matter from the point of view of the 'short haul,' so to speak. But as I have replied to him, I am vain enough, perhaps foolish enough, to be chiefly concerned with how things will go in the 'long haul.' That is to say, I am considering what will be the fate of my essays when my writing is done and the real account with time begins. In the long run will not such work be most effective and make a better fight for remembrance by its very bulk and massiveness?"[40]

"I tried Putnam's with the Nietzsche," a few days later, "but they would none of it. I may try some other house, but I doubt if any of them will care for it.[41] One finds it a bit tedious to hawk such wares about. Perhaps that is why I have grown

[40] To William Roscoe Thayer, Oct. 2, 1911; courtesy of Houghton Library, Harvard University.

[41] As a result of Thayer's recommendation of "Nietzsche" to Ferris Greenslet, Houghton Mifflin agreed to print the essay as a book at their own expense, with a ten per cent royalty to the author.

philosophical on the subject and speak magniloquently of the long haul."[42]

As fellow worker and editor More put several of *The Nation's* contributors virtually through a correspondence course in composition, so differently did their manuscripts appear in print from the way in which they had been submitted. "Style," he grumbled to Thayer, "is almost a non-existent thing . . . among university scholars in general, and I have to depend on them for the quality of *The Nation*."[43] ". . . on this whole matter of style, it must be as clear to you as it is to me, that the common sin of today is that form of 'inverted pedantry' which denies the authority of all rules and appeals to the indiscriminate authority of usage. A little reading shows the diversity of custom; only a large amount of reading in a kind of literature not much troubled by pedants will train the ear to the niceties of the best usage.[44] As a matter of fact at the present moment you may almost measure the pendantry of a man (witness Kittredge, Sheldon, *et al.*; witness the monstrous book recently published by Krapp, of Columbia, who knows Old English and Middle English to the ground, but no more *English* than a trained pig) by his repudiation, in theory at least, of the notion of a norm of good style. As a consequence the danger today is in nowise in the direction of too great purism but of cheap neoterisms and indiscriminate justification of whatever has been used sporadically. . . . I think *The Nation* can do a real service, in so far as its editors can feel the difference between . . . good English and . . . journalese. . . ."[45]

[42] To William Roscoe Thayer, Oct. 9, 1911; courtesy of Houghton Library, Harvard University.
[43] To the same, Nov. 26, 1912; courtesy of Houghton Library, Harvard University.
[44] As models of English More looked to Shaftesbury, Addison, Johnson, Cowper, Southey, and Chesterfield. [Cf. "English and Englistic," *Academy Papers*, Addresses on Language Problems by Members of the American Academy of Arts and Letters, New York (Charles Scribner's Sons), 1925, pp. 21-22.]
[45] To William Roscoe Thayer, Oct. 9, 1911; courtesy of Houghton Library, Harvard University.

The Nation

But of all his duties for the magazine More probably most enjoyed fostering the talents of Stuart P. Sherman, by constantly suggesting topics for him to write about and by carefully criticizing the results. Though Sherman's contributions so dazzled More with wit and irony that their author remained for him "something of a psychological problem," a man whose mask he "never quite penetrated,"[46] and though More had assured him, "Don't for a moment think that I wish to force any of my own opinions on the signed work in *The Nation*,"[47] occasionally the editor had to reject one of his articles.

"I hate to return any manuscript of yours," he acknowledged to Sherman, "but your title, 'Return to Nature,' points the way back to Illinois. . . . I am chiefly brought to my decision by an invincible feeling that your ideas are not quite clarified by reflection. These words 'nature' and 'reason' are notorious pitfalls, they may mean almost anything. Now Rousseau, it is evident, used the phrase 'return to nature' ambiguously: sometimes in a temporal sense, meaning back to the actual state of savage life; other times in a logical sense, meaning back to what is essentially nature in us. In the first sense he was, I think, confused, verging now to the not uncommon opinion of the day that primitive man lived in a state of ideal innocence, and now to the conception of primitive life as hard and inhuman. But in the second sense, he was, it seems to me, perfectly clear and fundamentally consistent. When he said 'back to nature' he was really concerned with the nature of Jean-Jacques. He used the phrase logically and not temporally, and his real influence has been in this direction. What was the essential nature of man to Rousseau? Manifestly it was his individual temperament, as something different from the temperaments of all other men. So that it seems to me your argument against those who derive the power of Rousseau from his temperament falls to the ground. 'The Social Contract' is in its logical scheme obscure and diffi-

[46] To Prosser Hall Frye, Feb. 17, 1912.
[47] To Stuart P. Sherman, May 27, 1909; courtesy of the University of Illinois Library.

cult. I defy anyone to give a consistent and clear definition of the working of the *volonté générale*. And, as a matter of fact, it is the logical ambiguity in this idea that has led to divergent theories of socialism and anarchy, both of which contend for Rousseau as their father. But the notion of human nature underlying the 'Contract' and the *volonté générale* is clear and has had an entirely unambiguous influence, is indeed to-day responsible for much that is dangerous in our educational and political practice, its influence of course being due in large measure to the fact that it expressed with marvellous eloquence the ruling sentiment of the age. The conception of human nature in the 'Contract' is developed, but not essentially changed, in 'Émile.' It is simply that a man's temperament is the fundamental element of his nature, is of itself totally good and needs only to be released from restraint to be totally good in act. You compare Burke and Reynolds and Rousseau and Bergson. It seems to me that the conjunction of these names ought to have shown you the fallacy of your argument. If anything is clear, it certainly is that Rousseau, equally with Burke and Reynolds, was at bottom inimical to the rule of abstract reason or wit. He, equally with Burke and Reynolds, appealed to intuition as a power having greater authority than reason. But the intuition of Burke and Reynolds was as different from the intuition of Rousseau as Burke's political doctrine was different from the Rousselian doctrine legitimately developed in the revolution. To Burke intuition was a centripetal and restraining force pointing to an ultimate unity, as opposed to impulse and temperament and instinct, in the lower use of the word. It meant subordination of the emotional nature to reason and subordination of reason to superrational intuition.[48] That, ultimately. In general he spoke in the language of Reynolds, contrasting abstract logic with 'accumulated experience' and 'habitual reason.' Now, to Rousseau as I see him,—and I do not see how any other interpretation can be put on 'Émile'—intuition meant the guid-

[48] Cf. *SE* VIII, 228.

ance of temperament, impulse, individual emotion. It was centrifugal and abhorrent to restraint. It certainly cannot be expressed by 'accumulated experience' and 'habitual reason.' Really to imply that Burke and Reynolds stood for instinct and that Rousseau stood for reason is to abdicate common sense."[49]

Work left More little time for family and friends. He lunched usually with Fuller, Fabian Franklin, and some of the staff of *The Evening Post*. He found an opportunity to thrill Darrah by letting her watch *The Nation* roll off the clanking press in a strange blue light. Sunday afternoons he often walked with her around the reservoir in Central Park. He used to sing with his little girls, and would play all sorts of card games with them, later teaching them bridge, which became a favorite family diversion. After children's books he read aloud to them from Dickens and Trollope. As one who in youth had "been drilled painfully in 'Paradise Lost' day by day" until in manhood he turned naturally "to Milton for refreshment and for refuge from worry,"[50] he tried it on his daughters, only to conclude: "All great poems, even those most universal in their human appeal, require a fairly high-developed historic sense for their appreciation, and it is idle to suppose . . . that *Paradise Lost* can ever be interesting except to scholars."[51] Also he started on *Pilgrim's Progress*: " 'As I walked through the Wilderness of this World, I lighted on a certain Place where there was a Den: and I laid me down in that place to sleep: And as I slept I dreamed a Dream.' To how many of us those words are an open-sesame to the enchanted caves of childhood. Hearing them we remember how all a sabbath afternoon we would hang upon a dear voice repeating the adventures of Christian between the City of Destruction and the heavenly Jerusalem, and how in a child's exquisite anticipation of the future we felt ourselves languish in

[49] To Stuart P. Sherman, Feb. 1, 1912; courtesy of the University of Illinois Library. Cf. *SE* VIII, 230.

[50] "Celebrating Milton and Reading Him," anonymous editorial by P. E. More, *EP*, Dec. 9, 1908, p. 8.

[51] *SE* X, 134.

Doubting-Castle and knew the fatal drowsiness of the Enchanted
Ground. Naturally we cherish these memories and hesitate to
believe that the new generation will never pass through that
experience; we grieve to see one of the reservoirs of fruitful
emotion dried up. But other times, other books. . . ."⁵² Always
concerned with what the girls read, when Darrah was about
twelve he insisted on her finishing Goldsmith's *History of Rome*
before she began her choice of Conan Doyle. Though seldom
angry with his daughters, he was constantly exacting, especially
about their speech and manners, and, when necessary, severe
in a quiet, decisive way. But they could count on his indulgence
towards their playmates. He and Mrs. More went out together
about once a week. As members of a dinner club they joined
their group at regular intervals at the Cosmopolitan and other
clubs, and more rarely entertained friends at home. Fairly often,
however, he would have the "Roaring Boys," Fuller and a young
Oxonian, Stanley Went, his assistant editors of *The Nation*, in
his study for "a wild debauchery"⁵³ of three-handed bridge and
whisky, though he himself drank little.

"One night I took dinner with Henry Sedgwick and a very
typical gathering of New York men of the intellectual sort. It
was tolerably interesting but I came away in the end with a
feeling not far from disgust. Sedgwick is a kind of rarefied Em-
ersonian, whose independence takes the form of a wild and
silly radicalism. Emma Goldman, the anarchist, was to speak
in New York, and he was expressing a kind of childlike rapture
at the thought of hearing her, the Rev. Percy Grant helping him
on. All this was over a costly and delicate dinner, and the incongruity of the scene, typical of so much that is going on to-day,
saddened me a little—there was nothing funny in it. I sat at
Sedgwick's right; at my other side was John Jay Chapman who
back in his Cambridge days burnt off his own right hand because he had struck a friend with it. I have a strange feeling
when I am with men of this standing. It is just as if I were two

⁵² *SE* VI, 206-07.   ⁵³ To Irving Babbitt, Jan. 22, 1914.

persons, one the old St. Louis boy whose wildest dream was to live in New York and talk with a man who had written a book, the other my present self, who has lost most of his humility before men and has found New York very sordid and rather dull and has learned that the writers of books are in general a pretty small folk. The interchanging views of these two persons is sometimes curiously entertaining."[54]

More's happiest hours away from home were probably those at the Century with Henry Holt (the publisher), Fuller, Went, Franklin H. Giddings (a Columbia professor of sociology), William A. Dunning (a teacher of history at Columbia), Henry Osborn Taylor (author of *The Mediaeval Mind*), Henry Rutgers Marshall (architect and psychologist), George Haven Putnam (publisher), William Peterfield Trent (the authority on Defoe), and, from Princeton, where he was now a professor of art and archaeology, that "obstinate little chap"[55] of impish wit, Frank Jewett Mather, who was forever "breaking in on the conversation with some irreverent but brilliant quip." The sociable "Uncle Henry" Holt assembled them on Saturday nights before one of the fireplaces, where they drank and talked until the club closed at two. There, as Thomas F. Woodlock said, More kept "open house in his ivory tower." With rollicking brusqueness he provoked debate. "Back to the harem!" he would cry, if someone defended "female suffrage,"[56] which he opposed on the ground that American politics were already too emotional. In regard to literature he liked to indulge "in summary judgments of an uncompromising kind, expressed in direct and salty language." When Major Putnam quoted Horace, as he thought, at impressive length, More drily observed its resemblance to Juvenal. He was always exposing factual and logical errors and furnishing apt allusions. If everyone there knew more than he about some field outside literature and the classics, none had so

[54] To Alice More, Feb. 8, 1912.
[55] To Irving Babbitt, Jan. 10, 1910.
[56] Cf. *SE* VIII, 237-38, 242.

labored to acquaint himself with at least the outline of general knowledge. He would never, for example, have cared to search a title, yet no lawyer could have been better read in Blackstone. If Uncle Henry's genius for friendship brought and held the group together, More was its source of intellectual stimulus. "The wild thought" occurred to one of his fellow Centurions, "that there was a mixture in him of Doctor Johnson, Porson, Charles Lamb and Sydney Smith."

The initial glitter of winning and holding an editorial job had long since been tarnished by fatigue and boredom. Except for a few studious weeks in the summer, More had now for almost a dozen years worked twice as hard as most men. He so greatly needed refreshment that, though he would have preferred his usual "quiet unemotional month at Essex,"[57] Nettie prevailed upon him to "go to England for eight or ten weeks."[58] He addressed[59] a joint meeting of Phi Beta Kappa and Tau Beta Pi at Lehigh University, Bethlehem, Pennsylvania, on April 18, 1912, and at last on May 25th boarded in New York the Hamburg American Line's *Cincinnati*.

[57] To Alice More, March 1, 1912.   [58] *Ibid*.
[59] Part of this talk, called "Philosophy is a Science of Life," he later included in his essay on Thomas Henry Huxley.

8

RELEASE FROM JOURNALISM
(1912-1914)

"MY dear Net . . .

"I was glad you were not on the pier as we slowly backed out. The scene pretty nearly broke me down, and if you had been there I think I should have disgraced myself. I don't know why it is but this separation by water seems infinitely worse than by land, and I think I shall never do it again. I am not demonstrative, as you know, but I do a good deal of concealed feeling inside, and as I sail away my wish is that sometimes I made more effort to show my emotions."[1]

"My account of the voyage will be the short and simple annals of the miserable. . . . I have been bored almost to madness. Dr. Johnson used to say that being on board a ship was like being in prison; I should change it to being in a combination of prison and summer hotel. There are so many people always about that you can't read with any *recueillement*,[2] and the people have that peculiar restlessness and fatuous idleness that make me despise humanity in summer resorts. . . . I am rather fortunate in my dining table. My companions are an innocuous widow, and a Mr. and Mrs. Hillerman. . . . The gentleman laughs tremendously at my least pretentious jests, so that I might with a little effort gain the reputation of a wit. I have been modest in my efforts in that direction. The Rev. Dr. (or Mr.) Smith, in full canonicals that conceal a suffering liver, is also a passenger. I thought his face was familiar, but only last night learned that he was a curate of St. Agnes'. He was on

[1] To Mrs. P. E. More, undated [May 25, 1912].
[2] "I have my *Odyssey* in my pocket, and this with a few novels has furnished my reading. . . . Now I am in Fogazzaro's 'Leila'; but I must say I find the Italian sentiment of it not to my taste." [To Alice More, June 1, 1912.]

[128]

deck this morning, jolly but fearful, and I introduced myself to him. Next year he expects to study theology—bless his simple, unvexed brain! The best company I have found is a young handsome Frenchman who has been in New York studying our electrical street railways. His father is an engineer, and he himself, a Parisian, is one of eight children. He is intelligent though little versed in books. With him and a young American engineer, of typically alert mind, I have had a few good games of bridge. . . . There are several girls and young fellows aboard who amuse themselves after the usual manner of those creatures. My steamer chair happens to be between those of two good old maids. . . . We pass the time of day politely, but not much more. No doubt I am reckoned unsociable. The worst of all is my stateroom. There is absolutely no air in it and I wake every morning with a heavy head in consequence thereof. I might get relief from the electric fan, but the noise of that, when I tried it, drove me to a state of exasperation which made me reflect on drowning for peace. Unfortunately my neighbours having better nerves than mine keep the detestable things screaming all night, with the result that I lie awake in a condition of suffocation instead of strangling in my sleep—which would be pleasanter. . . . The Lord never meant me for a traveller, and I am wondering what annoyances await me now by land."[3]

From Plymouth he took a train to Tavistock, from which by dog cart he drove over Dartmoor's "great rolling hills with gaunt bare summits" to Princetown and back. Then by train to Salisbury, with "for the first part of the way the rich Devon fields to the left and the wild downs to the right. . . .

"This morning I went over the cathedral carefully. The building itself is wonderful, but I was even more impressed by the close with its soft lawns, great trees and surrounding buildings. One could live here in peace, if anywhere. But England, this part of England at least, strikes me as being dull. One gets the feeling that the people have forgotten the stress of life. As Wil-

[3] To Mrs. P. E. More, June 2, 1912. Cf. *SE* IX, 42-43.

ton house is open to visitors on Wednesdays, I went out this afternoon to Wilton by train (3 miles) and walked to the house. . . . The rooms are large and handsomely appointed, but somehow I should not care to live in them, perhaps because I am used to smallness and comfort, and was not born an Earl of Pembroke. But the view of the lawn and garden from the windows was like a dream, the sort of thing one thinks of when one reads of these places. I saw a group of young men practising at cricket in the distance, and envied them. I walked back and stopped to see Bemerton, which lies half way between Wilton and Salisbury. I sent my card in at the rectory and was received most graciously by the rector. He took me into the church, and showed me over the house which had been the home of George Herbert and my beloved John Norris. On the wall of the church is an inscription which will be of service to me when I come to write about the latter. He also told me that Norris was much disappointed because, being a high churchman, he was kept from advancement by Bishop Burnet. You see one reason why the bishop was antipathetic to me by anticipation. Tea was announced when we crossed the street from the church to the rectory, and the old gentleman asked me so cordially to take a cup that I went into the dining room and met his wife and daughter."[4]

At Winchester "I went to the cathedral and then across to the school. I wandered about the courts of the latter, seeing no one but expecting every moment to be haled before some awful authority for trespassing. At last I came upon the porter who was conducting a party through the public rooms, and joined myself to them. The school as a whole is not impressive, although it has beautiful gardens where a lot of boys in white were playing cricket. The desks and other appurtenances are of the plainest, cheapest sort, and the study rooms would drive American boys to revolt."[5]

In London the next day at the British Museum "I went through the Roman and Greek rooms and felt myself for a while at least

4 To the same, June 5, 1912.   5 To the same, June 9, 1912.

at home. One of the statues that caught my attention was the bust of Faustina, wife of Marcus Aurelius, a round girlish face, which reminded me curiously of Sadie Brank, only with less strength of character. The face is an enigma, as was the woman herself. Then into the Elgin room, and the spoils of the Parthenon! Do you know the tears were streaming from my eyes so that I had to face away from the other visitors. The cathedrals do not move me deeply. At bottom they seem to me relics of an incomprehensible past, anachronisms now which we preserve and cherish as exquisite toys. But this Parthenon is eternal; it stands for the one perfectly right and good thing the human mind has conceived; and the spectacle of its pitiable ruins just made me blubber like a baby. Saturday morning I took the Underground to Westminster, changing twice *en route* and in doing so wandering through miles of corridors in the bowels of the earth. The House of Parliament is open to visitors on Saturday, so that I was able to see a good deal of the building. Then I crossed over to the Abbey, and by paying sixpence (the sixpences drip out of one's pocket incessantly) got into the choir and chapels. The Abbey itself, especially Henry VII's chapel, is imposing and beautiful, but the clutter of monuments was to my eye merely a nuisance. To see them with the work of Phidias fresh in memory was to feel the utter barbarousness of our civilization. I doubt if the British Empire is worth the time-worn stone of the Three Fates."[6]

"My dear Darrah,—

"Was it you or Alice who wanted me to call on the King? Well, I have not just called on him; but I have spoken to him and he has taken off his hat to me most affably. It was this way. Sunday afternoon I rode on top of one of the busses to Hyde Park Corner, which is one of the entrances to the principal park and not far from Buckingham Palace where his maj-

[6] *Ibid.* Cf. "Humanism," anonymous editorial by P. E. More, *N*, Aug. 15, 1912, vol. 95, no. 2459, pp. 140-41, and *SE* IX, 97-100.

esty lives. I was sitting in a chair on Rotten Row, as they call it, when I heard a woman cry out, Here comes *our* King! Sure enough, an open carriage dashed into the park, and there on the back seat was the King, dressed just as I am when I have on my cutaway coat and silk hat, and with him the Queen in white. On the front seat was the Princess Mary, just a sweet-looking young girl whom you would love to play with. I took off my hat and said, How's your royal majesty today, and where's your crown? not speaking very loud, however. He raised his hat to me, and drove on. I shouldn't like to be a king. He has to look straight before him and never turn his head to one side, for that would not be dignified. Yet he has to be on the alert to take off his hat whenever he is greeted. And the little princess! She sat bolt upright, and she has to keep as quiet as a statue, never moving her head or even her hands. I thought how you would enjoy such restraint. But that is the way of the world. To be a lady you have to learn to suppress signs of curiosity, and to be a great lady you have to learn to sit like this little princess—poor wriggling Darrah.

"London is terribly big and noisy, and I don't believe I like it. A hundred times I would rather be on the beach with you and Alice this minute.[7] The sea is noisy too, but there is something wholesome in its sound.

"I am expecting a long letter from you to cheer a lonely, tired father, for so I may sign myself.

From your daddie."[8]

"Monday came from Lou a letter from President Taft introducing me to Ambassador Reid. This got cards for Trent and me to the Distinguished Strangers' Gallery in Parliament, and yesterday afternoon and evening we sat there for five or six hours watching the bear-baiting—the bears in this case being the Irish members. . . . The chamber is smaller than you would

[7] The summer of 1912 Mrs. More and her daughters went first to Biddeford Pool and then to Essex.
[8] To Mary Darrah More, June 11, 1912.

expect, and more familiar, the Government and Opposition front benches being opposite each other and so close that members could lean over the table and shake hands—if so disposed. The personnel of the House is mixed, and I believe neither in dress nor in character would appear better than our Congress. . . . I saw the full bench of the Government at question hour, but none of them spoke except to answer questions. Birrell has a beautiful face, like a lesser and more reputable Thackeray. Asquith has a fine face, but to me did not seem strong or commanding. He is notably nervous with his hands and face as he sits listening. But for sprawling indecorum (with legs high up on the table) Bonar Law and one or two other Tories take the prize. I have met and talked with several M. P.'s since then. Wednesday evening I took dinner at the Shorters' (he edits *The Sphere* and writes about Charlotte Brontë, etc.; she is Dora Sigerson, the Irish poetess, a large, fat, blond creature, with a roguish eye), and met Edward Clodd, a Mr. Wale (who had been legal adviser for Gissing and was one of the founders of the Omar Khayyám Club), and Sir Laurence and Lady Gomme. Shorter has an extraordinary collection of books and manuscripts, the latter including masses of unpublished letters of all sorts of people. I took luncheon with him today at the Devonshire Club, and besides meeting various people heard the story of Gissing's career, which includes three unfortunate marriages and a term in prison for theft. I will tell you the details some time.[9] On the whole his misfortunes were due rather to a visionary and unpractical mind than to viciousness. Thursday I took luncheon with E. V. Lucas. . . . Lucas is cold in manner and a bit blunt, but I liked his way of asking questions. Tonight I go to see a play of Pinero's on a pass presented by Shorter."[10]

"My letter to Ambassador Reid has brought me so many

[9] Cf. p. ii of More's introduction to *The Private Papers of Henry Ryecroft*, by George Gissing, The Modern Library, New York (Random House), no date (1918 or later).
[10] To Mrs. P. E. More, June 14, 1912.

cards from secretaries, Mrs. Reid, etc., that I am really embarrassed. Having no clothes I could not go to Mrs. Reid's Thursday afternoon at home. . . ."[11] "I felt bound however to accept an invitation to luncheon at Dorchester House, and went yesterday—with some misgivings. It was, I fancy, a kind of formal function they employ to cancel just such obligations as they felt towards me. Twenty or thirty persons sat down, mostly Americans, and the whole thing was a dreadful bore. It was interesting of course to see the house, and to tread haughtily among an army of flunkeys, but I am glad I don't have to do it again."[12]

"Yesterday Trent and I took luncheon with E. V. Lucas; but of the men he invited to meet us, only C. L. Graves, assistant editor of *The Spectator*, could come. We had some talk, and I rather like Lucas. Curiously enough three several people here have observed that I remind them of him. I cannot see much resemblance except that we are both smooth-shaven. In the evening I dined with Chilton[13] at the Passmore Edwards settlement where he lives. A number of men who lecture and teach there, dine together—a dreadful crowd of boorish young reformers. They made me sulky. Then Chilton and I called on the Meynells. They live in a flat near Portman Square, up four pair of stairs. I thought of 99th Street as I climbed up, but their living room is three times as large as such a flat would have in New York. . . . We talked a good deal of Cardinal Newman, Francis Thompson, Coventry Patmore, and other Catholic writers, and Mr. Meynell insisted on giving me one of Thompson's books (the *Life of St. Ignatius*), with an inscription in it."[14]

"Sunday noon I took my luncheon at the Athenaeum, having received a card from that august club as a 'distinguished stranger.' It is, you know, the heavy-weight literary and learned club

[11] To the same, June 18, 1912.
[12] To Louis T. More, June 20, 1912.
[13] Described in an entry of June 15th in More's 1912 notebook as "the Bach enthusiast who is living here and working at the Museum."
[14] To Mrs. P. E. More, June 21, 1912.

of London, full of bishops and that sort of cattle. The building is perhaps a little larger than our Century but not so attractive, and made so as to exclude sociability. The library however is very fine, and an excellent, quiet place for work."[15]

"Well, I have been in London for more than two weeks, and am satiated with pictures and people. One picture I should love to have: I wonder if Alice remembers it. It is an Annunciation in the National Gallery by Filippo Lippi, the most exquisite example of innocent loveliness I think I have ever seen. But these galleries are at bottom a terrible weariness. There is something perfectly unnatural and inhuman in a lot of pictures hung together in these public places, with no relation to anything and no meaning in life."[16]

After a visit to Minehead and a view of Exmoor near Porlock, the traveller and Trent strolled about Bath and Wells. Leaving his companion at Bristol, More reached Oxford on the evening of June 28th, having taken "a long walk in the morning up the valley of the Usk at Brecon. The scenery is wonderfully beautiful there, and I shall always hereafter read Henry Vaughan with a more vivid appreciation of his love of nature.[17] Fortunately the sun shone at intervals while I was out, and the shifting light on the river and hills was inexpressibly lovely. . . . The colleges are fascinating but somehow I cannot reconcile myself to their mediaeval, monkish character, which is enforced by the strong contrast of the newer city which is not attractive and very modern. I feel though as I see more and more of the country, how small and well-knit England really is. It is like a big family, with all its interests intertwined in a thousand ways. Tradition and custom well may govern such a land and take the place of ideas. To make this feeling stronger I have been reading Mozley's gossiping reminiscences of the Oxford Movement and Oriel College. I have not often read anything more amusing than the chapters on the condemnation of Hampden's Bampton Lectures,

[15] To the same, June 25, 1912.
[16] To Mrs. Enoch Anson More, June 23, 1912.
[17] Cf. *DA*, 144, 161.

which nobody could understand and scarcely anybody had read!"[18]

In London again, "after expending enough thought and anxiety to write a book, and tramping innumerable miles," More assured his wife, "I have probably got the wrong thing for everybody to whom I am bringing remembrances. The fact of the matter is that you take so much of this sort of thing off my mind that when I come to shop, my wits go to pieces. . . . I have been doing a good deal of thinking in the intervals of my running about, and I see more [and] more clearly than ever I have seen before how far short I have fallen of doing my full share towards making a good and cheerful home. Part of that is due, I know, to my necessary absorption of mind, but not all of it. They say it is never too late to mend."[19]

"My last days in London were not very profitable. But I made rather an amusing acquaintance. Stark Young, an English instructor in the University of Texas, is in London, and, as an old pupil of Trent's, came to our hotel. He is gay and vivacious and stirred us up a bit. He is a votary of the Muses also, and Sunday morning he read a lot of his verse in manuscript. The sentiment of it was nice, but it had no invention to speak of, while the execution was often slovenly and ignorant. Yet the poor fellow was filled with the most exalted notions of its value. He had come over in the boat with E. K. Rand, of Harvard, who had not only taken an interest in Young himself, even asking him to Oxford, but had praised the poetry extravagantly. It was rather embarrassing for me to criticise the stuff after what Rand had said of it, but I tried to be discreet.[20]

"Sunday evening Trent and I went out to Hampstead to dine with Mr. and Mrs. Aitken. He has edited Marvell, written the authoritative life of Steele, edited Arbuthnot, etc., having got

[18] To Mrs. P. E. More, June 30, 1912. Cf. *SE* IX, 81.
[19] To Mrs. P. E. More, July 5, 1912.
[20] Cf. "Dear Mr. Wilson" and "Art and Decision," by Stark Young, *The New Republic*, vol. 91, pp. 130-31 and 307-08, June 9 and July 21, 1937, respectively.

together an extraordinary lot of fine editions from the seventeenth and eighteenth centuries. I looked at a number of his books, and was duly impressed. Several of them are absolutely unique copies. He himself is a dry little fellow, and talked bibliography with Trent in a manner which would have made you smile."[21]

"After my ever beloved Elgin marbles the most beautiful thing I have seen in England is King's College Chapel at Cambridge. I went into this at every opportunity, and Tuesday evening heard the five o'clock service. The choir and priests were in the chancel which is separated from what would be called the nave in another church by a heavy wooden screen. The chanting came to me very clear, but softened, and without any echo. From where I sat well towards the western end my eye got a perspective view of the southern windows of the chancel over the screen. The building is long and narrow, so that I did not see the glass of the windows, but only the colored light streaming in and reflected from the stone mullions. The whole wall seemed to glow like a subdued opal. Anything more inexpressibly beautiful you could not imagine. I confess I grew very sentimental. The thought that kept running through my mind was the words of Addison's *Cato* which I read a thousand times in my reader in the old Stoddard School: Plato, thou reasonest well. It must be so; else whence this pleasing hope, This longing after immortality.[22] I cannot see why we should give to the negations of reason any authority above the force of such emotions as I felt on that day."[23]

After admiring York cathedral and being bored in Durham, "I came to Edinburgh this morning. . . . I have the same impression of the city that I had twenty-five years ago or so. It certainly is majestically situated. One could live here. What

[21] To Mrs. P. E. More, July 9, 1912.

[22] More misquotes these lines again in *HP*, 180.

[23] To Mrs. Enoch Anson More, July 11, 1912. Cf. Wordsworth's sonnet beginning, "Tax not the royal Saint with vain expense," and *SE* X, 267.

more I see of it must be told by word of mouth in Essex, for this is my last letter. . . . I have felt grieved for your sadness this summer,[24] and have wished many times that I might have taken this long rest and holiday with you in Essex. As it is, I suppose this trip will set me up for the winter, but, as I have said before, I really do not enjoy travelling; I would far rather be quietly at home with you. Next time I come over you shall be with me. I return to my work a little anxious and perplexed. I fear *The Evening Post* in its advocacy of Woodrow Wilson will run into greater and greater extravagances of radicalism until my position is intolerable. However, there is no need to worry over that till it comes. I have something much pleasanter to think about—your love.

P. E. M."[25]

By sailing from Glasgow July 20th on the *Hesperian*, of the Allen Line, and by debarking "at Quebec and travelling all day by rail, I got to Essex Monday night, July 29. Wednesday night Net came down with me to the city, and just this morning she has gone back to Essex."[26]

"Here I am back at my desk and it seems already as if I had never been away. I feel more deeply every year the littleness of what we carry with us from the past. Sometimes I try deliberately to call back old emotions and experiences, but for the most part they come vague and blurred and as if alien to me. That has its advantages no doubt, for there is plenty we are glad to forget, and yet on the whole this loss of our past seems to leave life very thin and meaningless. If it is true that the past becomes more vivid again as we grow older, age has its compensation for many bereavements."[27]

"I wish you, with your artist's eye," he wrote to his sister that

---

[24] While mourning her sister, who died Feb. 9, 1912, Mrs. More suffered also on account of her bereaved brother-in-law and mother, both of whom became ill that summer soon after her husband left for England.

[25] To Mrs. P. E. More, July 15, 1912.

[26] To Alice More, Aug. 15, 1912.   [27] *Ibid.*

autumn, "were in my office at this moment to describe what can be seen from my window. The air is misty with a peculiar dull yellow suffused through it. Only down Church Street which opens out to sea, the fog is of a clear steel gray. The office buildings banked up across St. Paul's churchyard are showing golden lights at every window, and the steam from a hundred escape pipes is drifting through the mist in white lines and weaving strange figures on the face of the buildings."[28]

Leaving his desk at *The Nation*, the editor lectured each afternoon from February 17 to 21, 1913, in the chapel of the University of Kansas, speaking about William Beckford, Newman, Pater, Thomas Henry Huxley,[29] and Fiona Macleod. The five lectures, with his "Definitions of Dualism"[30] and his reprinted essay on Nietzsche, were published by Houghton Mifflin Company in March 1913 as *The Drift of Romanticism*, with the subtitle, *Shelburne Essays*, Eighth Series. Babbitt, the proofs of

[28] To the same, Nov. 1, 1912.

[29] "I make him [Huxley] a scientific naturalist at a time when the scientific naturalist was very hostile to the romantic naturalist. My theme is that as both science (philosophical science) and romanticism are the offspring of naturalism there is a way by which they can be brought together—have indeed been brought together. Huxley believed in the old mechanical evolution, which goes properly with rationalism. When this mechanical notion of the world was given up for the vitalistic notion, science was ready to join forces with romanticism. Now Huxley's office here was twofold. In the first place he gave the hypothesis of evolution currency, and the vitalistic notion of the world is still evolutionary, however contrary to rationalism it may be; and he gave to the very word science a kind of religious awesomeness in the minds of the half educated—that is, most of mankind save thee and me. . . . with all his noble ardor for the truth, his real legacy has been confusion and superstition. I do not think he is properly the sceptic. As I understand the sceptic, he is one who may be pretty certain of what is in his own brain and heart, but refuses to believe that he has in his thoughts and feelings a key to unriddle the source and laws of the world. You may say what you will, but the whole direction and weight of Huxley's writings were to impress a very unsceptical belief in evolution as [the] process by which a very small part of man's logic is made the law of the universe, a true *deus praesens*. At bottom he was one of the great dogmatists—not a sceptic in any but a most superficial sense of the word." [To Frank Jewett Mather, Jr., May 17, 1913. Cf. *HP*, 344, and *DA*, 67.]

[30] So he called the "aphorisms" or "epigrams" referred to on p. 115 above.

whose book, *The Masters of Modern French Criticism*, More had gone through, proofread the "Definitions" and with Mather looked over the preface—"an introductory letter to Mather, in which I take up his condemnation of my attitude towards Pater. It is an extremely difficult piece of writing, because I am attempting at the same time to make a kind of personal apologia and to sum up in a formula my attitude towards romanticism."[31]

As a young man More had been "immersed in the current of romanticism,"[32] whose contributions to "the world's sum of beauty and sublimity"[33] he gratefully acknowledged. But having, as he thought, "barely escaped" from the intellectual and moral dangers of the movement, later he attacked with "violent revulsion"[34] its insidious elements: "the infinitely craving personality, the usurpation of emotion over reason, the idealization of love, the confusion of the sensuous and the spiritual, the perilous fascination that may go with these confusions. It is like a dream of fever, beautiful and malign by turns; and, looking at its wild sources, one can understand why Goethe curtly called romanticism disease and classicism health. He might have added that disease is infectious, whereas health must be acquired or preserved by the effort of the individual."[35]

At the University of Michigan on April 4th More lectured on the conflict between the classical and the medieval Christian traditions, which had impressed him at Oxford and which he found wherever occidental education had not limited itself entirely to science and humanitarianism.[36] After two days, later that month, in Cambridge, Babbitt's "pleasant way of being hospitable"[37] and the steady strain of "entertainment" left him "ready to cry with fatigue and curse humanity for keeping me smiling."[38] At his wife's behest he went with her briefly in the middle of May

---

[31] To Irving Babbitt, Feb. 29, 1912.
[32] *SE* VIII, 83.   [33] *SE* VIII, 36.   [34] *SE* VIII, 83.
[35] *SE* VIII, 30.   [36] Cf. *SE* IX, 71-100.
[37] To Irving Babbitt, May 3, 1913.
[38] To Alice More, April 30, 1913.

to Mohonk Lake, New York. Then, while she and Darrah took a trip to Biddeford Pool, he and little Alice held "the fort bravely.

"I must tell you an amusing story about her. Two nights ago she, caught by the pictures, asked me to read to her, after she had gone to bed, from Seton's big animal book. I told her it would not interest her, but she insisted, and I complied. For half an hour I read out the dryest catalogue of measurements and other stuff of which she could have understood scarcely a word. She looked as if rapt in joy, and would say over and over: I just love this! We will read it every night! I made no remark. Last night I asked her what we should read. I could see her looking at me furtively out of the tail of her eye, and after a long silence she said, I think we'll have the Yellow Fairy Book. I have no doubt if I had smiled by the sixteenth of an inch, she would have exclaimed for the animal book. What little frauds children are."[39]

"*The Nation* comes out this week," its editor announced to Sherman, "with your entertaining and somewhat puzzling disquisition on 'Education by the People.' . . . I could not quite make up my mind whether the lift in the thing was from real conviction or in part from the intoxication of ink—whether, to speak brutally, you had not your tongue in your cheek when you wrote certain of the resounding paragraphs. Do you really believe the people—that is the great, busy majority—have any magnanimous desire for pure education? Do you see any signs of that in the kind of journalism they ask for, the kind of books that sell, or in anything else? Now, you know as well as I do, that higher education always has been and always will be the desire and reward of a comparatively few men. If the people support an institution of higher learning which has no practical value, they will do so because in one way or another they have been cajoled into it. By people I do not mean a distinction primarily of caste or birth or money, least of all do I mean to distinguish the East and the West. . . . But I do distinguish sharply between

[39] To Alice More, May 31, 1913.

Release from Journalism

the few and the many, and I know, as you do, that to get from the many the support needed for the higher task of the few requires, as I said, some kind of cajolery. Religion has done great things of this sort in the past. At present so far as I can see, the chief motive is that lurking spirit of jealousy which comes closest to being the mainspring of human action.[40] I suspect that the support of culture in popular institutions, so far as it gets such support, comes primarily from mere habit and mere imitation of older methods, and secondarily from jealousy of other institutions. And I observe that, whether slily or innocently, the whole gist of your article is a shrewd appeal to this motive of jealousy. 'Here, good honest people of the West, are you going to allow a few institutions in the East, founded as they are on the proceeds of rapine and plunder, to boast a higher purer form of education than you are willing to offer to the offspring of your own unsullied loins?'—It is magnificent; but did you have your tongue in your cheek?"[41]

Washington University on June 12, 1913, conferred on More the honorary degree of Doctor of Laws, which it had offered to him in 1909 on his appointment as editor in chief of *The Nation* but which he had then been too busy to receive. On this, the fifty-second, commencement of his alma mater he gave the principal address, "Aspects of Reaction," which drew its inspiration, as had his comments on Sherman's article, from George Savile, first Marquess of Halifax. His speech being on politics and education, in the latter he defended the humanistic tradition on about the same grounds as in the former he idealized the law. ". . . the firm and slowly changing reason of a nation contrasted with the inconsiderate impulse of the moment . . . the experience of time against the desires of the present, a restraining force imposed upon the action of the nation comparable to the habits grafted upon the individual man in childhood . . . law is a se-

[40] Cf. *SE* X, 63-64.
[41] To Stuart P. Sherman, May 8, 1913; courtesy of the University of Illinois Library.

[142]

curity for men not only against one another, but against themselves."[42]

Visits and visitors varied More's vacation with his family in July at his camp on Lake Champlain. He and Nettie stayed awhile with James R. Wheeler, who summered in "the fine old house" in Burlington, "where he was born when his father was president of the University of Vermont."[43] Wheeler, a professor at Columbia, belonged with More and some twenty others to a Greek Club, which met at the Century and for which More used to write Greek verse. From Burlington the Mores went to near-by "Fairholt, the great house built by Henry Holt on a hill behind the city, with a view of wonderful range and beauty. In the afternoon he took us seventy miles in his machine to the foot of Mt. Mansfield and through the lovely valley of the Lamoille (?) river. Seventy miles over hilly roads in two hours and a half is a bit strenuous, but the experience is something to remember. There was quite a party at dinner, including the Bishop of Vermont, a very reverend Englishman. The next morning we came back by the early boat, satiated, and rather tired, and quite pleased with the sheltered repose of The Cedars. Just before our visit the Wheelers had been over for dinner and a night and Marshall had been with us for three days, so you see we have been rather gay.

"I am working modestly at clearing up my place, but Lou is going at things with a reckless zeal that makes me feel old. . . . A little Homer[44] or Euripides in the morning, with a rubber of bridge in the evening, makes up the day. I have just read Seeley's 'Ecce Homo,' which, you may remember, made a great sensation in the middle of the last century. Do you know the book?

[42] *SE* X, 53, 55-56. Some of More's remarks in this address supporting constitutional government and independent courts are echoed, in rather different notes, in *SE* IX, 23-25.

[43] To Mrs. Enoch Anson More, July 24, 1913.

[44] "I am going through *The Iliad* again for my holiday reading. I long for the sound and sight of the sea when reading Homer, but the wonder and magnificence of the poetry are not lost, even here among the motionless pines." [To Prosser Hall Frye, July 15, 1913.]

Release from Journalism

It begins handsomely, with an extraordinarily clear analysis of Christ's authority and mission, but the second half degenerates into a depressing study of religion as a purely humanitarian instrument."[45]

In August he sent Alice "news which will certainly please you. I have handed in my resignation and am editing *The Nation* only until the office can be reorganized. I shan't go into all the details, but in a general way I was led to the act by two causes, the feeling that my health was suffering from this double work[46] and the knowledge that the literary department of *The Evening Post*, and hence indirectly *The Nation*, was to be made more subject to the demands of the business office. They are contemplating a regular Friday literary supplement for *The Post*, similar in form to that of *The Times*. To this end they are getting contracts from the publishers in such a way that we shall be under virtual obligations to them. As most of the matter for this supplement is to come from *The Nation* I shall be under constant pressure from Villard and Strunsky, the latter of whom . . . is to edit it. The position would be intolerable."[47]

For many months the resigning editor had contemplated "the old idea of the gentleman and scholar. . . . It is an astonishing thing that more of those who are blessed with independence . . . do not see the joy of an intellectual purpose steadily followed year after year . . ." uniting "toil and leisure in so perfect a bond as to make them scarcely distinguishable one from the other. Such a life is not debarred from the accomplishment of other duties. In its even, unhasting course it leaves time for the obligations of family and state; it may further bring to these the large outlook and sane tolerance of an intellect purged by sweet association with the wise and great, and steadied by the influence of a long-cherished, unselfish purpose. Nor does such a life deny the just relaxations of amusement; it may rather add to them a

[45] To Mrs. Enoch Anson More, July 24, 1913.
[46] ". . . of editor and scholar, and, to me at least, the latter work is much the more important." [To Irving Babbitt, Aug. 29, 1913.]
[47] To Alice More, "Sunday afternoon"; postmarked Aug. 17, 1913.

new zest; but its great and unique pleasure is that which comes to the man each morning as, returning to his study, *'perfumed with many such days before,'* he sees before him the familiar implements and, with free heart and unhampered energy, enters once more upon that mental pursuit which has become a part of his very being."[48]

But for the last ten or more weeks he had hesitated to resign, partly for *The Nation's* sake[49] and partly for his family's, since if he gave up his salary as an editor his family's expenses would have to be met by the income from Mrs. Richardson's bequest to his wife. That income, however, being ample, Mrs. More could endure no further restrictions on her husband's health and ambition. As a concession to masculine pride it was understood that he would pay his personal bills from his earnings as a writer and lecturer but that the family as a whole would enjoy the advantages they could now afford.

Had there been no threat to his independence as an editor and had he been granted more time for his own writing, he might well have remained longer with *The Nation.* But from beginning to end there existed between him and Villard, beneath their polite behavior sustained by distance, a deep antipathy. Whatever may have been its ultimate source, it was sharpened by the dissensions that sometimes divide "a little Conservative" from "a little Liberal." Everything about More announced his honest, disinterested, and, to those disagreeing with him, not merely amusing conviction that "conservatism is in general the intuition of genius, whereas liberalism is the efficiency of talent."[50] The president of The New York Evening Post Company considered

[48] "The Air of Quiet Study," anonymous editorial by P. E. More, *EP*, Aug. 17, 1912, p. 6, and *N*, Aug. 22, 1912, vol. 95, pp. 162-63.
[49] He tried to induce Sherman to take the editorship. "With you at the helm here I feel that *The Nation* would not degenerate and I should not suffer the self-reproach of being a traitor to the cause." [To Stuart P. Sherman, Sept. 6, 1913; courtesy of the University of Illinois Library.] But Sherman refused on the ground that he lacked the necessary experience, scholarship, resourcefulness, and fortitude.
[50] *SE* IX, 186.

his editor, despite his undeniable ability and probity, a smug, stubborn, reactionary intellectual. The editor in turn was disgusted by what seemed to him the reformer's fanaticism and gush.

More than a clash of temperament, however, was involved in his resignation. He had maintained the literary section of *The Nation* at so high a level that many then deemed it the best critical review in the English language. Under him, though its circulation increased, it had no chance of becoming very profitable. He loathed the subtleties of format and simply could not put his mind on the newer methods of make-up and display. Despite his insistence on the mediocrity of the many, instead of diverting "his talents to the popular market, with all the misery of such a conscious degradation,"[51] he exacted the best from those who chanced to turn his pages; he relied suicidally on quality. "His intellectual conscience," one of his editorial assistants and a close friend noted, "was as formidable a thing as were the religious consciences of his New England ancestors. For the shoddy, the second-rate or the merely pretentious in intellectual pursuits he had neither use nor patience. For intellectual dishonesty his scorn was devastating."

On January 23, 1914, the president of The New York Evening Post Company notified More that he would be relieved of his editorial duties on March 15th, but asked the favor of retaining his name as an advisory editor. Fuller, he was informed, would become acting editor, aided and supervised by Mr. Villard and Mr. Strunsky, and the magazine would be improved by a new policy and new features.

"My feeling of relief is very great, yet not unmixed with a sensation of failure. . . . Eleven years of journalism lie behind me like a nightmare, and I have got out just in time."[52]

"The simple fact of the matter is that I have been editing *The Nation* with my left hand, and have thus let many opportunities

[51] *SE* VII, 51.
[52] To Alice More, Jan. 24, 1914.

go by. But I am very much afraid (this, of course, entirely *entre nous*) that Villard's influence will cheapen *The Nation* and deprive it of its unique quality."[53]

On February 28th the secretary of the board of trustees of The New York Evening Post Company sent More a resolution expressing their appreciation of his service. A few days before his retirement they gave a "dinner to the staff,"[54] which he dutifully attended as guest of honor.

[53] To Louis T. More, Feb. 24, 1914.
[54] To Mrs. Enoch Anson More, March 2, 1914.

9

PRINCETON AND PLATO (1914-1917)

"YOU will be wanting to know how I am getting through these days of leisure," More wrote to his mother about three weeks after leaving *The Nation*. "My time has been somewhat broken by my visit to Cambridge[1] and Ainsie's visit here, but even apart from that, the twenty-four hours might be lengthened to forty-eight without becoming tedious. To begin with, I have just completed in twelve days an essay for *The Nation* which under the old régime would have taken my spare time for six weeks. Then I have written reviews; read essays for a prize given by Wells College; played cards with Fuller and Went several times until three in the morning; and begun a stiff bit of study for the first of my volumes on Plato. . . .

"Last Wednesday night I went to a big dinner at Delmonico's given by John Quinn in honor of William Butler Yeats. . . . Yeats read some of his verse—second-rate stuff which he mouthed grandiloquently—and told stories of his apprenticeship in literature. He spoke well and entertainingly; but I could scarcely refrain from getting on my feet and roaring at the pernicious ideas of art and life he divulged. He made one good epigram—fairly true, moreover—in comparing the Rhymers Club, which he and Ernest Dowson and Arthur Symons and other decadents formed some twenty years ago, with the young, very young, poets of to-day. We had, he said, the morals of bandits and the manners of bishops, whereas these have the morals of bishops and the manners of bandits.—I am not so sure about the bishops in either case; but the bandits are right."[2]

Present when his mother died suddenly of pneumonia on

---

[1] To attend the meeting on March 20th of an advisory committee on the Graduate School and to stay awhile with the Babbitts.

[2] To Mrs. Enoch Anson More, April 6, 1914. Cf. *SE* X, 294, and *OBH*, 45.

April 10, 1914, in Bridgeton, he "carried her out to St. Louis
for the last rites"[3] on the 13th.

". . . we cannot afford to rent a house in New York large
enough to hold both my books and the children. Madam won't
give up the children and I won't give up the books, and there
you are. As a result of this difference we are looking for a
roomier home where property is cheaper; the quiet atmosphere
of Princeton, with its very mild flavor of intellectual business,
attracts us, not to mention the fact that we have the Mathers
and other good friends there."[4]

Mrs. More finally decided to buy the comfortable Barsetshire
rectory at 245 Nassau Street, Princeton, New Jersey, secluded
in nearly an acre and a half of shrubbery and towering trees, its
yellowish-brown brick walls covered with ivy and wistaria, with
pointed, diamond-paned windows downstairs, round chimneys
among the gables, and a library "set off at one side in delightful
isolation."[5] While its attic was converted into a stack room for
thousands of volumes and while the rest of the house underwent
renovation, the former editor swam with his family in Lake
Champlain, visited the Holts and the Wheelers, enjoyed the
Trents' company at the Crater Club, and prepared his book on
Plato, which he likened to "setting out to sea in a cockle shell."[6]

In the summerhouse of thuja logs by his cottage in Essex he
struggled through the *Parmenides*[7] and the *Laws* during the
German invasion of Belgium. "What a strange comment is this
war on all our talk of peace! And no man can tell what the

[3] To Stuart P. Sherman, April 22, 1914; courtesy of the University of
Illinois Library.
[4] *Ibid.*
[5] To Louis T. More, Nov. 19, 1913.
[6] To Alice More, July 7, 1914.
[7] "I have finished a long essay on Plato's *Parmenides* which I am
going to send to the *Philosophical Review*. It was great sport writing it,
and taught me, what I had long suspected, that ordinary metaphysical
writing is vastly easier than aesthetic criticism or character-analysis. It
is such plain sailing comparatively, when one does not have to balance
the *nuances* at every step." [To the same, Dec. 13, 1915. More used
this essay as chapter VIII in *P.*]

political and ethical upshot is to be; but I have little hope of wisdom accruing. . . . I sit in my little study among the trees in a profound peace, thinking of things very ancient and withdrawn, and cannot realize in my imagination what is actually taking place in the present. Yet I presume that hidden under the quiet-seeming growth of these trees and grasses the same spirit of strife and envy is at work. I used to wonder why the prohibition of covetousness should have been placed among the Ten Commandments, but I have come to understand that in that passion lies the root of all evil."[8]

With Louis he feigned a little golf. Except to play with him, Paul rarely stepped onto the links. During his days at *The Nation* he was persuaded to follow Fuller and Went for a few holes on a course near New York, when they were playing Montrose J. Moses, who wished to establish himself as a literary critic in More's estimation. As Moses braced himself tensely to drive at a water hole fringed with reeds, More did not improve matters by correctly predicting, "Here's where we see Moses in the bulrushes."

"The Fullers and Wents have been spending the week-end with us," he reported from 245 Nassau Street, "our first guests and very enthusiastic over what Mather calls my 'Georgian setting.'[9] Whiskey and cut-throat until three o'clock Sunday morning,[10] followed by a day of talking, visiting and eating, have left

[8] To Irving Babbitt, Aug. 31, 1914. Cf. *SE* VI, 114-16.

[9] The exterior of the house at 245 Nassau Street was "of terrible American Gothic architecture"; inside, since the furnishings inherited from Mrs. Richardson were too costly to replace, it was "Victorian to beat the band." In both respects it testified to More's adaptability more than it exemplified his taste.

[10] As advisory editor of *The Nation* More several times asked Fuller and Went out for a bit of cut-throat when Mrs. More was away. On one occasion the visitors golfed in the afternoon, dined with More and Mather, and, when the latter had left, settled down to the rigor of the game. As time and whisky fled, the play became wilder and wilder, "a wholly unscientific gamble for 'dummy,'" mostly "luck and impudence," lasting until breakfast, after which the visitors returned by early train to New York and *The Nation*. [To Louis T. More, "Sunday morning," postmarked March 8, 1915.] "It was a glorious debauch, and three

my brain in just the state of sodden repentance that we choose to bestow on our correspondents, and here's to you. But you shouldn't," he warned Louis, "try your little prevarications or misrepresentations where you are sure to be found out. You write that Fuller has congratulated you on winning 'a shekel or thereabouts' from me at bridge this summer. He had already informed me of your boast that you were indulging in the luxuries of civilization on your earnings. I told him that civilization in Cincinnati was the one thing I knew of which was both cheap and rare. . . .

"In the few lucid intervals of yesterday I finished off a paper for *The Nation* on Nietzsche and the Lust of Empire; not bad in part, but the end has a smell of whiskey and cards. I may complete it with something for Holt on war and humanitarianism,[11] if he can stand my heterodox views on that theme."[12]

For a few years after leaving *The Nation* More gave much attention to *The Unpopular Review* (by 1920 called *The Unpartizan Review*), which Henry Holt in his seventies financed and edited as an antidote to old age. Though, aside from being a regular contributor to it, he had at this time no official connection with the quarterly, he was virtually Holt's assistant editor. He discussed with "Uncle Henry" the articles to be pub-

---

naps the next day made me as fresh as if nothing had been done. But I shouldn't care to repeat the joy too often. I lost about a dollar and a half, having the lowest score." [To Louis T. More, Feb. 23, 1915.]

Three months later he had the men back again. After watching Brown beat Princeton in baseball and after playing tennis awhile on the court the Mores had built near their house for their daughters, they dined, "having Alfred Noyes for a fourth. He is a nice honest fellow, but not brilliant. I never saw a poet who seemed to have much brains. Plato discovered that long ago, and he was right. Their talent, like the artist's, is of a special sort, though not so narrow as the painter's. Mather and Kemp Smith came in after dinner and stayed late—too late for those of us who were looking forward to a table of obstreperous cut-throat. But we did *not* sit up all night." [To Alice More, May 29, 1915.]

[11] Cf. *SE* IX, 221 ff. More read his "rather languid" paper on the war at the Cliosophic Society in Princeton on Nov. 19, 1914, and was elected an honorary member of the society. [To Irving Babbitt, Feb. 15, 1915.]

[12] To Louis T. More, Oct. 19, 1914.

lished, read the proofs, and maintained a friendly barrage against intrusions of Holt's "evolutionary-system-cum-spooks."[13] "I tell H. H. that every record I have read of communication with the other world has no other effect on me than to add a new terror to death—is man never to be released from his follies? Spirits are more foolish or more mawkishly sentimental than flesh and blood. If there is any 'progress' in the universe it ought to be in the passage from this world to the other."[14]

"The move to Princeton has proved eminently wise," More stated to Sherman. "It has quite made over my health. The children are living a normal life, and my wife has already a large circle of acquaintances of the sort she enjoys. And then the joy! Right after breakfast I go into my study where a wood fire is burning; 'ich steche mir eine Cigarre an'; I open my Greek book (Plutarch, just now), and settle down in a mood that combines all the delights ever promised by Epicurus and all the feeling of self-righteousness ever promised by Zeno. My only complaint is that the days are too short. I can't honestly say that I have entirely banished my old enemy, the diabolus mesembrinus, but by throwing the labor of writing into the afternoon I manage to keep the devil at the galley oar where he belongs, while my forenoons and evenings are left with long spaces of free and comfortable time. My writing capacity is pretty well mortgaged for a good many months to come, but before summer I am going to squeeze out six or seven weeks for my Plato, and get that book well under way. And so, I hope you can see me as a fairly happy man, as men are happy in this λειμῶνα ἄτης.

"And yet for several months after I came here it seemed as if everywhere about me was nothing but calamity and dissolution. My sister, to whom I owe my education and many other things, was suddenly laid low and for a while it looked as if she had a cancer. That fear proved untrue, and she is now regaining her

[13] To Alice More, July 17, 1915.
[14] To Stuart P. Sherman, May 25, 1917; courtesy of the University of Illinois Library. Cf. *SE* XI, 157-58, and *RP*, 134.

health. But for weeks I was making constant visits to her home in Bridgeton, N. J., and then to the hospital in Philadelphia whither we[15] carried her. Then came other illnesses, and deaths, none of the latter very close to me, yet near enough to make life become more than ever shadowy and uncertain. I have not allowed myself to worry over the war. Hideous as it is, it has not shocked me with surprise. . . .[16] But I can only foresee a general loosening of ties and moral license as the outcome of the war, with perhaps a return to an unwholesome asceticism and a futile withdrawal into their own περιωπή among those of the small minority. So much of men's decency is only habit, and the things that are happening now will not leave much of the old habits and restraints. And I want Germany to be thrashed to her knees; yet I am forced to admit that it will be a terribly dangerous thing for us all to see her system of command and obedience shattered.

"And so you are writing on Franklin for the Cambridge History while I am doing Edwards. . . .[17] As for the eighteenth

---

[15] May came from St. Louis to stay with Alice during her illness.

[16] Cf. *SE* IX, 41, and *HP*, 195. "There is so much sheer terror lurking under the surface of life at its best, that I hate to dwell on this hideous and wanton addition to it." [To Louis T. More, Dec. 28, 1917.]

[17] ". . . I have been rereading Leslie Stephen, with a confirmation of my old views. His human criticism, so to speak, as exhibited in his essays on Johnson and Pope, is supremely good; but when he comes to philosophy he is distinctly clever but almost always superficial, as befits a Utilitarian. Take his Jonathan Edwards. Here, so long as he deals with the man and with the influence of doctrine on character, he leaves nothing to be desired, but the moment he touches on the metaphysical problem he shows an acute logical faculty with complete inability to grasp the central issue. As I understand Edwards, that portent of New England had one of the clearest and profoundest conceptions of the dualism of good and evil the world has ever known. So far, good. But he was led by the spirit of the age to hypostatize these infinite principles of good and evil as two persons, God and the devil. In doing this there was nothing singular; all theologians have pretended to do the same thing. But Edwards was horribly logical and monstrously brave. The consequence is one of the most disastrous nightmares in history. Most men either do not conceive good and evil, whatever their professions may be, as absolutes. However they may talk of infinity, they really never transcend in their imagination the relative quantities of the flux. Or else, if

century and the deists, I always come to them joyfully. They are so wise, so sane, they have so perfectly the supreme comforts of limitation. And then, some day, this limitation galls me, and I turn back to the seventeenth century. And for a while those giants fill me with their enthusiasms and I rattle about the universe as if there were no walls of flame to hold me in. And then I long for my quieter friends, and go back to them, only to have the old experience. And that to me is the tragedy of English literature, of all modern literature, with the exception of a few, a very few, individuals who rose above their age. Milton came nearer than any other man of England, nearer than Shakespeare, to combining the law of limitation with the law of enthusiasm,—which is only the great law of the imagination; but Milton made no school, was never a real centre, and has in him also some extravagances of the mind pretty hard to pass by. No; the Greeks did that thing once for all. . . . They themselves made for us the synthesis of the seventeenth and eighteenth centuries, which in English literature we have to make, if we make it at all, by the painful welding together of two diverse and hostile ages. And that is the reason that every year I am more and more convinced that, in the strict sense of the word, there has been, and is, only one literature."[18]

After devoting most of a day to Plato, More worked in his garden—"Plato and a garden, what more should human nature

---

they are true dualists in their conception of good and evil, they do not really connect their absolute ideas with their religious personifications. They are illogical, but remain human. Not so Edwards. And, once grant that it is legitimate to accept a rigid personification of an absolute dualism, what is there left but the tremendous picture of a God dangling the poor souls of men gleefully over the mouth of an everlasting hell? Edwards is thus one of the most instructive illustrations in history of the consequences of mingling an unflinching mythology with a rigid philosophy, that is of confusing the personal and the super-personal. I do not find a word of explanation in Leslie Stephen of the real problem. And as he has treated Edwards so he has dealt with others." [To Irving Babbitt, May 3, 1913.]

[18] To Stuart P. Sherman, March 1, 1915; courtesy of the University of Illinois Library.

desire?"[19]—or for a change would walk an hour, jauntily swinging his cane. Impatient in little ways, when he was ready to leave the house he wanted to leave at once, whether anyone else who intended to go with him was ready or not. If his slim, energetic wife accompanied him at too fast a pace, he might have to restrain her by putting his cane in front of her as they went down Nassau Street. When he encountered Professor and Mrs. George M. Harper on their daily strolls, he used to tease him about the hat, perfectly good though out of style, that Professor Harper had found in a forgotten box and put to use. This continued until Mrs. Harper asked: "Why don't you wear your own hat as other people do, instead of perched on the top of your head as though it were too small for you?" "I'm high hat," More replied. He walked often with Edward Capps, a professor of classics and the American editor of the Loeb Classical Library. By persistent attacks in *The Nation* on "the scandalous appearance," "the bad type, bad paper, and unintelligent printing"[20] of some of the earlier volumes of that series More provoked James Loeb and the publishers to make needed improvements.

Were he sauntering by himself he would drop in for tea with women whom he found entertaining or would return home for that purpose. Preferring bright, vivacious women like his wife, he loathed the bluestocking who studied his books in order to discuss them with him. On the other hand Mrs. More would look sad when, having discovered that she had not read some masterpiece, he intimated that she might have been more intellectual than she was. Clear-headed and efficient, just and kind,

[19] To Alice More, May 29, 1915. "This afternoon I got my ladder up in the walnut tree and by scrambling about like an ape contrived to trim away a number of dead boughs. It is surprising how much work even a small place like ours calls for. I begin to understand when Milton says that Adam and Eve found the care of Paradise almost too much for four hands. The rest of my time I have been getting my exercise sawing up a cord of oak wood." [To Alice More, Oct. 17, 1918.]

[20] "The Loeb Classical Library," anonymous letter by P. E. More, *N*, May 20, 1915, vol. 100, no. 2603, p. 565. Cf. "The Loeb Classical Library," anonymous review by P. E. More, *N*, March 25, 1915, vol. 100, no. 2595, pp. 334-35.

she avoided any appearance of being "modern." When guests were present, she deftly turned the conversation into channels in which her husband shone. After tea he might take men from the drawing-room to his study to smoke and talk. He liked to make his own position on any matter clear and to have the last word. This was usually allowed him except by Mather, who defended contrary opinions partly, it seems, to provoke More's customary retort: "Frank, I never heard such damn nonsense in all my life!"

Because Ruth McLinn, who could not always leave her music pupils on the dot, once arrived late at his house for dinner, he thereafter called her "A. T." (artistic temperament). When she appeared punctually, he pretended to be astonished: "Why, what's happened to A. T.? Is she reforming?" The whole family would "cuddle" Miss McLinn a week each winter and sometimes also in the spring, giving her the best guest room and providing her with breakfast in bed and other little luxuries. Their evenings passed in banter (his wife and daughters affectionately ridiculing him)—in banter, cards, or music; for Mrs. More played the piano well and Darrah had a fresh, sweet tone in singing. When they sat down to bridge before the study fire, with the world shut out by heavy, red curtains, if Miss McLinn, lulled by peace and comfort, inadvertently lost a trick, Mr. More would exclaim: "You'd better stick to music, A. T.!"

After bedtime for the girls he would fill his pipe, tamp down the tobacco "scientifically" with a piece of wood he had whittled for the purpose, puff away with little pp-pp-pp sounds, and pause frequently to relight it. An additional narcotic he found in ecclesiastical reminiscences. "Alas, I have just finished the fourth volume of Liddon's *Pusey*, the best book to soothe the mind for bed I have laid hands on for many a month. It has all the advantage of being filled with thought without any of the vexation of thinking. Such is the beautiful result of authority."[21]

[21] To Louis T. More, Dec. 8, 1916.

Except for *The Times Literary Supplement*, which he examined with care, he scarcely glanced at newspapers; for though the general significance of political and social movements interested him, their daily details bored him. While he rested on the uncomfortable old couch in his study for an hour or so after lunch, "powerfully attracted," "like some other good and great men," "by the mysteries of crime and imposture,"[22] he would skim through a detective story, a form of fiction he had begun reviewing anonymously in 1910. " 'Wholesome' boys are spanked every day," *The New Republic* proclaimed, "for reading detective stories which delight Elihu Root and Charles E. Hughes and Paul Elmer More. . . . If, as may be suspected, they give undue excitement to Paul Elmer More, it is he who needs a reminder as to the true meaning of culture, and not the avid child who can digest literary green apples where later he won't be able to stand the delicate monstrosities of Katherine Fullerton Gerould."[23]

More relished detective stories as a diverting escape to prosaic common sense. The world usually appears in them as it appears to be to the reader of relaxed intelligence for whom they are designed. ". . . about the only form of literature today wherein you may be sure that the author will not play tricks with the Ten Commandments is the detective story . . . there alone murder is still simply murder, adultery simply adultery,

[22] Anonymous review by P. E. More of *Life and Memoirs of John Churton Collins*, by L. C. Collins, *N*, Nov. 23, 1911, vol. 93, pp. 497-98, and *EP*, Dec. 2, 1911, Saturday Supplement, p. 8.

[23] *Op.cit.*, Nov. 18, 1916, vol. IX, no. 107, part 2, p. 1. Cf. *DA*, 4-5. "Last night we had Marshall (who is lecturing here this semester), the Geroulds, and two others at dinner. The talk ran fast, and Marshall and the Geroulds stayed till well on towards midnight. Did you read Katherine Gerould's story of 'The 83rd' in the December (?) *Harper's*? It is pretty nearly the most offensive thing I have ever seen in print— a horrid, filthy nightmare—and the good people of this town are shaking their heads over the scandal. One lady confessed to me the other day that she had called on Mrs. Gerould just to see if she could see any point of contact between the author's home manners and her fiction. She candidly, and I think disappointedly, confessed that she saw nothing of 'The 83rd' in the lady herself." [To Louis T. More, March 8, 1916.]

theft simply theft, and no more about it."[24] In them "the love motive . . . is usually a sheer nuisance."[25] ". . . the detective, or crime, story is tolerant of some mixtures, but intolerant of others. The detective plot goes well with humour and with an idyllic setting, but just cannot be conjoined with the psychological method of narration or character-drawing; and this is particularly true of the Meredithian psychology which forces one to stop and consider the cause and implications of the parts of a dialogue. And I am almost ready to affirm that the novel of crime and detection suffers just to the extent that the author employs the psychological method with literary skill and subtlety. In fact subtlety is totally out of place in the detective story."[26] Often he sent wooden boxes full of these books to sick friends, begging them to keep them.

On March 17, 1915, at the Nassau Club, in Princeton, to which he had been elected the preceding December, he argued "that philosophy and the classics ought to be the backbone of education."[27] Five days later in an address on "Property and Law" delivered at a Princeton Phi Beta Kappa dinner he insisted, in opposition to advocates of socialism, that "the private ownership of property, including its production and distribution, is with very limited reservations, essential to the material stability and progress of society."[28]

He left for St. Louis on April 16th to take part on the 18th in the exercises ("perdition seize their inventor!"[29]) opening the library that Mrs. Richardson had bequeathed to the St. Louis Art Museum in memory of her husband. "As a delicate atten-

[24] *DA*, 99.

[25] Anonymous review by P. E. More of *The House of the Whispering Pines*, by Anna Katharine Green, *N*, March 10, 1910, vol. 90, no. 2332, p. 238, and *EP*, March 12, 1910, Saturday Supplement, p. 6. Cf. his anonymous review of *The Paternoster Ruby*, by C. E. Walk, *N*, Nov. 3, 1910, vol. 91, p. 418, and *EP*, Nov. 5, 1910, Saturday Supplement, p. 7.

[26] To Seward B. Collins, April 25, 1935.

[27] From More's notes for this speech, some of the ideas of which reappear in *SE* IX, 47.

[28] *SE* IX, 147.

[29] To Louis T. More, April 6, 1915.

tion to the dead I shall wear one of Uncle Clifford's neck ties when I make my address!"[30] "The hall . . . was open at the end and at the side, hard to speak in, and filled with an utterly miscellaneous crowd made up largely of children, nursemaids, and paralytics. I was so bored trying to talk to them that I just stopped before I had finished my subject—but of course no one knew that."[31]

He made another long trip "for little money and little honor"[32] to read on June 7th for the chapter of Phi Beta Kappa at the University of Indiana a paper on "that compound of the genius and the quack,"[33] Disraeli. "I . . . tried to give a personal characterization of the man while making his works the vehicle for all my philosophy of conservatism."[34] "As a negative force conservatism is based on a certain distrust of human nature, believing that the immediate impulses of the heart and visions of the brain are likely to be misleading guides; whereas . . . liberalism . . . rests on the assumption that, practically speaking, all men are by nature good and need only to be let alone to develop in the right direction. But this distrust of human nature is closely connected with another and more positive factor of conservatism—its trust in the controlling power of the imagination.[35] These, as I analyse the matter,—the instinctive distrust of uncontrolled human nature and the instinctive reliance on the imagination,—are the very roots of the conservative temper, as their contraries are the roots of the liberal and radical temper, the lack of imagination, if any distinction is to be made, being the chief factor of liberalism[36] and confidence in human nature being the main impulse of radicalism."[37]

[30] To Alice More, April 15, 1915.
[31] To the same, May 7, 1915.
[32] To Louis T. More, June 4, 1915.
[33] To Ellery Sedgwick, Jan. 18, 1915; courtesy of *The Atlantic Monthly*.
[34] To Alice More, April 15, 1915.
[35] Cf. *SE* IX, 16-20, 36 f.
[36] See the comments on Lord Morley in *SE* XI, 224-25.
[37] *SE* IX, 167-68. More's conservatism is discussed in *The Case for*

Bridge beguiled the sultry weeks in Essex, varied by a motor trip in the Adirondacks. "Much of the scenery was beautiful of course, and the whole thing was a lark, but I wouldn't do it again for a good deal. After two or three hours the mind simply fails to be affected by new scenes, and the only thing left is the rather vulgar sensation of whirl and hurry. Seeing how people live, I do honestly believe that these automobiles are a menace to civilization. After all, there is a fatal end to this delight in whirling, as we used to find out when we were children, and spun ourselves about till we dropped down dizzy and exhausted. This is gloomy moralizing, but it fits in with what I am writing for the Belgium relief book.[38] I am calling my little contribution 'A Moment of Tragic Purgation,' based on the plays of Euripides that deal with the Trojan disasters. They have been my reading this summer, diversified with the barbarous works of Clemens Alexandrinus."[39]

The More brothers kept the presses moving. Ainsie put out another novel, *A Vision of Empire*. Jim's first volume of poetry, *Gods and Heroes*, appeared early in 1916. Of his own first book, *The Limitations of Science*, Louis wrote to Paul that it derived from his criticism many of its ideas and much of its expression. In October 1915, after Babbitt had proofread it, Houghton Mifflin published the Ninth Series of *Shelburne Essays*, a medley which, "in despair of a better title,"[40] its author called *Aristocracy and Justice*.

"The great I. B. spent the month of January here," More in-

Conservatism, by Francis Graham Wilson, Seattle (University of Washington Press), 1951, pp. 72-74; *The Conservative Mind from Burke to Santayana*, by Russell Kirk, Chicago (Regnery), 1953, pp. 377-86; and *Conservatism in America*, by Clinton Rossiter, New York (Knopf), 1955, pp. 167-68.

[38] At the request of Edith Wharton he contributed to *The Book of the Homeless*, edited by her, New York (Charles Scribner's Sons), 1916.

[39] To Alice More, Sept. 13, 1915.

[40] To Irving Babbitt, June 27, 1915. *SE* IX contains essays on "Natural Aristocracy," "Academic Leadership," "The Paradox of Oxford," "Justice," "Property and Law," "Disraeli and Conservatism," "The New Morality," and "The Philosophy of the War."

formed Sherman from Princeton on March 6, 1916, "being the close of his semi-sabbatical. He had until then been in Dublin, N. H., working on his *Rousseau and Romanticism*, which promises, I think, to be a work of first-rate importance."[41]

"I am much pressed for time by the preparation of my lectures on American Poetry for the Johns Hopkins. Just now I am in the agony of a particularly hard question. It was stipulated that at least one whole lecture should be given to Sidney Lanier, and now I am perplexed to know how I may treat that poet *manqué* without rousing the ire of the loyal Baltimoreans."[42]

The Percy Turnbull Memorial Lectures,[43] however, at Johns Hopkins University "went off well enough, and one has large audiences there, but there is something false and upsetting in this direct appeal which is decidedly disagreeable to me. I find myself looking to see how I affect my hearers instead of thinking only of what I ought to say—and by 'affecting' I mean something different from 'making myself understood'; you know what I mean."[44]

Debating with Willard Huntington Wright on "Nietzsche and Progress" before the Get-Together Club in Hartford, Connecticut, on May 15th, More argued for self-control against humanitarian self-abnegation on the one hand and the Nietzschean Will to Power on the other. "The idealism of Christ and Plato was their strength, not their weakness, and it is because this is lost

[41] To Stuart P. Sherman, March 6, 1916; courtesy of the University of Illinois Library.

[42] *Ibid.*

[43] March 29, "The Spirit and Poetry of Early New England"; March 31, "Emerson"; April 3, "Whittier and Longfellow"; April 5, "The Influence of New York"; April 7, "Three Poets of the South"; April 10, "Sidney Lanier"; April 12, "The Modern Movement."
Persuaded by his sister, Alice, on Jan. 10, 1920, More took his evening clothes and "the disagreeable little journey" from Princeton to Bridgeton to read there (without remuneration) the last of the above lectures, renamed "The Modern Tendency in Poetry." [Alice More to P. E. More, Jan. 24, 1920.]

[44] To Alice More, April 15, 1916.

that mere human sympathy has usurped the place of justice, and that democracy, instead of being the school of virtue where true distinction of character is honored, tends to show an hostility to distinction and a levelling downwards."[45]

He dropped everything to be with his sister a few weeks in July when she submitted to an exploratory operation at the Maine General Hospital in Portland. As soon as Alice was out of danger, Mrs. More, whose activity and courage concealed from her friends and almost from her family her own chronic suffering from diseases of the heart and the kidneys, with her practical devotion at once set about finding quarters in Princeton for her sister-in-law, whose health, the surgeon had predicted, could never radically improve.

As her brother offered to pay her expenses, Alice remained at the hospital until the first of October, which gave him an opportunity to leave Essex in the middle of September for a brief visit to Babbitt at Squam Lake, New Hampshire; to rest at "The Cedars" after finishing the first draft of his *Platonism*; to tutor Louis's son, John, in Latin; and to arrange, together with Lou, for the purchase and the clearing of some land by his summer cottage for a tennis court. Then, having met Alice's train in New York, he took her straight to his house in Princeton. Delighted with the apartment that Mrs. More had found for her at 293 Nassau Street, by the end of October, with her sister-in-law's help, Alice moved herself, her maid, and her belongings into it from Bridgeton, where, with reluctance at leaving her friends, she sold her little house. As Ainsie, now retired and pensioned, and his wife were visiting Paul, Alice rejoiced in her return to family life.

In November the two brothers and their wives "took in the exercises of the National Academy[46] and Institute, including a

---

[45] From More's notes for this occasion.

[46] More was elected to the American Academy of Arts and Letters on Nov. 18, 1915. A few years afterwards he got W. C. Brownell, "for diplomatic reasons," to act as Babbitt's first sponsor for the National Institute of Arts and Letters. "Mather acted as second sponsor and I

long speech by Roosevelt in which he laid down the law on all
matters aesthetic and moral with an amount of half-knowledge
veritably amazing. What a jolly thing it must be to possess un-
bounded self-assurance, an inexhaustible flow of words, and no
distinction in one's mind between what one knows and what one
does not know. In the afternoon Net and I went to the reception
at Frick's and saw his house and pictures. He has a palace front-
ing on a whole Fifth Avenue block, and such pictures!"[47]

More invited Sherman, who was then in New York, to the
Authors' Club[48] on New Year's eve and to Princeton for a week-
end, which "the very distinguished writer and teacher from
Urbana"[49] unexpectedly cut short, because, his host said, "he
couldn't stand Francesco," the Mores' swarthy, hook-nosed, gray
haired, Italian butler.

On Twelfth-night Alice, who passed January 1917 in a New
York hotel, made Paul up for "the great costume ball given by
the Century Club. He wore the beautiful Chinese costume which
Mrs. Richardson brought from China. I tried my best to make
him look like a snub-nosed Mongolian but his profile looked
more and more like a red Indian's. He was stunning however.
The ball was magnificent, about 1000 men there in costume.
They hired Sherry's big ball room and had a bridge built to it
from the club, and a grand supper. Paul got back . . . at 4 a.m.
and had a swelled head when he waked up, from too much
smoking."[50]

At the University Club in New York on February 22nd he

---

as third. You are now on a level with Edgar Lee Masters and Robert
Frost!" [To Irving Babbitt, Jan. 17, 1920. Cf. *DA*, 53, 69.]

[47] To Louis T. More, Nov. 21, 1916.

[48] More, who had joined this club in 1912, regularly attended (often
with William P. Trent and sometimes with Henry Holt) its fortnightly
meetings held after the theatres were over. He served on the Committee
on Admissions of the Authors' Club in 1913 and of the Century for
three years beginning in 1912.

[49] To Stuart P. Sherman, Dec. 26, 1916; courtesy of the University of
Illinois Library.

[50] Alice More to Louis T. More, "Sunday" [postmarked Jan. 14, 1917].

delivered to the Academy what W. C. Brownell described as a "beautiful" paper "beautifully" read in a "beautiful" voice.[51] In fulfillment of other Academic duties More served in 1918 and 1919 on a jury for the award of one of the Prizes in Letters established by the Pulitzer Foundation, and for a few years afterwards he had the thankless task of persuading Academicians to write obituaries of their deceased fellows, who otherwise might "lie in Hades unknown to the world, unwept, unsung."[52] "Academicians may be immortal," he conceded to Brander Matthews, "but theirs is an immortality of crookedness, perversity, indolence, indifference, cussedness, egotism— and I leave you to supply the rest from your larger vocabulary. I have written nine hundred and ninety-nine letters, and two of the obituary notices—Hopkinson Smith and Henry James—are still a begging. One immortal is sick, another has a father to bury, another will bid farewell to his family, another admits ignorance, another answers by his secretary. What am I to do? I have myself supplied one notice[53] and do not like to appear more than once—and indeed I am incompetent for both the Smith and the James.[54] Have you contributed anything to this particular rogues' gallery, and, if you have not, will you not, in the name of heaven, come to my rescue? Take either Smith or James; do him up in four or five hundred words; curse him or bless him. I don't care. At any rate let me have a line by early mail to know what I may expect."[55] Matthews apparently came to the rescue; for More laid it on with a trowel: "Your immortality sits on you like butter on hot toast, like treacle on sausage, like

[51] Cf. Stuart P. Sherman to P. E. More, May 1, 1917.
The paper was "English and Englistic," referred to in n. 44 on p. 121 above.
[52] To Brander Matthews, Dec. 21, 1921; courtesy of the Head of Special Collections, Columbia University.
[53] On Henry Adams, published in *Academy Notes and Monographs*, New York, 1922, pp. 1-7.
[54] Cf. *DA*, 112.
[55] To Brander Matthews, Dec. 18, 1921; courtesy of the Head of Special Collections, Columbia University.

bay leaves on the brow of Apollo."⁵⁶ But for the rest: "Confound the crankiness of these immortals anyway; give me to live with responsible mortals."⁵⁷

Norman Kemp Smith, who (before the war caused him to return to England to enter his government's intelligence service) had formed with More, Mather, George McClean Harper, and Charles Grosvenor Osgood a little discussion group in Princeton,⁵⁸ wrote to More repeatedly and in detail, urging him to create as informally and privately as possible a small committee in New York to counsel the British government about its war propaganda and to supply it with mailing lists. He asked also for advice about establishing a network of such committees throughout the United States, to develop a rapprochement of American and Allied thought during the war and the subsequent period of reconstruction.

After consulting a few men in the city, More answered that he believed such an organization might do as little good and as much harm for the British cause as German propaganda in America had done for the German cause. Though convinced that the best interests of America and the British Empire required them to work closely together, he advised, in view of America's distrust of foreign conspiracies, against an organization directed by and reporting to London. If individuals here and there, moved by their own convictions, wished to help Britain, that was a different matter, and he was glad to count himself among them. He suggested a magazine article and, through friends, furnished names for a mailing list. But his outspoken disposition and his aversion to guile unfitted him for secret action, which became unnecessary on his part, since Americans favoring the Allies organized openly and America soon entered the war.

⁵⁶ To Brander Matthews, Dec. 21, 1921; courtesy of the Head of Special Collections, Columbia University.

⁵⁷ To the same, Feb. 13, 1924; courtesy of the Head of Special Collections, Columbia University.

⁵⁸ Edwin Walter Kemmerer and Augustus Trowbridge later took part in this group.

Princeton and Plato

"Saturday I was in New York, and it was exhilarating to see the British and French flags displayed together with the American all up and down Fifth Avenue, in honor of the coming of Balfour and Joffre. It has been interesting to note the different behavior of the French and English. Balfour, wisely conscious of the latent jealousy of Americans, has been extremely careful to avoid saying anything that could be construed as advice; whereas Joffre and Viviani have blurted out, with no ill effect, whatever was in their minds. If there is any hope for this world, we may hope that one good result of the war will be the bringing together again of England and America in peaceful brotherhood. . . . I have a horrible feeling that France is almost bled white. Russia cannot be depended on, and Italy has, I fear, played the part of a poltroon from the beginning. I suspect that the war will be brought to an end by England and America fighting side by side. Probably we can do nothing until next spring—nothing really to count, that is—but a couple of millions of men thrown into the field then ought to make a vast difference—and the American boys will fight, when they once get started. The pity of it is that our government has allowed the country to drag on with no preparation—and still Congress is talking—*labitur et labetur*! I would give a good deal to hear Balfour's real opinion of Wilson. The man carries a terrible responsibility for our evil state, yet is likely to go down in history as a hero.[59] It makes me think of old Walpole's com-

[59] "I have disliked various politicians, Roosevelt for instance; but I have never felt towards any other man, not even Bryan, as I do towards Wilson. He has certain qualities which appeal to the intelligence of men otherwise clear-sighted and straightforward, and as a consequence he seems to have corrupted the nation at the top, and lowered our whole mental and moral tone. . . . One hateful aspect of the matter is the probability that in a generation from now Wilson will be regarded as one of our very great men. These subtler moral effects (not easily detected, but of frightful consequence) will be forgotten. . . ." [To Louis T. More, Feb. 25, 1917. Cf. *SE* IX, 22-23, and *SE* X, xii.]

"It appears that Wilson is a great hero in France and England. . . . My own feeling is—and many Americans are with me—that Wilson is a dangerous factor in the forces at work. Just last night Dr. William

plaint to his son Horace: Don't read me history, for I know that it lies."[60]

After lecturing on March 23rd on "The Spirit and Poetry of Early New England" at Trinity College, the predecessor of Duke University, on the 19th of the next month More attended *The Nation's* semicentennial dinner at the Biltmore in New York. ". . . I had the good luck to sit at table with a party of chosen spirits, with Henry Holt at my right, Dr. Franklin (the biggest-hearted and best-brained Jew of my acquaintance) at my left, and Giddings, Lawrence Godkin, Haskins, and A. C. Coolidge completing the circle. The first part of the evening was exhilarating, naturally; but then the speeches! They weren't so bad in one way; representatives of half a dozen of the allied countries spoke, and said some things worth hearing—especially the Chinese ambassador, Wellington Koo, whose English was extraordinarily correct and fine, better than [that of] the Americans from whom he had learnt it. But it was all terribly solemn and serious, gradually becoming tiresome. Why do we try so hard to amuse ourselves, and why, doubly why, do we seek to be 'up-lifted' in our amusement? . . .

"I too am reading Plato: but this has grown to be a habit with me. Still every day, the first thing after breakfast, I go into my study, and for about two hours smoke my cigar and morning pipe, and read in one or another of the dialogues. To-day I began the *Laws* again. There is something wonderfully comfortable and clarifying in this constant association with a chosen

Adams Brown was insisting to me vehemently that Wilson stands for the highest ideals of humanity. I contended—to Brown's apoplectic rage —that Wilson's sentimentalism was not a true ideal and was likely to be an important element in the horrible spread of Bolshevism that threatens the world. For a man in Wilson's position to say, and insist as one of the terms of peace, that all peoples have the right of determining their own government strikes me as nonsense, and perilous nonsense. It is impracticable, the sort of sentimentalism that does not conform with fact or utility yet may be the cause of endless confusion and anarchy. And this sort of thing underlies the whole Wilsonian brand of humanitarianism." [To Norman Kemp Smith, Nov. 3, 1918.]

[60] To the same, May 12, 1917.

master; gradually one gets in the way of thinking in his grooves, and the everlasting botherations of the mind acquire a certain order and focus. I think I learn as much from Plato's errors as from his truth. My mind is naturally like his—I mean of course in quality, not in power—and when he goes astray I seem to know exactly why he did so and what ὁρμή was for the moment unduly strong; and to follow him then is a kind of intellectual purgation. I often ask myself what he would say if he were living now. And I think his sentiment would be in the words which—as I may have told you in my last letter—I have set up over my mantel: ἔστι δὴ τοίνυν τὰ τῶν ἀνθρώπων πράγματα μεγάλης μὲν σπουδῆς οὐκ ἄξια, ἀναγκαῖόν γε μὴν σπουδάζειν· τοῦτο δὲ οὐκ εὐτυχές.[61] It is the thought of his old age, but it was said almost in the same words in the *Republic*, and is implicit in many other passages. It is the Greek way of saying what forms the burden of the *Bhagavadgītā* and Hindu philosophy generally: Work, without attachment to the fruits of work. Not an easy rule. It is comparatively easy to lose one's self in the stream of the world, and equally easy to retire into the 'ivory tower' of the romanticists; but to be serious, when we know that life itself is not serious, there's the rub. There is no happiness without a sense of the universal illusion, but can a man be happy if he permits himself to sink into that illusion, instead of looking upon it, by some legerdemain of the soul, from without? Is not this the very essence of the σπουδαιότης of poetry? What you say of the difficulty of living in philosophic calm amidst a world gone mad, is terribly true. Perhaps, however, we exaggerate the present madness of society; has it ever been much different? Certainly, horrors were everywhere when Plato was writing, and

[61] *Laws*, VII, 803, b. Cf. *P*, 29, and *RP*, 332 f. Sherman referred to "the thesis, somewhat wearily stoical, which he [More] has carved in tall Greek letters across the wide face of his mantel shelf—a thesis of which this is the gist: 'Man's affairs are really of small consequence, but one must act as if they were [serious], and this is a burden.'" ["Mr. P. E. More and The Wits," by Stuart P. Sherman, *The Review*, Jan. 17, 1920, vol. 2, no. 36, p. 54.]

'the end was everywhere.' The sixth book of the *Republic* has always had a particular interest for me, owing to the perplexity of mind it exhibits over this very question. Two theses run through the book: That a State cannot be happy unless it is governed by the philosophers (and the same of the individual, unless he is governed by the philosophic element of his soul), and That it is difficult, if not impossible, for the philosopher to develop except in a well-governed State. It is a nasty dilemma, and Plato never really solves it except by his θεία μοῖρα. Which is as much as to say, I suppose, that there are no solutions of anything in this world. Our only solution is a παράδειγμα ἐν οὐρανῷ. But it is a good deal to know where we are, and to understand the terms of the seriousness that is imposed upon us. And if Plato was never quite a happy man, Socrates was—was, so far as I know, the only happy man whose life is recorded, unless we add Buddha.[62] It is this practical philosophy of Socrates that inclines me to regard the biographical dialogues—*Euthyphro*, *Apology*, *Crito*, and part of the *Phaedo*—as more valuable finally than the most splendid of Plato's own developments of the Socratic faith."[63]

After delivering his William Vaughn Moody lecture, "Standards of Taste," at the University of Chicago on April 26, 1917; repeating it before the Middlesex Women's Club in Lowell, Massachusetts, on December 31st, which gave him an opportunity to see the Babbitts in Cambridge, a visit that Babbitt returned when he lectured in Princeton on January 30, 1918; receiving the honorary degree of Doctor of Letters from Columbia and Dartmouth in June 1918; and passing a summer of rest, reading (Anthony Trollope[64]), exercise, and bridge at Essex,

[62] Cf. *CF*, 43.
[63] To Prosser Hall Frye, April 21, 1917. Cf. *P*, 304-05.
[64] "Despite his *longueurs* I wonder whether he does not stand much higher as an artist than we are commonly disposed to admit. He comes nearer to reproducing a whole national society than does any other novelist I know—nearer than Balzac, if genuine realism is a criterion of success—and to have accomplished that is certainly no mean feat. And

Princeton and Plato

More used his *Platonism* (which Babbitt had criticized in manuscript[65]) as his Vanuxem Lectures in October and November at Princeton University.

The book aims less at being an historical or critical exegesis than "an invitation . . . to the practice of philosophy."[66] "I can foresee no restoration of humane studies to their lost position of leadership until they are felt once more to radiate from some central spiritual truth. I do not believe that the aesthetic charms of literature can supply this want, nor is it clear to me that a purely scientific analysis of the facts of moral experience can

---

then, if you take him with the other major novelists of the Victorian era, what a world you have. I wonder whether in time we shall not come to recognize English Victorian fiction as the great achievement of the century. With all the finer qualities of French fiction as judged by the narrower canons of art, and despite its universal acceptance, I question whether it really touches as closely the deeper springs of human conduct as does the English, whether it is as great as the English in the terms of life. Contemporary novels I can scarcely read; almost without exception they impress me as unreal." [To Prosser Hall Frye, Nov. 27, 1917.]

[65] More in turn had been criticizing Babbitt's writing. "Now, my general position, that your work does not carry as it might for the reason that you do not sufficiently lay bare the skeleton of your argument and that you tend to conceal the rigid cold syllogism under a mass of allusions and illustration,—my general position in this respect is undoubtedly true. Your work would be more effective if you first *wrote* out a skeleton of your argument, with an 'it follows' at the head of each section and subsection, and if then, in putting flesh on the skeleton, you were diligent in keeping out of each section or paragraph every sentence that did not bear on the subject in the narrowest sense of the word. . . . But this is only one half of what I have to say; and the other half is far the more important. As you know, I owe my whole mental direction from what I have got from you in conversation, and some day, in the proper place, I shall state this in print. Now, in my criticism of your writing, I have that fact in mind. When I say that your writing is not so effective as it might be, I mean, not so effective as I have known you to be in another medium. And in my criticism of your method I am trying to lay my finger on the cause of this difference. But it does not follow that your writing, with no change in your method, may not be effective— ultimately, as readers get inside your circle of ideas so to speak, very effective. I repeat that my comments were not intended to discourage, nor ought they to discourage. You are certainly winning your adherents, though slowly. Could you expect to get them rapidly in the present state of society?" [To Irving Babbitt, Sept. 14, 1917.]

[66] *P*, viii.

furnish the needed motive; the former is too apt to run into dilettantism, and the latter appeals too little to the imagination and the springs of enthusiasm. Only through the centralizing force of religious faith or through its equivalent in philosophy can the intellectual life regain its meaning and authority for earnest men. Yet, for the present at least, the dogmas of religion have lost their hold, while the current philosophy of the schools has become in large measure a quibbling of specialists on technical points of minor importance, or, where serious, too commonly has surrendered to that flattery of the instinctive elements of human nature which is the very negation of mental and moral discipline.

"It is in such a belief and such a hope, whether right or wrong, that I have turned back to the truth, still potent and fresh and salutary, which Plato expounded in the troubled and doubting days of Greece—the truth which is in religion but is not bounded by religious dogma, and which needs no confirmation by miracle or inspired tradition."[67]

The general point of view of *Platonism* is about the same as that of the "Definitions of Dualism," not, More protests, because he would squeeze Plato into his "pint cup," but because the "Definitions" were a product of his study of the *Dialogues*. Although his Vanuxem Lectures are six times longer than his "Definitions" and contain chapters, among others, on Plato's psychology, science, cosmogony, and metaphysics, and discussions of the complexities of Plato's thought and of its influence on and interpretation by subsequent thinkers, More's deepest personal interest in *Platonism* concerns intimations of the ideal world.

"The beginning and end of philosophy are contained in the spiritual affirmation that it is better to be just than unjust, better to suffer all things for righteousness' sake than to do unrighteousness. . . ."[68] Socrates, when condemned to death, overcame the

[67] *P*, ix-x.   [68] *P*, 302.

temptation to obtain liberty through bribery, not by balancing opinions about pleasure and pain but by the superrational intuition, or the "higher knowledge" of morality, as More called it, that "it is better for a man to be just than to be unjust, and better if needs be, to suffer wrong than to do wrong."[69] "This is the last and supreme *argumentum ad hominem*: It is *better* to do justice simply and solely because you are *happier* so doing than otherwise."[70]

Socrates accepted and acted upon that sort of knowledge or insight as something compared to which everything else is questionable opinion and can be renounced. Plato, on the whole agreeing with him, tried to understand the implications of the dualism between "pleasure and the rapture, or peace, or happiness—the word is naught but the fact is everything—of obedience to a higher law than our personal or physical desires."[71] ". . . besides opinion, whether true or false, man has also knowledge. The operation of this faculty we may not be able to analyse, but it is there, within our souls, giving us certain information of the everlasting reality of righteousness and loveliness in themselves, as things apart from the flux, and bidding us look to the God of these realities for the measure of our nature."[72]

Although, More believed, there is no logical explanation of the relation between pleasure, opinion, prudence, and "the concupiscent element of the soul" on one side of our dualistic nature, and happiness, knowledge, morality, and "the inner check,[73] or spirit" on the other side,[74] "nevertheless, some sort

[69] *P*, 18; cf. *ibid.*, pp. 61, 120, and *RP*, 116 f.
[70] *P*, 77.   [71] *P*, 99.   [72] *P*, 113.
[73] The "subjection of the lower will to the higher" is "an exercise of the function which Emerson, quoting I know not what Eastern source, calls the 'inner check.'" [*SE* II, 118.] Besides "the great self-moving, incessant flux" of "inner desires and outer impressions" there is also "that within man which displays itself intermittently as an inhibition upon this or that impulse, preventing its prolongation in activity, and making a pause or eddy, so to speak, in the stream. This negation of the flux we call the inner check." [*SE* VIII, 247-48.]
[74] *P*, 168.

of reconciliation the heart of man craves and will not, perhaps cannot, forgo; and the Platonic Ideas, as the dualist understands them, are primarily just the labour of the imagination to effect practically what could not be effected intellectually."[75]

Though Plato postulated the reality of several kinds of Ideas, he "was brought to his doctrine of Ideas by ethical rather than logical considerations, and . . . despite what may be called his period of metaphysical stress, his chief interest lay in this direction."[76] ". . . in the procedure of science we are interested in acquiring a knowledge of the Ideas, whereas in the procedure of philosophy we are interested in possessing the Ideas themselves. Ideas, as Plato was supremely concerned in them, and as they constitute the essence of what the world has rightly known as Platonism, are not derived intellectually, but are an emphatic assertion of the unchanging reality behind moral forces, a natural development of the Socratic affirmation of spiritual truth."[77]

"If you admit the reality of the Idea of justice, you will love the Idea, and your love will be established on something fixed; you will not only be confirmed in your readiness to act in accordance with the principles of justice as these are formulated by your own experience and by that of the society in which you live . . . but you will be led to search deeply into your consciousness for principles that approach more nearly to the absolute standard and authority of an Idea. You will be a promoter of your own welfare and of society's, a guide and governor among men who are groping towards wisdom, a philosopher. On the other hand, if you reject the Idea of justice and say there is nothing fixed and unalterable behind the changing fashions of law and custom, nothing at once the cause and goal of these fashions, if you say that justice is merely a name for acts which may have nothing in common, you are taking away all that gives to justice a firm hold upon the human heart. You will scarcely

[75] *P*, 169.　　　　[76] *P*, 176.　　　　[77] *P*, 183-84.

retain any deep love for what is only a name; you may conform to the popular rules of justice from habit or for prudential reasons, but, really, one may well be slow in trusting you very far out of sight, or in placing much reliance on your character—indeed, one may ask whether, properly speaking, you have such a thing as a character. . . .

"These Ideas, then, which play so important a rôle in Plato's philosophy and have for these thousands of years haunted the world as impalpable embodiments of truth, are primarily ethical in their nature; and we have this pragmatic proof of their existence, that without them we can discover no sound basis of morality. . . . But in what does their reality subsist? . . .

"Justice, which to the reason was only a negation of our positive impulses, is, like the creation of the artist, projected outside of the soul so as to become a positive entity with a life and habitation of its own, and the soul under control of moral force seems itself to be reaching out to touch and take into possession that to which it has given form and motion from its own experience.

"These imaginative projections of the facts of moral consciousness are the true Platonic Ideas. Hence their peculiarity: though the most intimate realities of experience, things of which our knowledge is so firm and sure that of other things we seem in comparison to have only opinion, yet the moment we apply our discursive reason to them, the moment we undertake to describe them in intellectual terms, they melt away into nothingness, like the dew in the clear dry breath of the morning. . . .[78] Ideas are the product of the imagination, but of the imagination working upon material given to it by the immutable law of morality; the truth is present to our consciousness before this act of transformation, and has no more authority, though it may be clothed with more persuasion, after it has been evoked for the inner eye as a form than it had previously to that evoca-

[78] *P*, 185-89.

tion.[79] . . . the Ideas, though known in time, are eternal, and though seen by the eye of the spirit, are not to be found among the phenomena that fill the boundaries of physical space. They are as gods sitting on their unshakable thrones, seen through the drifting snow-storms of illusions. . . . The true philosopher is he who, having in memory the vision of the celestial images, possessing them yet not possessing them, feels the whole current of his being turned to the one supernatural desire to . . . make them the present palpable realities of his life. Every act, every wish, every thought, should be the perfect imitation, rather the complete embodiment, of an Idea. Imagination is not an empty dream, not a vacant and wandering liberty, but the master of things as they are and the moulder of his will.

"It is this emotional element that distinguishes Platonic philosophy from the other schools, and has made it an undying force in the practical world; and this emotional element must be regarded, I think, as the indispensable servant of truth, if philosophy is to be a life and not an idle disputation."[80]

After the lectures, the wedding of his niece, Anne Heard, at his house on the Saturday before Christmas, and the constant anxiety caused by the condition of Mrs. Beck's heart,[81] by the end of the year More felt rather weary. ". . . the task of composing my *Platonism*, taken up immediately after the double fatigue of trying to be an editor and a scholar at the same time, was almost too much for me. It has cost me exactly eighteen pounds in weight.[82] But the book is finished, thank heaven," he

[79] *P*, 193.
[80] *P*, 198-200. Cf. *SE* VI, 352-54.
[81] During the winters Mrs. Beck lived with the Mores in Princeton.
[82] A medical examination revealed "signs of colitis, a trouble which I have as a matter of fact always had." [To Irving Babbitt, Dec. 9, 1917.] Not infrequently More suffered from "colly-wobbles" or indigestion. Sore throats and colds, which made his eyes water, he would use as a pretext for stumbling blindly about the house, in order to be laughed at. And each book that he finished nearly finished him, so white and exhausted did he appear at its completion. Yet, though never robust, by heeding his limitations he kept in reasonable health throughout most of his mature life.

exclaimed to Frye; "and a copy of it will soon be in your hands. The worst of it is that I am not sure the work in itself was worth while. I cannot escape an uneasy doubt that it is a waste of energy to attempt to express in the logical terms of reason what ought really to be left in the vague penumbra of the feelings—that, perhaps, the sort of truth I have been endeavoring to define ceases to be truth as soon as it is defined."[83]

[83] To Prosser Hall Frye, Nov. 27, 1917.

10

LECTURER AND TORY (1918-1921)

AFTER several months of illness, early in 1918 Mrs. Beck died. Alice came from Bridgeton[1] to stay with Darrah and little Alice in Princeton, so that their parents could leave with their niece, Katherine Heard, on February 13th for the burial in St. Louis, from which Mrs. More returned "completely prostrated"[2] by an inflamed and floating kidney.

When he had thought of moving to Princeton, More had acknowledged to Mather that, though he expected to have no connection with the university, what "would please me most of all would be to have a course in Princeton on Plato and the history of Platonism, or on 17th century English literature and ideas."[3] Until his Vanuxem Lectures drew them into his audience, his contact with the students had been slight. It seemed to President Hibben and Professors Capps and Fite, however, that the university could benefit by his presence. Would he increase its lustre as a "Lecturer on Greek Philosophy"? If some qualified students cared to hear him talk on his current interests, he would gladly share with them the thoughts at his disposal, provided that his inclusion in the department of philosophy did not necessitate his participation in committees, faculty meetings, and the rest of the university routine. On such an understanding he began, with the second term of the academic year 1918-19, his course on "Platonism and Christian Theology."

[1] About the end of 1917 Miss More moved from Princeton to a hotel in Bridgeton, to look after her elderly aunts, the Misses Jane and Caroline More, towards whose support she, her brothers and sister, and some of their cousins, contributed. Her decision to move was reinforced by her conviction that Paul's family life suffered from the time and attention he devoted to her (though her keen, sympathetic criticism helped him in his work). In leaving Princeton on the first impenetrable pretext she subordinated, for her brother's as well as for their aunts' sake, her happiness to a greater extent than even he may have surmised.
[2] To Louis T. More, March 23, 1918.
[3] To Frank Jewett Mather, Jr., Jan. 23, 1914.

Lecturer and Tory

To the students who went to his study, while Don, his collie, lay at their feet, their host seemed less a professional teacher than a genial and respected friend. He sat in a large chair with books piled on its arms and within reach. Before him, on an adjustable stand or lectern, lay his notes and the volume from which he read aloud, first in the Greek and then in his own easy translation. His pride in an ancient set of Chrysostom, which he had bought at some sacrifice, communicated itself to the boys as they stared at its enormous pages. He walked with them companionably at his own pace, enjoying their company when they followed him, resignedly talking on when they heard only his voice.

"The other evening after tiring my combined graduate students and theologues[4] with Platonism, I asked the poet of the group . . . whether he was acquainted with the works of William Maginn (a recent discovery of mine). He said no. Whereupon I gave him and his colleagues an account of that whimsical scholar and genius, and as an illustration of his manner read them part of one of his vicious attacks on the Cockneys, Shelley being the particular victim in this case. I observed that, whatever one might think of Maginn's general attitude towards the so-called Cockney poets, his ridicule of the quoted passages from *Adonais* and *The Cenci* was well founded. . . . [The poet of the group] and the other graduate both replied that Maginn had selected for abuse two passages which they had always specially admired. Now, the curious fact is that at their age I am sure I should have agreed with them. I should have regarded the empty expansiveness and vapid intensity and absence of concrete intelligibility as of the very essence of poetry. Our difference was nothing in the world but that between youth and maturity."[5]

Whatever he discussed he was apt to relate to its forebears,

[4] Two of his students were "nascent divines" from the Presbyterian Princeton Theological Seminary.

[5] To Stuart P. Sherman, May 5, 1918; courtesy of the University of Illinois Library. Cf. *SE* VII, 25-26.

collaterals, and descendants, ranging widely through the history, literature, and philosophy of the ages. The extent of his reading, outside the sciences, was as amazing as the power of his memory. If he could not quote it verbatim, he could find a needed passage at once, "without any cumbrous apparatus of note-taking." Long after they had forgotten the subject of their lesson, his listeners remembered his tracing of modern poems to their classical sources; his comparison of the different styles of Greek in the New Testament; his account of the sensation caused by the publication of Hobbes's *Leviathan*, a huge copy of which he would pull down from his shelves to show them; his reading of Lanier's "Into the woods my Master went" or of "The Fool's Prayer," by Sill;[6] and his amusement when he passed around a card on which Father Tabb had written some humorous verses.[7] Those who not infrequently remained for lunch or dinner remembered also how pleasantly formal education could blend with family life.

". . . poor Sherman is getting the most ruffianly treatment in many quarters for his temerity in dedicating his essays[8] to me. I never thought I was popular, but I had no notion of the active hatred I had aroused until this occasion brought it out. The Chicago papers in particular have been spewing the venom of blackguards. I am sorry for Sherman, but perhaps it won't hurt him.

"Alas for *The Nation!*" More lamented to Mather. "That door is closed for us, and, for me at least, there are not many other doors open. Personally, it matters little, but it is really tragic to think of *The Nation* in the dirty hands of Villard and Mussey. Franklin was out on Tuesday, and is still hopeful of raising the money for the new weekly contemplated by Fuller and him. I am contributing what little cash I can spare."[9]

---

[6] Cf. *RP*, 258.   [7] Cf. *SE* XI, 171-72.
[8] *On Contemporary Literature*, New York (Holt), 1917.
[9] To Frank Jewett Mather, Jr., April 6, 1918. "Fuller is out of *The Nation*. Villard, apparently, expects to make it his personal organ, which will mean a perfect riot of isms and a feast for all the ists. It will be a

Lecturer and Tory

He gave critiques as well as cash to Franklin's and Fuller's venture, which began as *The Review*, continued as *The Weekly Review*, and merged into *The Independent and The Weekly Review*. Samuel Strauss, who ran *The Villager*, of Katonah, New York, so interested More in that little periodical that he not only wrote gratis for it but recommended to Strauss, as among possible contributors, Sherman, Norman Foerster, Mather, Louis More, and Warner Fite. As for magazines in general, however, he inclined to "give them up entirely. I get little profit from reading them or writing for them. And the years remaining to a man begin to shorten."[10] He avowed to Babbitt a longing to practise, with Greek moderation, the Hindu doctrine of detachment,[11] which means, "so far as I dare apply it to myself, that I am concerning myself more wholeheartedly with my work and thinking less about its effect—or perhaps I should say, less about praise and blame. I do feel too that the world for the present has gone beyond any care that I can offer; but nevertheless it is vastly important to keep the tradition alive for those who come after us. That also is a way of keeping up the fight, but perhaps it may not satisfy your more belligerent nature."[12]

Referring to the reviews in which he was taken as a club to beat Sherman with, More retorted: ". . . what a medley of lies and blackguardism! Even the sedate *Springfield Republican* goes out of its way to quote a piece of hateful nonsense from the London *Nation*: 'If a navvy's child is to die for lack of proper food in order to enable Mr. More to read Pindar in comfort,' etc. The insinuation in the words 'in order to' is nasty, and the whole thing is the sort of sentimental lying that gives me a dis-

---

real calamity if *The Nation* loses even what pretensions it had to be an organ of intelligence and sound taste. Fuller has fought a good fight against terrible odds." [To Stuart P. Sherman, Jan. 4, 1918; courtesy of the University of Illinois Library.] More's own nominal connection with *The Nation*, as advisory editor, soon ceased.

[10] To Irving Babbitt, Sept. 12, 1919.
[11] Cf. *SE* VI, 56-57, 60.
[12] To Irving Babbitt, Jan. 17, 1920.

gust in general of the humanitarian movement. Does any sane man eat his dinner or read his Pindar with discomfort because people all the while are starving all over the world? We simply could not live on that basis, and nobody does live on it. I dare say my reviewer took his guinea for his pious work, and cracked a bottle of wine in some tavern with a perfectly clean conscience, despite the starving navvy's children—and what else should one do, unless one sets up to be a Christ or Buddha to whom the sins and sufferings of the world are present as they cannot be, and ought not to be, to the ordinary man? . . . There is no end to this sort of lying and misrepresentation. However, it really annoys me scarcely at all. It is part of the game and shows that we," so More included Sherman, "if I may couple our names together as these gentlemen do, are getting under their skins. I should be very sorry only if this kind of abuse should injure the sale of your book, for I think the men and questions you have considered, and your acute manner of dealing with them, may open the minds of a good many of the young men who are simply drifting with the current. . . .

"As for the connection between naturalism and democracy, perhaps that . . . at least as it lies between us two, is largely a matter of definition. I am not so undemocratical as you may suppose, certainly not as the wolves of Chicago proclaim. But I do maintain that the kind of democracy represented by them is pure naturalism, just as the Nietzschean aristocracy of Mencken is pure naturalism. Why do they and a man like Mencken consort together so readily, when as 'democrats' and 'aristocrat' they ought to be at one another's throats? Evidently, they come together on the common ground of naturalism.[13] So far as I have any quarrel with your position, it is because, so it seems to me, you show some inclination to take the word democracy as self-defined and blessed in itself. These gentlemen of the *Tribune* and the *Examiner*, honorable gentlemen all, ought

[13] Cf. "Theodore Dreiser, Philosopher," signed "P. E. M.," *The Review*, April 17, 1920, vol. 2, no. 49, pp. 380-81.

to open your eyes to the fact that democracy is a thoroughly ambiguous word and, as assumed by one class of men, not blessed at all—or, rather, not open your eyes, for you are as fully aware of these distinctions as I am; but they might emphasize the need of defining your terms more sharply than you have yet done."[14]

At Essex that summer, "through all the beauty of the scene it seems to me that I never before felt so strongly the illusory nature of the world.[15] Sometimes this feeling has come to me in my little reading house, when, looking at the green curtain of the trees before me, I was curiously conscious of the lake and the white light and the hills in the distance, as if only a breath were needed to blow aside the curtain and reveal what lay beyond. Sometimes the feeling came to me while on some elevation which gave me a view of the whole panorama. Then again it seemed to me as if I was looking at a brilliant curtain, which might roll up at any moment and exhibit a great stage on which the powers and gods of the world would be seen playing the drama of fate. . . ."[16]

"My conviction grows more and more firm and clear of a reality of which this life is only the shadow, in relation to which pain and disappointment are almost meaningless, and into which death may be, now or some time, the initiation. Perhaps my reading of Chrysostom has been strengthening this feeling in me. Certainly I find him inexhaustibly interesting, one of the few writers of true religious insight."[17]

After looking over the proofs of Babbitt's *Rousseau and Romanticism*,[18] entertaining its author at "The Cedars" in the

[14] To Stuart P. Sherman, March 8, 1918; courtesy of the University of Illinois Library; quoted in part in *Life and Letters of Stuart P. Sherman*, by Jacob Zeitlin and Homer Woodbridge, New York (Farrar and Rinehart), 1929, vol. 1, pp. 344-45; this book contains a photograph of More opposite p. 510 of vol. II.

[15] Cf. *SE* VIII, 291.

[16] Cf. *RP*, 320.

[17] To Alice More, Aug. 20, 1918.

[18] "It certainly has elements of greatness, and exhausts the subject;

middle of September, and returning to Princeton—"merely a
war camp with nothing of the glamour of war"[19]—to repeat his
course on "Platonism and Christian Theology," More read "the
Last Lectures of Wilfrid Ward. . . . It may perhaps sound presumptuous, but for pages I seemed to be reading about myself,—not so much about what I have accomplished or what I
have made of myself, as about what that group of writers are
so fond of calling the ἦθος. Newman's whole life was a protest
against the modern invasions of materialism and epicurean scepticism, and in that respect he seems often to be speaking
words that I should speak myself if I had his power of lucid
expression. His sense of the illusion of this world also comes
very close to me; and I was particularly struck by Ward's quotation of a passage at the end of the *Idea of a University* which
is almost a duplication of the great passage in Emerson's *Illusions* which has always meant so much to me and which I have
quoted in my chapter on Plato's Ideas.[20] I can sympathize too
with Newman's desire for a clear voice of authority and for
some escape from the limitations of our individual experience.
'Truth,' he said, 'is wrought out by many minds working freely
together.' That is my notion of the long tradition of philosophy,
in so far as philosophy remains true to human nature and does
not go awhoring after the strange gods of Plotinus[21] and Kant.[22]
But when Newman jumps to the conclusion of a Church which
has in its charge the revelation of clear absolute truth, then I
draw back. We have no such precision of knowledge, no such
guide, no such visible monitor. There is where the philosopher
needs a courageous heart—to preserve his reverence for the
hidden truth which is involved in clouds of ever-shifting error.
With all that my notion of the traditional experience of human-

---

whether it will exhaust the reader also I cannot tell." [To Louis T. More,
March 28, 1919.]

[19] To Irving Babbitt, Oct. 2, 1918.
[20] Cf. *P*, 197.   [21] Cf. *P*, 289-91, and *RP*, 307, 337.
[22] Cf. *CNT*, 118 ff.

ity is not so very far from Newman's idea of the Church. He has come to mean more to me, on the whole, than any other writer of the past century."[23]

"Last night I finished off my class work for the week, and this morning, when I awoke at about six, I found myself in a glow of excitement at the thought of getting into my Museum (to use the words of the Renaissance scholars for their work room) with nothing to interrupt long hours of Greek. It really is strange, isn't it? Darrah is scarcely more excited over her parties, of which by the way she is having a plenty."[24]

As Christmas cheer for his sister, who basked in any beam that lighted on her "baby," he reported some "honors that have been coming to me. At a dinner at Dean West's[25] the other day, at which Shipley, the vice-chancellor of Cambridge, was present, I was mentioned as the most distinguished essayist of this country, and Shipley replied that I was so recognized in England. (Query: why don't they buy *Shelburne Essays*?) And, then, I have just received the circular of a new book for Freshman reading, containing selections from English and American authors on *The Great Tradition* of 'ordered liberty' among English-speaking peoples. The last section includes essays by Viscount Morley, Wilson, Lloyd George, Earl Grey, John Dewey, and myself.[26] Some of these gentlemen may not be reckoned great writers, and Dewey[27] is detestable, but they are all very

[23] To Alice More, Nov. 8, 1918.
[24] To the same, Dec. 5, 1918. Cf. *SE* XI, 15, 25.
[25] Andrew Fleming West, professor of Latin and from 1901 to 1928 dean of the Graduate School of Princeton University.
[26] Part of More's essay, "Natural Aristocracy" (*SE* IX), was reprinted on pp. 620-23 of *The Great Tradition*, edited by Edwin Greenlaw and James Holly Hanford, Chicago and New York (Scott, Foresman), 1919.
[27] "I do not question what you say of the admirable personal traits of a man like Dewey, but I hold him nevertheless in reprobation. It is not that I am intolerant of differences of opinion within certain bounds. I should lead a sadly solitary life—any one would who should demand like views with his own on all points. But there is a degree of difference, or rather there are matters on which a radical disagreement must mean a sharp break between men, or else a lukewarmness of soul such as I do not care to foster. To me a philosopher who preaches in season and out

great names to the present world. I do not repeat these things to anyone but you, having learned that mankind is as jealous as Jehovah, but I know it gives you pleasure to hear them. I must add, rather sadly, that they bring a very languid pleasure to me."[28]

In the opening address of the Latin Conference of Mount Holyoke, Smith, Vassar, and Wellesley colleges, held March 21, 1919, in Northampton, Massachusetts, and again before the chapter of Phi Beta Kappa at Allegheny College, Meadville, Pennsylvania, on June 3rd, More upheld humanism and the humanities. At Vassar (where the next November he visited his freshman daughter, Darrah) on April 25th he expounded the importance of Greek for ideas and of Latin for language. But the more he reflected on the matter the more he became convinced that " 'discipline' and 'taste' and 'stability of judgment'—all of them intrinsically sound arguments for the older curriculum—are still only in the periphery. I do not believe there is the slightest chance for a return to the Classics until we have got some of the conceit, the 'illusion of the present,' knocked out of us, and have come to realize that at heart we are, and always have been, barbarians, save for the modicum of

---

the sort of doctrine of education proclaimed by Dewey, who boldly proclaims that he wishes to see the world 'with the lid off' (to use his elegant quotation from the language of the Tenderloin), is striking at the roots of everything that makes life worth while or even tolerable to me. Great God, what is this maniacal war but a world with the lid off? What is it that is making a farce of education and is threatening all the decencies of life, but this contempt for restraint and discipline and the austerities of order which is the professed animus of Dewey's philosophy, as it was the professed animus of James's? I don't care anything about Dewey's private life; I am ready to grant that he may have written well on epistemology (though I suspect that to say a man has written well, unless by well you mean sceptically, on that subject is a contradiction in terms). I have never supposed that Dewey was a fool—I wish he were a fool—but I do feel intensely that he belongs to the most mischievous group of men now leading the public, and I hold it the first duty of a philosopher to fight this utter negation of the philosophic life. . . . Forgive . . . my outburst of metaphysical ill temper. . . ." [To Norman Kemp Smith, Aug. 13, 1916. Cf. *SE* VII, 253.]

[28] To Alice More, Dec. 19, 1918.

Greek influence we have carried with us. It is simply the fact that Greece had something which we have not, and without which we shall fly apart into the distractions of anarchy or into brutal imperialism. Essentially that *unum necessarium* is religion. . . ."[29]

After he had received on June 16th from Princeton (on nomination by Moses Taylor Pyne) an honorary degree of Doctor of Letters, and while visitors interfered with writing at Essex, More devoted himself to Plutarch's *Moralia* and to "playing tennis and otherwise taking violent and foolish exercise. I am resolved to go home this autumn totally exhausted physically, so that no one will ever dare say exercise to me again."[30]

The publication in November of *With the Wits*, the tenth of the Shelburne series, with essays on Beaumont and Fletcher, Halifax, Aphra Behn, Swift, Pope, Lady Mary Wortley Montagu, Berkeley, the Duke of Wharton, Thomas Gray, and Decadent Wit, drew from his own familiar friend, Sherman, an "infernally clever" and "curious criticism and character-sketch" of More, "the bishop of our criticism,"[31] who found the praise "too thick," the Toryism "too black," and "the etherialism . . . a dream of the writer."[32] After an ironically amusing page designed to present More as a reverent, reasonable, conservative, austere, pure, decorous, serene, aloof, mystical, moral, philosophical, retired, meditative man—everything apt to make the gallery giggle—Sherman then, in a disinterested moment, describes a Shelburne essay. "It is criticism, it is history, it is philosophy, it is morality, it is religion, it is, above all, a singularly moving poetry, gushing up from deep, intellectual, and moral substrata, pure, cold, and refreshing, as water of a spring from the rocks in some high mountain hollow. . . . By its compression of serious thought and deep feeling it produces the

[29] To Percy H. Houston, Sept. 12, 1920.
[30] To Irving Babbitt, Aug. 20, 1919.
[31] "Mr. P. E. More and The Wits," by Stuart P. Sherman, *The Review*, Jan. 17, 1920, vol. 2, no. 36, p. 54.
[32] To Norman Kemp Smith, Feb. 6, 1920.

effect of one speaking between life and death, as the Apology of Socrates does."[33] But he quickly returns to his audience and his attack: More is not easily understood or widely popular; therefore More is at fault. Were he really "a great man of culture," he would not remain on his own level but would express "the *best* knowledge and thought of the time" in a tongue "suppled and vulgarized" to "chat with the work-master and carpenter and the driver of oxen." How different, Sherman intimates casually, from the ease with which I talked to two carpenters whom I employed and "a Northern peasant farmer of my acquaintance"! How regrettable that More sitting "in external and internal placidity under a pallid bust of Pallas in a comodious library" in "that quaint little imitation-English city, striving so bravely, amid the New Jersey oil refineries, to be a home of lost causes"[34]—how regrettable that More has not "enjoyed opportunities such as these"! "Somehow," candor adds, "he seems always to have evaded them."[35] If " 'P. E. M.' had a bit more of that natural sympathy,[36] of which he is so distrustful,

[33] *Op. cit.*, p. 55. [34] *Ibid.*, pp. 54-55. [35] *Ibid.*, p. 56.

[36] Notwithstanding his reserve, sympathy with those around him was so natural to More that in mere prudence he had to distrust and check it somewhat. Morality dissolved into good affections "in contradiction to moral obligation and a sense of duty," he believed, in the words of Sir John Hawkins (whose *Life of Johnson* "deserves far more credit than it has ever received for its critical discernment"), "is that of Lord Shaftesbury vulgarized, and is a system of excellent use in palliating the vices most injurious to society. . . . that cant-phrase, goodness of heart, which is every day used as a substitute for probity . . . means little more than the virtue of a horse or a dog." ["A Scholar's Life of Fielding," anonymous review by P. E. More of *A History of Henry Fielding*, by Wilbur L. Cross, *The Villager*, Dec. 13, 1919, vol. 3, no. 28, p. 127. Cf. *DA*, 92.]

More was not one to advertise that he had no difficulty in talking to all sorts and conditions of men and that he usually got on well with those who had to work for or with him. Wherever he found excellence, he appreciated it as spontaneously as he despised an empty appearance of it. "I reserve most of the damning articles for myself," he remarked after in one of his earlier reviews for *The Independent* he had demolished an eminent clergyman's discourse on immortality; "it is the only writing I thoroughly enjoy! Such a huge lot of shams come to me that it is fun to prick one now and then." [To Alice More, May 9, 1901.] In *JL* [pp. 115-17] the father of Jack O'Meara is a reflection of "a poor

he would have perceived that what more than anything else to-day keeps the average man from lapsing into Yahooism is the *religion of democracy*. . . . I am speaking of the average man and traits of his which I can never contemplate, being one myself, without a lift of the heart"—and so on.[37]

"My first knowledge of the article," More informed its writer, after begging Sherman to send a short notice of a volume to *The Unpartizan Review*, the book section of which Henry Holt had suddenly asked More to edit, "came to me at the Century where I happened to be taking lunch Saturday a week ago. The men there were buzzing over it. Naturally I went down to the lounge room as soon as I could leave the table, and got the magazine. I had a strange sensation. It was as if I saw my own soul set free of the body and immortalized, but with the bloodless dehumanized immortality of the ghosts in Homer's Nekyia. Certainly the flattery was abundant enough to satisfy the vainest of authors; but you are a sly dog too, and did not forget the use of malice as prescribed by the book in hand.[38] It is a bril-

---

broken-down Irishman . . . a victim to the demon whiskey that has dragged him down to the very gutter," who used to shuffle through the office of *The Independent* to More's desk; for the young editor recognized in the "besotted tramp" "a high ideal of literature and conscience in writing" and ability, in his sober moments, to express them, and also a compassion for humanity surpassing that of the Pharisees and strangely uncorrupted by too intimate acquaintance with human weakness. He gave the old man books to review and, it is believed, "loans" when needed. At home, too, where his conduct was less likely to be known to the public, More was kinder than prudent men often are. As a matter of course he paid his servants' hospital bills, even when there was little or no likelihood of their returning to his service, even when he might have left them to the mercies of a charitable institution, even in his early married life when he could afford it little better than they. He devoted several long-suffering years, in vain, to straighten out one of them, a periodic drunkard. He could, therefore, testify in print to the "instinctive, unreasoned relation between man and man, which recognizes the dependence of the lower on the higher and of the higher on the lower, together with that communism of the imagination which softens the asperities of fortune as no chilly abstraction of rights has ever yet succeeded in doing." ["Der Alte Jude," anonymous article by P. E. More, *The Villager*, Dec. 11, 1920, p. 117.]

[37] *Op. cit.*, p. 56.   [38] Cf. *SE* X, ix-x.

liant portrait; how true it is, I can not very well say. . . . As a matter of fact I am not quite so stubborn a Tory in theory as you suspect, and I rather fancy that in practice I can meet your carpenters and teamsters with as little condescension and with as much sympathetic understanding as you can. As a matter of fact the intellectual Tory is ordinarily better fitted for such intercourse than is the academic Liberal. Nor have I quite so gloomy a view of human nature in general as you like to believe. I like the consistency of Swift, I can't say I approve of his misanthropy. On the other hand I am affected by a sort of moral nausea when the sentimentalist begins to pour rose water into the sewer. What I least like in democracy is its undoubted tendency to shirk the truth. All the heroisms are in man, *est deus in nobis*; there is something admirable, noble if you wish, in the steady life of many an ordinary worker. . . . See the good, yes; but in God's name don't deny the evil, don't get slushy. Human nature is of a strange mixture, and the one thing it cannot stand is too much flattery.[39] Whatever other sins we may uproot, we shall never get rid of vanity, οἴησις κενοδοξία; and the sure way to turn democracy from a blessing to a curse is to puff it up with conceit and call it heroic and curse those who criticise it. I do not like to see a man of your ability and insight, deliberately taking up the job of whitewasher; and you'll never carry it off without bartering your soul for popularity, as you may judge from the way the young wits of Chicago love you. There's a Roland for your Oliver! But I'm really not in a disputatious mood. I ought to be letting you know how flattered I was by the resounding epithets of your eulogy. You have made me 'as popular as a man can be, three quarters of whom is in the third century and the rest in'—'heaven' was the word applied to Bishop Wordsworth, but I fear you would change it to 'up the chimney.'—Now be good, and send me that review."[40]

[39] Cf. the excerpt from More's letter of Feb. 8, 1920, to Stuart P. Sherman, *Life and Letters of Stuart P. Sherman*, by Jacob Zeitlin and Homer Woodbridge, New York (Farrar & Rinehart), 1929, vol. I, p. 376. See also *RP*, 256; *HP*, 150-53, 160, 201, 231; and *CW*, 293 ff.

[40] To Stuart P. Sherman, Jan. 25, 1920; courtesy of the University of Illi-

Lecturer and Tory

In the second term of Princeton's academic year 1919-20 More gave his course, for seniors and graduate students, on "Hellenistic and Patristic Philosophy." "If I were a younger man, with a less heavy task of writing upon me, I should love to get a group of students about me to work in the Greek fathers, and issue a series of volumes of readable compass which should make those old Christian sinners live again as the real men they were, not, of course, neglecting the theological ideas for which they fought and sometimes became saints and very often showed themselves *menschlich allzumenschlich*. Do you know Synesius?[41] Are you acquainted with the letters of Basil, and the strange sensitive unstable character of Gregory of Nazianzus as it comes out in his correspondence and poetry? For human interest, let alone its religious and philosophical importance, I know nothing like this literature until one comes to the memoirs of the French seventeenth and eighteenth centuries."[42]

Besides teaching, reviewing regularly for *The Villager*, editing the book section of *The Unpartizan Review* (until in 1921 Holt dropped the magazine), and writing occasional essays, More generously bore his burden of correspondence. People with little or no claim on him constantly begged him for criticism of their prose and poetry or sought his help in family and personal difficulties. Though some of the less intimate matters

---

nois Library; quoted in part in *Life and Letters of Stuart P. Sherman*, by Jacob Zeitlin and Homer Woodbridge, New York (Farrar & Rinehart), 1929, vol. I, pp. 375-76, which mistakenly copies the word "steady" as "sturdy."

[41] "He was a philosopher, who loved nothing so much as learned leisure, and who passed his life between books and sport (mainly hunting). When called to the bishopric he was reluctant, and in fact consented only after receiving assurance that he might retain some of his philosophical heresies without molestation. The office threw him into a tangle of administrative business, over which he is continually lamenting in the most amusing manner. One of his complaints is that as a philosopher he felt that his prayers were answered, but now as a bishop he gets no answer at all. And he adds, ruefully: When I was a philosopher my life with God was my own, my play was public; now my life with God is public and my play must be private." [To Louis T. More, Nov. 20, 1919.]

[42] To Norman Kemp Smith, Feb. 6, 1920.

thus brought to his attention he would occasionally discuss in a general way, matters of confidence he did not divulge. He might protest in words "that scandal is the breath of my soul,"[43] but in fact sordid behavior so repelled him that when, as happened only a few times, he had to deal with it at all, he did so effectively. For the more innocent aspects of gossip, however, he displayed a rich, warm, human curiosity.[44] "What delicious morsel have you brought back today?" he would ask his wife on her return from a feminine gathering. And he was not above repeating such morsels to those who knew, as Jowett had observed, that "every amusing story must of necessity be unkind, untrue, or immoral."[45]

On his twentieth wedding anniversary his sister congratulated him, calling him "blessed indeed" to be able to describe his house as "a nest of singing birds."[46] In August, leaving Mrs. More and Darrah at Essex and taking his daughter Alice to visit the Gausses[47] in Greensboro, Vermont, More went on to Chesham, New Hampshire, to stay with the Babbitts for a week. Remembering More's former comments, like, "I never saw such colossal ignorance as in that fellow you had in to tea," or, "So-and-so doesn't know anything," his hosts selected with trepidation those whom they asked to meet him and invited only a few at a time lest he be bored by the trivia of general conversation.

"It will be a proud moment when I see my name in your book," he declared to Frye, "with 'to' or any other preposition before it, and it will be a true pleasure to see the book itself. As I have said before, our only hope of accomplishing anything at all is to give the impression that there is a considerable group of us hanging together. That in fact is already the case. Menck-

[43] To Louis T. More, June 16, 1916.
[44] Cf. Stuart P. Sherman to P. E. More, postmarked Jan. 17, 1922.
[45] "A Daughter of the Walpoles," review signed "P. E. M." of *The Life and Letters of Lady Dorothy Nevill*, by Ralph Nevill, *The Unpartizan Review*, March-April, 1920, vol. XIII, no. 26, p. 428.
[46] Alice More to P. E. More, June 12, 1920.
[47] Christian Gauss was a professor of modern languages and, after 1925, Dean of the College at Princeton University.

en's last volume of essays[48] opened with a thundering diatribe against Brownell and Babbitt and Sherman and myself as a nest of conspirators. I will give myself the credit of saying that I am the chief devil in his hell. . . .[49] And I have enemies all up and down the country who never miss a chance to get a fling at me. These are the things after all that make life livable. Gass[50] can easily make a place for himself in the circle of the damned, and another book from you, especially if you care to open with a belligerent preface, will raise you to be one of the captains in the ranks. . . .

"I have been driving pretty hard to finish the revision of a new volume on Plato[51] before my lectures[52] here begin (February 24th). The task is done, though there is a good deal of filing still needed. I shall probably bring it out next autumn, and meanwhile the eleventh volume of *Shelburne Essays* is about to appear. You will admit that I am at least damnably active. The feeling you describe—what is the use of it all?—does come to me whenever I am about to publish; but I think of those that hate me and am cheered. We ought to take for our motto Butler's magnificent audacity: 'In that I write at all I am one of the damned!' "[53]

"Robert Frost was in Princeton yesterday reading and talking to the Freneau Club, and I had him here over night.

[48] *Prejudices*, Second Series, by H. L. Mencken, New York (Knopf), 1920.

[49] So, too, in the next volume of *Prejudices*: "More . . . is, perhaps, the nearest approach to a genuine scholar that we have in America, God save us all!" [*Prejudices*, Third Series, New York (Knopf), 1922, p. 178.]

[50] In 1919 Sherlock Bronson Gass, a friend of Frye's, had published *A Lover of the Chair*.

[51] *The Religion of Plato*.

[52] In Princeton's academic years 1920-21 through 1923-24 More, as Lecturer on Greek Philosophy, continued his course on "Hellenistic and Patristic Philosophy." "Did Net tell you, or have I told you, that the university is giving me an honorarium of $1000 for my course? This will seem a pitiful sum to a Harvard professor since the new wealth has poured in, but it is a very comfortable addition to my income and a welcome sign that the work is approved." [To Irving Babbitt, June 18, 1920.]

[53] To Prosser Hall Frye, Feb. 13, 1921. Cf. *SE* XI, 183.

1918-1921

"I have always rather admired his poetry, which is modern in some respects, but has balance and measure and deals with the real things of life. It was a pleasure to talk with him—we sat up until about one—and hear how sound his views of art and human nature are. He knows all the wild men now snorting up the sides of Parnassus, has heard the infinite scandals of their life, and can prick them out in epigrams to the king's taste. It was rather exhilarating to listen to him, and I think too he went away somewhat encouraged from his contact with a kindred soul. . . . I was interested in seeing how Frost managed some of our ultra esthetes who gathered about him after his lecture and asked him the old foolish questions: Does not thinking dull poetic genius, and must not a poet welcome all (particularly the base) experiences of life?[54] He handled the boys with a good deal of tact, but made them feel rather silly."[55]

"The learned author," H. L. Mencken announced of More's latest volume of essays, *A New England Group and Others*, "undismayed by the winds of anarchic doctrine that blow down his Princeton stovepipe, continues to hold fast to the notions of his earliest devotion. He is still the gallant champion sent against the Romantic Movement by the forces of discipline and decorum. He is still the eloquent fugleman of the Puritan ethic and aesthetic. In so massive a certainty, so resolute an immovability there is something almost magnificent. These are somewhat sad days for the exponents of that ancient correctness. The Goths and the Huns are at the gate, and as they batter wildly they throw dead cats, perfumed lingerie, tracts against predestination, and the bound files of the *Nation*, the *Freeman* and the *New Republic* over the fence. But the din does not flabbergast Dr. More. High above the blood-bathed battlements there is a tower, of ivory within and solid ferro-concrete without, and in its austere upper chamber he sits undaunted, solemnly composing an elegy upon Jonathan Edwards, 'the greatest theologian and philosopher yet produced in this country.'

[54] Cf. *RP*, 239-40. [55] To Alice More, March 10, 1921.

Lecturer and Tory

"Magnificent, indeed—and somehow charming."[56]

Sherman, though defending a humanitarian or social service sort of religion against More's otherworldliness, recognized that "Mr. More is important to those who care for 'the whole truth,' precisely because he meets current popular tendencies with an inveterately 'antagonistic mode of thought.' It is popular nowadays to scoff at the Puritans and their sense of sin; in his essays on early New England poetry and Jonathan Edwards, Mr. More treats the stammering Puritan muse almost tenderly, and he inclines to think that a revived sense of sin is the need of the hour. It is the mode to speak with relief at our emancipation from 'the fear of God'; through nearly all of the essays, especially through those on Emerson, Norton, Henry Adams, Economic Ideals, and Oxford, runs the sense that we must, somehow or other, 'get the fear of God back into society.'[57] The current social watchword is 'universal sympathy'; Mr. More preaches individual self-respect and a stern discrimination of values. The keynote of contemporary education is 'power and service,' a phrase which Mr. More, championing an older ideal of self-realization, characterizes as 'maleficent.' It is the fashion to

---

[56] *Prejudices*, Third Series, New York (Knopf), 1922, p. 176.

[57] "I do not mean to be a foe of charity and human kindliness and justice and institutions that mitigate the hardship of man's fate. My only quarrel with humanitarianism is when it sets itself up definitely, as it often does, as a substitute for or an enemy of religion—using the word religion in a broad sense. . . . However crudely men may have thought of the Ideal world, τὰ μὴ βλεπόμενα, however at times they have identified their God with cruel or hard thoughts, in the long run religion has not only given to men the only peace that can satisfy the heart, but out of that peace, and out of that alone, has come any true and wholesome sense of the brotherhood of mankind. . . . To set up an antithesis between religion, or Idealism, and humanitarianism, as the prevalent school of John Dewey does, must end at the last—at least such is my earnest conviction—in letting loose the baser instincts of men and in lowering life at every point. The results may be deceptive for a time, but not for long; nor do I think they ought to deceive anyone today. To think that humanitarianism, natural sympathy, or whatever you choose to call it, will avail alone without the fear of God, seems to me unwarranted by history and highly chimerical. At the best it will take from life its purest joy. For I cannot see much joy in this world if left to itself." [To Stuart P. Sherman, Jan. 20, 1922; courtesy of the University of Illinois Library.]

magnify 'the people' at the expense of their leaders; Mr. More intimates that the first step towards wise and effective leadership is a renascence of the old-fashioned contempt for 'the vulgar herd.' . . . Most of the agreeable people today profess themselves sex-equalitarians; Mr. More mildly protests against being taken for a misogynist, while at the same time he reminds us that the Puritan Church started toward the innocuous desuetude of Unitarianism when Anne Hutchinson undertook to explain the sermons, that Henry Adams lost his head when he began to worship the whimsical Virgin, and that English gentlemen lost Oxford and God when Mrs. Humphrey Ward and the rustle of petticoats were heard in the cloisters."[58]

Depending on how they weighed the book's faults and merits, other reviews of it ranged from the commendation of *The Times Literary Supplement* ("Mr. Paul Elmer More, who wields with urbanity one of the most graceful pens in all America"—"reflections of a mind whose culture is sound, whose humour is gentle but charming, whose philosophy is sturdy, and whose criticism is quietly forcible"[59]) to the abuse of *The New Republic* ("For the present generation . . . he has nothing but uncritical rudeness and sneers"—"What he feels is usually meagre and grudging. What he thinks is almost always one-sided and illiberal. His temper is censorious"—"Mr. More's pressed flowers of speech"—"He knows nothing of . . . poverty"[60]—"Being

[58] "The Religion of the Day," review by Stuart P. Sherman of *SE* XI, *The Independent and The Weekly Review*, Nov. 12, 1921, vol. 107, p. 167.
[59] "A Critic of Character," anonymous review of *SE* XI, *The Times Literary Supplement*, Sept. 15, 1921, p. 592; reprinted Sept. 17, 1954, p. lxxxi.
[60] ". . . we need . . . a clearer perception of, and a firmer insistence on, those immaterial values which it is within the power of every man to make his own, whatever may be the seeming injustice of his material condition. We need . . . to emphasize the simple truth that poverty is not the only, or indeed the worst, of mortal evils, that happiness does not consist mainly in the things which money can buy, that the man of narrow means may enrich himself with treasures which only he can give to himself, and which no one can take from him, that the purest satisfaction is in the sense of work honestly done and duties well met, and a mind and conscience at ease with itself. . . .

rather unusual in the slowness and dryness of his imagination, having a deficient emotional equipment"—"What he needed much more than the classics was a variety of human experience"—"His ignorance being preserved, however, and fortified by egoism"—"Mr. More for what he is, an exasperated provincial"—"it was men like Paul Elmer More who gave Socrates the hemlock"[61]).

While reviewers stirred their caldrons, More (who had gone to Cincinnati to speak there on April 18th to a chapter of Phi Beta Kappa on "Scholarship") sweltered through a Princeton July "with lowering skies and dripping trees and a general air of depression. . . . Fortunately, or unfortunately, I have been kept pretty busy writing the lecture I am to give at Columbia this Thursday. It is more or less old material, the subject being criticism, but three or four good weeks have gone to getting it in shape. I really have a feeling of shame for the labor I must expend on trifles."[62]

Despite an impression that his young friend had "a kind of raging jealousy in his vitals of anything 'undemocratic,' almost of anything consciously distinguished," and without concealing a conviction that Sherman's "brilliance seems quite to have outrun his judgment,"[63] More signed at the end of July and returned to W. C. Brownell a blank the latter had sent him nominating Sherman to the American Academy of Arts and Letters.[64] At

---

"If there is any truth that needs to be reiterated today, it is the simple truth that a man may heap up riches and increase his power indefinitely, and command all the visible sources of pleasure, and still be a poor, mean creature, a mere beggar in the veritable joys and honours of life." [OBH, 141-42.]

[61] "Mr. More Moralizes," review by Francis Hackett of SE XI, The New Republic, April 6, 1921, vol. 26, pp. 163-64. Cf. DA, 3-4.

[62] To Louis T. More, July 11, 1921.

[63] To Prosser Hall Frye, Feb. 13, 1921. "Sherman's recent work, by the way, Americans, is no less than a compact signed with the Devil." "It seemed to me markedly inferior in literary quality from his earlier work." [To Irving Babbitt, Jan. 2, 1922, and Feb. 9, 1923, respectively.]

[64] More had facilitated Sherman's entrance into the National Institute of Arts and Letters. His letter of March 21, 1923, to Ernest Bernbaum

the same time More tried, but too late to complete the formalities that year, to get support for the nomination of Irving Babbitt to the Academy.

Throughout August and September he corrected in Essex proofs of *The Religion of Plato*, a set of which he had mailed to Babbitt for criticism. "Parts of the book will scarcely meet with your entire approval," he cautioned his friend, whom he visited the last week of August at The Ark in Jaffrey, New Hampshire; "something in their tone I fear will displease you; but as a whole I hope you will think the work is better constructed than the *Platonism*."[65]

He discussed Plato's religion under the aspects of philosophy, theology, mythology, and "as a composite whole."[66] To the Platonist "philosophy was the dominating element; here was the starting point of religion and the sphere of whatever certainty is attainable by man; here he thought he was dealing with facts and was standing on a foundation of proved knowledge. In theology he believed he was still close to ascertainable truth, yet removed a step from the region of immediate experience. Mythology carried him further afield from positive assurance, though it might be indispensable as the expression, more or less symbolical, of necessary truths."[67] The knowledge of justice or of righteousness, "the clear simple truth, that which we learned from immediate experience and intuition, has been given to us by philosophy; this we can possess without theology and without mythology, but, having this, we have laid the foundation for the superstructure of religion."[68]

---

on the occasion of a dinner celebrating Sherman's election on Feb. 22, 1923, to the Academy is quoted in *Life and Letters of Stuart P. Sherman*, by Jacob Zeitlin and Homer Woodbridge, New York (Farrar & Rinehart), 1929, vol. II, pp. 559-60.

[65] To Irving Babbitt, June 23, 1921.

[66] *RP*, 4.   [67] *RP*, 17.

[68] *RP*, 109. "We must begin with philosophy, as the more immediate certainty of our inner experience, and regard the drama of the Incarnation as a less certain, or less obvious expression of that experience in mythical form, instead of following the common procedure, which places

Lecturer and Tory

In his theology Plato shows a "reticence before the divine mystery," a "confessed ignorance of God's nature as revealed to the Jew by prophecy and to the Christian by the incarnation," which "leaves the Platonic Deity a pale conception by the side of Jehovah or of the divinely compassionate Father, a conception lacking comparatively in driving force and wanting in some of the deeper human consolations, although, in compensation, it is free also of the sharper incentives to fanaticism which have maddened so many religious communities. We may grant so much; but still for all that is necessary to the religious life of a man, for the large things of the spirit, the theology of Plato is sufficient. Thus much we know—and it is the gist of the whole matter—that the souls of men are not set adrift in a soulless world, either to fortify themselves in the harsh pride of indifference or to sink down in abject terror at the thought of their loneliness."[69]

Mythology "combines with theology and philosophy to round out the religious life. . . . A myth is false and reprehensible in so far as it misses or distorts the primary truth of philosophy and the secondary truth of theology; it becomes more probable and more and more indispensable to the full religious life as it lends insistence and reality to those truths and answers to the daily needs of the soul. Perhaps the first requirement of sound religion is just the due recognition of these two elements in mythology, neither on the one hand giving to myth the character of philosophic truth, nor on the other hand carrying over to philosophy the conjectural character of myth. By the former error faith assumes the hard rigidity of fanaticism, until doubt creeps in, and then, when the myth has lost its grip upon us, the whole fabric of religion crumbles away together. In the second

---

mythology first, as a fact demonstrably true in itself, and builds up a philosophy from this fact as best it can." ["The Revival of Mysticism," review signed "P. E. M." of *The Philosophy of Plotinus*, by W. R. Inge, *The Villager*, May 24, 1919, vol. 3, no. 5, p. 20.]

[69] *RP*, 125-26.

case, by seeing in philosophy nothing different in kind from the probabilities of mythology, we leave faith without any solid foundation; religion may be a useful illusion, to preserve if we can, but it will speak to us without authority or power."[70]

". . . though religion may be thus analysed into its elements, still no one of these elements alone is religion in any full or satisfactory sense—not philosophy, which, pursued separately, leaves the soul friendless in a world of austere impersonal law; not theology, which of itself is in danger of forgetting the eternal primacy of the moral law; not mythology alone, which too easily falls into a vain, even a degrading, superstition. Nor yet is religion a mechanical juxtaposition of the three, but an emotion, an aspiration, a faith, a knowledge, a life, a something born of their intimate union and coöperation."[71]

Religion being both public and private, "it must ever remain the delicate task of the worshipper to be diffident of his personal beliefs and at the same time to judge for himself between the settled deeper conviction and the floating opinions of mankind. Perhaps there is an unresolved paradox in this appeal at once to the individual conscience and to common consent; if so it is a difficulty not peculiar to Plato but one that has persisted to the present day. I should say that the fairest example of it in modern times, *mutatis mutandis*, is the endeavour of the Anglican profession to hold a middle course between the Romanists, who accept absolutely the authority of the Church, and the Bible Protestants, who, practically, reject such authority for a document which each man must interpret for himself. And I should venture to assert that, not indeed in all dogmas, but in what may be called the *êthos* of religion, no book of theology comes closer to the spirit of Platonism than Hooker's *Ecclesiastical Polity*. It may be irksome to the imperious demands of the reason to rest in this undetermined ground of compromise and adjustment; but so it is, in this as in all things else, religion is a

[70] *RP*, 165-66.
[71] *RP*, 278.

part of the sense of the divine as a law of measure and mediation."[72]

As soon as his proofs were out of the way, he could send to his sister an edition of the *Life of Samuel Johnson*, which she had asked him to buy for her. "I am sure you will thank me for starting you again in Boswell. You may remember that Jowett boasted he had read the book through fifty times. I myself must have read it ten or twelve times, and it never palls. I don't know what there is about the fellow Johnson that enthralls me. He was cantankerous, often headstrong and perverse in judgments (though much oftener right), not over nice in his habits, but you can't help feeling in him something very great and high.[73] Perhaps he attracts me by his combination of humble fear before God and pride before men. At any rate, he is one of the few who speak in a language I completely understand—as do Newman and Henry More and Henry Vaughan and Trollope—a sufficiently mixed company, you will admit."[74]

In Lake Forest, Illinois, where in November he spoke on "Religion and Social Discontent" at Lake Forest College, More by good luck was "quartered with a Mr. and Mrs. Martin, who are charming hosts. Martin, a lawyer by profession and a bookworm by love, has the finest private library I have ever seen (barring, of course, such display collections as Hoe's). . . . My address . . . was pretty thin and shabby *au fond*, but it was tricked out with some rhetorical devices *ad captandum*, and caught the audience.

---

[72] *RP*, 294-95.

[73] "To me the central fact of the man Johnson is so big, so overpowering, that his minor faults, which are many, sink into—shall I say, esthetical?—insignificance. That personality of his, that mysterious inexplicable something, is itself one of the greatest facts in literature. . . . You see how this fact of character, or personality, outweighs with me all other matters. Hence perhaps my undue leaning on the side of ethical criticism. Critically to me the great question is how the imagination deals with this fact. In classical literature it seems to me to have dealt with it supremely well; in romantic literature generally not at all well. Hence the common saying that classical literature is strong in judgment whereas romantic literature is strong in imagination always seems to me a crude error." [To Percy H. Houston, Dec. 3, 1923.]

[74] To Alice More, Nov. 12, 1921.

Having arrived at the mature age of sixty—nearly—I just begin to see how entirely easy it would be to make a reputation as an orator; I can tell exactly what will hit. But unfortunately it needs a Burke or a Cicero to hit an audience (and Burke himself was not too successful in that) and at the same time to say anything that will bear reading in cold blood.

"In the evening there was a banquet, at which six presidents of Illinois colleges spoke on end. The effect was terrible, overwhelming, crushing, nauseating. One after another they got up, and in bad English glorified the small *Christian* college as the great American institution; I did not know there was so much Christianity in the land, and was ready to pray for less. One after another they declared that truth and life lay with the new generation and that the faculty had more to learn from the students than vice versa; I wanted to ask them o' God's name what they and their faculties were for. I rather doubt they were right. There was to be a procession and inauguration ceremonies the next morning; but I did not, could not, go. For the hope of my soul's salvation I stayed away, and read Mr. Martin's books."[75]

"The Academy you know has received money from an anonymous donor whose name everybody knows for a building by the Hispanic Museum on 155th Street. Well, we were to have great doings. Marshal Foch, as a French *académicien*, was to lay the corner stone, and some of his glory was to be shed upon our somewhat factitious immortality. By consulting with Sloane I learned that a silk hat was your only token of immortality. This did not trouble me much because I had just received Ned's handsome new Dunlap,[76] and as I have worn his hat several times in St. Louis I thought I was well fitted out. What was my dismay, on trying the thing on, to find it two sizes too small. Either his head has shrunk in the last five or six years, or my head has swelled, manifestly. I took the hat round to our Dago on Witherspoon Street and asked him to stretch it.

[75] *Ibid.*
[76] More's brother-in-law died earlier in 1921.

Lecturer and Tory

Naw, he said; it crack. I insisted. Finally he said: You put it on block; it crack, then you responsible! I did put it on the block, and turned the screw until the brim bent ominously, and so left it for the afternoon. When I called for it, I found I could just put it on my head and keep it so in calm weather. My Italian friend looked at me, and exclaimed: Why you buy so small hat? Well, that was the beginning. I lugged the thing into New York, having paid $2.50 for new straps on my antique hat-box. Friday at a meeting of the Academy I received my marching orders. We of the Academy were to be at the Indian Museum at 4:15 Saturday afternoon, where we should find five or six ambassadors to escort to the ceremony. At exactly 4:30 Foch was to arrive from Columbia University where he was to receive his fourteenth LL.D. (grotesque!), the bugle was to sound, and we were to march with him to the sacred spot, all crowned in shining black—not Foch, of course, but we immortals. I got there in good time. Nobody looking immortal was in the Indian Museum, nor did the curator seem to know of the existence of any such persons. He insisted that the ceremony of laying the corner stone was then going on, and that Foch had arrived at four. I swore it was impossible, that that stone could not be laid without my presence, and so on. At last I went out, and sure enough, there over a vast sea of heads, beside a gaunt derrick, I could just see the noble white (and empty) head of R. U. Johnson emerging into the air. He was reading a sonnet as I afterwards learned. Fortunately our literary Bolsheviks have not yet dared to tamper with the sonnet or add to its fourteen lines. And there about me, shouldered and elbowed by the ignoble crowd, were other immortals in their well-polished tiles, among them President Hadley, and Mead, the architect of the building. It came out that Foch was under his physician's orders to rush things through and get home to rest. Hence this foreshortening of time; hence these tears. There was to be a grand reception after the ceremony, but this was cut out entirely. I stood with Net and Darrah and Alice and Katherine Heard in base obscurity, having expected to inspire them with awe for my sublime importance."[77]

"Fifty-seven years old today, and just beginning the work I have been preparing for all my life. It is rather a disquieting thought that in a few years my strength will begin to grow less, although up to the present time I have felt myself gaining in power, mentally at least, as each birthday came along. It is a truth you cannot understand," her father told Darrah, "and will scarcely credit that happiness, if I may judge from my own experience, increases with age. One finds that so many things that seemed vastly important, are rather insignificant, and one learns that peace of mind and clarity of knowledge mean so much more than the desires which used to fret one. But I do not mean to preach, or to impose the lessons of age on the heart of youth; although, it is true, that the saddest burden we have to carry is the knowledge that what little experience we gain must be for ourselves only and cannot be passed to another. Each must learn for himself, and it often is so hard to learn—πάθει μάθος. . . ."[78]

[77] To Louis T. More, Nov. 21, 1921.
[78] To Mary Darrah More, Dec. 12, 1921. Cf. *PB*, 46; *SE* II, 252; and *CW*, 324.

11

FROM PLATONISM TO CHRISTIANITY
(1922-1925)

AT THE beginning of 1922 on "an excursion to Cambridge to sit in the Visiting Committee of the Graduate School," More found Babbitt looking "old and troubled, but the spiritual fire burns undiminished."[1] Some weeks later, on March 9, 10, and 11, the Platonist spoke to Princeton undergraduates about the religious imagination, the beauty of holiness, the reality of the invisible world, and the light and peace manifested in Christ. And with April came the thrill of tulips. ". . . they are my favorite flower; I love them better even than roses. Their straightforward clean colors and their simple geometrical forms appeal to my senses in some mysterious manner I can't explain. And there they are on the table at every meal."[2]

"I have been indulging in terrible dissipations, and have come to the conclusion that virtue is more agreeable than vice. Saturday night the Century celebrated its seventy-fifth birthday. . . . Root gave an address which was really very fine for the occasion, and after that were moving pictures of various old members and groups of men. Most of the subjects were familiar to me when I first joined the club but are now disporting themselves in other worlds. The sight of their faces was rather saddening; indeed the house is already peopled for me with ghosts. . . . Several newly elected members from Princeton—Atwood and Gauss and Stuart—were there, and we came out together in the owl train, reaching the junction at 2:20. Gauss had his car waiting there, so that we drove home, an hilarious party. Sunday I rested. Then Monday afternoon Net and I went into town . . . for the Molière celebrations of the Academy. Monday night there was a

[1] To Alice More, Jan. 14, 1922.
[2] To Louis T. More, April 20, 1922.

grand dinner at the Ritz-Carlton. . . . Both Donnay and Chevrillon, of the Académie française read long, long papers in French, which fatigued me and gave me nothing I cared to hear despite my painful attention. Fortunately the eating was notably fine. Then Tuesday afternoon came the literary exercises, with an address by Brander Matthews and again two long papers by the French guests and a recitation by Gus Thomas. The whole thing lasted nearly three hours, and almost finished me. Sitting on the platform in full view, I had to keep quiet, with the result that corns seemed to be growing on a part of my anatomy half-way up from my feet. Jusserand and Joffre were present on both occasions. I had an opportunity to study Joffre's face at close range. I have never, I think, seen a much sadder eye than his. Certainly that man looks upon ghosts—as why should he not? Then came Sloane's dinner Tuesday evening. There were about twenty-five of us crowded in a small room. My chance was to sit with . . . a cheap Irishman who got into the Academy by one of those strange lapses that come over bodies of men. David Joyne Hill however was near me, and his talk was fairly good. With it all I got home Wednesday noon, feeling that I had wasted time, tired my body, soured my temper, and deepened my pessimism. How true it is that the things which really satisfy are simple and easy, and we labor hard to bore ourselves. But I have a very interesting History of Dogma by a French Roman Catholic to solace me."[3]

After attending the June wedding of his niece, Katharine Hay More, to Wilmon Brewer, in Hingham, Massachusetts, where about 1921 James Brookes More had bought "one hundred thirty-six acres within sound of the sea,"[4] More devoted most of his energy to cutting his grass, "and as for weeds, I just leave them and count them an ornament to the garden. Withal I manage to do my regular stint of writing in the morning, and, D. V., I shall have the first draught [of *Hellenistic Philosophies*] fin-

[3] To Alice More, April 27, 1922.
[4] To Louis T. More, July 11, 1921.

Platonism to Christianity

ished by the end of next week. Just now I am engaged with Plotinus, who is hard in every way, desperately hard Greek, desperately hard metaphysics; and I dislike him thoroughly. To get the atmosphere I have [been] reading up various medieval and modern mystics, who all derive from him directly or indirectly, and every day I am more utterly convinced that mysticism is a false way[5] and one of the maleficent parasites of true religion—it and asceticism[6] that belongs with it. Ah, these mystical ascetics were sweet creatures. There's Jacopone da Todi, for instance. He wanted some liver. To mortify his taste he hung the meat up in his room, and would smell it and lick it without eating. Then it went bad, and made such a stench that the brothers in the convent finally found it, hanging there filled with worms. The brothers snatched it away and carried it to what the old *Vita* calls the necessario, where they told Jacopone he might enjoy it if he liked. And he did like. He stood in there praising God with a loud voice: 'O joy of the heart which thou makest to sing of love!' It's typical, and it's nasty. I see no religion in it, but a hideous caricature. And Plotinus—though I admit his asceticism was not excessive or nasty, only foolish—

[5] In return for More's gift to him of a copy of *The Religion of Plato* Norman Kemp Smith sent von Hügel's *Essays and Addresses* to More. ". . . [von Hügel's] dialectical acuteness I admire, his learning is manifest, there is undoubtedly a fund of genuine religious experience in his mind, but his method of dealing with that experience, I am bound to say, leads him into regions where I at least cannot follow. Mysticism inevitably implies a metaphysic of the absolute, which like Kronos devours its offspring. Absolutes have no meaning, they correspond to nothing we know, or can know—at least to nothing that I know. And I am inclined to think that the Christian theologians' conception of God, a compound of the Aristotelian absolute and the Jewish Jehovah is one of the most monstrous products of the *intellectus sibi permissus*. Deprive God of his attributes, call him 'infinite,' and He ceases to bear any relation to my life, or to any life. I prefer to leave the notion of the divine in a state of fluidity, and to reject all these attempts to associate him with the absolute of reason. Then, when this metaphysically conceived God is made the object of mystical ecstasy, I shudder." [To Norman Kemp Smith, Dec. 5, 1922. Cf. *CW*, 71 ff.]
[6] Cf. *HP*, 368-69, and *CF*, 263-67.

they say was a true follower of Plato.[7] Really, when I think of the perversions of history and criticism, I feel perfectly hopeless, and wonder why I write at all. If only anybody would listen! So much for grumpiness, due to Plotinus."[8]

In Essex Paul let Louis, then engaged on his *Dogma of Evolution*, use "my brain as if it were his own. This is interesting; it gives me the pleasure of composition without the labor. If Lou really gets himself together, he may make a great hit. The time is every way ripe for just such an attack on the biological and evolutionary superstition as he is planning. It is curious that, despite his scientific training, he is clearest and most original when he deals with the motives and human traits of Darwin, Huxley, et al. His criticism of the fanaticism and bad faith of these men is subtle and, I think, sound. It will make something of a sensation, since they have been canonized in the popular faith, and a good deal of the reverence for evolution grows out of a quite erroneous reverence for the evolutionists. . . .

"My great excitement has been the discovery of Holtzmann. He gives in wonderful form the results of the Biblical studies of the past fifty years, and on the whole his work[9] seems to me about the most beautifully constructed I have ever met. One thing stands out clear: the results of the higher criticism have been to reestablish in large and larger measure the historical validity of the Synoptic Gospels. Having gone so far, the critics are obliged to indulge in an almost bewildering subtlety of thought and interpretation to avoid the old-fashioned dogma of Christ's divinity. It is an exciting pursuit."[10]

[7] More thought Plotinus misinterpreted Plato's doctrine of Ideas, superimposed the mystical trance on Platonism, and followed "a method of reasoning which was introduced by Aristotle, and which, combining with certain Oriental currents of theology and merging into Neo-Pythagoreanism, carried philosophy in a direction quite contrary to the true implications of Platonism." [*HP*, 205. Cf. *HP*, 172-259, and *CF*, 222-30, 235-45, 250-51.]

[8] To Alice More, July 20, 1922.

[9] *Lehrbuch der neutestamentlichen Theologie.*

[10] To Alice More, Aug. 19, 1922.

Platonism to Christianity

"Since I wrote last I have been to Aurora to give a lecture at Wells College. You almost lost me in transit. About midnight on the way up we ran full speed into the rear of a standing freight train. As I was in the last car the shock was not very great, but the caboose of the freight was totally wrecked and several men burned to death. We were due at Ithaca (where my sleeper was to be switched off) at 4:37 a.m., but did not reach there until noon. I had a hard scramble to get to Aurora in time, but with the aid of an automobile managed it. I was the guest of a young fellow named Shafer who as an undergraduate here had found his chief intellectual stimulus in my Essays. The visit was very pleasant."[11]

His fifty-eighth birthday sent More "over the lengthening past" to return "to the present with some very uneasy questions. It seems clearer to me every year that in some way I never made quite the right choice, or never made it whole-heartedly. I have wavered between things secular and things sacred, with the result that I have not found myself planted firmly in either world. I think of the title of my early book, *The Great Refusal*, and ask myself whether in a manner—though in a manner different from that of the book—I have not refused to meet the issues squarely. I might have been happy aiming to be a saint; I might have succeeded in the world. But this is rather morbid, and, now at least, leads to nothing."[12]

"I have read your book[13] through with absorbed interest," More reported to Frye, "and have passed it on, by way of a loan, to Mather, hoping he may be inspired to write an adequate review of it, a task from which I am rather debarred by the dedication. . . . I am obliged to say that the dedication may work you a mischief. I have gained the rather sad preeminence of being at once the least read and the worst hated author in the country. There are some writers no doubt who are less read than I am—

[11] To the same, Oct. 25, 1922.
[12] To the same, Dec. 15, 1922. Cf. *CNT*, 139-40.
[13] *Romance and Tragedy*.

I hope so—and there may be some who are more hated, but the combination in my case is, I fear, unique.[14] The stream of abuse that pours over me is quite beyond my deserts from any point of view. And some of that abuse may be attracted upon you. . . .

"The other night—my birthday—I was summing up the good things of a scholar's life, and I put down these four moments of the day as the chief recurrent blessings. First comes the moment when you settle down in your chair after breakfast, set a match to a scientifically filled pipe, and turn to the page of Plato where you left off the day before at the end of that same first smoke. That is a pleasure I am forgoing for the present, but not for long. Perhaps the omission brings me with greater zest to the second moment, when, after luncheon, I stretch out [on] the sofa with well piled pillows under head and a warm blanket over body, and open the novel or biography or what not —anything not remotely related to what I am working at—that happens to be in hand. Half an hour of reading, half an hour of sleep, half an hour of dozing, and a little time for reflection—it breaks the back of the day and brings me to Greek or German in the evening with a fresh heart. I have found the lives of the bishops superbly suited to afternoon siestas. Who would not sleep deliciously over the life of my Lord Cantuarius or Eboracensis? And they are so long; they give one a sense of everlasting rest such as I could never get from Baxter. Bishops today are becoming a hard-worked and not too erudite sort of universal correspondents, but it was not so with the older set who counted the editing of a Greek text above cleanliness. . . . But carried away by my episcopal hobby, I have not finished my day. The third high moment is when, as midnight approaches, I browse over my shelves and pick out one book or several for an hour's quiet reading—some poet or essayist or the like. And then, last and, I think, sweetest of all, arrives the moment when your bed has got thoroughly warmed, and the cool air from the window strikes your face, and you feel yourself slipping away into the

[14] Cf. *DA*, 3.

long sleep of the night—with Plato and pipe and all the rest awaiting you with the coming day. There are still some fine things in this crazy old world. And then I remember that a grain of sand or the *gutta serena* in my eye might ruin the whole building of my happiness. Could I be a philosopher and blind? The question tantalizes me so that at times I almost pray to be put to the test. But I beg you not to offer any such prayers of intercession for me."[15]

Having delivered the manuscript of his *Hellenistic Philosophies*[16] to the publishers, More, "reading and thinking furiously,"[17] found himself "all on fire" to get at his "next volume, on Christianity."[18]

"I can never be an ordained preacher, but I am coming as close to it as possible. Not long ago I gave a talk to the ladies, and some men, at Mr. Weber's[19] on the history of the eucharist. Wednesday I spoke at the luncheon of the Present Day Club on the Demon of the Absolute, and now I have promised to address the Clerical Club which meets here April 23rd on the Greek, Roman, and Anglican Churches.[20] My head is so full of

15 To Prosser Hall Frye, Dec. 29, 1922.
16 According to *HP*, of "the three main theses of the Socratic teaching"—namely, scepticism, spiritual affirmation, and the identity of virtue and knowledge—the Epicureans and the Stoics "followed the rationalizing tendency of the third thesis taken alone"; the Neoplatonists "rationalized the spiritual affirmation"; and the Pyrrhonists "clung to the scepticism and rejected the other two theses. . . . Plato alone developed the full doctrine of the master by uniting the three theses into one harmonious system of thought." [*HP*, 356-57.]
17 To Alice More, March 15, 1923.
18 To the same, March 9, 1923.
19 Shirley Howard Weber, associate professor of classics at Princeton University.
20 "I dropped a bomb among them by denying the right to personify the Holy Ghost and by ejecting the Trinity from Christian dogma. They fought a bit but all in good nature." [To Louis T. More, April 23, 1923.] "The more I read and study, the more deeply am I convinced that the *personification* of the Holy Ghost was a vast blunder. Out of it grows the tangled metaphysics of the Trinity. It overshadows and almost abolishes the true and beautiful meaning of the Spirit as the instrument of the divine and human communication. It runs counter to the genuine utterances of Christ. I know that the surrender of this dogma of faith

these topics, that I talk on them without difficulty, and the practice helps me to get my thoughts in order. I still fumble a good deal for words, and often omit the principal point I had in mind to make, but I gain in ease. It wouldn't take a great deal of experience to turn me into a ready speaker, but I am too old to learn new tricks. And on the whole I am inclined to believe that fluency in that direction has some dangers for one whose first aim is to write."[21]

The same lack of fluency appeared in his course on "Hellenistic and Patristic Philosophy." As from 1919 onwards the number of his students increased to twenty or thirty, instead of talking to them in his study he addressed them about three times a week in a classroom. Occasionally he would arrive long before the scheduled hour, to cover the blackboard with diagrams or passages in Greek needed to illustrate his subject. Neatly dressed, with a stiff white collar, he would begin reading his limpid, cadenced prose in a matter of fact, dignified manner, with deep, richly modulated voice and precise pronunciation, at that part of the manuscript of *Hellenistic Philosophies* where the bell had cut him short on his previous lecture. When his eyes grew tired or an idea pressed upon him too insistently, he used to put down his papers, take off his glasses, look into space or out of the window, and digress awhile on Buddha, Dean Inge, Chesterton, Dreiser, H. L. Mencken, Jonathan Edwards, or "the theories of the man whom our inquisitive college youth are beginning to speak of reverentially as 'Frood,' "[22] with acute insight and a

---

may seem to invalidate the creeds and otherwise make trouble with the traditional forms of worship. But I think not immediately. The triune formula might still be used, with the understanding (even with the 'reservation' where necessary) that the H. G. is not a separate person but the indwelling and grace-giving spirit of God." [To Paul R. Coleman-Norton, Dec. 9, 1924.]

[21] To Alice More, March 9, 1923.

[22] "Theodore Dreiser, Philosopher," signed "P. E. M.," *The Review*, April 17, 1920, vol. 2, no. 49, p. 381. Cf. "Dr. Freud Bowdlerized," review signed "P. E. M." of *The Secret Spring*, by Harvey O'Higgins, *The Weekly Review*, April 20, 1921, vol. 4, pp. 368-69.

violence of half-opinionated and half-humorous expression that diverted or exasperated his auditors.

Openly or silently they might oppose his opinions as energetically as he condemned views that he deemed incomplete or mistaken, but, except for those for whom he was inevitably "just another professor," as an individual he fascinated them. In his dryness and his constrained avoidance of emotion, even more than in his outbursts of vehemence, they sensed an evangelistic intensity.[23] He did not analyse ideas for their own sake. Though he delighted in distinctions, though he admitted a large range of shadings and gradations, despite his intellectual scepticism his spiritual affirmation invariably triumphed. In the end he saw only a right direction or a wrong direction,[24] truth or falsehood, order or chaos, health or disease, life or death. Every step, every turn, counted, bringing one nearer to or farther from reality, happiness, and God.

For students who called at his house he would put aside whatever he was doing and devote his time unstintingly to them, inviting them to join his family at tea or any other meal that occurred during their talk. Were a boy preparing a paper on Newman, for instance, More would show him "some five or six portraits of the man taken at different ages,"[25] and on returning to his chair would remark: "There is something wrong when religion makes a man's face look like that." His formality in public in no way lessened his enjoyment in private of a parody of "Abou Ben Adhem" by one of his undergraduate auditors,

[23] "I have never felt that my lectures at Princeton were really successful. For one thing, they touched so near the quick of one's own inner life that I have always been conscious of holding myself very much in reserve." [To Irving Babbitt, March 7, 1925.]

[24] Cf. *SE* VI, 321-22.

[25] To Alice More, April 26, 1921. In the end Newman's "face took on a look of something close to spiritual anguish. Why was it? I can't imagine such a look on the face of a good Platonist. Perhaps Newman desired too much, was unwilling to see only enigmatically as in a mirror, and could not wait for the clearer vision. Perhaps he forgot that after all the αἰώνια must be μὴ βλεπόμενα now." [*Ibid.* Cf *POD*, III, XVIII, and *DA*, 77.]

who, incited by the lecturer's attacks on cant about "the brother-hood of man," substituted More's name for Abou's and revised lines like, "Write me as one who loves his fellow-men," to ex-press the Platonist's less complacent sentiments. He helped sev-eral students with loans (sometimes exceeding a tithe of his small annual earnings). On their behalf he wrote innumerable letters, frequently without their knowledge. Moved by a Quixotic notion that Princetonians should speak passable American be-fore they graduated, he coached some of his pupils with pa-ternal persistence, trying to save them from the common blund-ers of "shall" and "will," the use of "toward" for "towards" (a point he had not noticed before his trip to England in 1912), the corruption of "behind" into "back of,"[26] and strange sounds, like "wock" and "tock" for "walk" and "talk."

His greatest gratification as a teacher came perhaps from bringing light to other minds. One of his students who had sailed so far into the seas of philosophy that, until he saw More's guiding star, he felt himself lost, wrote him "a letter about my course which I shall keep as a kind of diploma to hand down to my children's children."[27] "It was overdone, but in the main sincere I think, and encouraged me when encouragement was very welcome. So many of the men sit looking at me with an expression of dumb stupidity and are so evidently merely bored, when they are not wondering what it is all about, that I really at the end of this year was ready to throw the whole thing over, but for the salary. One needs to be shocked occasionally into a modest optimism."[28]

More's writing and lecturing in the spring of 1923 did not prevent his criticizing Babbitt's partially completed draft of *Democracy and Leadership* and the manuscript of Louis More's *Dogma of Evolution.* After attending Darrah's graduation at

[26] Cf. *Academy Papers,* New York (Charles Scribner's Sons), 1925, p. 24.
[27] To Louis T. More, May 6, 1923.
[28] To Alice More, May 25, 1923.

Vassar, he gave the commencement address at Oberlin College.[29] "The heat was terrific. I sat on the platform inrolled in my heavy silk gown and resplendent hood. Then I talked for three quarters of an hour, straining my voice to make myself heard in a large hall whose acoustics are none too good. Meanwhile I was sweating abundantly. My legs shrunk in dimension and otherwise became like two well-greased poles. When we arose to march out to a sonorous recessional, I felt that my garters were slipping down. What could I do, there on the platform before two thousand pairs of eyes? Nothing, I simply stalked down the chapel aisle at the head of the procession trailing two very conspicuous garters as I went. Wasn't it awful?"[30]

The Mores, who had originally planned to go to Europe that summer (where Alice and her sister, May, were then travelling) and had rented "The Cedars" before they decided to postpone their trip, remained during August in Princeton.

"Poor Francesco, you know, went over to Italy in June. He did not take out proper papers, and now he finds he cannot return until he gets into the regular quota of immigrants. He has been writing the most pitiful letters of appeal, and last Monday I got a document signed at the Italian consulate in New York which, I hope, will expedite his return. You should see his letter to Mary:[31] 'Me no lak Italy, me lak America, me morto in good America. Pleas Mr. More, please Mrs More' . . ."[32]

[29] His speech on "The Demon of the Absolute" differed from the opening essay in *DA*. The general thesis in both instances was the same, namely, that "reason" unleashed from the "actual data of experience" runs to extremes. At Oberlin he illustrated this in literature and theology, with special reference in the latter to the humanity and the divinity of Christ. He there opposed views of Christ as either exclusively divine or exclusively human, "preferring the inexplicable dogma of the combined humanity and divinity of Christ." [*The Oberlin Alumni Magazine*, July 1923, vol. 19, p. 11.]

[30] To Mary Darrah More, June 24, 1923.

[31] The Mores' Negro cook since about 1904. About 1922 they began to employ William Stephens, "Mary's latest husband, a capable smart fellow." [To Louis T. More, April 20, 1922.]

[32] To Alice More, Aug. 21, 1923.

On Labor Day More and his family went to the cottage they had rented for September at Hurricane Lodge, at Hurricane in the Adirondacks. They turned 245 Nassau Street over to Maurice Baum, one of More's best students, who that spring had married and brought his bride to Princeton.

More's hoped-for month of rest in the mountains "with a little Greek and Hebrew"[33] and some "golf—or near-golf"[34]— was disturbed by the receipt of pounds of such slovenly proof of his *Hellenistic Philosophies* that he had to return much of it unread. But "the view at Hurricane during the last two weeks when the foliage had turned"[35] "was unspeakably lovely. I used to say that I did not know what we had done to merit such goodness from the Old Man. Certainly such beauty is an argument for a divine purpose not easy to overcome. I think it had a good deal [to do] with Plato's doctrine of Ideas, which to me is just pure philosophy and the only philosophy.[36] Without it, what place is there in the world for any hope of spiritual things, or why should we say anything but, Let us eat, drink and be merry, for tomorrow we die?"[37]

A test of this cheerfulness came rather suddenly. "Net has had a lump in her breast with some soreness under the arm. Day before yesterday she was examined by a Philadelphia surgeon, who says that almost certainly it is a malignant growth, though not of the most dangerous kind. We go down this afternoon to the Presbyterian Hospital in Philadelphia, and the doctor will operate tomorrow. The whole breast and perhaps more

---

[33] *Ibid.*
[34] To Henry Holt, Dec. 10, 1923.
[35] To Maurice Baum, Oct. 5, 1923.
[36] He wished Plato "had not made of beauty an Idea in the same category with justice, and truth, and temperance, and the other moral qualities, but had regarded it as the effluence, the effulgence, the perceptible sign of the Ideas as these are embodied in phenomena. It is the intimation of these poetic powers in the things of the material world that lends a divine charm to them, an appeal to the soul, a sense of something lost and now vaguely discovered, or discoverable." [From one of More's notes. Cf. *SE* III, 233.]
[37] To Henry Holt, Dec. 10, 1923.

will have to be taken away. It is not the sort of thing to confirm one in an optimistic view of this blessed world. . . .

"P. S. Net knows exactly the nature of the case. She is naturally a good deal affected, but brave. . . ."[38]

Without referring to his anxieties about Mrs. More, he tried to encourage one of his recent students, who had found his first year out of Princeton hard sledding. "The wind is whistling about my north window and intruding through all the crevices of my room in such a way that I fear the chill of the weather may get into my ink; but I trust still to get some warmth into my words. I have not forgotten, nor put your name in my black book, nor lost your first letter in which you tell of your search for a domicile along with your quest of a philosophical solution of the universe. You seem in a manner to have found both. As for poverty, remember you have in your possession the greatest counterpoise of all—youth. Life is young for you, and you can temper suffering and disappointment with hope. I was poor enough once. For two years I lived in the country in a little shanty the rental of which was $3 a month. But of course I was alone and without responsibility—that took the sting out of deprivation. Tell your good little wife that I believe in you and have no doubt of your future. Tell her that all your future— yours and hers—depends on her trust and courage now. Tell her that the real curse of poverty is the undue stress it forces one to lay on material things and bid her fight against that and hold fast to the things that really make life worth while. Tell her all that; but I do not think she really needs to hear them from me."[39]

Having read in *Civilization in the United States* an attack on his former teacher by an Irish poet named Ernest Boyd, More's young correspondent asked him whether he had ever stepped on Boyd's toes and also why More ignored current writers in favor of those who, as Boyd insinuated, were safely under ground.

"I certainly never wrote anything about your Ernest Boyd,"

[38] To Louis T. More, Nov. 14, 1923.
[39] To Maurice Baum, Jan. 6, 1924.

More replied, "and I am pretty sure that I never printed anything about him. He has really never swum within my ken. But then I used to have a big parcel of newspaper clippings filled with rancorous abuse written by earnest panting young souls all over the country. Sometimes they amused me, because the critics had evidently taken such desperate pains to say what they thought would cut me most deeply. It was not so long ago that a 'paragrapher' in California asked what sort of mother and wife I must have who could write such things; and I happened to see a notice of my Plato in a Brooklyn paper which described the book as nauseous when it was not imbecile.[40] I have not subscribed to a clipping bureau for some time, but occasionally my friends send me these choice bits. On the other hand I generally get one or two excellent reviews in England, and the highest praise I ever received was from Robin, of Paris, one of the foremost Platonists of the world. As for your question why I had deserted authors of our own day for those of yesterday,—I haven't. I never set out to write serious criticism of contemporary literature. I have of course reviewed hundreds of new books, but only as a journalist. I have pretty thoroughly confined my essays to writers who were worthy of serious consideration, and who would be remembered twenty years from now. Can you name any author living in America today whose books are likely to be read twenty years from now? And besides, criticism of the essay sort is a different thing from reviewing, and has a purpose of its own. Why should not a man write about Shakespeare or Milton or Wordsworth, if he chooses? Is there any crime in that? I never set out to be nurse to the sucking poets of the day."[41]

On February 11, 1924, before the Twentieth Century Club in Pittsburgh, More spoke again on "The Demon of the Absolute," apparently repeating his commencement address of the preced-

[40] Seward B. Collins in "The Eagle Eye," *The Brooklyn Daily Eagle*, March 18, 1922, p. 3, col. 7, described More's work as "pathetic at the moments it is not disgusting." Cf. *DA*, 3.

[41] To Maurice Baum, March 31, 1924.

ing spring at Oberlin. The rest of February, while Mrs. More, under the care of a trained nurse, struggled against tonsilitis, laryngitis, and grippe, her husband, "pretty well worn,"[42] besides delivering his regular university lectures, proofread *The Christ of the New Testament,* which Babbitt had criticized in manuscript.

The purpose of that book was not to "prove" the truth of the Incarnation but to show that "the so-called Definition pronounced by the fourth ecumenical Council at Chalcedon, in A.D. 451"—to the effect that "Christ was a person who embraced within himself the full nature of divinity and the full nature of humanity"—is "the one essential dogma of Christianity, that the philosophy underlying it conforms to our deepest spiritual experience, that it is the mythological expression (using the word 'mythological' in no derogatory sense) of the Platonic dualism, and thus forms a proper consummation of the Greek Tradition."[43]

Christ's teachings about repentance, purity, humility, and love[44] rang true for More, convinced as he was that they are prerequisites to spiritual progress, though human conduct, short of saintly martyrdom, shows little regard for them. But the fundamental question about Jesus, provoked by his alleged arrogation to himself of "something more than belongs to humanity,"[45] is whether he "was or was not in some way superhuman."[46]

A materialistic preconception makes, for many people, such a question absurd. If, as they assume, our ethical and religious ideals have no significance beyond their existence as activities in our brains; if the only realities are those in time and space;

[42] Alice More to Louis T. More, Feb. 20, 1924.
[43] *CNT,* 1-2. Believing "that Greek literature, philosophic and religious, pagan and Christian, from Plato to . . . the Council of Chalcedon . . . is essentially a unit and follows at the centre a straight line" [*RP,* vi], More gave the name, "The Greek Tradition," to his series of books, *RP, HP, CNT,* and *CW,* to which he added *P* as an introduction and *CF* as a conclusion.
[44] Cf. *CF,* 35 ff., 172 ff.
[45] *CNT,* 243; cf. *ibid.,* pp. 236, 244.   [46] *CNT,* 248.

if our minds somehow belong entirely to that natural order; if there is no order of spiritual realities that may, in contrast, be described as supernatural and superhuman; if God simply cannot be—why, on such assumptions, Jesus must have been, as those so persuaded have asserted, an impostor, a paranoiac, or a deluded dreamer.

Impostor and paranoiac More rejected. Delusion involves the question of its kind and extent. But first going to the source of these difficulties, he tried to show that the materialistic "preconception philosophically is unjustifiable, that, on the contrary, the supposition of a higher nature resident within our human nature is of itself no more irrational than that operation of mind in body which every act of existence forces us to accept." Why, then, he seems to ask, balk at just one more paradox? "But . . . because the union of the divine and the human is not to be rejected out of hand as psychologically impossible, it does not therefore follow that Jesus of Nazareth was actually divine, as he claimed to be."[47]

If, however, the materialistic hypothesis is a shallow dogmatism, we can, at least theoretically, consider the claim of Jesus and "weigh the consequences."[48] Let us, then, in an attempt to understand the Christian point of view, assume that Jesus was not entirely deceived in his divine pretensions. "Suppose that the Son of man was also, in some ineffable manner, the Son of God!

"Oh, the supposition is large,"[49] More granted. The eschatology of Jesus, far from being divine, "was simply that of his country and his age."[50] "The Messianic predictions of Jesus were erroneous."[51] To that extent he was deluded as every man is by the clouds of his time. ". . . the limitations of his knowledge are so manifest, that the problem has been rather to discover his divinity through the veil of his mortal nature."[52] But on account

47 *CNT*, 248-49. Cf. *CW*, 241.   48 *CNT*, 249.
49 *CNT*, 247.   50 *CNT*, 69.   51 *CNT*, 247.
52 *CNT*, 251.

of such limitations alone we "should not simply dismiss him as one of the long list of human fanatics. . . ."[53] Such limitations alone, in More's opinion, do not preclude, unless the scriptures and the convictions of Christians may not be trusted to that extent, the possibility of there being some spark of truth in his allegations of divinity. "If you ask how this can be, how the divine and the human could dwell together without the one cancelling the other, how knowledge and ignorance can abide in unison, I will say frankly that I do not understand. Neither do I comprehend any better how my own body and soul exist together. But I repeat that, unless we descend to a purely humanitarian view of Christ or lose our hold of reality in a metaphysical theology, we have simply to accept the mysterious fact in the humility of faith."[54]

The analogy of the coexistence of body and mind may have little bearing on the coexistence of the human and the divine. The disparaging phrases, "descend to a purely humanitarian view" and "lose our hold of reality in a metaphysical theology," may do less than justice to those and other possibilities. But, More insists, whoever finds God in the man Jesus, whoever hears in that voice a tone that, if anything, can be called divine, and to that extent accepts "the mystery of the Incarnation," though unable to understand and explain it, must hold fast to that divinity and that humanity. Beside this "one essential dogma of the universal Church, western and eastern, protestant and catholic . . . all other questions are of secondary importance."[55]

". . . whether Jesus was deceived or not in his claims, that is a question . . . to be answered individually by each man as the voice of conscience responds to the words spoken so many ages since by the lake of Galilee. Only, thus much I would urge: if the supposition of Christianity be not true, then we have no sure hope of religion. The Ideal philosophy of Plato waits for its verification upon no belief in anything outside of what we can test and know in our immediate experience, and he to whom the

[53] *CNT*, 249.   [54] *CNT*, 251-52.   [55] *CNT*, 289.

otherworld of Ideas is a reality possesses a spiritual comfort beyond which it may be presumptuous to search—I do not say. But the full scope of religion requires a theology and a mythology as well as a philosophy, and if the crowning element of religion is to be more than a reasonable conjecture, as ultimately it was to Plato, then I see not whither we are to turn save to Christianity."[56]

The Christ of the New Testament "was written under great pressure in a state of intense concentration,[57] so much so that now, as I read it over, it seems like the product of some other brain than my own. In one respect it has not added to my ease. Years ago when I went to the Harvard Graduate School I came into close contact with a man of my own age, but more mature than I intellectually, Irving Babbitt, whose books you may know, certainly ought to know. He turned the whole current of my life, saved me from something akin to mental and emotional suicide. Since then we have worked more or less on the same line, fighting side by side. But now there is—at least he strongly feels there is—a break. He puts it in the terms of Aristotelianism and Platonism. To him the only way by which the world can be brought to sanity is the Aristotelian positivism, though with this he harbours a sympathy with a thoroughgoing mysticism. As a consequence he is really offended with the last part of my chapter on Plotinus,[58] and has been made still more uneasy by my volume on the New Testament. I cannot see things as he does. To me the only possible release from the present trend towards materialism and dissipation seems to lie through the awakening of the sense of what I call otherworldliness.[59] I do not believe

---

[56] *CNT*, 291-92.
[57] When he ended the book with the words, "The alternative is the Faith of the Greek tradition or no religion of Christ," More lay on the floor exhausted.
[58] *HP*, chap. V.
[59] "You once told me that you found it idle to introduce your California students to the great things in literature until you had brought them to a consciousness of the fundamental tragedies of life. . . . Now in religious jargon that sense of tragedy is simply the conviction of sin.

the mass of people ever was or ever can be rational or positive; I do not believe the positive scientific view of life will ever have the power to restrain the passions—and there we are. He is coming to visit me soon, and we shall have long nights of hot discussion—for he can talk like Samuel Johnson and S. T. Coleridge rolled into one."[60]

"Our difference—his and mine—is rather, I think, a matter of emphasis than of fundamental disagreement.[61] Our views are still about the same in most respects, as indeed can be seen by comparing his book[62] with my *Aristocracy and Justice*, but he takes a different view in regard to the strategical point of attack, as he calls it. To him it seems wisest to lay the stress on the humanistic virtues and to let the religious questions lie in the background. . . . The 'positive' attitude with him tends to exclude the belief in a personal God; I do not see that to be positive excludes such an experience. . . . Babbitt has just been with me for several days, and we had some high talk—in which I played chiefly the humble and proper rôle of listener."[63]

Their intellectual differences causing "not the slightest personal friction,"[64] in the spring of 1924 More sought the signa-

---

I do not see how this feeling, whether one is to sympathise with it in Sophocles or Shakespeare or Johnson or Newman, can be evoked by an approach through pure humanism; I think we must dig deeper. At bottom the sense of tragedy is the child of religion, of the realization of the pathetic or grim insufficiency of our life amid sensible, palpable, ephemeral things under the light of an order of things utterly different in nature and value, whether we firmly believe in that other world or passionately long to believe in it. Of course humanism is not antipathetic to religion in that sense, may even be founded on it; but ordinarily it is a substitute for it." [To Percy H. Houston, Jan. 10, 1926.]

[60] To Maurice Baum, June 9, 1924.

[61] "He [Babbitt] thinks the emphasis should be on judgment; I am inclined to argue that first of all we must arouse the imagination." [To Percy H. Houston, Jan. 10, 1926. Cf. *HP*, 299 f.]

[62] More regarded Babbitt's *Democracy and Leadership* "as quite the strongest piece of work he has done . . . epigrammatically brilliant and at the same time weighty." [To Percy H. Houston, July 4, 1924.]

[63] To Percy H. Houston, July 4, 1924.

[64] To Maurice Baum, June 29, 1924.

tures of Brander Matthews and Stuart Sherman for the papers nominating Babbitt—"a tower of strength,"[65] "my best friend," and "the strongest intellectual power in America"[66]—to the American Academy of Arts and Letters.

Having obtained a leave of absence from Princeton University and arranged for William and Mary to remain at 245 Nassau Street, which, as well as "Stonecliffe," was conveniently rented, More with his family sailed from New York July 12, 1924, on the *Orbita*, of the Royal Mail Line. Reinforced at Southampton by Louis More, his wife, and their children, Catherine and John, they went through Salisbury to Stratford on Avon.

". . . at the tomb of Shakespeare I received something of a shock. Ordinarily I am not very sensitive to local associations, but here, rather to my amazement, I was overcome by a rush of emotion.[67] It seemed to me that here in this old church where Shakespeare lies—that here, if anywhere, I stood at the heart of England. And since then I have felt again and again that the true life of the country is symbolized in the churches. And I have felt that if there is to be any genuine unity between England and America, as indeed between any peoples, it must come through concord of worship. Visiting the rural churches, and the cathedrals too, though these affect one rather as mere museums of antiquity, I have had my old opinion confirmed that the greatest and most characteristic product of the English genius is its Prayer Book. And the conclusion? It is simply the query whether in these days of mental confusion and insolent materialism the first and most effective protest may not be simply to go to church. A lame and impotent conclusion, I fear you will say; but there is something in it, believe me. The greatest obstacle of course is the brainless character of most of the clergy, but then

[65] To Brander Matthews, April 15, 1924; courtesy of the Head of Special Collections, Columbia University.
[66] To Clement K. Shorter, Sept. 24, 1924; courtesy of the Brotherton Library, University of Leeds.
[67] He wept.

that would soon remedy itself if intelligent men took part in the service."[68]

The "two families knocked about England—chiefly the cathedral towns—without knocking each other's sensibilities,"[69] moving up the east coast to Edinburgh and through the Lake District to Chester, staying about three days at each stop. After Chester they visited Canon Went at Birstall, the father of More's former assistant on *The Nation,* Stanley Went. They next remained in London about two weeks before "Net and Eleanor took Alice and Catherine over to Lausanne, where the children are now in school."[70] From Oxford the women flew off again, Mrs. Louis More to winter in France, and Mrs. Paul More in Florence, where Darrah took singing lessons. The three men remained at The Isis, on Iffley Road, Paul deep in Hebrew and the Old Testament, Louis reading Italian until he left early in January 1925 for his Vanuxem Lectures[71] at Princeton, and John studying Greek until in November he joined his mother in Paris.

"Reggie Harris has been very hospitable, inviting me to dine in hall at Corpus and at All Souls, introducing me to various people. . . . All Souls . . . you know, is a college of dons without any students, which is the original conception of a college and still the ideal. There were about twenty men at the board. Members of the college in their gowns, guests in full evening dress. There was a good deal of handsome silver on the table and the lighting was entirely by candles. The dinner, including the wines, was good, but at the end Reggie persuaded me to drink a mug of their famous home-brewed ale, which I didn't like at all. The talking, at least at my end of the table, was dull. After dinner we retired to the common room for wine and dessert. In this college

---

[68] To Irving Babbitt, Sept. 5, 1924.
[69] To Frank Jewett Mather, Jr., Oct. 16, 1924.
[70] To Irving Babbitt, Sept. 5, 1924.
[71] As *The Dogma of Evolution* found no ready publisher, Louis suggested that, if invited, he could read the manuscript as the Vanuxem Lectures at Princeton and let that university print them; so Paul proposed this to one of the men in charge of the lectures.

they sit at two long tables on which fruit of various sorts is laid out. Sherry and port are in carafes set in a heavy silver boat, which they religiously slide about the table, so that each man may fill his glass as he pleases. No smoking: the Englishman, you know, would sooner mix his parts of speech than smoke and drink port at the same time. I must say the common room was deadly dull. But after they had solemnly consumed the proper amount of wine, we passed on to the smoking room; and here, before good fires, and under the influence of whisky and to-bacco, things really began to move. I had a long chat with the Warden, who proved a jolly soul well stocked with amusing stories. Later he, or rather his wife, invited me to dine at the Lodgings. . . . It was pretty slow; except for the time I was talking with the Warden's young daughter, who was both pretty and vivacious."[72]

"Lou and I sit and read most of the day, going out twice to walk. The crown of the twenty-four hours is the midafternoon when they bring in our tea. The sun is low on the horizon, and by four o'clock it begins to grow dark. Then, with lights burning and a clear fire on the hearth, we put down our books, and chat over tea and thin bread and cake. It is delightfully cosy."[73]

"The pleasantest dinner I have had was given by Macgregor . . . in the Fellows room at Balliol, to which J. A. Smith of Magdalen was invited in order that we might meet. He is regarded as a prodigy of learning, and indeed he does know endless things, can quote nonsense or philosophy in all sorts of languages. But like most men of vast memory he is not always aware of his limitations, and made numerous funny blunders in recondite matters where he supposed no one could follow him. However he is very entertaining. . . ."[74]

After two weeks with Louis in London at the end of 1924, More returned to Oxford.

[72] To Alice More, Nov. 4, 1924.
[73] To the same, Nov. 21, 1924.
[74] To the same, Dec. 11, 1924.

Platonism to Christianity

"My impression of the place is that we are quite on a par with the men here in exact scholarship, but that we fall behind them in imagination. So few of our scholars have any large undertaking in hand, but most of them are squandering their energies in a succession of ephemeral papers. This is no doubt due in part to our system of forcing quick and constant publication; but in part also I should attribute it to lack of imagination and patience.

"Clifford Moore has asked me to give Gulick's courses [at Harvard] in Plato and Aristotle and some other subject for advanced students the second term of next year. I have replied that I should like very much to accept, but must first consult the Princeton men, and that at any rate I could not give more than two courses. As I must keep the first term free for my writing, acceptance of the offer would mean the suspension of my course at Princeton for two successive years. And then there is the question of family. They will scarcely wish to pull up stakes again so soon after returning, nor should I like to be separated for most of four months. I should be expected to reside in Cambridge. What draws me most," he admitted to Babbitt, "is the chance I should have to be near you for so long a period."[75]

Sitting in his room at The Isis during the first six or so solitary weeks of 1925 More began the notes that later were published as *Pages from an Oxford Diary*. As he looked back over the course of his life he saw "that through all the changes of belief and interest the old flame flickered within me, the hidden fire of religion which was kindled in my soul at birth. . . ." Burning brightly in his childhood, it was almost smothered by the romanticism and the rationalism of his adolescence and by the "miscellaneous curiosity" of his early manhood. "It flared up again when my curiosity waned, and at first tormented me with a vast uneasiness.[76] If life is an end in itself, then why do all singular lives conclude in a confession of futility? If these earthly forms are all, then why the ever-present sense of evanescence?

[75] To Irving Babbitt, Dec. 30, 1924.
[76] Cf. *POD*, xviii.

[226]

Is illusion the final word, and beyond the illusion nothing? Then began a passionate search to discover the eternal verities behind the veil—the realm of Ideas which Plato taught, and in which my soul could move, some day if not now, in liberated joy. I can say simply and without reservation that to this goal I attained, and that I shall end my days a conscious, as I was born, an unconscious, Platonist. The visible world of things has contracted into comparative insignificance save as a symbol of that which is unseen; the Ideal world has become the vivid reality upon which all my deeper emotions are centred. I have no valid doubt, only at whiles the impediments of a sluggish brain."[77]

"Only slowly did the incompetence of such a belief, in itself with no connecting link between the two realms, dawn upon me. It was just the perception of purpose in the evolution of the world, as something above and beyond the static imitation of Ideas, that finally led me to the quest of a dynamic, personal agent at work. That made me a better, as well as a more complete, Platonist, and it set me again on the road to Christianity. Now, the thought of a naked soul journeying forever on and on through inanimate Ideas, with no personal guide or consoler, with no glimpse of the majestic Spirit whose eternal home is there,—the thought of such a journey sends a shudder and a chill through me. I cry out: Lord, I believe, help thou mine unbelief!"[78]

". . . purpose implies . . . two things. It means an end consciously conceived and proposed; and it means obstacles and difficulties in the way of carrying out the proposed end. These are the two factors, as I see it, that distinguish evolution from a mere succession of events or from a static immediacy. And they are the factors that at the last will make teleology only another name for a true theism.[79] For the sense of design in the world as an unfolding purpose implies a person effecting his will through some obscurely resisting medium or material. In simpler language that would be God, but it would be a Creator stripped of

[77] *POD*, v, vi.   [78] *POD*, xv.   [79] Cf. *CF*, 70.

those paralysing terms of a metaphysical theology,—infinite, absolute, omnipotent, and the remainder brood of a licentious reason.

"I do not hold this as a proof of the existence of God; there is no proof. If another mind, studying the history of the earth and of humanity, does not receive that unshakable impression of purpose working itself out through thwarts and hindrances, or if he thinks purpose can be thinned down to an accidental emergence of new events, for him my argument will have no force; it is sufficient for me. It may come from an emotional reaction, from the imagination, or what you will—I care not."[80]

". . . I can find no key to the Incarnation unless it reveals God as a personality somehow involved in the failure of His own handiwork and somehow redeeming the evil of the world by participating in the penalties of imperfection."[81]

"I do not pretend to fathom the mystery of evil and pain, I leave them unexplained as part of the dark Necessity; but we know that in some way evil and involuntary pain are bound together, and we seem to see that in some way also evil may be redeemed by voluntary suffering. . . . I believe that on Calvary . . . the demands of Necessity were satisfied, the awful responsibility was acknowledged, the debt of creation was paid."[82]

"So was the Incarnation for us a work of vicarious atonement. This too I see dimly as part of the terrible Necessity. How else save by this divine condescension should we learn the full meaning of sin and holiness, and see how our deeds reach out in their consequences into the eternal world of the spirit, to the very heart of God?"[83]

"We cannot escape the ultimate responsibility of choosing our path, and no true man would wish to do so. But to know that we have a great Friend at our side who voluntarily shares with us the consequences of our faults, who will not abandon us though we err seventy times seven, who shows us that the evil

---

[80] *POD*, XIV. [81] *POD*, XXIV.
[82] *POD*, XXIII. [83] *POD*, XXIV.

we do is a breach of trust between person and person,—to know that is to gain a new insight into life and death, and to be inspired with new hopes; it may mean rebirth from above. O Lamb of God, that takest away the sins of the world!"[84]

On Lou's return from Princeton, where his "lectures on the Dogma of Evolution were a howling success, and drove the biologists to a frenzy of rage,"[85] the two brothers and their families spent the spring of 1925 in Italy and Greece. "Here I am at last in . . . Florence. . . . Only one thing is unexpected—the amount of beauty crowded together in this little place; it is astounding. . . . But I am puzzled by what I see—not the town itself, but the pictures. I cannot make out the mind and heart of these people. The Gothic I can understand, Oxford I can understand, and Greece, and Rome, and other things, but I am balked before a people who built San Marco and developed the Dominican discipline, and then adorned the cells with the pictures of Fra Angelico. What were the thoughts of the monks before those sweet, fragile angels and madonnas? It intrigues me. I suspect there is something incongruous and even wrong in the whole thing. In fact the whole Renaissance is something of a mystery, a kind of glinting and ephemeral transition that must fill a thoughtful mind almost with alarm. I do not think this is due to insensitiveness to beauty on my part, for I can feel the beauty of Greece and China to the full; it is something else— beauty without character behind it, which, when all is said, is *malsain*. There is character in the frescoes of Giotto and the early Italians; one sees it slowly slipping away and reaching its ebb in Leonardo—though I have not seen the Last Supper."[86]

"I cannot find the connecting link between the religion of the Middle Ages, or indeed of Christianity generally, and the peculiar beauty of the late fourteenth and fifteenth centuries. . . . I went out to see Berenson, at his request, and put the problem

[84] *POD*, xxv. Cf. *CF*, 105-06.
[85] To Irving Babbitt, March 7, 1925.
[86] To Alice More, March 14, 1925.

to him, but got no answer. With all his subtlety, he had not felt the incongruity at all. I was uneasy in Italy for this reason. Greece affects me differently. I go up on the Acropolis here, and at once I am a Greek. I can imagine myself in the Panathenaic procession winding up to the Parthenon; all the intervening ages are wiped out, there is nothing to trouble. . . . The Parthenon, as one sees it again and again, seems to grow larger and to take on almost a defiant aspect, as if it were planted there against all the threats of time. Standing before it, I lost every doubt and became assured in my mind that the world some day will return to its allegiance to Greece. This little folk, in their barren land, did something unique after all. But the best of our experiences was the trip to Delphi. The position of the town, high up on the slope of Parnassus, looking down over a great valley to Itea and the Gulf of Corinth, is beautiful beyond belief. And there one stood, at the centre of the world, as the Greeks believed, on the ruins of the temple where Apollo gave his oracles. I cannot tell you what I felt;[87] I hardly know myself. We all felt, without exception, that there was nothing to equal that place."[88]

"Rome I enjoyed. I don't know just why, for the city has very little beauty to show. In fact the Romans have about as vicious taste as any people in the world. St. Peter's affected me as perhaps the most monstrously vulgar exhibition of ugliness that I have ever seen. How anyone can be drawn to the Roman church by what he sees there, is beyond my comprehension. Nevertheless the city itself got hold of me; I felt it was a delightful place to live in. As a contrast I thought the Piazza [di] San Marco at Venice about the most magnificent and beautiful thing in Europe. The Duomo appealed to me with an inexpressible charm. Of all the pictures I saw the Mystical Crucifixion of Perugino touched my religious sensibility the most, and I sent home an excellent photograph in a hand-carved walnut frame representing the architectural framework. The sight of the picture, with the

[87] At Delphi, too, he wept.
[88] To Alice More, April 16, 1925.

adorable grace of the figures and the glimpse into a far spacious country, gives me a thrill every time I stand before it.[89] How did that man Perugino do it, for I believe he was anything but religious in his life. . . .

"When I left the family in Paris, I went straight to a house kept by a Mrs. Bishop in Shepton Mallet among the Somerset hills. The place was well kept, only a few 'paying guests,' and the country all about offered endless beautiful walks. But the house itself was right in the town with no view at all, and I found it very boresome to be polite. After two weeks I went, at the suggestion of Canon Went, to Malvern Wells. Here the hotel, which I had almost to myself, stood on the hillside overlooking the broad flat valley of the Severn. The scene from my window was marvellous with changing lights over the farms and hedges and groves.[90] After a while Net and the girls joined me there. We had separate bedrooms and a sitting-room, and altogether our stay was too short. A motor drive over to Hereford was about the loveliest I have ever taken. . . . The English churches and cathedrals were wonderfully attractive to me after the florid buildings of Italy. I revelled in their cool gray stone and lack of flummery."[91]

Before he and his family left Southampton August 3rd on the *Arabic*, he roomed at Balliol between July 24th and 27th for a joint session of the Aristotelian Society and the Mind Association. "The meeting . . . was . . . an expense of spirit and a waste of words. It confirmed me in the opinion that modern philosophy is an intellectual nuisance. I never in my life felt so much out of place and so hopelessly stupid as when attending these sessions."[92] "My own addition to the ματαιότης was to open a symposium of Plato and Aristotle as representatives of two modes of thought which I distinguish as 'philosophy' and 'metaphysics.' "[93]

[89] Cf. *DA*, 36-37.
[90] Cf. *POD*, xxviii, and *SAR*, 78.
[91] To Alice More, Aug. 14, 1925.
[92] To Irving Babbitt, Sept. 15, 1925.
[93] To Robert Shafer, Aug. 16, 1925.

Platonism to Christianity

Although in the notes for his talk More admitted in theory, "names philosophy & Metaph. arbitrary" for "2 modes of philos.," which seems to imply that discrimination between them depends on one's curiosity, purpose, vision, and blindness, nevertheless in practice he complained: "The distinction I draw between 'philosophy' and 'metaphysics' seems to me perfectly simple and clear,[94] and yet I cannot make anyone . . . understand me. There's something wrong; either I'm stupid or all the rest of the world is; and I haven't quite reached the point of setting myself *contra mundum*."[95] He did not hesitate, however, to charge his Oxford audience with "inability . . . to appreciate the point at issue. I suppose one should not expect a group of professional metaphysicians to admit out of hand that the labor of their lives is nothing more than an empty logomachy. . . . As for me, when the issue stands between the philosopher and the Philistine I am frankly with the Philistine, which may only mean that I am not a philosopher."[96]

Except for his weeks of reflection in England and his experiences at Stratford and Delphi, he acknowledged little value in "seeing an enormous mass of objects, most of which I shall speedily forget. At the end I came to recognize that my mentality is about the same as that of the bewildered shopkeeper from

[94] Cf. *P*, 240-41, and *RP*, 10, 340 ff.

[95] To Seward B. Collins, Dec. 8, 1930. The trouble lay not in More's stupidity nor the world's. As philosophy for him was overwhelmingly a personal matter, a way of salvation, his attempts to explain his convictions were hindered partly by his own intensity of feeling or lack of detachment, partly by a certain indifference or half-heartedness springing from the belief that unless a man himself recognizes reality no one else's efforts can greatly help him, and partly from the resulting disinclination to take the trouble to treat in a technical or conventional way the problems involved as formulated in his day. Chapter X of *Therapeia, Plato's Conception of Philosophy*, by Robert E. Cushman, Chapel Hill (University of North Carolina Press), 1958, a book that contains no reference to More despite several similarities of spirit in the interpretation of Platonism, probably makes clearer some of the reasons why More preferred Plato's philosophy to Aristotle's metaphysics than do More's discussions of the subject.

[96] To Robert Shafer, Nov. 8, 1925.

1922-1925

Oshkosh, who goes through galleries and cathedrals with a mute but eloquent eye upon his wife, as if to say: Oh when will you take me home out of all this?"[97]

[97] To Henry Holt, July [mistake for Aug.] 11, 1925.

12

PARTINGS (1925-1928)

HAVING passed the rest of August in Princeton and much of September at Essex, by October More sat again in his study at 245 Nassau Street, "buried in the Greek Fathers, and writing a book which nobody will want to read. We do fashion our lives in strange ways. I think if I had to shape mine over again, I should set out to be a thoroughgoing saint, at least so far as withdrawal from the world, or, if not that, a complete Epicurean. These halfway houses are always drafty and uncomfortable."[1]

"Probably I have told you that Krans in Paris has asked me to send over a selection of my essays, which he thinks he can get translated and published.[2] I have been going over the volumes for that purpose, and it has been a queer experience. They go back to 1904, the last volume being 1921. As I read I wonder where I got my knowledge, and that interests me. And then I find that my views, philosophical and religious, have changed surprisingly.[3] I could write an essay on that subject! It is not strange that readers who remember my 'Newman' (which I did not) should be rather disconcerted at the turn of thought in my *Christ of the New Testament*. But I think the grip of ideas is stronger in the later work, and represents my native bent better than the earlier essay. For one thing I see everywhere the traces of Babbitt's influence, until very recently, and though that influence was salutary in the main and helped to pull me out of the slough, it has certainly led me to emphasize several ideas which would have been quite secondary with me if I had developed more naturally."[4]

[1] To Henry Holt, Oct. 23, 1925. Mr. Holt died in 1926.
[2] Horatio S. Krans, associate director of the American University Union in Europe, did not succeed in getting the essays translated into French.
[3] Cf. *POD*, xxix.
[4] To Alice More, Nov. 3, 1925.

1925-1928

On Miss Katharine Babbitt's death in an automobile accident:

"November 27, 1925.

"Dear Babbitt,—

"Your news is heart-breaking indeed, it leaves me dumb, like Tiberius not knowing what to say and what not to say. At least I can respond to your words about Katharine; I was well enough acquainted with her to know how loyal and helpful a sister she had been, and how utterly unselfish she was. To me she can be a beautiful memory, but I understand what her loss is to you. These years that are coming now take away one thing after another, and to that we have to grow reconciled; but there is something unspeakably painful in a death, so sudden and so cruel and so needless. I have never been, am not now, able to take the common Christian view of these evils and say they must be providential and somehow for our good. Often they seem to me to bring irreparable loss. But on the other hand I cannot look at them as the Buddhist does and regard them as the essential of life. They strike me rather as hateful accidents, or as the working of some no less hideous fatality, breaking through and thwarting the real purpose of the world. Strange as it may sound, they have come to be for me in that way the last bulwark of faith and hope. Taken with the large beauty and many benevolences of the world they force me to believe that the universe is not governed by a dull, inhuman, passionless law, nor is yet a thing of chance and blank illusion, but is the result of purpose, understood quite anthropomorphically, working through mysterious obstacles of evil.

"But I am not in a mood to preach or to philosophize, least of all to you. I am sure you know how deeply I sympathize with you. There is no one in the world whose sorrow would mean so much to me. Nettie desires me to express her sympathy also.

Faithfully yours,
Paul E. More."

[235]

Partings

"Day before yesterday Capps called on me and made me a definite offer to take a course in Greek—Plato and Hellenistic philosophy—in the Graduate School. I accepted provisionally, and proposed that I should also offer an undergraduate course in Plato. He was more than willing, and the matter has gone through. I am transferred to the classical department, and am to have $2500 for the semester, beginning next year.[5] I told him that I had been groaning under the difficulty of teaching Greek philosophy to students who had no Greek, but that now I should probably suffer a like agony from students who knew no philosophy. My fate seems to be a hard one. Last night Bowman gave a dinner to the philosophic department, and I made my farewells. They are a pretty fair lot, and I hate to leave them."[6]

More changed from one department to another chiefly because, no matter how much philosophy may have been to him a secular piety or "a psychological therapeutic, a private bulwark against the ravages of spiritual and political *Angst*,"[7] he was not a "professional" philosopher—not a Doctor of Philosophy of the then Teutonic type, who, he thought, exchanged precision and thoroughness for imagination and significance. Platonic scholars like John Burnet, Léon Robin, Paul Shorey, and A. E. Taylor received his *Greek Tradition* with respectful appreciation and many reserves.[8] They or others complained of his relative

[5] ". . . something more than double the money I now get . . ." [To Alice More, July 30 (mistake for Jan. 31), 1926.]

[6] To Louis T. More, Jan. 30, 1926.

[7] "The Roman Stoic," *The Times Literary Supplement*, July 18, 1958, no. 2942, p. 408.

[8] Patient and generous with those who genuinely and privately sought his opinion, as a rule More did not allow published comments about himself or his work, no matter how misleading, to draw him into controversy. But in his run-down condition in 1917 and 1918, when querulousness somewhat marred his correspondence, he wrote to the editor of *The Times Literary Supplement* an over-sensitive complaint (not to be printed but to be forwarded to the reviewer) about the "dishonesty," as he called it, of the notice of his *Platonism* in the April 25, 1918, issue of the paper. The reviewer, A. E. Taylor, answered him with cogent specificness in a sharp letter of June 14, 1918, which More described as "a furious reply." [To Louis T. More, Oct. 26, 1922.]

neglect of Plato's ideas about art, mathematics, education, and politics; his inadequate attention to the relation of the *Dialogues* to their historical environment; his failure to give due weight to interpretations of Plato by his nearest successors; and his warping hostility towards the mysticism of Plotinus. They questioned the validity of an ethic dependent on feeling, even on one so exalted as happiness, peace, or rapture, noting that the easily satisfied are more prone to it than are those of sensitive and conscientious temperament.[9] Here and there they would light on an error of fact or of interpretation, one of More's most characteristic being his magnification of the negative sign that warned Socrates of ill consequences into a spiritual intuition of right and wrong. More apparently never retracted this imposition of an Oriental inner check, or of Babbitt's *frein vital*, upon Platonism, but thereafter he ceased to emphasize it. And many more personal animadversions were or could be made about the Princeton lecturer's recourse to "lower and higher reason" and to what Shorey called the "vocabulary of mysticism and irrationality";[10] about his tendency to beg questions by assuming his point of view to be a "superrational intuition"; about his uncritical attitude towards "spiritual affirmation" and the alleged data of experience; about his distaste for what he called "metaphysics" and his inclination to damn rather than to refute certain opinions by attaching that epithet to them; and about the impression sometimes inadvertently conveyed that his distinctions and the patterns of thought that he utilized to order his complex material were distinctions and patterns of thought used

[9] This objection applies more to the *Shelburne Essays*, the first edition of *P*, and *RP* than it does to More's final position: ". . . not happiness but the potentiality of happiness should be the immediate aim of conduct. . . . he who demands the actuality of happiness here and now is doomed to . . . disappointment. . . . Plato . . . restored the judgements of God in another world to their place as executors of the law of righteousness and as the everlasting keepers of happiness." [*SAR*, 87. Cf. *P*, 90; *RP*, 46; and *CW*, 254-60.]

[10] Paul Shorey's review of *P*, *N*, Feb. 21, 1918, vol. 106, no. 2747, p. 210.

by Plato himself. Even More's virtues had their defects: in correctly accenting the significance of morality for Plato, he tended to underestimate the importance of Plato's many other interests; his own dualistic point of view made him keenly aware of the Hegelian vagaries of interpreters of Plato like Green, Caird, and Bosanquet,[11] and rightly led him to stress Plato's otherworldliness, but it also caused him to picture Plato as being as deeply concerned as himself in a subjective moral dualism.

No wonder a critic to whom we are indebted for some of these less debatable strictures should conclude that "as an expositor and interpreter of the religious thought of Plato, More is thoroughly unreliable. He obtrudes his own preconceptions upon Plato not to illuminate him, but to distort him almost beyond recognition. To interpret Plato exclusively in terms of a moralistic and obscurantistic dualism has nothing to recommend it except the quality of being an ingenious *tour de force*. . . . More is no better an expositor of Christianity than he is of Platonism, and for the same reason: he brings to his subject neither the erudition nor the originality required."[12]

That this critic could devote a chapter to More, as he does to each of Dean Inge, A. E. Taylor, William Temple, Whitehead, and Santayana, as persons influenced by Plato and playing prominent parts in recent Anglo-American religious thought, suggests that More's importance is not confined to exposition. If allowance is made, as it must and can be made in regard to any in-

[11] "At one moment in the *Republic* Plato was evidently drawing very near to a monistic metaphysic. His modification of this monistic idealism by the theism of the *Timaeus, Philebus,* and *Laws* x is one of the most significant and surprising events in the history of philosophy; and also it is, for very obvious reasons, surprisingly overlooked or viciously interpreted away by commentators of the nineteenth century who are almost all, despite their occasional protests, dominated by Hegel. It is a curious fact that Aristotle, *in his religious metaphysic,* derives from *Republic* vi and *Laws* xii, and brushes aside the intervening position of the *Timaeus* and *Laws* x." [To Irving Babbitt, Nov. 27, 1929. Cf. *CW,* 251-61, and *SAR,* 68-71.]

[12] *Platonism in Recent Religious Thought,* by William D. Geoghegan, New York (Columbia University Press), 1958, pp. 45, 51.

terpreter, for the effect of his preconceptions, to the extent that More felt obliged to be an expositor of Plato rather than to speak for himself, his erudition, despite some inevitable gaps, is as dependable as that of most reputable Platonic scholars. Nor does he lack the desirable amount and kind of originality attached to independence of judgement and deep concern for his subject. As he would have balked at being merely a translator of Plato, so the intensity of his individuality and the width and vigor of his interests caused him to subordinate exposition to assimilation. His first concern lay less in the letter than in the spirit—in making vital in current terms to himself and to others certain aspects of Platonism that he considered spiritually nourishing—in being in his own way and to some degree a Platonist rather than in parroting the master. His treatment of Platonic Ideas, for example, is "thoroughly confused,"[13] if one imagines it to be primarily an exercise in analysis, an attempt to dissect minutely what they once meant to Plato rather than to convey the emotional power they can now have for us. "The Platonic ideas are at bottom no empty abstractions of logic, but a searching vision of 'the heavenly life.' "[14] Probably the consensus of his best qualified critics is that he enriches as well as obscures a literal interpretation of Plato (as far as one is possible) by reflections and fancies, by wisdom and errors, drawn from his own vast reading and study.[15] His appeal here, as for better or worse in most of his writings, is predominantly personal: "What have we to do with the discordant voices of the world? I alone speak to you alone, and unless the solitary witness within you con-

[13] *Ibid.*, p. 166.

[14] Quoted from *John Inglesant* in More's review, "Fixed Points of Light," of a new impression of the *Dialogues* of Plato translated by B. Jowett, *New York Herald Tribune* Books, Section VI, p. 5, Nov. 29, 1925.

[15] "I should like to make it clear beyond all question," A. E. Taylor, for example, despite his reserves wrote in "a laudatory notice of *The Religion of Plato* . . . in which he virtually apologized for the tone of his previous review of the *Platonism*" [to Irving Babbitt, Feb. 9, 1923], "that I fully sympathize with Mr. More's central position. . . ." [*Mind*, Oct. 1922, new series, vol. 3, p. 518.]

fesses to my words, I speak to no purpose."[16] To the extent
that the solitary witness does so respond, the faults in More's
treatment of Platonism may be compatible with what Robin
called a *"valeur originale et puissante."*[17]

Not the discordant voices of the world but technical questions
of philosophy brought to him by his students, for which in many
cases he did not have the required erudition and which as often
as not simply bored him, caused More to switch to the department of classics. From a narrowly pedagogical view his decision
might not have been regretted. Instead of "cramming" his boys
and testing them every few days, he lectured and talked delightfully for half a term or more. When he belatedly examined them,
the revelation of their ignorance and of his negligence in meeting it would, by their anxiety and his asperity, disturb the tenor
of the remaining classes. His colleagues in the department of
philosophy were loath, however, to be deprived of his "un-
usually full and fine personality," his "rounded enjoyment of all
the best features of life," his high degree of practical efficiency,
and his broad and deep learning. Regardless of their theoretical
differences, most of them would probably have concurred with
Dean Andrew F. West's statement about More: "Never have I
met a man more completely and wholesomely intellectual," and
with Dean Gauss's assertion: "As a human and a social being
I know very few people who are personally more genuine and
really attractive."[18]

Having leased 245 Nassau Street to Professor Kenneth Mc-
Kenzie, More rented, at Mrs. Babbitt's suggestion, the house of
Professor James Hardy Ropes at 13 Follen Street, Cambridge—
"right in the centre of things yet very quiet," the street in which
he used to visit the Goodwins in his "old Harvard days."[19]

[16] *RP*, 292, quoting Socrates.
[17] Quoted and repudiated in *Platonism in Recent Religious Thought*,
p. 45.
[18] *The Papers of Christian Gauss*, edited by Katherine Gauss Jackson
and Hiram Haydn, New York (Random House), 1957, p. 278.
[19] To Alice More, Nov. 3, 1925.

In addition to his three courses—two at Harvard (one on Plato to about a dozen undergraduates, another on Hellenistic philosophies to about twenty people, half of them graduate students, the rest hearers) and one at Radcliffe ("Greek 8" to "two schoolmarms . . . and a professor's wife"[20])—More made a few speeches. "The other day I met a joint meeting of the Classical Club and Modern Languages Conference, to whom I unburdened myself of my indignation over the present system of teaching English literature in our graduate schools.[21] My diatribe awaked sympathetic echoes among the students, and won me round applause. My next appearance will be before the graduates of the Theological School on their return for Visitation Week."[22] "Dean Sperry asked me to address them on the subject of Individualism and the Church, and as my wisdom seemed to him to be worth $100, I consented."[23] "He informed me that their graduates are a good deal worried over the sort of impasse and sterility to which the conclusions of New England individualism had brought them. I said that my opinions on that head might be summed up in the advice to go over to the Episcopal Church. He thought such counsel would be, under the circumstances, neither helpful nor palatable."[24]

That winter in Cambridge Babbitt, then in mourning for his sister, called on him almost every evening.[25] Formerly, when they had more closely agreed, Babbitt's method of argument, which was to storm about, stooping slightly, with strong changes in his facial expression, and to shout down his opponent, had been somewhat less exhausting because the barrage fell elsewhere. But their estrangement in regard to religion took on a poignancy proportional to the depth of their friendship. Frequently they discussed Wordsworth, the spell of whose poetry,

20 To Irving Babbitt, Jan. 8, 1926.
21 Cf. *DA*, 75-76.
22 To Prosser Hall Frye, March 28, 1926.
23 To Alice More, April 27, 1926.
24 To Prosser Hall Frye, March 28, 1926.
25 Cf. *OBH*, 34.

Partings

Babbitt believed, concealed unsound thought. More, on the contrary, began to suspect that Wordsworth had moral and religious values that Babbitt did not appreciate. "I can convince the whole world," Babbitt bellowed from the doorway one rainy night, waving his umbrella at More and talking with the exaggeration they occasionally assumed, "but I cannot convince you!" When he seemed about to go, "How about a little cheese?" his host would ask, and the guest would stay an hour longer until More walked home with him.

Despite his disappointment at More's lapse into Christianity, Babbitt, who was ever recommending his friend's books and ever admiring his style, sent to him for literary advice one of his own students, "a pretty and charming poetess from Radcliffe,"[26] named Roberta Swartz. "Now," More asked her when they first met, "have you any religion?" And, in view of the surfeit of secular and the dearth of religious poetry, he suggested she might do well to express her faith, if only in simple couplets.[27]

In May he gave two more addresses, one to the Harvard Philosophical Club on "The Demon of the Absolute,"[28] the other to the Harvard Classical Club on humanism's battle against romanticism and humanitarianism and on religion's battle against naturalism and religiosity. By religiosity he meant "a luxury of emotion" that fails to convert conduct and character[29] —"something that will give the moral warrant and the spiritual peace afforded . . . by Christianity, yet without surrendering to the Christian dogma,—that is to say . . . a purely psychological substitute for a religion which demands objective and concrete faith. . . ."[30]

[26] To Louis T. More, June 22, 1926.
[27] In similar vein More wrote on June 24, 1929, to Austin Warren: "Literary criticism from a religious point of view is almost a virgin field in English, and it might bear a rich harvest."
[28] This address of May 3, 1926, like his talk at Oberlin in 1923 (cf. p. 214 above), emphasized the need of dogma (especially the dogma of the divinity and the humanity of Christ) as a defence against the excesses of reason.
[29] Cf. *OBH*, 72.   [30] To Robert Shafer, June 20, 1926. Cf. *CW*, 8.

1925-1928

Someone mentioned Babbitt "with Kittredge and G. F. Moore and Pound as the four outstanding scholars of the university. My reply was that Kittredge, the great English scholar, had reduced the teaching of literature to a killing pedantry, that Moore taught the history of religions without, so far as one can see, a spark of religion in his soul,[31] that Pound at the head of the Law School was undermining the very principles of law, and that only Babbitt had a true message for the hungry student."[32]

"Princeton looks very lovely, but somehow I return with rather a sinking heart. I shall undoubtedly miss the intellectual stimulus of Cambridge. Towards the last Babbitt softened so much and seemed to cling to my society so earnestly, that I suffered a pang at tearing myself away. When all deductions are made he is one man in a million. I shall meet no intellect in Princeton to which I can defer.[33]

"To pass the time I am working hard at the revision of my MS. [of *Christ the Word*]. But, do you know, I cannot for the life of me, get up any genuine enthusiasm for the work. I keep asking myself *cui bono*."[34]

As the greater part of *Hellenistic Philosophies* concerns conflicting developments of Platonism, so most of *Christ the Word* concerns heresies that transformed the unrationalized monotheism of the Old Testament into a monistic theism and that sought to reconcile such a theism with the New Testament's evidences for the humanity and the divinity of Christ—itself "an insoluble enigma of faith," which More maintained should be believed

[31] Cf. "Religions without Religion," More's unsigned review of *The History of Religions*, by George Foot Moore, *The Villager*, Jan. 24, 1920, vol. 3, no. 34, p. 152.
[32] To Percy H. Houston, July 6, 1926.
[33] "It is disheartening to think that in this whole university I can go to no single person for intelligent consideration of the matters in which I am interested. The lack of any such companionship makes the contacts of life very superficial and unsatisfactory." [To Archibald Allan Bowman, June 10, 1929.]
[34] To Alice More, July 7, 1926.

or rejected according to its "conformity with, or . . . repugnance to, the deepest intuition of our spiritual experience."[35] Every way that the heretics tried to reconcile the Incarnation, "that 'thing truly paradoxical' as Athanasius[36] admitted, with the monistic demands of reason . . . ended in logical confusion and moral disaster. . . . There was needed just such a statement of orthodoxy as that provided by" the Council of Chalcedon in 451—"a formula which, in hard, precise, immitigable terms, should set a check upon the claims of reason to extend the faith in one direction to the exclusion of the other. It had come to this pass: either the central fact of Christianity had to be abandoned, or such claims of reason had to be transcended."[37] The Council decided "on two affirmations—the affirmation of the duality of natures, and that of the unity of person. That was all, and by the mercy of Providence there was no more."[38]

In the Incarnation thus described More found "the authority of revelation from above" confirming "the plausibility of persuasion from below"[39]—"the fulfilment of Hebrew prophecy," as Christians have claimed, and, what has rarely been so zealously asserted, "the consummation of Greek philosophy."[40] One of the senses in which he describes how the Incarnation may be thought of as a consummation of Platonism springs from "the assimilation of the personal Logos with the genuine Idealism of the Academy," whereby "the doctrine of Ideas is, as it were, illuminated from two sides. On the one hand Plato had always insisted that we know Ideas, and only them, yet he had never, unless through an obscure myth, been able to give a satisfactory account of the manner in which we possess this knowledge. Now the Word of God, as Wisdom itself and Beauty itself and Holiness itself, as the way and the truth and the life, had shown itself embodied in a human character. So and only so can we really see the Ideas, at least in our mortal state; and so we saw them in Jesus."[41] ". . . in this personification of Ideas in the

---

[35] *CW*, 132. [36] Cf. *CW*, 181. [37] *CW*, 240. [38] *CW*, 247-48.
[39] *CW*, 29. [40] *CW*, 249; cf. *ibid.*, pp. 9, 12, 84. [41] *CW*, 262-63.

divine Logos, while they yet, as the impersonal law of justice and beauty, continue to be entities by their own right, and in this symbolical use of Ideas as the place and furniture, so to speak, of the spiritual life of the soul in communion with other souls and with God, we have the fine flower of Platonism blossoming after long centuries in a strange garden."[42]

For the infant Church the relationship between the Father and the Son was the main theological question, the Holy Ghost not becoming personified in trinitarian doctrine until early in the third century.[43] Though much that More wrote "in regard to the Trinity would be acceptable to the most sensitive orthodoxy . . . orthodox historians would insist that the dogma of the Trinity, though not fully comprehended or formally defined by the early theologians, is implicit in their words, and that it was the proper office of the Church, under the guidance of the Spirit in question, to develop and elucidate the sacred truth. That, obviously, is a thesis not easily settled or even discussed. To me it seems quite plain that the dogma has no justification in the words of Jesus or in Scripture, that it was forced upon the Church by the mythopoeic tendency of the age, and that it introduced needless perplexities into theology. It seems to me equally clear that the rigid personification of the Holy Ghost is at bottom even unchristian, since it tends to conceal the true nature and function of the spirit as the power of God manifesting Himself in the world, and as the voice of God speaking to the spirit of man and so opening a mystic channel of communion between the divine and the human. In this way only is the majesty of the Holy Ghost reverently maintained, and its importance magnified, as that attribute of God whereon the very life of the Church and the validity of true religion hang. So taken, the trinitarian *formula* may be used in worship with a force and meaning which have almost been lost under the sway of a wrongly schematized theology."[44]

[42] *CW*, 265; cf. *CF*, 234, 308.
[43] Cf. *CW*, 116, 127.   [44] *CW*, 129-31; cf. *ibid.*, p. 117.

Partings

"Shortly after Chalcedon the scholasticism of Aristotelian logic, hitherto the weapon of heresy, was definitely introduced into orthodox theology. . . . That way lay the devious course of medieval scholasticism, the top-heavy metaphysics of Thomas Aquinas, and the Nessus shirt of irrational rationalism from which Rome can escape only by a miracle."[45] ". . . no more vital task confronts the Church today than to recognize the urgent necessity of insisting on the unreserved acceptance of the one dogma of the Incarnation as the definite, clear, and common mark of a Christian, while leaving to the conscience of each individual how far he will interpret the accessory articles of faith as literal or symbolical, as fact or poetry," as "essential and permanent and immutable" or as "that which must change with the changing modes of thought."[46]

In August and September at Essex despite running into a ditch More gradually learned to "feel pretty safe at the wheel" of his pheasant green Dodge touring car with buff top. "I detest the machine. While driving one has to sit rigidly with eyes fixed on the ground and mind centred on a horrid combination of levers. . . .

"After a house full of company we are now alone and quiet. Alice goes over to Greensborough next week for a visit. . . .[47] I am reading Ruggiero's *Storia della Filosofia Contemporanea*, and really the metaphysics since Kant is about the most futile and exasperating product of the human brain. I am utterly at a loss to understand how men, highly educated and well endowed with brains, write seriously and read seriously books in which the hoariest old fallacies of logic are concealed—scarcely concealed—under barbarous verbiage."[48]

[45] *CW*, 244-45; cf. *HP*, 214-15.
[46] *CW*, 275-76; cf. *CF*, 76, 84.
[47] When she visited the Gausses in Greensboro, Vermont, whom a week before the Mores had entertained in Essex, Alice met an Englishman, Edmund Gilbert Dymond, who had been taking graduate courses in physics at Princeton.
[48] To Alice More, Aug. 25, 1926.

"If I may say it," her father wrote on August 18, 1926, to Darrah More, then happily looking after young cripples at the Children's Island Sanitorium in Marblehead, Massachusetts, "I do not see how anyone can go into the sort of work you are at without growing utterly hardened or utterly sentimentalized, unless he, or she, brings to it some spirit of religion. And I have seen these effects often enough. Unless, to use words from which as you know I rather shrink, one can bring to such charities something more than mere sympathy for suffering, some faith in the larger issues of another world and some love of God—without that such work in the end has a deplorable effect. And there's my little sermon."

Besides ferociously felling trees, he put the finishing touches on a revised or second edition of his *Platonism*. "As I read the book over it seems to me for the most part hard to understand and stiff in construction, with the exception of two or three chapters. I shall add a second (short) preface, admitting that in some respects the ideas of the book are not in accord with the later volumes of the series."[49] The change in attitude, he noted in his thanks to Babbitt for criticizing the new preface, occurred "between the writing of the *Platonism* and of *The Christ of the New Testament*. The former volume was composed from my reserve of study, and presents almost completely the same point of view as the sixth volume of *Shelburne Essays*."[50]

From Essex to Dublin, New Hampshire, where for a few days he talked with Babbitt, played cards with Mrs. Babbitt, and chattered with her four year old nephew, More went on to Cambridge for the International Congress of Philosophy. "I managed to listen through about two lectures a day; but it took heroic resignation on my part. Really, this philosophical game is ended. Some of the papers . . . were just rotten; and I heard

[49] To Irving Babbitt, July 23, 1926.
[50] To the same, Aug. 29, 1926.

nothing, absolutely nothing, that had the slightest value. . . .
The pleasure of the Congress was in meeting the men."[51]

"Stuart Sherman's death shocked me. He had gone into paths
which seemed to me a betrayal of his gifts, yet after all he was
a writer born and could marshal phrases. At one time we were
very close together and I was his first editor, in fact discovered
him; but he was restive under the abuse heaped on him as associated with my name, and perhaps was driven further in the
way of revolt for this reason than he otherwise would have gone.
That of course was some years ago, when my name was taken
seriously enough by the roaring young bloods of the press to be
hated.

"The *Revue de Paris* has asked me to contribute an article on
present tendencies in American literature. After some hesitation, owing to the fact that I really am not competent to deal
with the subject, I accepted; and now I am wondering what I
shall say. I wish," he told Shafer, "I could talk with you about
Dreiser, Cabell, Dos Passos, Lewis *et id genus omne*."[52]

"Have you by chance read Dreiser's *Book About Myself*?"
Paul asked Louis. "I have got hold of it by way of posting myself up, and have found it really very interesting. For one thing
he was in St. Louis, on the *Globe-Democrat* and the *Republic*,
just when we were leaving the city. His account of the place,
the streets and buildings, and such men as 'little Mack' of the
Globe, is amazingly realistic and true, and brings back the whole
time to me in startling fashion. I am sure you will enjoy reading
it. Another book I have got half way into is *Jurgen*, which I find
tantalizingly dull—I say tantalizing because it always just misses
being good."[53]

"I feel very much as the traitor must have felt in the old days

[51] To the same, Sept. 19, 1926.
Later in the year F.C.S. Schiller and J. A. Smith lectured at Princeton, the former staying with More, who gave dinners for them both.
[52] To Robert Shafer, Oct. 8, 1926. The order of these two paragraphs
has here been reversed.
[53] To Louis T. More, Nov. 21, 1926. Cf. *DA*, 65.

when his hands were hitched to one horse and his feet to another, and then they pulled. Why I ever promised to write on modern American fiction is more than I know—except that I. B. and Net overpersuaded me. To read Gregory Nyssen and write about the Logos in the morning, and then to pass the evening trying to make out what Sherwood Anderson and Dreiser and Cabell stand for, is a soul- and body-wracking distraction. And I get no forarder. These Americans perplex and trouble me. It would be so easy to condemn them *en bloc* as unclean and unartistic; and it would be equally easy to praise them lustily for their frankness and Americanism and other qualities which most critics find in them so abundantly—but to strike the balance! and to see what it is all derived from and pointed towards!"[54]

". . . the snow has been wonderfully beautiful on the trees and vines. The view from my bedroom has been all a white glory morning after morning. I say to myself, that is the breath of the λόγος transmuting the world into loveliness."[55]

"Mercier[56] has sent me the MS. of his book on Brownell, Babbitt, and myself—at least the sections on the two latter. It is laudatory enough in all conscience. He really takes my work as supplementing Babbitt's and giving the necessary religious content to humanism. . . . It will be a great thing for me, if he gets a publisher, as I hope he will."[57]

[54] To Alice More, Dec. 4, 1926. On Jan. 18, 1927, he sent off to Paris his article (translated into French by Louis Cons, an associate professor of modern languages at Princeton University), which was published as "Le Courant moderne dans la Littérature américaine" in *Revue de Paris*, Dec. 15, 1927, 34 année, tome vi, pp. 858-79, and later in *DA*, 53-76.

[55] To Alice More, Jan. 18, 1927.

[56] Professor Louis Joseph Alexandre Mercier, of Harvard, in "The Challenge of Paul Elmer More" (*The Harvard Graduates' Magazine*, June, 1926, vol. 34, pp. 556-69) wrote the first comprehensive article published about the philosophy of the *Shelburne Essays*. In his chapter on More in the book referred to above—*Le Mouvement Humaniste aux États-Unis* (1928)—he presented also a summary of More's religious development from *P* through *CNT*.

[57] To Alice More, Feb. 3, 1927. At Babbitt's suggestion and in return

Partings

"I have just been reading a review of Newton's life and work in the London *Times Literary Supplement* for March 17, and it has given me an idea. The writer of the article . . . remarks that we have no satisfactory book on Newton. Now it occurs to me," Paul informed Louis, "that here is your chance. The subject is just suited to you—much better in my opinion than a general history of science or of physics. It is interesting from many points of view. His scientific achievement can be expounded as a consummation of much previous work; it can be made the text for a critical discussion of present-day theories. Personally Newton seems to offer a very pretty psychological and religious problem. It seems to me that here you have the chance of your life."[58]

"The winds are let loose and the floodgates are opened," Paul announced to Louis, who had immediately adopted his suggestion about writing a biography of Newton, "and I dwell in a house built on the sand. Which is semi-biblical language to express my feelings at the thought that both of the girls are planning to be married within a few months. . . . Both the men are acceptable—more than that. Harry Fine[59] is straight and clean and entirely trustworthy, and he has every prospect of succeeding as a schoolmaster. Gilbert Dymond,[60] from all I can hear, is an exceptionally brilliant student and good fellow. He has a university demonstratorship at [St. John's College] Cambridge next year. All this is satisfactory, and of course one cannot but be glad to think that one's daughters are to be happily married—only somehow the happiness doesn't extend to the father. . . . the expected sale of this place has fallen through, but we hope for other offers, and meanwhile we are buying one

---

for some copies of Mercier's book, More contributed one hundred dollars towards the cost of its publication.

[58] To Louis T. More, April 1, 1927.

[59] Then taught history and mathematics at Princeton Preparatory School, where he later followed his father as headmaster.

[60] ". . . a physicist engaged in the metaphysical disintegration of the atom. . . ." [To Percy H. Houston, July 3, 1928.]

hundred feet in Battle Road[61] preparatory to building when the time comes. But most disturbing of all is Net's condition. She has been suffering a good deal of pain for ten or twelve days with a renewal of pyelitis, and both eyes are affected so that she cannot read at all. We have a trained nurse, and are simply waiting. . . .

"Saturday my lectures end, and I shall plunge instanter into the writing of a volume of Shelburne Essays. I must keep my mind occupied. Meanwhile I practise two or three hours a day on that flute you helped me to buy, and am already playing simple airs with the piano.

"I feel like Nero fiddling over the flames of Rome."[62]

August and September More passed at Essex, the two months being "about the laziest, intellectually, of my life."[63] He "did however go through Cicero's *De Senectute*, which is fine rhetoric but quite misses the real sting of old age," and "was annoyed to find *The Georgics* difficult."[64] As Mrs. More, who stopped at a hospital in Philadelphia before going to "The Cedars," was obliged to rest almost continuously and as suffusions of blood caused by the kidneys made her almost blind, her husband "had to take in hand all her business correspondence" and give "a good deal of time to reading [Trollope] aloud to her."[65] Early in August "little" Alice returned to them from about half a year in Europe, and her fiancé joined them later that month.

On September 1, 1927, at St. John's Episcopal church in Essex, which More and his family attended during the summers, he gave his daughter, Mary Darrah, in marriage to Harry Boehme Fine, son of John Burchard Fine, of Princeton, the Reverend Leonard Hodgson officiating.

---

[61] On June 25, 1927, Howard Russell Butler and his wife, for $7,000 conveyed by deed to Henrietta More the lot known as 59 Battle Road, Princeton, with a frontage of one hundred feet on the northwesterly side of the road and a depth of two hundred twenty-five feet.
[62] To Louis T. More, May 19, 1927.
[63] To Irving Babbitt, Sept. 26, 1927.
[64] *Ibid.*
[65] To Prosser Hall Frye, Aug. 26, 1927.

Partings

A few days later Mrs. More had an acute attack of nephritis. At home in Princeton by September 25th, concealing her weakness she lunched and dined downstairs and bore her share of entertaining those who streamed in before her second daughter's wedding. Two or three of her friends called regularly to read to her, "so that her days will not be so intolerably dull."[66] Apparently they read little; for though at times pain overcame her, the warmth, decision, and gaiety of her vivid conversation generally prevailed. She may even have let them come in order to lessen her husband's feeling of responsibility for her and to give him an opportunity to plunge into the volume of essays, *The Demon of the Absolute*, which he wanted to have "ready for the press by Christmas."[67]

Some years before, when college or their other interests had deprived him of his daughters' company and had reduced the social sufficiency of his own hearth, More became one of The Gentlemen Dowagers. He, Christian Gauss,[68] Duane Reed Stuart (a professor of classics), and Julian Street, the writer, who, after he went to Paris, was succeeded in 1927 by Percy Addison Chapman (an assistant professor of modern languages), used to meet every fortnight or so about half past eight at one another's house for five rubbers of bridge topped off by sandwiches and drinks. Talk was the *pièce de résistance*—sincere, humorous, free—the cards merely serving as garnish. More played rather a cagey game of poker bridge, relying less on metaphysical conventions than on the certainties, or at any rate the certitudes, of intuition, judgement, and bluff. Claiming he must see red at least once a night, without warning he would bid wildly, bringing his partner crashing down with him in outrageous and hilarious defeat.

But at this anxious time he needed something else to occupy his mind. "I hope that you and Dennis[69] have taken up the

[66] To Louis T. More, Sept. 29, 1927.   [67] *Ibid.*
[68] Cf. *The Papers of Christian Gauss*, p. 278.
[69] Holmes Van Mater Dennis, III, was an assistant professor of classics at Princeton University.

matter of a religious or theological group and that you will see
me about it before long," he urged Paul Robinson Coleman-
Norton.[70] "I rather think Longwell[71] would be a good associate.
He knows the medieval field pretty well, and is personally concerned with religious questions." The little group, including also
Albert M. Friend, Jr. (an assistant professor of art and archaeology), Theodore M. Greene (an assistant professor of philosophy), and Robert Scoon (an associate professor of philosophy),
met once a month to discuss a paper on a religious topic that
happened to interest its author. At the first of their few meetings
(for they talked themselves out in the course of a year), at 245
Nassau Street, Mr. More, as the oldest member and the organ-
izer of the group, "pontificated." Though various people read
papers and though they met in their respective lodgings, so inevitable was the deference shown to him and so definite and
articulate were his convictions that, for all his efforts to keep
the talk "open and lively," the meetings usually culminated in a
"clear, competent, forceful" but "rather dogmatic restatement
by Mr. More of his own position on the question at issue."

That autumn he saw his *Christ the Word* published in September, read Babbitt's manuscript of an article on Buddhism,[72]
played his flute whenever Darrah could accompany him on the
piano, and, moved by "that last infirmity" more than by a nine
cent royalty on any volume sold, kept several series of the *Shelburne Essays* in print at his own expense.

On December 17th his daughter Alice was married at home
to Gilbert Dymond. About a month later, on Saturday, Jan-

[70] In a letter of Oct. 12, 1927, to this assistant professor of classics.
[71] Horace Craig Longwell, associate professor of philosophy.
[72] "What is the permanent, or is there any permanent, that Buddha
offers when the impermanent is escaped? Does Buddhism totally elimi-
nate the sense of cosmic *purpose*? How is the doctrine of sympathy or
love related to his doctrine of the will? What is the passage from inner
to outer ἐνέργεια? The first of these is of course the fundamental question, and is scarcely quieted by declaring Buddha's repudiation of metaphysical curiosity. He should have gone further and confined karma to
this life only, or he should have gone further in the other direction and
left room for a continuing ψυχή." [To Irving Babbitt, Oct. 12, 1927.]

Partings

uary 14, 1928, "Nettie was struck by an acute attack of nephritis with dilatation of the heart. She rallied, but had a second attack Sunday, and since then has been gradually failing. The first days were very distressing. . . . Fortunately Darrah was near and of course has been sleeping here in the house. I don't know what I should have done without her."[73]

While a day nurse and a night nurse watched the unconscious patient, anyone who then found Mr. More reading aloud poems and bits of Plato to Darrah might never have guessed their suffering, so determined was he to keep weakening emotions at bay. On the night of January 20th he came downstairs dry eyed and bewildered. At dinner with Darrah, Louis More, and Harry Fine, he asked for a little whisky. The sounds made overhead by the undertakers put him on edge. He talked wildly or sat in black depression.

On Monday afternoon, the 23rd, Paul Clement Matthews, the bishop of New Jersey, and the Reverend Hugh H.F.O. Morton, the assistant at Trinity Church, Princeton, conducted Mrs. More's funeral at 245 Nassau Street, which was followed by interment in the old cemetery on Witherspoon Street, Princeton.

[73] To Irving Babbitt, "Friday morning" [probably Jan. 20, 1928].

13

RECOVERY (1928)

"WHAT one has to struggle against is the evil which the Greek Christians called ἀκηδία, or accidie in Chaucer's English, the feeling of depressed indolence," so More described it to Trent, "the terrible disillusion of discovering that one's efforts to do anything are really not worth while, that the prizes we strive for bring no satisfaction. That is an evil that age alone can bring; it becomes acute when such a loss comes to one as you and I have suffered. However I am not going to succumb to the temptation. I have withal a strong faith in that all-surrounding otherworld which Plato talked about as Ideas, and believe that our true reward is 'as he pronounces lastly on each deed.' But we need our friends to help us in our resolution, and I have always counted you as a very close friend, despite the fact that we saw each other so seldom.

"Darrah and her husband have come to live with me until I can dispose of this place and build myself a snugger home. She has been to me all that a daughter could be. . . ."[1]

Alice also moved into 245 Nassau Street from Bridgeton, "an old and broken woman. She can do practically nothing and is pretty deaf. It is not cheerful to live in the presence of decaying age, but she has done so much for me in the past, and depends on me so in the present, that I have no choice but to make her declining years as comfortable as may be."[2]

"Zeitlin is writing a monograph on Stuart Sherman, and has asked me for any letters I might have, as he particularly wishes to know why Sherman broke with me and went over to the camp of the enemy. Yesterday I got out his letters—what of them I had kept—from the dusty packages of correspondence in the attic, and went through them to see whether I should send

[1] To William Peterfield Trent, Feb. 12, 1928.
[2] To Prosser Hall Frye, March 24, 1928.

Recovery

them to Zeitlin. It was rather a sad adventure to read over the old record of so warm a friendship. There were no letters from him written after he had turned renegade to his humanistic faith. And indeed there was never any open rupture between us. . . . Then for several days I have been going over my books, selecting those that I shall give to the university library to lighten my shelves—probably two or three thousand volumes. . . . The sight of so many volumes long forgotten calls back all my old enthusiastic curiosities. How eager I was to master every field of learning, how keenly I sought here and there for the secret of life, how I searched through biographies to discover if I might the meaning of happiness—and how little I found.[3] The thought of it all depresses me, and these are not days when I need to add to my depression. Scholarship is a pretty empty business at the last; we must learn to make our peace with the world otherwise. For months I have read very little except such books as would pass the heavy hours, and it needs a large amount of good will thrown in. I have, however, got a MS. of a volume of essays—*New Shelburne Essays*, Volume 1, I call it—to the printer, and have recently read through the first proof. It is partly old stuff, but with some new pieces, particularly a long essay on Trollope to whom I have tried to pay my deep debt of gratitude. I have too paid my respects to the modern vulgarians and witless aesthetes who are roistering on the slopes of Parnassus. The book will make me a new batch of enemies—whom God knows I do not need. Now I am writing on the last

[3] "Aristotle has taught me why biography, which I used to read with exhilaration, now depresses me. These men whose lives are told are for the most part such as fulfilled some purpose and were able to shape their own destiny. They climb and climb, and then at the last, when they have reached the summit, one sees them slip over the edge, a brief struggle, and then the plunge into the abyss. That is it, the everlasting oscillation of birth and death, the few years of purposeful living, the attainment, and then the defeat. Despite the gift of προαίρεσις and πρᾶξις how does human nature differ from the fateful and meaningless oscillation between contraries and opposites which is the law of φύσις? Unless there is something more, and the something more is so hard to realize." [From one of More's notebooks, after an entry dated March 15, 1929.]

volume of my *Greek Tradition*; but the work, with many interruptions, goes slowly. When that is finished, I scarcely know
what I shall take up. . . . You will see that at least I am not
idle; but there is little joy in it all, a kind of dull mechanic
exercise."[4]

The "old stuff" in *The Demon of the Absolute* includes
"Sâvitrî," More's translation from the *Mahâbhârata* (probably
made during his engagement to Henrietta Beck) of a tale of
wifely devotion. The essays on George Borrow—"essentially a
picaresque character" yet clean "as the wind on the heather"
and fearless as a Jesuit missionary—and on Henry Vaughan—
"my much-loved swan of the Usk"—appeared in *The Nation*
in 1912 and 1916, respectively. "A Note on Poe's Method"—
that "combination of nervous irritability, running even into the
morbid, with rigorous intellectual analysis"—had first been
printed in the July 1923 issue of *Studies in Philology*.

The Demon of the Absolute, the villain of the title essay, "is
'reason run amuck.' Reason, properly our 'guide and friend,'
has a perennial tendency to leap beyond 'the actual data of experience' and 'set up its own absolutes as the truth.' It craves
to explain life in terms of some single formula. Thus it blurs
that 'double consciousness,' as Emerson called it, that inexplicable sense of the opposition of dust and deity in human
nature, from which great art and great conduct take their rise."[5]
The first three sections of the essay—on standards, tradition, and
the criterion of taste—go back substantially to 1917. Former material about the humanity and the divinity of Christ was deleted,
perhaps as out of keeping with the rest of the book or as included
in *The Greek Tradition*. In its stead appeared new sections
called "The Fetish of Pure Art"—illustrated by reference to
Benedetto Croce and José Ortega y Gasset—and "The Phantom
of Pure Science"—for which Alfred North Whitehead served

---

[4] To Prosser Hall Frye, June 19, 1928.
[5] George Roy Elliott, review of *DA, The Saturday Review of Literature*, Jan. 26, 1929, vol. 5, p. 618.

Recovery

as the whipping-boy. Although the last two sections strike some sharp blows against the divorce of art from the higher human faculties[6] and against the relevance to religion of Whitehead's "principle of concretion" and the adequacy for philosophy of his concepts of "organic mechanism" and "events," nevertheless, as their contemptuous titles suggest, they are personal and polemical in a rather contracted sense.

To More's desire to speak without paltering must be attributed his somewhat cursory and intemperate treatment in "Modern Currents in American Literature"[7] of Amy Lowell, Joseph Hergesheimer, Sherwood Anderson, John Dos Passos (whose *Manhattan Transfer* he called "an explosion in a cesspool"[8]), Sin-

[6] "Can or cannot art be divorced from ethics? The 'moderns' of the present passing moment, as I see them, differ chiefly from their immediate predecessors in their greater insistence on the possibility, even the need, of such divorce. . . . No doubt there are other differences of a more technical character. Well, I say flatly that art, any art, worth considering very seriously cannot be so divorced. Of course you will understand that by ethics I mean no narrow or specific code of morals, but the laws of man's ἦθος. And another point: I do not mean that ethics and aesthetics are the same thing. They are not. And it is perfectly possible, and may be valuable, to study a work of art, or a movement of art, from the purely aesthetic point of view. Only, in my opinion, it should be remembered that such a study is abstracting for a special purpose what in practice cannot exist separately. . . . I would not for a moment deny that technique and aesthetic enter into the criterion of art and are factors of tradition. Indeed I have said as much. But I think you will find that of the two, aesthetic is far more changeable than ethic, and that the continuity of taste depends more on the latter than on the former— though I would not press this point too far. But, after all, the great enduring things are the primary emotions, and about all I would say is that the higher emotions feed the better and more enduring art." [To William Mode Spackman, Feb. 16, 1929. Cf. *P*, 180; *SE* II, 217; *SE* VIII, 112; and *DA*, 100-02.]

[7] He recognized as a "disability inherent in" his "theme" that some of the abler writers of the day, like Edith Wharton, Edwin Arlington Robinson, and Robert Frost, were neither so "modern" nor so "American," in the peculiar senses given to those words, as to fall within the scope of his essay.

[8] Cf. "Notes on Babbitt and More," by Edmund Wilson, in *The Critique of Humanism*, edited by C. Hartley Grattan, New York (Brewer and Warren), 1930, pp. 56-57; "Pupils of Polonius," by Burton Rascoe, *ibid.*, pp. 113-15; and *The Confident Years: 1885-1915*, by Van Wyck Brooks, New York (E. P. Dutton & Co.), 1952, p. 392.

clair Lewis, and, less hastily, James Branch Cabell and Theodore Dreiser. If "the hardest test of the critic, in the exercise of his special function, is his tact and sureness in valuing the productions of his own day,"[9] More's revulsion from Cabell's "cunningly suggestive lubricity," Dreiser's would-be literary style ("a miscegenation of the gutter and the psychological laboratory"), and Sherwood Anderson's "almost complete impotence to check the flood of animal suggestions from his subconscious self"[10] made less for tact than for a cutting discrimination between these writers' qualities and their defects.[11] Of the various causes contributing to their failure to write lasting literature "the deepest and most universal . . . is that strange theory . . . that there are no moral laws governing life, or that, if such laws are, they have no jurisdiction in the artistic representation of life."[12]

"You think," More retorted to a young friend teaching English at the University of Illinois, "I might accomplish something worthwhile if I would come out openly as a champion of the Anglo-Catholic Church. I rather doubt it; I was not made to be a champion of anything so definite as that. As you probably know, I am not even a communicant, and it is not likely that I ever shall be. The reason why is too long, and in part too intimate, to tell. I am fixed now, and my habit towards matters of that kind is, and will remain, primarily intellectual—though my nature is emotional enough, heaven knows. On the other hand, I do honestly believe that the best service I can render the Church is by arguing for her fundamental truths as an unconcerned advocate. I think my position gives me a certain claim on educated readers, which I might not have if I were a

[9] *SE* VIII, 84.   [10] *DA*, 59, 65, 71.

[11] Admitting skill in *A Story Teller's Story* and in *Winesburg, Ohio*, even though he felt that some of their author's "books are a painful illustration of what 'the stream of consciousness' means when it is allowed to grow putrid" [*DA*, 71-72], More joined Mather and Sherman in nominating Anderson to the National Institute of Arts and Letters. [Cf. the letter by Frank Jewett Mather, Jr., in *The Saturday Review of Literature*, April 5, 1941.]

[12] *DA*, 72.

recognized member of the organization—I think that, while admitting that the claim has not been widely heard. . . . As for Rome, I feel that either you or I have a right to hear its mass and accept its message. But I feel very deeply, and more and more deeply every year, that for a man of your or my position actually to 'go over' is a sign of weakness and an act of treachery to our better nature. Rome has committed herself to theses that are simply impossible; she is the clearest and most admonitory example in history of the mischief that comes from yielding to the human craving for absolutes. Do you think that if we were meant to have any absolute revelation, the life and words of Jesus himself should have come to us in so broken and imperfect and at times contradictory a record? In the end we shall see that Christianity could never have endured, had it come to us in clearly formulated terms; and we shall see the claims of Rome to absolutism become a fatal impediment to her—but that will not be for some time."[13]

On July 28, 1928, More sailed from New York with the Stanley Wents on the S. S. *Cedric* of the White Star Line. Reaching Liverpool on August 6th he accompanied his friends to Leicester to visit Canon Went, "a wonderful old man of eighty-four."[14] On the 8th he arrived at his daughter's house, 10 Hills Avenue, Cambridge.

While Gilbert Dymond walked with friends in the Pyrenees, More hired a car and a chauffeur, who drove Alice and him to Ely, where they viewed the cathedral with the Babbitts. From there father and daughter continued their motor trip through Bury St. Edmunds, Ipswich, Yarmouth, Norwich, and King's Lynn, in "the Eastern counties, the home of FitzGerald and Borrow and Crome and Constable. . . ."[15] But "neither Peterborough nor Rugby nor Worcester, through which" they passed on their way from King's Lynn to Hereford, where at Hampton

---

[13] To Marcus Selden Goldman, May 23, 1928. Cf. *CF*, 181-99.
[14] To Prosser Hall Frye, March 24, 1928.
[15] To the same, Sept. 24, 1928.

Grange they stayed three days with Gilbert's parents, "was very interesting. Of course we were glad to see the home of Tom Brown and Thomas Arnold, but the buildings themselves have no beauty or value. And the cathedrals at Peterborough and Worcester are rather flat after Norwich. We attended service at Worcester Sunday morning, and heard a sermon which contained, in my judgement, some doubtful etymology. On the whole the cathedral services are not so impressive as are those of some of the smaller churches. Friday afternoon we made a short excursion from Peterborough to Little Gidding, the home, as you will remember, of the Ferrars and Collets in *John Inglesant*. The house itself is gone or altered out of recognition, but the little church—it must be one of the smallest in England—still stands, quite solitary except for a single farmhouse near by, looking out over a wonderfully beautiful slope. Inside the church, panelled in oak, is quaint and charming. Altogether it stirred me as few other sights have done. Then coming from Rugby to Worcester we went a little astray and so stopped at Stratford on Avon for lunch. The church moved me almost as deeply as when I first saw it. Certainly the heart of England lies there. . . . Yesterday we went down the Wye to Tintern and Chepstow, through magnificent scenery. The old ruined abbey at Tintern is a grand sight. . . ."[16]

Via Bath, Cheltenham, and the Cotswolds, More and his daughter returned to Cambridge by September 9th, where he remained a week or so longer. ". . . I quail before the solitude of my life here," he admitted to Frye from London. "Seven or eight million people all about me, each intent upon his own concerns, and not one of them would grieve for five minutes if I should disappear. It is [a] terrible symbol of the world, and it frightens me, though it would not have done so ten years ago. How I wish you and Nellie[17] were here; what a cosy time we could have together, and what things to talk about now that the

[16] To Mrs. Harry B. Fine, Sept. 4, 1928.
[17] Mrs. Prosser Hall Frye.

road from youth has grown so long. I think of you very often, and hope and even pray that you have got back your health. My friends grow fewer. Some time soon we must be together. We will sit on the ground and talk of kings and philosophers."[18]

"I have dined already with T. S. Eliot. . . . Tomorrow I have luncheon with him and a Father D'Arcy, who is a theologian of high standing and head of the Jesuit Society at Oxford. I want to draw him out on the question of papal infallibility.[19] So far as I can make out, the Encyclical *Providentissimus Deus* of Leo XIII has committed the Roman Church irrevocably to a fundamentalism as absolute and as abject as anything known among the extreme Protestants of America. Yet the proceedings at Dayton afford amusement for the world, while Rome goes unscathed. I want to learn from D'Arcy whether any distinction can be made between such an Encyclical as that of Leo XIII and such a pronouncement *de fide*, as, say, the Immaculate Conception (a dogma by the way which, I believe, originated in the Koran). Yesterday I took tea with Alfred Noyes and his new wife. . . . Then, too, my old friend Graves has put me up at the Athenaeum, where I shall probably spend most of my noon hours. . . ."[20]

"My two days at All Souls," during a visit to Reggie Harris on October 6th and 7th, "were rather exciting. The first night we sat up in the smoking room until two thirty, debating chiefly that same question of infallibility. One of the dons, a leader writer on *The Mail*, is a Roman Catholic, another is an agnostic, and so we had it from all sides. The next night was milder, but we did not break up until nearly one."[21]

From October 8th until the end of the month, while he stayed at the Isis Hotel in Oxford, More wrote in the morning, walked along the river to the Trout Inn for tea, and read in the evening.

---

[18] To Prosser Hall Frye, Sept. 24, 1928.
[19] ". . . I could not corner him." [To Mrs. Harry B. Fine, Sept. 27, 1928.]
[20] To Christian Gauss, Sept. 21, 1928. Cf. *CF*, 190, 192-93.
[21] To Mrs. Harry B. Fine, Oct. 14, 1928.

Now and then he knocked at the door of Miss Roberta Swartz's sitting-room at the hotel, saying he was so lonely that he wondered if he might come in. Were she busy with her university studies, he would, after having obtained her permission, quietly smoke his pipe. At other times, glancing over her few textbooks, he would cry out ravenously: "Haven't you anything to read? Haven't you any detective stories?" She offered him a series of sonnets she was composing. In return he gave her lessons on poetical diction and construction. "I think I was not offensive, and she seemed extremely grateful."[22]

He read Latin aloud to her and, putting down his pipe, leaning back in his chair, and touching his finger tips together, recited "O fons Bandusiae" and other poems from memory, in a deep, moving voice between speaking and singing. Milton he intoned mightily, with long breaths. And the recitation of

> Rose Aylmer, whom these waking eyes
> May weep, but never see,

or of Vaughan's

> They are all gone into the world of light!
> And I alone sit lingering here,

would force him to restrain his tears. Speaking often of his wife, he observed that since her death he felt keenly the need of Christian dogma.

"Last Wednesday I had tea with Father D'Arcy and the Jesuits at Campion house. We did not talk much theology, but I was interested in observing the type of men,—priests and students,—who gathered there. What impressed me was a certain strength of will stamped on their faces, together with a something which set them apart from the ordinary Englishmen, a something not easily explained and not to my taste. The next day I dined at Pusey House, across the way in [St.] Giles['s] Street, with Darwell Stone, the Principal, especially to meet Father Walker, a Dominican from the house next door. . . . After the meal we went up to Dr. Stone's private study, accom-

22 To the same, Oct. 26, 1928.

panied by a young priest who has been working in the same field as myself. There I opened my batteries on Father Walker, but with no great success. I did not draw from him the admission that the Encyclical of Leo XIII must be taken as an infallible utterance and so does commit the Church irrevocably to the inerrancy of Scripture. But when it came to the question of what is meant by inerrancy, neither I nor the young priest could get anything very definite. But squirm as the poor fellow would, he had to admit that the definition declared that there could be no error in the Bible in matters of history or science. Dr. Stone, who came down to the door with me after the discussion, said the truth of the case was that scholars like Father Walker—and he is a scholar—were in a cruel position and just had to make the best of it. At the last it comes down to the question: what is meant by truth. And Father Walker tried to throw dust by instancing Aristotle's and St. Thomas Aquinas's definition of truth as concerned with a 'judgement.' More simply stated I should say that they play fast and loose with their admissions and have quite juggled any sense of plain, simple veracity out of their minds. Well, I have done with that inquiry. In fact my paper is finished, and has been sent to Tom Eliot for publication in *The Criterion*, if he cares for it."[23]

In "the horrid locution of the day," More found the men at Oxford "suffering from something like an inferiority complex. They seemed to feel that the university was in the doldrums and was effecting nothing. As I interpret the situation, the old humanistic and religious ideal of education, for which Oxford has always stood, has been shattered, they are half-hearted in their assumption of science, and so feel as if they were doing nothing. I may be wrong, but I cannot help believing that the only sound solution of their embarrassment would be to bring back the church into authority, and let the old place maintain its 'lost illusion' until perhaps it ceased to be an illusion. It would be a

[23] To Alice More, Oct. 20, 1928. Cf. *CF*, 189 f.

1928

great thing to have one such place standing for an idea distinct from the main trend of thought."[24]

"Last Sunday I dined in Hall with Spens, the Master of Corpus Christi. This is the smallest college in the university," More explained to his sister, Alice, from Cambridge, where he had returned on November 1st, "but it has a mighty spirit, in fact has made itself at once something of a jest and a trouble to colleges like Trinity and St. John's (much the largest and admittedly the leading institutions here) by its assumption of importance. The Master and some of the Fellows are also very High Church, which does not endear them to the scientifico-agnostic spirit of the place. Nevertheless, or perhaps therefore, I had on the whole the gayest evening I have ever spent at an English college. It seemed to me that the Fellows were of an altogether better and finer type than, for instance, the very plebeian and dull looking crowd at St. John's. Among others I met a Fellow named Smyth, who had been at Harvard and in the West, and who showed something of the *élan* and free expansiveness one expects from the better men in America. I went up to his room after bidding good night to the Master in his drawing room, and had a good discursive and argumentative talk. To my surprise it was half past eleven when I left. Then of course I got lost. No bus runs out here [to 10 Hills Avenue] after 9:30, and as the weather was good, except for fog, I undertook to walk. Well, after a while I seemed to be getting out into some unknown country. Nobody was about, until I saw a bicycle approaching. Stepping out into the middle of the road, I waved my stick violently and threateningly, and when the man stopped, thinking me no doubt a highwayman, I asked him if I was heading for Hills Road. No, says he, you are half way to Newnham. I contrived to get back into town without mishap, and then supposed myself lost again—though I wasn't. The only persons I could see were occasional students galloping at full speed for their colleges to get in before the gates were finally locked at

[24] To Archibald Allan Bowman, Dec. 13, 1928.

[265]

midnight. I did not dare stop one of them for fear of consequences, but plodded on, and by the grace of God reached Hills Avenue at last."[25]

"This noon I had luncheon with . . . Smyth in his rooms at Corpus, and enjoyed myself very much indeed. . . . Smyth is . . . one of Eliot's contributors to *The Criterion*. . . . Eliot himself, in the preface to a new book of essays which he has sent me, comes out clearly on his new platform; it is summed up in three words: classicism, royalism, and Anglo-Catholicism. This is the sort of thing that is going on in England. There is some claptrap mixed up in it, but they mean something serious too—at least there are elements of a wholesome reaction from the maelstrom of follies that has almost engulfed the world. With their classicism they contrive to mix the freest of free verse, with their royalism an ultra democracy, and with their Anglo-Catholicism a good dose of scepticism plus bravado; but they may come to terms with themselves later on."[26]

Alice "has been very sweet in the way she has done everything possible to make me feel at home and as if I were really wanted. It has touched me deeply. Indeed I have no words to express my thankfulness for the love of both my daughters. I am not too proud of my career as a father—indeed, as I look back, my life seems to have been largely a succession of stupid blunders—but the comfort that has come to me from you and her is inexpressibly dear. Without it I think I should just throw up the sponge. May you have the same joy when the years of decline come upon you in your turn—which is looking a long way into the future, is it not?"[27]

". . . my cherished desire to see something of English university life is satisfied. My conclusion is that the students as a body average well above ours in maturity of mind and thoughtfulness, but the dons certainly are not above ours in scholarship or manners or culture. I should judge that most of the young

25 To Alice More, Nov. 7, 1928.
26 To Mrs. Harry B. Fine, Nov. 18, 1928.   27 *Ibid.*

men coming into academic life are of an interior stamp, very crude, if anything cruder than our recruits, and that is saying a good deal. . . .

"Just now I am in correspondence with Philip S. Richards (a schoolmaster at Portsmouth) who wrote a long article on Babbitt for *The Nineteenth Century*, and, at Babbitt's suggestion, is now doing the same thing for me. It was a magnanimous suggestion of Babbitt's, as Richards is more in sympathy with me, being a Platonist and Anglo-Catholic, than he is with him, Babbitt. I hope to see Richards in London on my way to Southampton. I shall certainly see T. S. Eliot with whom I have contracted rather an intimate acquaintance."[28]

"December 12, 1928, my 64th birthday, I went up to London from Cambridge to meet P. S. Richards. . . . We had tea together, then dinner at the Holborn Restaurant, and he left to catch his train at about nine. I had rather dreaded so long a visit, but as a matter of fact the talk never dragged, and I enjoyed every minute of it. This was due to our sympathetic views in religion and literature and philosophy. . . . I found him a devoted admirer of *John Inglesant*,[29] and urged him to try his hand at supplying what is strangely lacking in English literature, that is fiction imbued with the spirit of Anglo-Catholicism as a bal-

[28] To Alice More, Nov. 30, 1928.

[29] ". . . my own noetic growth has been, like Inglesant's, shaped by this triple strand of Quakerism (which so easily merges into the Platonic Logos), of Platonism also, and the sort of Catholicism to which Inglesant returned at the last and which has been slowly, with much fumbling but with steady progress, worked out by the Anglican Church." [*M*, 8.]

By Quakerism, in this connection, "I mean those intimations of the Otherworld such as Whittier describes so beautifully in his 'The Pennsylvania Pilgrim' as coming to Daniel Pastorius:

> . . . a Voice spake in his ear,
> And lo! all other voices far and near
> Died at that whisper, full of meanings clear.

> The Light of Life shone round him; one by one
> The wandering lights, that all-misleading run,
> Went out like candles paling in the sun." [*Ibid.*]

ance to the popular Roman Catholic stories of the type of Father Hugh Benson's, of which we have an abundance. . . .

"In the evening after he had left, I sat up till a late hour, recounting to myself the strange experiences of the months before and after my grand climateric,—the bleak fits of depression, partly caused by a great sorrow, partly the result of a suddenly heightened sense of the lapse of time,—at bottom inexplicable to me. That is past, or at least seems to be past; and so much the four months in England have done. I think the real change came at Oxford, something of the spiritual exhilaration that I felt there and recorded four years ago—no, not exhilaration, but a kind of emanation of peace.

"My birthday was Wednesday, and on Friday I sailed from Southampton. The home-coming was happy, yet at first a terrible shock. I remember the words used by Charles Eliot Norton on a similar occasion—I had said them to myself many times on the voyage: ἡ χώρα τὸ μὴ ὂν ποθήσει. What words, τὸ μὴ ὄν, what they mean! This grievous absence will not be filled; but the bitter, senseless, strangling waves of depression that have rolled me over for these two years—I think I have escaped them."[30]

[30] From one of More's notebooks.

14

HUMANISM (1929-1930)

"RECENTLY I had four of the younger members of the classical department here for dinner. We got talking about T. S. Eliot, and I told them of my meeting him in London.[1] One of them was immensely interested, and avowed himself an enthusiastic admirer of *The Waste Land* et cet. Well, I took up a volume of his poetry, and read *The Hippopotamus*—at least I read part of it, and then turned the book over to the enthusiast, who intoned it as one might Milton. Do you know the verses? They make some sort of contrast between the Church and a hippopotamus (!) ending:

[1] "Two things are to be considered in judging his [Eliot's] work. In the first place some time between *The Waste Land* and *For Lancelot Andrewes* he underwent a kind of conversion, due largely I believe to the influence of Maurras and the *Action Française*. And in the second place, he seems to cherish the theory—very heretical in my eyes—that ethics and aesthetics are to be kept rigorously separate. I remember that last summer, after reading his *Andrewes* with its prefatial program of classicism, royalism (the divine right of kings!), and Anglo-Catholicism, I asked him whether, when he returned to verse, he would write the same sort of stuff that he once called poetry, or whether he had seen a new light. His answer was: 'I am absolutely unconverted.' The situation is complicated by the fact that many of his most ardent followers were won by his verse and are very dubious about his later critical views. This he knows, and I think he feels himself in an embarrassing strait. How he will extricate himself remains to be seen. He is avowedly and, no doubt, sincerely religious; but just what his religion means to him, I do not know." [To Austin Warren, Aug. 11, 1929.]

"The kind of criticism you have given," More remarked to Frye on the publication of the latter's *Visions and Chimeras*, "—and which I give—is at present demoded. That, needless to say, is nothing against it intrinsically. In the lack of any philosophy of life, or the conception of the possibility of such a philosophy, the younger men have frankly turned aside to purely aesthetic criticism and to the discussion of the means of producing artistic effects. . . . On the other hand T. S. Eliot who has a philosophy of life in the form of religion seems to despair of connecting it with art, and so compromises by the same sort of disjunction." [To Prosser Hall Frye, Oct. 3, 1929.]

[269]

Humanism

He shall be washed as white as snow,
By all the martyr'd virgins kist,
While the True Church remains below
Wrapt in the old miasmal mist.

But, said I, when he stopped, with a look of rapture on his face,—but what is the Hippopotamus? None of us could guess. And then: 'What difference does it make?' said the enthusiast. I suspect that what enthralls them is just a succession of sensational images or expressions, while they never stop to think at all."[2]

After conferring in 1927 with Babbitt, Norman Foerster took up the task of editing a volume of essays in line with Babbitt's and More's criticism, then often referred to as "the new humanism."[3] More's invitation to contribute to the symposium came, at Foerster's request, through Shafer, who, believing the volume should be written entirely by the younger humanists, urged More to decline. "I think your advice to me," More replied, "that I should not contribute to the proposed volume of essays on the New Humanism, is quite sound; the book will be more of a unit and more impressive if it is confined to the younger group."[4]

Shafer in the meantime had suggested to some publishers for whom he was working that a study of More be included in their series about American writers. As they welcomed the proposal, he asked More whether he might count on him to supply the necessary biographical material.

"My vanity—and perhaps not vanity alone—makes me . . . interested in your proposed volume on myself, if that goes through. Sherman was always urging me to drop my metaphysics

[2] To Prosser Hall Frye, Feb. 19, 1929. Cf. "The Cleft Eliot," by P. E. More, a review of Eliot's *Selected Essays, The Saturday Review of Literature,* Nov. 12, 1932, vol. 9, p. 235.

[3] Cf. *The Humanism of Paul Elmer More,* by Robert M. Davies, New York (Bookman Associates), 1958, p. 9 ff.

[4] To Robert Shafer, June 24, 1928.

and 'give the world' a history of my own spiritual development.[5] I have thought much of following his advice, but have been restrained by various causes. The theme has this interest, at least, that I have gone through a number of superficial changes, whilst never, so it seems to me, losing what is central to my mind and character. Perhaps some day I may undertake the task, but meanwhile I should really be keen to offer you what help I could—without of course expecting for a moment to bias your critical judgement."[6]

George Roy Elliott and Gorham B. Munson, who believed the leading humanists, regardless of age, should contribute to the symposium, were disappointed by More's decision. "A few days ago," More informed Shafer, "I received a letter from Norman Foerster with a schedule of the essays to be contained in the manifesto of humanism. No doubt you have seen it too. I confess I was somewhat surprised, not to say dismayed, to find that I was put down for a contribution, along with Babbitt and Mather. I think the book would be more effective without us, and personally I have a disinclination for that sort of thing. It appears however that the publisher insists on our inclusion, and I judge from the precision of the title after his name that Babbitt has already acceded. For all I know, he may be in sympathy with the plan of including us. I suppose there is nothing for me to do but to accede too. And then the question arises as to the subject I shall choose. I am inclined to take up the relation of humanism to religion. It is a delicate theme, I know, but I think it could be handled in such a way as to avoid cross purposes with the other contributors."[7]

"More and more I am driven to feel that . . . the effort to revive humanism without" religion "is perfectly hopeless. . . . But there is a huge difficulty. There can be no valid religion without believing something, without dogma. Many men, I sus-

[5] Cf. "Mr. P. E. More and The Wits," by Stuart P. Sherman, *The Review*, Jan. 17, 1920, vol. 2, p. 55.
[6] To Robert Shafer, July 17, 1928.
[7] To the same, Jan. 24, 1929.

Humanism

pect, agree with us in a general way about religion, but find it impossible to believe anything."[8]

In his correspondence with Foerster and Elliott early in 1929 More supported by Shafer's reiterated conviction that contributions should come only from the younger humanists, wavered between his disinclination to write and his desire to do what was best under the circumstances. Finally, convinced that the project could go ahead with or without him, he left his participation in it open.

"Your book[9] came yesterday," More notified Elliott, who had formerly entertained him at Bowdoin College[10] and who now, as a professor of English at Amherst College, was soon to be his host again, "and I have already read it through, with unflagging zest and, I need scarcely tell you, with almost entire agreement. You have struck the best blow for humanism and true art yet of any of the on-coming critics. . . . Of course your heart is most in the long essay on Milton. . . . Much you say in praise of Puritanism is sound—some of it I have myself said in my own way—but it is, I am bound to believe, the limitation as well as the strength of Milton. It severed him from whole-hearted participation in the great tradition; it to some degree divided his moral sense from his aesthetic sense; it ended, religiously, in an impossible individualism; it puts him a little to the side of the deeper—no, not deeper, but broader, current of English thought and life; it has prevented, and I fear will always prevent, him from holding such a place in our literature as Homer holds in Greek, and Virgil and Dante and Goethe hold. I say this unwillingly because I am afraid it is true; though I love Milton passionately and would not remit a sentence from what you have said. Still it would have been well for us, if just a strain of Wordsworth had been added to his nature. If this is treason,

8 To George Roy Elliott, March 28, 1929.
9 *The Cycle of Modern Poetry*, Princeton (Princeton University Press), March 1929.
10 On Dec. 7, 1920, More had read "The Spirit and Poetry of Early New England" as the Annie Talbot Cole Lecture at Bowdoin College.

make the most of it. Wordsworth is a poet about whom I am still very, very uncertain; I am still groping to get at the centre of him. Perhaps my difficulty is due to the fact that the true approach to him should not be central, but longitudinal. Perhaps his growth is more important than his achievement. I do not know. But I have a vague uneasiness that makes me ask whether your attitude and Babbitt's towards him is quite just, quite *comprehensively* just. After all, there is true healing in the man; he cannot be fundamentally wrong, as, in my view, Shelley is.

"I could not help thinking of my own critical work as I read. There was no such writing as yours, and in a minor way Agar's and Shafer's and others', coming out when I did most of my work. There was almost a critical vacuum in this country and in England, and I see now that my writing suffers from absence of the right kind of friction and emulation. Yet it was something of an achievement—I say it unblushingly—just to keep going in such a desert. The coming out boldly for righteousness and beauty among your group is to me quite a thrilling experience. Babbitt was there of course, a tower of strength; but his *French Masters* was not published until 1912, and our companionship was a kind of twin loneliness."[11]

"It was a surprise and a delight to see Dora at Amherst," More wrote of Mrs. Babbitt to her husband. "In fact my whole experience there was pleasant.[12] But this lecturing business is hard on the nerves. I had of course some talk with Roy Elliott about the humanistic book. As a matter of fact I should really prefer to keep out of the venture, and still may do so.[13] I feel sure that I shouldn't contribute anything of much value, and that

---

[11] To George Roy Elliott, March 31, 1929.

[12] At Amherst College on April 17th More repeated the rambling address on "Humanism and Religion" that he had given the month before at the Princeton Graduate School.

[13] "My only fear for the book, and indeed for the movement in general, is that we may all be taking literature a little too seriously. We must not forget that, when all is said, art is the adornment and not the substance of life." [To George Roy Elliott, July 28, 1929.]

Humanism

I could probably serve the cause better by writing *about* the book in some magazine than by writing *for* it."[14]

". . . Hibben and Jacobus[15] have persuaded, almost compelled, me to take the course on the Origins of Christianity. . . . I accepted with the utmost reluctance, for I recognize the intrinsic difficulties of lecturing to students on such a subject and am fully aware of my own deficiencies as a lecturer. However, so it stands, and I can only do my best. I must say that Hibben has treated me liberally in money and otherwise. I told him that my interest lay strongly in the direction of Anglo-Catholicism, and that, however I might try to avoid any note of propaganda, still something of my views would come out; but he merely said, Go ahead. Money also (I hope I shan't appear wholly mercenary) has led me to accept a call to give a couple of courses[16] at Berkeley, Cal., next year—a lecture course on Plato and a seminar on Aristotle."[17]

". . . now at last I have sold this house . . . the neighbourhood, since they have made Nassau Street part of the Lincoln Highway, has become impossible. As you know, I have a lot in Battle Road, and work on my new house there has actually begun. . . . The long wing, running back from the street, will have dining-room, pantry, kitchen, and garage on the first floor. Above will be two master bedrooms with bath between, and over the garage the maids' quarters. The other wing[18] will have the library on the first floor, and over it a study and bedroom, with bathroom cut off from the hall. I have done what I could to make book room, but even so may have to dispose of another large batch of volumes."[19]

During August, while Gilbert Dymond travelled in Montana

14 To Irving Babbitt, May 19, 1929. In a letter of July 5, 1929, More apprised Foerster of this decision.
15 Melancthon W. Jacobus, a trustee of Princeton University.
16 On the Mills Foundation at the University of California.
17 To Archibald Allan Bowman, June 10, 1929.
18 Running west, parallel to the street, and at a right angle to the south end of the long wing.
19 To Prosser Hall Frye, July 7, 1929.

[274]

and Harry Fine remained with his dying father in Princeton, More's "vacation for a month at Essex with ["little"] Alice and Darrah and the Baby[20] was a sweet oasis in my present life. We were very quiet; went out scarcely at all, and did almost nothing; but it was a delightful and companionable calm. In the evenings we read Trollope's *Doctor Thorne* with almost ecstatic enjoyment. There's a man for you, and, in an unobtrusive fashion, ethics and aesthetics and a philosophy of life."[21]

That summer, when rumors spread that More might receive a Nobel Prize in literature, T. S. Eliot reported he had as yet found no publisher for *Pages from an Oxford Diary*, a typescript of which its author had sent him the winter before. Though moved by the *Diary*, he suspected it would make its way slowly were it printed, as More wished, anonymously. Eliot hesitated to use his own name in any way to introduce the volume lest it give a clue to its source. Nor as a matter of principle did he care to recommend that a commercial publisher produce at its author's cost a book unlikely to earn its way, unless it were an expensive, scholarly work that ought to be published regardless of sales. Rejecting the suggestion that an agency might place a typescript of so little popular appeal, he begged More to let him keep it longer, assuring him that any attention devoted to the matter was purely a satisfaction to him.

After returning to Princeton to give, in the first term of the academic year,[22] an undergraduate course on Plato and another on the origins of Christianity, More acknowledged to Seward B. Collins (who that June had called on him in Princeton, to interest him in *The Bookman*, of which he was owner and editor): "It was very thoughtful of you to send me the copy of *The*

[20] Darrah's daughter, Mary Darragh Fine, was born in Princeton early in February 1929. "She adores her grandfather, who is perfectly infatuated with her." [Alice More to Marie R. Garesché, "December 30th" (1929).]

[21] To Prosser Hall Frye, Oct. 3, 1929.

[22] In the academic year 1928-29 More had taught, as usual, the second term only, giving an undergraduate course on Plato and a graduate course on Aristotle.

Humanism

Criterion, which for various reasons I had not yet seen, and I thank you accordingly. Naturally I turned first to Allen Tate's article.[23] I found it not easy reading; in fact I had to go through it a second time, and carefully, before I could see what he was driving at, and I am not quite sure that I understand him yet, or that he understands himself. Nevertheless I can see in a way that he has laid hold of some of the real difficulties inherent in the humanistic movement as it is now conducted. It is true that humanism, *per se* and practically divorced from positive values of a religious source, seems rather to be suspended in a vacuum and has great difficulty in declaring what it is all about and where its values lie. Perhaps Mr. Babbitt could answer such questions. He might quote Tate's own words: 'The man who supposes himself a naturalist may practise the Humanistic virtues (Montaigne); the Humanist in doctrine may exhibit the method of naturalism (More)', and he might reply: There are then humanistic virtues and why all this pother you are raising? For myself, I have been driven step by step to a position which seems to be not unlike Tate's, with one important exception—though he certainly does not recognize any such fact. His criticism of my own work is amazingly naïve for the reason that he has not read the books which give the key to my views. Apparently he had not even heard the name of the most important of these until he had read the proof of my own article in the same issue of *The Criterion*. A good deal that he says about my earlier views, especially as expressed in *Shelburne Essays* VI, really repeats the arguments that forced me into my present, fairly different, position. The religion I was seeking as a background and stay of humanism was somewhat of the vague, eclectic, contentless kind he criticises. I have come to see that time is a necessary element in religion, that it must be historical. I have come to see too that it must justify itself to reason. But the Absolute of faith

[23] "The Fallacy of Humanism," *The Criterion*, July 1929, vol. 8, pp. 661-81.

and revelation simply cannot be maintained. There Tate would, I conjecture, part from me. . . . I believe if I had been the editor to whom he first submitted the essay that I should have accepted it. It is confused, obscure, pretentious, insolently naïve, and all that; but the fellow is groping for ideas and challenges thought."[24]

In response to a telegraphic appeal from Norman Foerster, More consented to the reprinting in the humanist symposium of his essay, "The Demon of the Absolute," which, he learned later, Babbitt had suggested to Foerster as, in default of new material, a suitable contribution to the volume. As parts IV and V of the long essay could stand by themselves, Foerster published them alone, naming them (with More's approval) "The Humility of Common Sense."

"On his way home from lecturing in Atlantic City,"[25] Babbitt stopped at 245 Nassau Street "in his most genial mood and full of good talk—with the usual modicum of advice to take off my

[24] To Seward B. Collins, Sept. 7, 1929. Another instance of More's ability to distinguish between a simply malicious attack on himself and one (no matter how unsatisfactory in other respects) motivated by reflective difference of opinion appears in his comment on an article in *The Bookman.* "Newton Arvin's study of Sill is in my judgment admirable and thoroughly right. I have always felt, from the day when I first became acquainted with Arvin through a hostile criticism of myself—that there is mind in the fellow and honesty and that he has something to say. And here is a job for you as editor. If you can get the good out of him, detach him more completely from the influence of the New York intelligentsia, draw out the positive insight into life and letters that is now more or less obfuscated, you may produce something really worth while. He is worthy of encouragement and editorial patience. So it seems to me, though he is no friend to me." [To the same, Feb. 24, 1931. The "hostile criticism" was probably Arvin's review of *SE* XI in *The Freeman,* June 1, 1921, vol. 3, pp. 283-84.]

Though in writing to Mrs. Harry B. Fine on March 27, 1930, More described Edmund Wilson's "Notes on Babbitt and More" in *The New Republic* of March 19, 1930, as "the meanest article" printed about him during the humanist furore, that did not blind him to the merits of Wilson's essay on Proust in *Axel's Castle,* which in his letters of Oct. 10 and Dec. 12, 1931, he mentioned to Collins as worthy, with Seillière's study of the same author, of attention in *The Bookman.* [Cf. *OBH,* 65-68.]

[25] To George Roy Elliott, Nov. 19, 1929.

coat and get into the fight. Alas, what is a shy pundit[26] to do? I wish I had more of the strenuous spirit of my apostolic namesake; but I am only a groper—neither a prophet nor the son of a prophet. Mencken says I should be a good fellow if I had drunk more whiskey and begotten more bastards,[27] and Foerster tells me that Walter Lippmann admires *The Greek Tradition*. Between such denunciation and such admiration what can a puzzled critic do?"[28]

What he did was to move about November 22nd with Alice, his sister, to his "small house built about books"[29] at 59 Battle Road—"a pretty neighbourhood, and quiet save for prowling dogs."[30] Literature lined the walls of his library. Detective stories graded alphabetically[31] (as pupils' papers are graded by their teachers) and marked with the dates on which he had read them stood in the northern passage running westwards from the head of the front stairs, under the slanting roof and past his little bedroom. By allowing himself two detective stories a week and by rereading and regrading the A's every five years, he jestingly hoped to collect before his death five hundred incontestable A's. At the west end of this passage or Scotland Yard, in a plain, trim study stood his work chair with a wide wooden panel attached to one arm, which tilted for reading or writing, and, attached to the other, a rack full of pointed pencils and of pipes for every mood. On a projecting shelf rested a quadrilingual

[26] In an editorial of Nov. 18, 1929, a clipping of which More sent to G. R. Elliott, *The Daily Princetonian* had referred to More as "Princeton's own shy pundit."

[27] In the same late August 1929 letter to Hoffman Nickerson, Mencken had praised More as the best of the humanists.

[28] To George Roy Elliott, Nov. 19, 1929.

[29] To Alan Reynolds Thompson, Dec. 2, 1930.

[30] To Prosser Hall Frye, Jan. 19, 1930.

[31] If the villain cheated justice by committing suicide, neither ingenuity of plot nor grace of style could save the book from a low grade. When Mrs. William Mode Spackman, a friend of his daughters', who had travelled with them in Greece, questioned More's taste, he was quite severe: "Mary Ann, your husband may criticize my scholarship—but when it comes to detective stories, *I* am *paramount!*"

Bible, which, for some ten minutes daily, More would read standing, switching from tongue to tongue. About seven thousand volumes of philosophy and religion crowded the sides of the room from ceiling to floor,[32] leaving little space for his framed photographs of the Three Fates and of Perugino's Mystical Crucifixion.[33]

He was no sooner settled than he had to move to "a suite of bed, bath, and sitting rooms at the very reasonable price of $150 a month, including meals,"[34] in Berkeley, California, at Cloyne Court, "a fairly satisfactory place . . . but infected by radios and strange females who tramp up and down their rooms by the hour, treading as if in seven-league boots and humming in a loud stertorous voice. It interrupts Plato and Aristotle somewhat, and even chills my attention to a detective story."[35] "And I am a little embarrassed by the fact that I contribute to the confusion by blowing the flute. However I do this for only half an hour in the early evening."[36]

"I have tried two or three of my old jokes on my audiences, and they have gone off in a manner most encouraging."[37] "My two courses promise well. The undergraduate Plato"[38] "enrolls 48, more than twice the number they expected,"[39] "besides a number of auditors (some of the latter middle-aged): they are about equally divided in sex."[40] In the graduate seminar on Aristotle "are nine regular students and eleven auditors."[41] "The streets are thronged with really pretty girls with well-shaped legs —it is like walking through a revue."[42]

[32] Cf. *CF*, 213-15.
[33] Cf. *The Triple Thinkers*, by Edmund Wilson, New York (Harcourt, Brace & Co.), 1938, pp. 3-19.
[34] To Alice More, Jan. 14, 1930.
[35] To Frank Jewett Mather, Jr., Jan. 22, 1930.
[36] To Mrs. Harry B. Fine, Jan. 18, 1930.
[37] To Frank Jewett Mather, Jr., Jan. 22, 1930.
[38] To Christian Gauss, Jan. 17, 1930.
[39] To Frank Jewett Mather, Jr., Jan. 22, 1930.
[40] To Christian Gauss, Jan. 17, 1930.
[41] To Percy H. Houston, Jan. 21, 1930.
[42] To Christian Gauss, Jan. 17, 1930.

Humanism

"Somehow all this talk about humanism has given me a kind of notoriety, and people are crowding in just to see me. I don't care much for that sort of thing, as you know. Clubs are asking me to talk, three newspapers have interviewed me, and each new acquaintance inquires about the business."[43] ". . . so far as mere society goes I promise to have a sufficiency. But this sort of thing does little more than occupy stretches of time; somehow it quite fails to break through the stony wall of isolation that years and other matters have built about me."[44]

". . . for the most part the people I have met have been black-hearted pessimistic Tories. Some of them make me feel almost romantic and optimistic. Night before last, for instance, I dined with Brewer of the German department (he by the way attends my Aristotle seminar) and was first fed up with a double course of magnificently diabolical *hors d'oeuvres*, preceded by cocktails and accompanied with wine and followed by a Lucullan feast. After that I was regaled with such criticisms of democracy[45] and youth and the present age generally as I have never heard in Princeton. . . . I simply cannot understand how anyone conversant with what is going on over the country can fail to see that the present policy of Harvard and Yale and Princeton is suicidal. Their attempt to compete with these great state universities on a common ground means that ultimately they will lose their national position and sink to mere local institutions. Their only possible means of maintaining their position is by keeping themselves radically different from the state uni-

[43] To Alice More, Jan. 24, 1930.
[44] To the same, Jan. 29, 1930.
[45] So far as democracy means "an embodiment of liberty, I cherish it. The difficulty is that large masses of men seem to be incapable of living free for any great length of time. And certainly the one word almost taboo in politics today is just that—liberty. Who talks of it (except Belloc and a few of his kind)? What people fights for it? Who believes in it? Imagine a Patrick Henry today, if you can; he would be put in a lunatic asylum for his eloquence. Every turn in the sociological wheel is in the direction of one or another form of tyranny, and the success of a government appears to depend on the degree of centralized despotism—witness Italy and Russia." [To George Roy Elliott, June 24, 1932.]

versities; and the only practical way of doing that is by keeping up a cultural standard that will attract the finer and better bred men from everywhere."[46]

On March 7th before an audience in Berkeley More read aloud a revised version of his review[47] of *Humanism and America*. The contributors to the volume, he noted, recognized in the life and literature of their day futility and confusion derived, in his opinion, from a dogmatic, one-sided, naturalistic point of view, which deprived those blinded by it of confidence in their will and conscience. Against this "inflamed vision of a monocular Cyclops"[48] the humanists, denying that "man is totally submerged in natural law,"[49] affirmed the reality of individual personality, purpose, freedom, and responsibility.[50] While sympathizing so far with the humanists More went on to ask, in the latter half of his review and speaking solely for himself, whether humanism could stand steadily on its own feet without the support of religion. Granted that man does not belong entirely to the natural world, that he has a certain amount of characteristically human responsibility and freedom, nevertheless has his purpose, though different from the stir of a leaf, any significance beyond itself? "For purpose that will not end in bitter defeat; for values that will not mock us like empty masks, must we not look for a happiness based on something beyond the swaying tides of mortal success and failure? Will not the humanist, unless he adds to his creed the faith and the hope of religion, find himself at the last, despite his protests, dragged back into the camp of the naturalist?"[51]

Religions have not automatically produced humanistic eras nor are artists always religious as individuals. Indeed so "antagonistic to art and humane letters" has religion often been that "there is need also of a humanism, aroused to its own dignity

---

[46] To Christian Gauss, Feb. 23, 1930.
[47] "A Revival of Humanism," *The Bookman*, March, 1930, vol. 71, pp. 1-11.
[48] *OBH*, 6. [49] *OBH*, 7. [50] Cf. *DA*, x-xii. [51] *OBH*, 20.

Humanism

and ardently concerned with the beautiful representation of life as well as with life itself."[52] But, More concluded, a religious soil, as it were, that, though some be unaware of it, supports us in our best activities, in our quest of justice and beauty, in our search for meaning and value, is generally essential to the flowering of humanism.

"Do you know, I am really famous out here. It bewilders me; I don't know what to make of it, and wear it like a new shoe. Unfortunately I can't see that it adds one cubit to my stature and contributes more than a scant ounce to my happiness. A young preacher took me out driving this afternoon over an amazingly beautiful road. When we returned I thanked him and he replied: Not at all, the pleasure is mine; you are the first genius I have ever met!—That's the sort of thing they say to those young gloony-eyed Cubists and poets; but I didn't smile."[53]

On reading in *The Bookman* More's review of *Humanism and America*, Shafer charged him with having virtually surrendered the cause to Tate, with having betrayed humanism with a kiss.

"The phrase applied by me to Allen Tate 'ignorant and conceited' I regret," More avowed, "and should probably have struck it out had I had opportunity of seeing the article in proof. The words, I could maintain, are strictly true, but they have a personal animosity which rather lowers my position. On the other hand I would not admit that I have 'conceded his whole case.' Ultimately the question he raises is one of absolute authority, on which I disagree with him totally, nor is there anything in my article to intimate a concession there. . . .

"The real question as you know, and indeed state, is this: What is meant by religion? And here I think, rather I know, that Babbitt is evasive. His personal conception of religion is virtually Buddhistic, leaving no place for belief in a personal deity or immortality of the soul or for purpose in the world (though it does leave room for ethical purpose to escape the

52 *OBH*, 24.
53 To Alice More, March 29, 1930.

world); and all this he veils under such terms as 'higher immediacy.' . . . Furthermore he is evasive as to the relation of humanism and religion. On the one hand he persistently declares that Confucianism has produced a great humanistic art without religion (which I do not believe is historically true), with the implication that humanism today could do the same thing; while on the other hand he maintains that a man must take sides with the naturalists or supernaturalists, and proclaims that he himself stands with the latter, as an advocate of humanism. 'Under which king, Bezonian? speak, or die!'

"I do not at all know what you yourself mean by religion in general, or in particular by the kind of religion necessary for humanism. But I do know that to a great many minds of the recent age (I see this in exaggerated form here in California) religion has been thinned down to a kind of sentimental indulgence in revery by which they would beatify their moments of relaxation. It is little more than a laggard remnant of Babbitt's bugbear, Rousseauistic romanticism. It *costs* them nothing, and it gives them nothing; rather it laps them in enervating illusion. Frankly, I have grown very weary of the claims of this sort of thing to be called religion, and I believe that humanism is likely to suffer less from the outspoken agnosticism of a Mather[54] than from this bastard offspring of romantic naturalism.

"As for myself, I have changed, and I have openly and re-

[54] Of Mather's chapter in *Humanism and America* More wrote: "There is not a phrase or a sentence in your article with which I do not find myself in hearty agreement; and this may appear odd when one thinks of our disagreement on certain fundamental matters. It leads me to believe that perhaps our disagreement is not so fundamental as it at first appears to be. It comes in the end perhaps to this: that I find, or think I find, a more definitely concrete reality behind tradition, i.e. behind the accumulated wisdom of the generations; and that this objective reality assumes the form of religion. At the last you seem to me to leave life and art rather *in vacuo.* . . . The question, practically considered, would be: will men 'aspire' when they see nothing concrete and objective to aspire to, or will men 'live nobly,' as you better express it, without belief in a concrete and objective idea (not ideal) of nobility?" [To Frank Jewett Mather, Jr., Dec. 16, 1929.]

[283]

Humanism

peatedly acknowledged the change. I hope there is no sin in that. To me the choice is between non-religion and dogmatic religion; the middle ground of religiosity I spurn. And the final issue for dogmatic religion lies between the theism of Christianity and the moral atheism (thoroughly dogmatic in its way, despite Babbitt's protests to the contrary) of the Buddhist. I choose the former. Theism seems to involve some kind and degree of revelation (the nature of which it would take me too long here to expound). I believe in the Church, but not in an *absolute* Church. I believe that the future efficacy of the Church is bound up with a sacramental form of faith, but I do not accept the definition of sacrament as an *opus operatum* taken, again, absolutely. . . .

"Let me add that I have written nothing here about Babbitt which I have not often said to him in conversation; but naturally he would not like it if my remarks came to him through a third person. My friendship with him is quite as much to me as the success of humanism, which, to speak the truth, we may be in some danger of taking too seriously as a sharply defined programme. Personally I should prefer to fight for sanity, decency, truth, rather than for a word to which after all we have no exclusive claims."[55]

G. R. Elliott, in contrast to T. S. Eliot (who liked More's review), criticized "A Revival of Humanism" as heading for Rome, as not recognizing that happiness can exist without religious dogma, and as afraid to acknowledge that Christianity is a myth.

"In the first place," More answered, "humanly speaking, there is no danger of my going over to Rome. It behooves me to be modest on this head. A man who has changed as he never expected he would change ought not to be too certain of his future. Nevertheless I do feel secure in saying that my conversion to Rome seems to me impossible. . . .

[55] To Robert Shafer, April 1, 1930.

"And this leads me to the question of happiness. As I see it there is for man in this life no more claim for absolute happiness than for an absolute revelation. It is a question of degree, yet not wholly so. I should say that the pretensions to happiness uncomplicated by religious dogma, the pretensions of 'the comparative atheist who has attained some real inward (not worldly) happiness,' are simply false. I think you fail to discriminate between the Stoic καρτερία (resignation, endurance) and the theistic εὐδαιμονία (happiness). The former is attainable, has often been attained, by the pure humanist; but it is a poor substitute for the more positive feeling of happiness, and it can never move the world. At the same time I do not believe that the religious man, however far he may have progressed in true happiness, can ever quite pass beyond the end of καρτερία also. In that remnant of doubt which he can never escape, in the weakness of his mortal state, he must cling also to the sheer determination of the will, the pure unreasoning affirmation of faith, to hold the world a place where, despite all evidence to the contrary, there is a power, a divine will, making for righteousness—which is a different thing from the dogmatic affirmation of the Stoic that all things are right simply because they *are*. It is a different state also from the 'admiration' (so ably advocated by Thompson[56] as a substitute for faith) which we should bestow upon the strong man who persists in righteousness in a world where factually righteousness has no meaning. No, you are simply wrong—and you know you are wrong—in setting up happiness as a possible goal for the humanist who desires to live a life uncomplicated by religion. What otherwise would be the creed or function of religion, unless you wish to regard it as a pretty adornment, a nice luxury, to be toyed with in our hours of leisure? The humanist doctrine, in so far as it presumes to be adequate as such, is attached finally to nothing,

[56] "The Dilemma of Modern Tragedy," by Alan Reynolds Thompson, *Humanism and America*, edited by Norman Foerster, New York (Farrar and Rinehart), 1930, p. 127 ff.

if happiness is our test and goal.[57] On the other hand, I would not admit that religion is attached in the end to nothing unless it accepts the doctrine of absolute revelation through an infallible Church, or that religious happiness is for the same reason attached ultimately to nothing. Our human state is in the mean; let us make the best of it, neither crying for the impossible nor surrendering what we have.

"And next the question of mythology and illusion. It is one of the disadvantages of writing too much that an author cannot expect his arguments on any particular point to be remembered; yet really I have said a good deal on both these points. I have, for instance, said categorically that Christianity rests ultimately on a myth, meaning by that not that it has no historical basis, but that in some way there lies behind and beyond its dogma a truth which we can grasp only in symbols and signs. We cannot totally rise out of the realm of illusion. But here again let us avoid absolutes, or at least the wrong use of absolutes. If you mean by myth and illusion the sort of thing proclaimed by the German liberal school, whether of the eschatological wing or the contrary, i. e. that it makes no difference whether Christianity has any historical basis or not, whether Christ ever lived or not, or whether he ever taught anything about himself and God like what is recorded of him, if you mean that by myth and illusion, then I say you are usurping terms to which you have no right. Your myth is merely a lie, and your illusion is merely self-deceit (the $\pi\rho\hat{\omega}\tau o\nu$ $\psi\epsilon\hat{\upsilon}\delta o\varsigma$ abhorred of Plato[58]). I maintain that no Christian can escape the Definition of Chalcedon. In some way we have in the person of Christ what is truly human and what is truly divine (in the sense that there is here something different in kind from the divine in you and me). Without such an acceptance of the Incarnation one is only a Unitarian,

[57] "As for happiness, a word which I have used and abused in my own critical writings, I begin to doubt whether I know anything about it, what it is or who has it or why." [To Percy H. Houston, Sept. 25, 1930.]
[58] Cf. *RP*, 259.

and a Unitarian is about the poorest sham in the whole field of pseudo-religion. At the same time the Definition of Chalcedon (at least as I read it; *vide Christ the Word*) leaves the door open for the admission of illusion in the proper sense of the word, in so far as it places the Incarnation in a region beyond the powers of reason to define or analyse or, in a way, to comprehend. 'We see as in a glass darkly.' "[59]

Towards the end of the semester Edgar J. Hinkel, a graduate student who listened to More's course on Plato, asked him to dine with him and two other students, Edward E. Cassady and Joseph Chesley Matthews, who had also enjoyed the same course. Saying with a twinkle of the eye, "I must be in bed by ten," More accepted enthusiastically. From the moment he entered the car in which they drove about Berkeley before going to the Hotel Claremont, they found him a congenial companion, who talked as though he were of their own age and yet from a source of wide and tempered experience that braced and refreshed them. He satisfied their insistent questions, frankly telling them about his life; about the growth and the current state of the new humanism; about his disappointment in Stuart P. Sherman; about the rewards and the trials of academic life, including his loneliness at Berkeley;[60] about his course on Plato, which he characterized as "somewhat thin," because, having left his books in Princeton, he relied too much on his memory; and about detective stories ("Philo Vance is a dreadful prig").

At half past nine, when they reminded him of their promise to take him home early, he asked, "Where do we get cigars?" Then they sat talking and laughing on the veranda of the hotel, overlooking moonlit San Francisco Bay. When they parted after

[59] To George Roy Elliott, April 12, 1930.

[60] After describing some dinners that he attended in Berkeley, one of which was "large and quite gorgeous," More continued: "I am lonely, very lonely, and go out into society, and come back feeling if anything a little more lonely, and repeating to myself the words of Thomas à Kempis: I never go among men without feeling myself less a man. It is a horrid dilemma. But the people here are treating me very decently." [To Alice More, Feb. 9, 1930. Cf. *SE* I, 208.]

midnight at Cloyne Court, he gave them as their battle cry, "Sursum corda," which he inscribed in one of the autographed copies of *The Demon of the Absolute* that he sent to them on his return to Princeton.

Leaving Berkeley for San Francisco on April 26th, after his students had thanked him with fervent applause at the end of his course on Plato, and lecturing in Los Angeles on April 29th, More headed homeward early in May, visiting Louis a few days in Cincinnati, after the sight of the Grand Canyon had evoked a sonnet. "Alas, into what temptations an idle man is carried. . . .

> "To mock what men with paint and stone should do,
> Some power, with all of time at its command,
> Carved out this Canyon that we call the Grand,
> A myriad miracle of form and hue.
> Was it mere chance that travailed whilst it grew?
> Or did some Worker like an artist stand
> Exultant o'er the cunning of his hand?—
> The old insurgent question, here made new.
> Had it a purpose of itself, or lay
> It meaningless until some eye like mine
> Added the thought of beauty? who shall say?
> But this I know, that he who would divine
> One single purpose for the world and man
> Must risk a thousand doubts to find the plan."[61]

[61] To George Roy Elliott, May 8, 1930.

15

THE PLATONIZING CATHOLIC
(1930-1931)

"ONE of the first things I did after settling down at home was to take up your little book on Dante"—T. S. Eliot's *Dante*, published in 1929—"which has been awaiting me here for several months. I think you have done a thoroughly successful piece of work, and to me every page was interesting and provocative of reflection. Dante, for some reason or other, is the one great acknowledged master poet whom I have felt I could not fully appreciate. I read him and admire, I think I understand, yet somehow I am not drawn instinctively to him, as I am, for instance, to Virgil, whose *Aeneid* I am even now going through for the twelfth or twentieth time with undiminished zest. I have thought about this a great deal. I suspect the cause of my comparative coldness towards Dante is partly the allegory, a genre which rather repels me if it is serious enough—as Spenser's is not—to keep me guessing. But the more important cause no doubt is somehow involved in that matter of 'belief' and 'assent' which you analyse so carefully. My difficulty is just that I cannot assent to the treatment of what I believe; I am put out by what seems to me a false representation, or perverted interpretation, of a great body of fundamental truths. For instance those words inscribed over Hell Gate: *giustizia, la divina potestate, sapienza, il primo amore*—no, there is some twist here, some echo of a theology gone frightfully astray in the bogs of medievalism. Omnipotence and love did not combine to make Hell, nor did God make Hell. You see how—to my way of thinking—Dante is dealing with tremendous truths falsely—as the Roman Church, by its bondage to the Middle Ages, still does too generally. I can read Homer's Hades and Virgil's with joy, not Dante's."[1]

[1] To T. S. Eliot, May 20, 1930. Cf. *SE* II, 226.

The Platonizing Catholic

Eliot's comments drew this response:

"Ods bodikins, man; I am a humanitarian, am I? and my God is Santa Claus, is He? and I can't understand Dante because I am a half-Christian. Well, if it comes to slinging epithets, I'm with you through the dictionary, and there's nothing I delight in more. In reply I convict you of three gross errors and herewith denounce you to all and sundry:

"(1) Metaphysically, you are a monist;

"(2) Theologically, your deity is not the Jehovah of the Psalmist nor the [sic] of Christ, but an abortion sprung of the unholy coupling of the Aristotelian Absolute and the Phoenician Moloch; you are a Mohammedan or Calvinist, no Catholic.

"(3) Historically, you confound Christianity with Medievalism; and

"(4) you are not consistent (no monist can be) in your heresies. . . .

"Evidently the *fons et origo* of all this mischief is a form of that damnable sin of the reason called monism. For you the universe is God, or God is the ultimate unique cause of the universe, which two are about the same thing. He is, you say, above good and evil; in other words He is the source of both good and evil, and good and evil, as flowing from one fountain, are not ultimately distinguishable. Now, I grant that there are hints of such a belief in the more rhapsodical magnifications of Jehovah here and there in the Old Testament; but the Jews, totally lacking in the metaphysical sense, never carried these hints through to a rational monism, and in general Jehovah was to them the doer of righteousness and the punisher of evil (should He punish what He created?). And I maintain that in the words of Jesus there is not a breath of this false rationalism. Have you ever thought of the implications of that extraordinary prayer at Gethsemane: εἰ δυνατόν ἐστιν παρέλθῃ ἀπ᾿ αὐτοῦ ἡ ὥρα? Have you ever reflected that this δυνατόν implies what Plato meant by his ἀνάγκη (perhaps the profoundest intuition of any

[290]

philosopher),[2] that there is some dark necessity, some obscure residue of unmastered disorder in the nature of things, beyond the will and persuasion (πειθώ) of the divine purpose—rather giving meaning to the moral purpose (St. Paul's πρόθεσις) connected with the Creator? You will, no doubt, fling at me the rest of the prayer: 'Αββά ὁ πατήρ, πάντα δυνατά σοί . . . ἀλλ' οὐ τί ἐγὼ θέλω. . . . Superficially the two clauses of the prayer are contradictory, but not, I believe, essentially. The πάντα δυνατά may imply that the Father could, if He so willed, remove the cup, but only by shirking the terrible necessity that lay upon Him of meeting the mystery of evil squarely, and so of fulfilling His beneficent purpose by self-sacrifice (I am a Patripassianist to this extent). All of which means, if it means anything, that there is a terrible and inexplicable rift in the nature of things, and that God is not the universal cause, but the power that makes for righteousness, hampered, in some way it would be blasphemous to attempt to explain, in His love and goodness. . . . Let us leave the mystery of evil a mystery, admitting that it lies beyond the reach of the monistically impelled reason, the state of the soul *in articulo mortis*. I am not a believer in metempsychosis in the crass and naïve way; but I do believe that in some unimaginable manner the soul is capable after death of ascent and descent. Purgatory is no substitute for such a belief, but a mischievous doctrine which has done much to sap the morality of the Roman Church. I admit that certain parables of Christ seem to point to an immediate and final separation of the sheep and the goats, but I can explain them at least to my own satisfaction. And I do protest with all my mind that hell is not *giustizia, sapienza, amore*, as Dante meant. And here I catch you in inconsistency. You may, if you choose, remove God to some region beyond good and evil (Christ did not), and you may then conceive of God as the cause of what we, in our ignorance, regard as evil; and you may thus conceive of Him as the creator of hell as part of His eternal plan. But

[2] Cf. *SAR*, 76 f.

then, if you desire to swim in this ethereal plane beyond good and evil, by what right do you say that justice, wisdom, and love (human terms for good) are the cause of hell's being? I will connect hell (as a name for the consequences of sin) with God only in a world deeply bifurcated in its essence.

"What a letter! And I have a great deal I should like to tell you about my experience as a lecturer in Washington at the College of Preachers, and about a great project for an anthology from the 17th century to show the ethos of the Anglican Church; but I forbear. I am afraid to read this letter through, and am going to leave it unsealed until tomorrow, when I may amend or destroy it. I don't want to appear as an epistolary infliction. And I do want to tell you that I hate your theology, and love you as a theologian. After all theology is the only really interesting subject, and I get so little of it in conversation or letters. I try one bishop after another as I meet them, but they all shy off, being, our American Rt. Revs., as I suspect, densely ignorant.

"Believe me your very explosive and humorous friend and well-wisher, here and in eternity,

Paul E. More. . . ."[3]

After flaying "the intelligentsia of New York City" as "the most tawdry ever found,"[4] in a commencement address on "Philosophy, the Basis of Humanism," at St. Stephen's [now Bard] College, Annandale-on-Hudson, New York, and after next delivering his four lectures on mysticism at the College of Preachers, More (who had leased his camp in Essex) and his sisters, Alice and May, passed most of the summer in Greensboro, Vermont. Darrah and Molly, as her baby ("the dearest child in the world"[5]) was nicknamed, joined them there for a month, and "Lou came down from Murray Bay for a week."[6] ". . . I feel that the scenery within easy reach of this

[3] To T. S. Eliot, July 9, 1930.
[4] *The New York Times*, June 10, 1930, p. 33.
[5] To Prosser Hall Frye, Oct. 30, 1930.
[6] *Ibid.*

town is about the loveliest, though not the grandest, in New England."⁷ ". . . the hills . . . draw me most. The cloud-shadows passing over a valley and long acclivity have a fascination for me that nothing else in nature affords—not even the sight and sound of the great sea."⁸

Alice, his "invalid sister, now 81 years old, was surprisingly well there, and I gave a deal of time to playing cards with her and doing what I could to lighten what is probably the last outing she will ever enjoy. She had a pretty bad collapse, however, just the day before we started back [to Princeton] and as we had to get an express some thirty miles from Greensboro, her progress was made by the use of three ambulances. She is still in bed and very weak. The sight of the human machine breaking up before one's eyes is not a cheerful thing. It seems to me now as if I had had sickness about me most of my life. However the doctor pronounces all of my own organs and blood pressure perfectly normal."⁹

As far as nature was concerned, More scarcely regretted exchanging Greensboro for Princeton. West of 59 Battle Road a tangle of trees and vines bordered his lot, the northern end of which merged into a grove of locusts. Alice had had a flagstone terrace, roofed over on account of her weak eyes, built on the north side of the library. Now she enjoyed it vicariously, whenever her brother sat there for his after-breakfast pipe or his afternoon tea, which he liked also under the locusts. The "little covered loggia here, looking out over a bit of lawn, a few flowers, and into a back screen of trees, can hold me by the hour in something almost like a trance. The place is particularly desirable in the mornings, because the light and shade are then at the best, and the birds (never anywhere else in the world have I seen and heard so many) are most vociferous. I should not like to say how many morning hours I wasted there

⁷ To Robert Shafer, Aug. 25, 1930.
⁸ To the same, Sept. 22, 1930.
⁹ To Percy H. Houston, Sept. 25, 1930.

in May and June and again this warm September—and yet I should not say wasted for my brain was very active and my heart very light. (Am I a humanist, or a Romantic?)"[10]

Alice More, "a brave soul,"[11] died October 5, 1930. She "had been passionately devoted to me all my life," her brother reported to Philip S. Richards. "Her death spared her months, perhaps years, of decline and weakness, but it seems a bit hard that she had to go just when she had what always she most craved—the irony of Fate, which appeals to me less than the Sophoclean variety. My other remaining sister, a widow, is still with me; but must go back to her home in the West very soon. Then begins my experiment of solitude.

"While at Greensboro I got hold of a recent book by A. J. Macdonald on *Berengar and the Reform of Sacramental Doctrine*. It is an excellent book from the historical point of view, and I set out to write a review of it for Eliot's *Criterion*. The review waxed in length, and I decided to develop it into an article for *The Criterion*. The article began to expand beyond measure. In the end I rewrote it, and it now stands as an essay on the Sacramental Principle of the Eucharist ready for my next, and concluding, volume [of *The Greek Tradition*]. I wish I could read it to you and get your criticism. I am going to read it, despite its length, to a young reverend named Crocker who has come here as student chaplain at what is called the Foundation House[12] but has no official connexion with the university."[13]

"This term I have an undergraduate and a graduate course— the latter on Aristotle,[14] and on this I am putting my time and energy."[15] For recreation More walked to the Princeton Pre-

[10] To Robert Shafer, Sept. 22, 1930.
[11] To Irving Babbitt, Nov. 10, 1930.
[12] The house at 53 University Place was used as a Protestant Episcopal center for student activities by the William Alexander Procter Foundation, as a trustee of which More served from about 1932 to 1936 "with devoted interest and wise counsel."
[13] To Philip S. Richards, Oct. 12, 1930.
[14] The former on the origins of Christianity.
[15] To Prosser Hall Frye, Oct. 30, 1930.

paratory School to see Darrah, to talk with the masters, or to watch the boys at their games. His son-in-law (who in 1929 had been appointed headmaster) persuaded him to address the pupils that October on Shakespeare. As the school's problems increased with the deepening economic depression, Harry Fine discussed them with More, who, as a trustee of the institution for several years, provided moral and financial support.

"I had not been informed of your election to the Academy,"[16] he mentioned to Babbitt, who soon visited him in Princeton, "until your letter came this afternoon. I am glad that the 'immortals' have seen the light at last, but frankly I do not think you will get much profit from the honour. If they had not elected you this year, I was in fact on the point of resigning."[17]

Having previously dismissed the Sauk Center man as intellectually cruder than Theodore Dreiser and Sherwood Anderson,[18] More, even apart from a pang of disappointment, thought the selection of Sinclair Lewis as the first American to receive the Nobel Prize in literature was scandalous. He wondered sometimes whether Lewis, though a stranger to him, had used the names Elmer Gantry and Babbitt as a slap at him and his friend. Yet he repeatedly insisted that to introduce words, like "Main Street"[19] and "Babbitt," into everyday language was an extraordinary achievement. And in his own eyes More appeared to himself as "a very human and groping person, very much addicted to friendship, humble as to my efficiency as a writer and more so of my ability to teach. This is not cant, but simple truth."[20]

[16] The American Academy of Arts and Letters.
[17] To Irving Babbitt, Nov. 10, 1930. ". . . I take little interest in the Academy and cannot see that it has any real use. In fact the taste of its leaders and their methods so irritate me that several times I have been on the point of resigning." [To Irving Babbitt, Nov. 18, 1931.] In Nov. 1931 with Babbitt's support More also became a member of the American Academy of Arts and Sciences.
[18] Cf. *DA*, 63.
[19] Cf. *DA*, 69.
[20] To Alan Reynolds Thompson, Dec. 2, 1930.

The Platonizing Catholic

As to his ability to teach, opinions varied. By his synoptic approach he made Aristotle alive as a whole rather than as a sum of his parts. He presented the Stagirite not only in the context of his own day but in that of earlier and later, oriental and occidental, philosophical and religious, thought. He continually aroused his hearers' curiosity by suggesting tempting paths of research in Aristotle, Plato, Plotinus, and St. Thomas Aquinas. Some of them considered his course on Aristotle as in substance, though not in form and delivery, one of the most satisfactory and brilliant of any they had taken in Europe or America. Indeed it became almost a cult. A few of his students from the department of philosophy, however, reacting in part against the fervor of his disciples, urged a professor in that department to rescue Aristotle from More. They complained that More's failure to assign a definite program of study and to require periodical reports encouraged loafing rather than independent work. They disliked his cold, constrained manner of lecturing and even more the obstinacy with which he clung to some of his opinions, with the irritating implication that those disagreeing with him must be fools.

"I have, by the way," More related to Shafer, "been having rather a good time reading the essays of my present volume (on *The Catholic Faith*) to a select group. I have had the curate of Trinity,[21] the student chaplain,[22] and Bob Root[23] to dinner, filling them with wine and tobacco, and a number of young men later in the evening. Root has given me some valuable criticism —a keen mind."[24]

The next few years More held about once a month such little dinners at 59 Battle Road followed by a larger group to discuss a paper written and read aloud by him or by one of his guests. For these occasions he drew not on old friends, whose

[21] Roger Alling was then curate of Trinity Church, Princeton.
[22] John Crocker.
[23] Robert Kilburn Root, a professor of English at Princeton University and, from 1933, Dean of the Faculty.
[24] To Robert Shafer, Feb. 28, 1931.

thoughts he knew almost as well as his own, but on a new generation. "I wish it could be impressed upon . . . [the young] that in a way they can really confer more upon the old than the old can upon them. I do not mean by that any silly glorification of youth, but just that as one grows old it is highly stimulating to come in contact with younger, still searching minds, and to feel that one has even a little to impart from one's long experience."[25] Besides Alling, Crocker, and Root, he invited as his more regular participants, at different times and in different combinations, Albert M. Friend, Francis R. B. Godolphin, Theodore M. Greene, Asher E. Hinds,[26] Whitney J. Oates,[27] and Hugh S. Taylor,[28] from the university; Quitman F. Beckley, the Roman Catholic chaplain at Princeton; and Samuel P. Cowardin, Jr., Harry B. Fine, R. Prunty MacGerrigle, and Paul F. Vaka, from the Princeton Preparatory School.

A night a week he liked to reserve for music, with Darrah or Ruth McLinn or Vaka at the piano, and Mary Crocker or Cowardin or Louis F. Rahm[29] at the violin. When Rahm also played the flute, More insisted on taking the easier part, saying that a man of his age, who was always getting out of breath, had no business to blow a flute at all. Though he liked some of the music of Chopin, Schumann, Brahms, Debussy, and Ravel, the eighteenth century classics appealed to him more—Bach, Händel, Haydn, and, above all, Mozart. "But I should like to include Beethoven among them. To be sure one can detect in him hints of the coming decline, and certainly he lacks the seraphic purity of Mozart and the exhaustless genius of Bach, but after all he belongs among the children of light. Wagner

[25] To Bernard Iddings Bell, Feb. 11, 1934.
[26] An instructor in English.
[27] An assistant professor of classics, who later wrote "Paul Elmer More: A Quest of the Spirit," *The Lives of Eighteen from Princeton*, edited by Willard Thorp, Princeton (Princeton University Press), 1946, pp. 302-17, with a photograph of More opposite p. 308.
[28] A professor of chemistry, later Dean of the Graduate School.
[29] An assistant professor of engineering at Princeton University.

to my mind is the great corrupter, though again at his best Wagner has a reminiscent note of the divine. Most modern music to me is just liquefied ugliness, a moral and aesthetic poison gas. Nothing greatly good can come from an age that enjoys it."[30]

Among More's new friends was a graduate student of philosophy, Edward DeLos Myers, who in the winter of 1930-31 dropped in at 59 Battle Road several times a week—on a morning to discuss his doctoral thesis about Santayana, which the department of philosophy had asked More to supervise, on an afternoon for tea, and on an evening for bridge. At the start More admitted he had read nothing by Santayana after *Winds of Doctrine* in 1913. But from his understanding of Santayana's point of view until then, he outlined how he imagined his thought had developed since, which impressed Myers who, thoroughly acquainted with Santayana's published works, found More's conjectures amazingly accurate. Henry L. Shepherd, Jr., a graduate student of economics, usually accompanied Myers to the bridge games, the fourth being sometimes Ernest T. DeWald, an associate professor of art and archaeology, or another member of the faculty, or Barrows Dunham, George F. Luthringer, Graham C. Mees, or another graduate student. Convinced that economics was of little scientific and of less cultural value, More joked with Shepherd continually about economists, sparing only Tawney, whose *Religion and the Rise of Capitalism* proved, he stated, that even an economist might be a scholar.

"You may be interested to hear that a number of my *Shelburne Essays* are to appear, translated, in a Swedish newspaper,[31] and that two Stockholm houses are negotiating to print translations of *The Greek Tradition*—and this because the Nobel Prize went to Sinclair Lewis!"[32]

[30] To Austin Warren, Oct. 22, 1929.

[31] "Modern Currents in American Literature" (*DA*), "Justice" (*SE* IX), and "Pascal" (*SE* VI) were printed in *Nya Dagligt Allehanda* (Stockholm), Söndagsbilaga, on, respectively, p. 3, March 8, 1931; p. 3, Nov. 8, 1931; and p. 3, May 10, and p. 2, May 25, 1932.

[32] To Robert Shafer, Feb. 28, 1931. In *Nya Dagligt Allehanda*, Nov.

1930-1931

Having managed, by typing after midnight, to dispatch at the end of March the manuscript of *The Catholic Faith* to the printers, on April 4th More "sailed for England in the *Britannic*. Lou was with me and I also knew a Fellow of Magdalen, Oxford, so that the trip was less irksome than usual. We landed at Liverpool and I went immediately to Cambridge, via London, to be with Alice. Seven days later Alice had a son,[33] a sturdy boy, and as Darrah had a son[34] not long before my sailing, I am now a thrice venerable grandfather. Lou went to London, where he . . . worked at the Museum on his life of Newton. After a month I joined him at Brown's Hotel, from which centre —an excellent hotel—we knocked about town and saw various people. My chief interest in the latter way was with T. S. Eliot. He had written me that he was looking forward to long evenings"[35] "enlivened by whiskey and tobacco and countercharges of heresy. Ah, theology is the only interesting topic after all, and to convict a devout Anglo-Catholic of heresy is something for which I would surrender ten good dinners."[36] "As a matter of fact we had little whiskey and less theology.[37] But we did discuss

---

16, 1930, Söndagsbilaga, p. 4, Knut Hagberg, "one of the younger outstanding critics," published what More called "a strong rebuke for the awarding of the Nobel Prize to Lewis and claim for myself." [To Seward B. Collins, Dec. 13, 1930.] "I do not quite recognize myself as the inhuman philosopher living in inaccessible isolation; I seem to myself very human indeed. On the other hand Hagberg has shown real penetration in seeing that the ground of my inner life has been rather emotional than purely intellectual; in guessing that the letters of *The Great Refusal*, with some exceptions, are actual documents; and in tracing the development of my ideas." [To the same, Dec. 18, 1930.] *Det Nya Testamentets Kristus*, with an introduction by Knut Hagberg, was published by Wahlström and Widstrand, of Stockholm, in 1932.

[33] Paul Philip Dymond.   [34] John Burchard Fine.

[35] To Prosser Hall Frye, Sept. 8, 1931.

[36] To William P. Trent, March 24, 1931.

[37] "There were so many things that I really wanted to discuss with you seriously and at length. But that is life—my life at least—we are just tossed about on the surface of things and have so few chances to touch our deeper interests. And in this case the fault is entirely my own, for I cannot but be grateful for your hospitality and for the time you gave me. . . . You are for me, intellectually, a magnificent enigma, which I shall never unriddle to my satisfaction." [To T. S. Eliot, July 10, 1931.]

literature a bit, and I tried, and failed, to discover what he is aiming at in the wild mystifications that he calls poetry. He is getting a notable position in England. I should be inclined to rate him the most distinguished man of letters in the English-speaking world. . . . P. S. Richards, a schoolmaster and writer whose name may be familiar to you, dined with us one evening. Later I was his guest at the White Horse Inn, Storrington (where Tyrrell lies buried), and he drove me about the charming country of Sussex. From there I went to Exeter, where I joined Lou again, and where we hired a car for a tour from Tintagel to Taunton. There we dismissed the car and took train for Bath. From there to Liverpool, where Lou met his family. I went on to Glasgow[38] where I picked up an LL.D.[39] (and the most gorgeous robe imaginable, of scarlet and Venetian red). My next point was Edinburgh, where I stopped with Norman Kemp

[38] On his way to Glasgow to receive an honorary degree on June 17th, More bought in Chester a copy of *The Roadmender*. The book, like others of its kind, puzzled him. "This deep peace, this assured tranquillity, this strong realization in the present of the other world—is all this literature or life? Did the author live and feel what the pen puts down? I know quite well that I myself could write in such a vein (though without the genius of expression), and appear to the world as one in whom all troublesome doubts had been overcome, while the beasts of hell were ravening at my heart. I wish I knew how to take such literature. Shall I confess that *The Roadmender*, as I read it this time, gave me keen aesthetic delight but saddened me—but alas, so many things sadden me that used to exalt. There's something wrong in Denmark, you will say; and there is: old age first of all, and too much knowledge of human nature—though this last sounds like boasting. And for religion: is any man really religious? The will to believe, yes; the penetration of the world's illusions, yes; the desperate love of ideas, Plato's Ideas, and the Christian's God; a sublime and awed reverence of that enigma of history, Jesus, yes; an intellectual conviction of dualism (which sounds like an anticlimax, but is the keystone to the whole building), yes; but the joy and peace of religion? Is it that the faces of the great saints, and the terrible figure of the crucifix itself, should warn us not to look for joy and peace in this life? But then, what sublime faith in another life this compels, and who has it?" [To Philip S. Richards, June 14, 1931. Richards had taken More to the grave, in Ashurst, of "Michael Fairless" (Margaret Fairless Barber), the author of *The Roadmender*.]

[39] Archibald Allan Bowman at a meeting of the university senate proposed More for this degree.

Smith. At dinner there I met Grierson and A. E. Taylor, the latter being the most volubly continuous talker I ever tried to interrupt, but interesting and enormously learned. I went then by express to Oxford, where I engaged an assistant for the projected 'corpus,' and so back to Cambridge. Have I told you about the 'corpus'? It is to be an anthology . . . including sermons, chapters from books, documents of all sorts, to illustrate the *ethos* of the Anglican Church in the period from Hooker to Ken. It is to be published by the S.P.C.K. Through Bishop Rhinelander, of the College of Preachers, Washington, money has been raised to pay a salary to an assistant editor for two years, and it was this assistant I engaged at Oxford. He is a young priest,[40] now at Pusey House, who I think is thoroughly well qualified for the work. . . .

"Perhaps the most amusing adventure in England was a week[41] spent at Magdalen, Oxford, as guest of two Fellows. I had a Fellow's suite of rooms and saw life from inside as I never had seen it before. What interested me most was the intimate intercourse with the students. I dined and wined with them and was treated by them with a courteous familiarity for which no experience with American colleges had prepared me."[42]

[40] Frank Leslie Cross.
[41] Beginning May 11, 1931.
[42] To Prosser Hall Frye, Sept. 8, 1931. John Frederick Wolfenden, formerly a Davison Scholar at Princeton and in 1931 a Fellow of Magdalen, who had been invited to the twenty-first birthday dinner of one of his students, on excusing himself from attending, because he was then to dine with More, asked the undergraduate whether he might, later in the evening, bring in "the American professor" who was his guest. After the two parties had dined pretty well in their several places, Wolfenden went to see how things fared with the twenty-firster. Greeted there with "a concerted sing-song: 'We don't want you, we want the American professor,'" he left and fetched him. After an uproarious welcome, More was "induced to stand on a chair and make a speech," which was received "with suitable hilarity." The Fellow and his guest remained with the youngsters until early the next morning. On the following evening when More chanced to meet in Wolfenden's rooms some of his recent companions in revelry he told them that *The Atlantic Monthly* had commissioned him to write an article on "the relations between the faculty and the undergraduates at English universities" and that "the events of the

The Platonizing Catholic

More left London July 18th on the *Minnewaska* to read in Princeton the proofs of *The Catholic Faith*, which Babbitt had gone through with such "extreme care"[43] as to prompt extensive revision of its first essay, "Buddhism and Christianity." In regard to Buddhism "the point is this, and I insist on it: What is it that is reborn? Something is reborn, and yet over and over again, in the anattâ doctrine,[44] Buddha so analyses the constituents of being that nothing would seem to be left for rebirth where there is only a stream of cause and effect. It is true also that he rejects the question of *what* is reborn as not for edification. But his psychological analysis, nevertheless, forces the question, and did force the question upon his disciples as many passages show. I cannot help thinking that the Western acceptance of the soul as something namable at least, however unanalysable, is better logic and better psychology, unless one takes a purely agnostic position and denies any knowledge of moral responsibility carried into the future. Buddha's position is morally, to this point, irreproachable; it is philosophically impossible. And beyond this point the difficulties, both moral and philosophical, increase. His conception of Nirvâna does most certainly involve what I call an 'absolved dualism'[45] and does lead to the difficulties I enumer-

---

previous evening had given him just the slant he needed." He spoke with such solemnity that it took Wolfenden several days to convince his sheepish pupils that they had not been turned into "copy for an American magazine."

[43] To Irving Babbitt, Aug. 2, 1931.

[44] Cf. *CF*, 45 f., 54 f.

[45] "Any genuine dualism must be 'absolute' in the sense that it postulates a radical distinction between spirit and matter and between good and evil, with all that these distinctions imply. Admittedly a conjunction of such contraries involves an irrational paradox in the nature of things; but it is a paradox rooted in the nethermost stratum of human consciousness, and it may be the foundation of a perfectly reasonable superstructure of experience. Without it certainly the otherworldliness and morality of religion . . . correspond to nothing objectively true. By an 'absolved' dualism I mean that the absolute distinctions of dualism are maintained, but on the condition, so to speak, that the goal of religious endeavour shall be regarded as a final divorce of these opposites in such wise as to permit spirit to exist in perfect unity and immutability, absolved from

ate. Up to a certain point the fruits of Buddhism and Christianity are extraordinarily alike. . . . But I do not see how anyone familiar with history, and unprejudiced, can fail to see that Christianity (despite its fanaticism, etc.—*corruptio optimi pessima*) has produced a richer life than Buddhism. Nor does it seem to me possible to deny that this is because Christianity accepts the soul simply and refuses practically, despite the vagaries of certain metaphysical theologians, to advance to an absolved dualism. Whether Buddhism or Christianity is true in this respect is another question, though pragmatically the argument is on the side of the latter. . . .

"The last essay in the book . . . is a long discussion of mysticism in which I endeavour to distinguish its various forms. In clinging to an 'absolute' as against an 'absolved' dualism I mean to say simply that the absolute, abstract element of our being that we express as unity and immutability has no meaning for us apart from its conjunction with multiplicity and change."[46]

". . . the excesses of Christian mysticism must be condemned because they nullify the vision of purpose and the law of measure."[47] In a mood or seizure "in which all the variety of our impulsive being is swallowed up, for the most part only momentarily, in an abysmal sense of absolute unity,"[48] lies "a ground of psychological experience, potential in all men, actually realized in a few, common to the mystics of all lands and times and accountable for the similarity of their reports. But upon

---

any association with the feelings and thoughts and activities which pertain to the multiple and mutable element of normal consciousness. That of course is an ideal of mysticism wherever it appears, and is the special mark of Buddha's teaching only in so far as he carried it out with exceptional rigour of logic. The conclusion I would draw in that the right in Buddhism, and to a lesser degree in all other true forms of mysticism, depends on a sturdy adherence to dualism, while its wrong follows upon the attempt to pass from an absolute to an absolved dualism." [*CF*, 66-67, with corrections made by More in his copy of the book. Cf. *ibid.*, pp. 206-312.]

[46] To Irving Babbitt, Aug. 12, 1931.
[47] *CF*, 222.   [48] *CF*, 290-91.

that common basis we need not be surprised to see them also erecting various superstructures in accordance with their particular tenets of philosophy or religion."⁴⁹ "It is one thing to lift the heart towards God the Father in perfect love, to subdue the restless human will into obedience, so that at the last we may say, *la sua volontade é nostra pace.* That is the way of *homoiôsis*, of becoming like to God through the economy of atonement. . . . It is another thing to strive after union with the unqualified, impersonal, infinite Absolute by the suppression of all desire and love and by the transcendence of our personal individuality. . . . To attempt a combination of these two aspirations of *homoiôsis* and absorption . . . is to create a tension of spirit, an anxiety, an acute torment, an overshadowing of doubt and despair, from which few who enter upon that way can escape, and which no man should be asked to undergo in the name of religion."⁵⁰ ". . . the impulse to hypostatize the unifying energy of the soul into an absolved Unity must be regarded as a temptation of the reason just as surely as the impulse in the opposite direction must be so regarded; and the effort to lose our sense of conscious responsible being in the gaping abyss of the unconscious is a temptation of the spirit just as surely as the surrender in the opposite direction is a temptation of the flesh."⁵¹

Thus on somewhat similar grounds More rejected certain aspects of Buddhism, Christianity's closest rival as a world religion, and of mysticism, revelation's chief competitor as a claimant to religious truth. ". . . without revelation the belief of the Christian is a baseless assumption."⁵² Jesus claimed, according to Christian tradition, "some unique relationship to God, whether as Son or Logos. We may even assert, as the Councils of Nicea and Chalcedon did assert in no hesitating language, that in some way he is presented as having that in him which must be called very God of very God. But how? What is the

---

⁴⁹ *CF*, 294.   ⁵⁰ *CF*, 310; cf. *RP*, 38 f.
⁵¹ *CF*, 297.   ⁵² *CF*, 170.

character of this mystical relation? Why, if the whole fabric of Christianity is to be founded on this dogma of the Incarnation, should the formulation of the truth and its corollaries be left after all to inference? Why are not the statements of the fact so consistently categorical as to leave no loophole for evasion or misinterpretation or nuance of understanding or honest doubt? . . . Why should revelation so stammer in its speech?"[53]

"The morality preached by Jesus in his call to repentance . . . may be summed up pretty thoroughly under three heads: Purity, Humility, and Love. . . . He who sets out on the way of purity and humility and love will know beyond peradventure by the indubitable voice of conscience, that he is moving towards the God of Christ and into the heaven of spiritual peace. And if he will consider the intimacy with which these three principles are combined with the gospel message, and the completeness with which they cover the religious life, and if then from all these points of view he will compare the teaching of Christianity with the ethics of any other doctrine, even Buddhism, I think he will be inclined to admit that here he has found something which can claim the distinctive authority of revelation."[54]

For him who accepts it revelation must have an intimate note of finality, such as we find, for example, in "the indubitable voice of conscience." Without such "immediate" and "finer intuitions of the soul" "Church and dogma fall into a parody of religion."[55] There is, of course, nothing transparent about conscience or simple about intuition. "The vigour with which certain principles of the religious life are announced" in Christian tradition contrasts vividly with "the curious lack of precision in the application of these principles to the details of conduct."[56] Though we must live up to our convictions (or to such revelation as we can assimilate), doubt shadows our discovery and implementation of them. "It is futile to talk of an absolute inspiration," or of an absolute revelation, "which cannot, or will

[53] CF, 176-77.   [54] CF, 172-73.   [55] CF, 199.
[56] CF, 172. For a similar situation in the ethics of Plato, cf. RP, 284.

not, make itself indisputably clear."[57] Some such inevitable "mingling of vivid insistence with strange ambiguity"[58] seems to underlie what More calls his "mediatorial view of common sense,"[59] that there is no absolute authority or infallible revelation in scripture, church, or pope,[60] though any or all may possess "a certain amount of authority,"[61] depending, presumably, on how well they express "the accumulated wisdom of the race."[62]

"Thus it is that at the last religion can be neither purely individualistic nor purely determined. In one sense individualistic, yes, in so far as the ultimate responsibility of choice cannot be withdrawn from the conscience of each man, whether he shall accept this dogma and this form as complying with what seems to him the verity of his own inner life or shall reject them as expansions in a false direction; but determined also to this degree, that he will be extremely hesitant to set up his private judgement against a formulated tradition, and will prefer to abide in humble, yet not abject, submission to the authority of a wider experience than his own. He may even find his peace by uniting himself to a corporation with which he is not in complete sympathy, and by participating in a liturgy which he cannot interpret to himself quite in its literal sense, knowing that only by such concessions can any stability of worship be maintained. That is what I mean by an authoritative as contrasted with an absolute Church. No doubt there is something unsatisfactory in such a position; it demands the constant exercise of our will and intelligence in making an adjustment never quite final . . . there is no finality granted us here any more than in the other fields of life. As Emerson said: 'God offers to every mind its choice between truth and repose; take which you please, you can never have both.' "[63]

[57] *CF*, 172.   [58] *CF*, 174.   [59] *CF*, 169.
[60] Cf. *CF*, 171 ff., and *A*, xxviii-xxxii.
[61] *CF*, 169; cf. *ibid.*, p. 183.   [62] *CF*, 203.
[63] *CF*, 203-04, as emended by More in his copy of the book.

Repelled by the "infallible book," "the poorly nourished homily," "the extemporaneous prayers," and the "poverty-stricken service" of "the rationalizing Protestant," and by the infallible pope, the false expansions of dogmas, and the quasi-magic nature of some of the practices of the "rationalizing Papist,"[64] More found in Anglicanism a congenial kind of Christianity. In the Protestant Episcopal Church in the United States of America he had to determine how he would "accept this dogma and this form as complying with . . . the verity of his own inner life." If, as he contended, "the revelation of supernatural truth must come to us through our natural faculties," and if "its expression must be conditioned by what, in a broad sense, may be called the scientific belief at any particular period,"[65] then a Christian is continually obliged to reinterpret his ancient creeds in such a way as to express their truths in the language of his day.

"The degree and manner of believing vary with the content" of what is believed, and even where the content is identical, the grounds or the reasons for belief vary with different people.[66] This point of view prevails in More's treatment of the articles of the so-called Apostles' Creed, the only one discussed at length in *The Catholic Faith*. He reiterates and elaborates his position that a trinitarian formula rather than the later personification of the Holy Ghost in the dogma of the Trinity is a more Christian and orthodox way of dealing symbolically with an inexpressible mystery.[67] Having "committed himself to the

[64] *CF*, 170, 180-99.
[65] From a note written by More on the margin of pp. 112-13 of his copy of *CF*.
[66] *CF*, 79.
[67] *CF*, 81-84, 94-95. ". . . I am still convinced that for liturgical purposes the trinitarian formula is justifiable and valuable but that the attempt to deal with the ἅγιον πνεῦμα philosophically as a πρόσωπον or ὑπόστασις of the same category as the Father and the Son leads to mischievous impossibilities. That does not mean that I am, as some of my critics have called me, a 'binitarian' instead of a trinitarian. I prefer to leave the conception of the λόγος very much in the vague." [To Hugh H.F.O. Morton, Dec. 25, 1928.]

The Platonizing Catholic

supernatural" by his acceptance of the Incarnation, he has no
difficulty "so far as the mere fact of miracle is concerned," but
is obliged to question "what may be called the manner of the
miraculous."[68] Of the descent into hell, the resurrection, the as-
cension into heaven, and the judgement, while acknowledging
an important truth in the affirmations, he admitted of each:
". . . I do not understand it to have happened in the manner
understood by those who formulated the words I use, and to
this extent I reserve the right of private interpretation."[69]
Though heaven and hell, for instance, were not empty sounds
to him, he could not "conceive them locally and spatially as they
were conceived by the apostles, by the early Church, and by the
great divines of the seventeenth century."[70] With "the changing
views of the age," he confessed, "the sense of the words"
change too; so it is "a mere subterfuge to pretend that the
creed is quite the same thing" for us as it was for the early
Church.[71] Once, however, "the door is thrown open to a slid-
ing scale in the matter of belief," the question becomes not
whether reservation is permitted "but where the line should be
drawn between an honest use of reserve and a liability to the
charge of hypocrisy."[72] "I think the test of sincerity lies in this:
is there behind the metaphorical language a truth to which we
can give whole-hearted assent? If there be such a truth, then I
do not see why the most meticulous mind should hesitate to
make confession."[73]

[68] *CF*, 85; cf. *CNT*, 256 ff.   [69] *CF*, 86; cf. *CNT*, 269-80.
[70] *CF*, 87-88.   [71] *CF*, 88.   [72] *Ibid.*
[73] *CF*, 111-12. On the margins of pp. 112-13 of his copy of *CF* More
noted the difference between his position and that of the modernist. "The
modernist carries his rejection of literalism up to the fact of the Incarnation itself, which the genuine Christian must accept as an actual event
in history. Hence his interpretation . . ." of various articles of the creed
"deprives them of any relation to fact in such wise that they become
not different ways of expressing great truths but mere concessions to the
als ob. It does not reinterpret the articles, but says that, though they are
fundamentally false, we must act as if they were true. This difference
comes out even in the virgin birth where the two might seem to agree.
The genuine Christian takes the article symbolically in regard to the

Besides its discussions of Buddhism, mysticism, church, and creed, *The Catholic Faith* contains also a chapter on "The Eucharistic Sacrament." "The sacramental idea . . . rests ultimately upon a dualistic conception of the world, in accordance with which matter and spirit are essentially distinct yet mutually interdependent. It implies on the one side that matter can be indefinitely adapted to spiritual uses, and on the other side that spirit requires now and, so far as our knowledge and imagination reach, will always require the aid of some sort of corporeal instruments. It points to a divine purpose unfolding itself in a continuous process wherein the stuff of existence is miraculously transmuted into an ever finer medium of order and beauty and righteousness and joy. And in this scheme it holds that men are called to play a subordinate part under the eye of the supreme Artificer, and that their every act, even the least, may be dedicated to this end:

> A servant with this clause
> Makes drudgery divine:
> Who sweeps a room, as for Thy laws,
> Makes that and the action fine.

> This is the famous stone
> That turneth all to gold:
> For that which God doth touch and own
> Cannot for less be told."[74]

In regard to the Eucharistic sacrament More thought it "a reasonable attitude towards the faith to hold that the Spirit of Christ may descend upon the elements for a divine purpose in the same manner as, according to the theory of the *Timaeus*, Ideas are imposed upon the inert stuff of Necessity, not as a

---

birth of one who was truly and actually theanthropos. The modernist sees no historical fact behind it to justify the symbolism." [Cf. *CNT*, 267-69, and *CW*, 78-79.]

[74] *CF*, 122-23.

substance supplanting another substance, nor as a substance mechanically conjoined to another substance, but as actual powers of creative adaptation. It is a quieter of many doubts to hold that, as the Idea of Beauty is really present in material phenomena and renders them beautiful to the eye, while yet the Idea abides in its own unique and glorious integrity, so the Logos may be really present in the bread and wine, making of them its own body, and by their material instrumentality imparting itself to the embodied souls of men. In this way the miracle of the Real Presence becomes only one aspect of the ultimate mystery that confronts us in the dualism of mind and body and whithersoever else we turn."[75]

While he revised the proof of *The Catholic Faith*, More resorted to "a good deal of wire-pulling" to get Mary, his cook for more than twenty-five years, who had developed tuberculosis, "placed in a sanatorium, where I hope she will receive adequate treatment. She must remain there of course for many months, and indeed I am not too sanguine of her recovery at all. Meanwhile William will carry on for me alone, with occasional help from the outside. My housekeeping will go on one foot, but I trust not too lamely."[76]

After a "rather drab summer"[77] in Essex, More stayed a short time with the Gausses in Greensboro on his way back to Princeton to give two undergraduate courses, one on Plato, the other on the origins of Christianity, during the first term of the academic year 1931-32.

"I have been looking through the September *Bookman*," he wrote to Shafer, who had called at "The Cedars" some weeks before, ". . . and was disappointed to find nothing of yours in it and still more disappointed at Babbitt's attack on Wordsworth. This strikes me as an eminent example of failure to obey the two

---

[75] *CF*, 167-68.

[76] To Irving Babbitt, Aug. 12, 1931. More paid Mary's hospital expenses.

[77] To Robert Shafer, Sept. 13, 1931.

guiding laws which are the charter of humanism and of which Babbitt himself, rightly, makes so much: distinctions and mediation. Take the words 'wise passivity,' on which any sound discussion of Wordsworth's criticism of life must turn. Surely the phrase has a double meaning and calls for distinction: (1) all passivity, that is wise as opposed to any activity, and (2) a wise as opposed to an unwise passivity. Now I do not see how one can read the whole of Wordsworth without feeling that he uses the principle sometimes in the former, sometimes in the latter sense. For instance the famous stanza on the 'vernal impulse,' which I myself have quoted to Wordsworth's detriment, undoubtedly inclines to the former and more romantic interpretation of passivity. But innumerable passages could be cited tending in the other direction. Taken literally, the stanza is an absurdity. But understood as it may be from a larger reading of Wordsworth, to signify the need of opening the mind, by a wise kind of passivity, to the perception and influence of divine purpose in nature as opposed to the way of the 'sages' (the word is ill chosen) who cannot go beyond the drawing of shallow pedantic distinctions, who would peep and botanize on their mother's grave, the stanza hints at a great truth. So it is with the pantheistic revery of *Tintern Abbey*. The same question and need of distinction arises in connection with the doctrine of Grace. Taken as the quietists, and practically many of the accepted mystics (as I have tried to show in my treatment of Juan de la Cruz[78]), took it when they speak of 'infused grace,' you have a theory of 'wise passivity' in the first, and wrong, sense: i. e. the belief that man of himself can do nothing, that his will is totally evil and of no avail for salvation, and that religion demands a complete suppression of all the faculties and an utterly passive surrender to some arbitrary, if not freakish, influence out of the skies. The orthodox view of the Church has been to deny 'infused grace' in this sense and to mediate between the spirit of God and man's free will. So I

[78] Cf. *CF*, 253-83.

The Platonizing Catholic

think a true humanism should mediate between romantic revery which prescinds distinctions and floats away into a debilitating emotionalism in the manner of Schleiermacher and Rousseau who take this to be the essence of religion, and a cold harsh intellectualism which finds salvation in the bare distinguishing faculty of reason. And such a mediation is not a mechanical compromise or a flabby wavering between two moods, but an intimate marriage between passivity and activity, contemplation and self-direction, emotion and will, of which is born a certain *tertium quid*.

"Now undoubtedly Wordsworth in the course of his life and under the sway of diverse currents did waver in his allegiance. But I am convinced that the total effect of his work and the central drive of his mind leave the impression of just such a mediation as I have described, or at least that a wisely balanced criticism would so mediate. After all Arnold was right in lauding Wordsworth's healing power and in insisting on the value of his message for us of today, who are caught in a civilization bent on a purely mechanical wisdom and based on a philosophy that can find no centre of repose between vague dispersive revery and a slavish materialism. We need to be instructed in the orthodox doctrine of Grace and the true philosophy of divine purpose discoverable in impulses from the vernal wood. . . .

"Babbitt's one-sided treatment of the theme seems to me to lay the cause of humanism open to the charge of barrenness and imaginative dryness so often expressed. . . . There is a profound and fruitful truth in Babbitt's hostility; the question is whether what he condemns is the total and veritably effective element of Wordsworthianism."[79]

"As for my own early criticism of Wordsworth, I simply confess that it is one example out of many where I have said things that ought not to have been said or, more particularly in this case, left unsaid the things that ought to have been said.

[79] To Robert Shafer, Sept. 13, 1931.

The article is wrong rather, I think, in emphasis than in substance. I too, and more than Babbitt, need to be readjusted, though not for the same reasons. The key to understanding my essays—and I cannot blame those who do not possess it—is that my noetic life, if I may call it such, has been wrought out of separate strands which have appeared and reappeared in various combinations and antagonisms; so much so that to myself, when I dare to look back over the past, I seem to be not one but all mankind's epitome—not to mention Plato's many-headed beast. In my youth I was steeped in the rankest romantic literature of Germany, and suffered from it grievously, in ways that need not be described. Yet all the while there was a strong pull within me to the classics, at first the Latin and later the Greek. By the time I got to Harvard I had become acutely aware of the mischief done me, and had begun deliberately to refashion my taste on the classics. And in this Babbitt, who was born in Horace's cradle, acted as a powerful stimulus. Hence the note of personal bitterness occasionally in my attacks on the romantics, and such lapses of taste as the essay on Wordsworth.

"Another strand in this unstable compound was a hard, dry rationalism. While inditing tragedies and a huge epic in the romantic vein (fortunately long ago burnt), I was plotting out a rationalistic philosophy which should accomplish what Darwin and Spencer had failed to finish (and this too went to the flames). How in my one poor person I harboured three such clamorously diverse moods, the dominance of which was in part consecutive but in part also synchronistic, or how I contrived to have any intellectual character at all,—I do not know.

"But along with these three strands ran from the beginning a religious impulse—the strongest of them, I think, though often out of sight. This was emphatically dominant in childhood, suffered from scepticism in adolescence, and was mutilated and all but destroyed by rationalism. Its reappearance, I fear, shows signs of that mutilation. But even when most submerged it was there, pushing this way and that for egress and searching for some philosophical justification of its existence. Then, in 1891, I chanced upon Baur's *Das Manichäische Religionssystem*,— how I do not remember. Such mental excitement as that book gave me I had never known before and have never felt since. It was as if the religious sense, like a drowning man, had laid hold of something solid to which it could cling. This was the principle of dualism,—a crude mechanical sort of philosophy as taught by the Manicheans, but through the really magnificent allegory in which their mythology flowered hinting at a deeper and subtler truth.

"From that time what I see, looking at my writings objectively, is a series of studies in which, so far as they are literary, classicism is gradually strangling the old romantic remnants, while, so far as the religious interest appears, the newly discovered principle of dualism expresses itself in various affiliations. First it takes the hue of romanticism, seeking a medium in medieval mysticism more or less conflated with the mysticism of the Upanishads, as in *The Great Refusal* (genuine letters, I may say quite privately, though with some fictitious additions at the end and with local alterations by way of disguise). Then it purges itself of medievalism and finds its body in the Hindu contrast of Brahma and Mâyâ, *vidyâ* and *avidyâ*, as expressed in the *Century of Indian Epigrams*. As the sway of Oriental thought wanes, it next evaporates, so to speak, into a kind of thin velleity of absolute faith purified of all myth or dogma or even definite belief, as in the essay on Newman.[80]

"Up to this point the religious evolution seems to be strangely lagging behind the literary. But in the end classicism comes to its own in religious philosophy as well as in taste. The result is a transition from India and a sort of thin disembodied Hinduism to Greece, showing itself in attachment to the doctrine of Ideas and phenomena, first in *Platonism*, where the Oriental influence

[80] Cf. *M*, 26-27.

can still be traced, and then more clearly in *The Religion of Plato,* and finally in the Christian Platonism, or Platonic Christianity, of the later volumes. Here *The Catholic Faith* is the τέλος."[81]

[81] To Robert Shafer, Oct. 22, 1931.

16

BABBITT AND ANGLICANISM
(1932-1934)

"THOUGH I boast myself one of the best of Catholics" but "a damn poor Christian,"[1] "my . . . brief stay at Holy Cross" in late January 1932 at the mother house of the order in West Park, New York, "did not give me any real insight into the life. . . . It was all, I say candidly, very alien to me; but this of course is no criticism of the profession. And there are so many ways of serving God, and at the same time doing one's bit for men. The example of holiness is of inestimable value. The sacrifice utterly of worldly life for religion means much to the world. Certainly also an athletic training of the intellect can be made of highest value. I hope the good Lord does not despise the service of the brain any more than he does the service of a contrite heart—despite what St. Paul had to say. . . . often, very often, I regret . . . that circumstances prevented me from becoming a priest (I was, as you know, brought up a Presbyterian). It seems to me that I might have accomplished something real and significant if I had worked under such a check and with such an inspiration, instead of going a-whoring after all the strange deities of the intellectual life."[2] "I . . . might have approached the end of life without regrets for scattered aims and misused powers. I . . . have dabbled in religion all my years, and only now am beginning to know what prayer means!"[3]

"Spring is showing its face, despite the blustering winds and dull skies. Every morning, before dressing, I stand at my bathroom window and look out at the green and yellow outburst. This, you know, is the first time I have seen the season come in at this place,[4] and the spectacle fills me with almost an ecstasy

---

[1] To Edward DeLos Myers, Jan. 16, 1932.
[2] To the same, July 7, 1932.   [3] To the same, Dec. 24, 1932.
[4] 59 Battle Road, Princeton.

of joy. Pretty soon the tulips will be flaunting their scandalous colours, and then the roses, and then the peonies. It is good to see these miraculous returns and very wise to guess at their meaning."[5]

"I. B. was here day before yesterday, having been giving a lecture at Drew Seminary over at Madison. Crocker and Harry and Darrah came in during the evening and stayed pretty late. Then I. B. sat and talked with me until about one—having said repeatedly that he was dog-tired and going to bed early. From one to two I cooled my brain by reading a detective story. The next day he stayed until 2:08 p.m. talking all the while, with Mather as a third part of the time. I can tell you he left me pretty well exhausted. He himself, I am sorry to say, looks old and has a disfiguring eruption on his cheek; but he is venerable, amazingly handsome in his own way."[6]

As tactfully as possible More expressed to the author of *On Being Creative and Other Essays* his opinion of the book. He had not the heart to tell Babbitt, as he told P. S. Richards, that it was "a sad letdown," marked by "damnable iteration," symptomatic of a "narrowing and petrifying" mind. ". . . his treatment of Wordsworth—though all the things he condemns can be found in Wordsworth—is frightfully one-sided and warped and vindictive. His treatment of the 'supernatural' meanwhile grows at once more insistent and more cloudy. I hate to say all this—and indeed I have said it only to one other person, and to him with more reservation—but it is the truth—*quantum mutatus ab illo*."[7]

On the basis of the ideas they had long shared, however, and in regard to Babbitt's "inculcation of humanism on the purely human level of moderation, restraint, decency, etc.," More could assure him that he had read the book "for the most part with great satisfaction. . . . On one or two matters I think you

5 To Louis T. More, April 30, 1932.
6 To the same, May 3, 1932.
7 To Philip S. Richards, May 25, 1932.

still have something to say to make your position clear. For myself I am even yet a little cloudy as to what you mean by imagination and the supernatural, and their relation one to the other. . . . Certainly the imagination is not the perception of resemblances—that faculty, if it has any name, is the reason. You seem to agree with Joubert in his definition of it as that which 'gives access to the supersensuous,' and in this sense, I take it, you use the canon of 'imitation' for art. But what is this supersensuous, or supernatural? It cannot be 'a certain quality of will,' as elsewhere you define the 'superrational.' One doesn't get access to a quality of the will; the will of right quality is that which is directed to, or by, the supernatural. Is this 'supernatural,' 'supersensuous,' 'superrational,' a reality in the sense of the Platonic Ideas, or is it God, or what? Or is there only 'an illusion of a higher reality,' given by the imagination, in the Joubertian phrase?"[8] And what then is meant by illusion? Does it mean that the supernatural is a reality, which becomes through the imagination an illusion in the sense that it appears to us clad in natural, or sensuous, forms? Or does the imagination simply give us the illusion of something as existent which really does not exist? I cannot escape the feeling that you are a little inclined to play fast and loose with your supernatural, dealing with it as a reality at one time, and then retracting it to a mere quality of the will. One can't, in this world, have his cake and eat it. And I may say that it is just impossible to get the psychological benefits of Christianity while rejecting the Christian (and Platonic) conception of the supernatural as a reality. Nor from Buddhism either, for that matter. Nirvâna is erected upon a vast foundation of the supernatural accepted in the most concrete form, though Nirvâna may be an ultimate escape from that supernatural reality."[9]

In response to Babbitt's explanations, More conceded that religion and the supernatural "are indeed difficult to deal with

[8] Cf. *SE* I, 122-28; *SE* II, 25, 112; and *RP*, 328 ff.
[9] To Irving Babbitt, May 17, 1932.

sharply, yet, after all, the Socratic method must be applied there
as well as elsewhere. I think if you would define in writing your
notion of the higher will as clearly as you defined it to me in
conversation,[10] you would satisfy some of your readers who cannot quite make out where you stand and what you mean. It is
another question whether the higher will, so defined, would be
sufficient to supply the place, in any but an extremely few men,
of that sense of the supernatural which they need as a make-
weight against the world and the flesh—not to say the devil. We
are something more than bare will; we must reckon with the
desires, with those of both orders. However you may be *entirely*
right; and certainly you are half right."[11]

"A few days ago . . . [Babbitt] was here with me overnight,"
More wrote to Shafer on June 13, 1932, "having come down to
deliver the commencement address—of all places—at Drew
Seminary. We had a very satisfactory talk, in the course of
which he made his position clearer than he has done in all his
books.[12] There was an unwonted note of humility in his tone, a
note almost of pathos, which wrung my heart. His physical condition troubles me a little. After all is said, there is a great man.
Brewer, a friend I made at Berkeley and a pupil of Babbitt's,
was visiting me today, having just returned from a year abroad.
He tells me the younger men are turning away from Babbitt,
thinking that his mind crystallized years ago and that he merely
says the same things over and over again. There is truth of a

[10] Babbitt "holds that we are immediately conscious of a higher will,
'the ethical will' or the '*frein vital*,' which to us appears as a check upon
the natural will and as acting only negatively in respect of our lower,
impulsive will. So far we all agree. He holds also that we are immediately
and inexpressibly conscious that this higher will is at once ours, our essential self, and not ours, something super-personal. This is pretty pure
Hinduism, the sort of philosophy which I myself got out of the Upanishads, and which Babbitt clarified by his study of Buddhism. It runs, as
I see it now, into an impossible transcendental monism, and *The Catholic
Faith* is my public retractation of what can be read in some of my earlier
books." [To Marcus Selden Goldman, Sept. 9, 1932.]
[11] To Irving Babbitt, June 16, 1932.
[12] Cf. *OBH*, 40-41.

sort in the charge; but they ought to remember Socrates' retort to the same charge made by Hippias.[13] And they ought to know that his rigid inflexibility has been one of the elements of his strength."

During that hot, damp June More turned out "two or three pages a day for the Lowell Lectures. The fifth of these is well under way, and, D. V., will be finished before I leave for Essex. That will leave only three more to complete the course—and the book."[14] About July 11th he joined Darrah and Harry Fine and their children at "The Cedars." As Alice, her husband, and their infant son came over from England to be with him there, most of More's time "was devoted to *l'art d'être grand-père*"[15]—"a pleasant but ruthless distraction."[16] With Louis (whose wife's funeral Paul had attended in Cincinnati in November 1931) and his daughter, Catherine, next door at "Camp Barberry," what cards they had, "and what walks and drives and even picnics."[17] Besides that "I have been playing golf—or what I call golf—with Louis . . . and he wishes me to tell you," More informed Shafer, "that your book ought to mention my juvenile habit of drinking ice-cream sodas after exercise. I love them, as the girls say, with a passion."[18] All of which left time for only "a little reading this summer: Bradley, Hocking (who is Bradley sentimentalized), Kant. I also went through Hooker, making excerpts for the Anthology. But I wrote nothing."[19]

His salary being needed for the pay of younger men in the

[13] Cf. *SE* VI, 255.
[14] To Philip S. Richards, June 30, 1932. The lectures, "in the nature of a veiled confession" [to Percy H. Houston, May 4, 1932], and based largely on material reworked from his previous publications and from his lectures on the origins of Christianity, he called *The Sceptical Approach to Religion.* "You will smile when you hear that the subject of my lectures . . . is the teleology of faith, or the faith of teleology, whichever is the cart or the horse." [To Irving Babbitt, May 17, 1932.]
[15] To Irving Babbitt, Sept. 19, 1932.
[16] To Paul F. Vaka, Oct. 2, 1932.
[17] To Louis T. More, April 15, 1932.
[18] To Robert Shafer, Aug. 19, 1932.
[19] To Irving Babbitt, Sept. 19, 1932.

department of classics, More gave only one, and his last, course, "on Aristotle to graduates,"[20] in the first term of the academic year 1932-33. He officially retired from teaching at Princeton on April 13, 1933, without pension, living chiefly on property inherited from his wife, which he put in trust with a bank but the value of which the depression had so reduced that he had to relinquish some luxuries, including his car.

A rather vehement letter from G. R. Elliott criticized him for defending a "miraculous" view of the Incarnation. Elliott denied that Jesus had, unless mistakenly, "arrogated to himself something more than belongs to humanity." More's aim as a dualistic humanist, Elliott argued, should be not to harp on the hopeless old paradox of the human and the divine but to treat their union in Christ as representative of us all. Though Elliott barely sketched the notion that he and, so he asserted, many others held of a "representative incarnation," he implied it was the latest rage, of which More could know nothing on account of his "isolation." And he spiced his missive by charging More with special pleading, a secondhand atmosphere, fundamentalism, and a fifth-century point of view.[21]

"Your letter," More responded, "reminds me of one from S. P. Sherman written after reading the *Christ of the New Testament*. He thought my view of the Incarnation was a fitting consummation of my whole dualistic philosophy, and consistent in that respect,[22] while at the same time he rejected my conclusion. He would go with me so far as to see in the divine nature of Christ something different in *degree* from that of other men, but not different in *kind* or unique in this respect. To me it seems that I should have halted half way in the development of my philosophy if I had stopped where Sherman did and where you apparently do. . . .

[20] To Prosser Hall Frye, Dec. 29, 1932.

[21] For Elliott's position see his *Humanism and Imagination*, Chapel Hill (University of North Carolina Press), 1938.

[22] In writing to More on June 9, 1924, Sherman praised the "architectural" rather than the logical effect of More's use of the Incarnation.

Babbitt and Anglicanism

"To come to the heart of the question, your view seems to me to be in close affinity with the thesis of Harnack in his *Wesen des Christentums*, which was nothing less than the flower and consummation of the 'liberalische Theologie' developed from Protestantism. And I had supposed that the 'liberalische Theologie' had received its death-wound from Loisy and its *coup de grâce* from Schweitzer. I had supposed that nothing could be deader than the 'liberal' compromise, which you apparently would uphold as 'modern.' . . .[23]

"In conclusion a word about Chalcedon. . . . The 'Definition' (perfect God, perfect man, etc.), as I have attempted to show in *Christ the Word*, is to be taken as positive in the sense that it demands belief in a unique revelation of the divine nature in Christ, but negative in the sense that it denies the possibility of giving any metaphysical explanation of the singular and paradoxical fact of the Incarnation. It leaves the matter just there, and I for one see wisdom in the inhibition.[24] I cannot escape the feeling that your theory allures by appearing to render the fundamental doctrine of Christianity simple and credible, whereas in fact it does nothing of the sort. The operation of Grace, however taken, is just as miraculous, just as hard to believe, just as incredible as the orthodox view of the Incarnation. And the diminished, pseudo-rational theory simply cuts the nerve of religion as based on theism. Better Buddhism."[25]

About the middle of October More tried out the first of his prospective Lowell Lectures on some two hundred and fifty of "Bishop Manning's clergy at Lake Mahopac"[26] and completed

[23] Cf. More's review of *The Riddle of the New Testament*, by Sir Edwyn Hoskyns and Noel Davey, *The Criterion*, Jan. 1932, vol. XI, no. XLIII, pp. 351-55, part of which was paraphrased in *SAR*, 142-43; cf. also *SAR*, 165.

[24] He did, however, let his "limited intelligence . . . play upon the theme" [*SAR*, 159] in his article, "Liberal Catholics and the Incarnation," *Theology*, March, 1933, vol. 26, pp. 147-52, much of which was repeated in *SAR*, 160-67.

[25] To George Roy Elliott, Sept. 29, 1932.

[26] To Louis T. More, Oct. 11, 1932.

an article on Eliot,[27] who taught that winter at Harvard. In the meanwhile Shafer wanted to show More his manuscript about him, while More wished in no way to influence Shafer's critical judgements.

"Naturally I am curious to see the manuscript, and to know what you have made of the material. At the same time I still have a lingering feeling that it would be better if the book went to the press without any knowledge of its contents on my part. I can give you an instance of the sort of thing that may cause me perplexity. Last Thursday was the annual meeting of the Academy, and Babbitt came down the night before in order to attend. In the course of our conversation he referred to your article in *The Hound and Horn* and to your statement that from a comparison of the dates of publication it appeared that I had referred to Emerson's law for man and law for things before he had, with the inference or suggestion that I had been in the field earlier than he had. (I do not remember what you actually wrote, and so can make no comment from my own knowledge.) He was much hurt by this, and has asked me to see that no such statement gets into the book. All these things happened so many years ago that in truth I have a very vague notion of what took place between us and what ideas passed from one to the other. In a general way I should suppose that the initial move towards humanism was from him. He was born in Horace's cradle, as I may have said to you before, and has undergone no real change in position, though he has of course grown enormously in knowledge. I on my part have changed as often as a chameleon. But I suspect that the philosophic principle of dualism was brought to the partnership by myself. However this and that may be, you will understand that I may suffer some embarrassment if called upon to O. K. or veto whatever you may say about Babbitt and myself—if you say anything. Babbitt, I may add, is anything but a well man. He looks old and causes me anxiety. He read a

[27] "The Cleft Eliot," review of Eliot's *Selected Essays*, *The Saturday Review of Literature*, Nov. 12, 1932, vol. 9, pp. 233 and 235.

paper at the open meeting of the Academy on the Problem of Style in a Democracy. It was full of good allusions, but rambled unmercifully and never really touched the question at issue. It seemed to me that his stalwartness has hardened to something almost approaching petrifaction. . . ."[28]

"Christmas eve I took supper with the McClures[29] who have the habit of inviting in a group of lame ducks (the deaf and doddering chiefly) and regaling them with cocktails (excellent), spaghetti (good), charades (passable), and carols (very bad). The evening went cheerfully, and after it I attended the midnight service. Sunday morning Harry and Darrah brought the children . . .[30] "and a number of unopened presents, and there was a bit of the proper sort of racket for a while."[31] "Yesterday and today I have spent alone, reading and writing a review for *The Criterion*."[32]

At the beginning of 1933 while reports again spread that More might receive a Nobel Prize, he added to "the burden of friendship"[33] he had imposed upon Myers (who, having taken his Ph. D., often returned to Princeton to talk or play bridge with his aging teacher) by sending him frequent drafts of all his Lowell Lectures, some so confused that Myers had to let a typist decipher them before he proposed revisions. "As for your difficulties in writing," More encouraged Shafer, who was struggling with his book on P. E. M., "don't worry over that. I can assure you, if it will afford any comfort, that with all my scribbling I have never made the least progress in facility—rather the contrary. The Lowell Lectures I am now writing are costing me daily agonies. Five hundred words are the best I can

[28] To Robert Shafer, Nov. 15, 1932.
[29] Charles F. W. McClure, professor of zoology at Princeton University.
[30] To Louis T. More, Dec. 27, 1932.
[31] To Mrs. Irving Babbitt, Jan. 3, 1933.
[32] To Louis T. More, Dec. 27, 1932. The review was of *Prayer: A Study in the History and Psychology of Religion*, by Friedrich Heiler, *The Criterion*, April 1933, vol. 12, pp. 492-94.
[33] To Edward DeLos Myers, Feb. 7, 1933.

do in a day; and some of the lectures have been written over four or five times, and the end is not yet. My labour is to be clear, and that goal I rarely attain."[34]

In March he lectured at the preparatory school in New Lebanon, New York, where Cowardin was then teaching, and, on "A Sceptical Approach to Religion,"[35] at Williams College. On the 23rd of that month, in Princeton, he introduced Eliot at great length and with undisguised pleasure, "recalling their common origin and background in St. Louis."[36] After Eliot's "thoughtful and scholarly but not particularly exciting discourse on the influence of the Bible on English literature"[37]—"rather disappointing as a whole, though lightened here and there by neat epigrammatic sentences"[38]—the tired visitor returned to his headquarters at 59 Battle Road, where his host had invited fifteen or twenty men, mostly from the university's departments of English and classics, to meet him. Nobly playing his rôle, the guest read aloud from his "Sweeney Agonistes." As whisky loosened tongues, however, a few local savants took over, talking loudly of where they had lectured and of how well they had been received. Now and then they tossed a question to Eliot about his poetry, which, for all More's efforts to develop a discussion, the long-suffering celebrity simply ducked.

The April 1933 number of *The American Review*, established by Collins after *The Bookman* had succumbed to the depression, brought out More's article on Proust, about whom he had talked too precipitately before the philosophical club of Princeton University in January 1932.[39] The essay, reprinted July 2,

---

[34] To Robert Shafer, March 14, 1933.

[35] Substantially the same as the first of his Lowell Lectures.

[36] "Conversations with Paul Elmer More," by J. Duncan Spaeth, *The Sewanee Review*, Oct.-Dec. 1943, vol. LI, no. 4, p. 533.

[37] *Ibid.*

[38] To Mrs. Irving Babbitt, March 24, 1933.

[39] He infuriated his audience, with whom Proust was then much in style, less by his still limited knowledge of Proust's works than by the implication that if Proust's "trailing meditations on sodomy and sadism" [to Edward DeLos Myers, Feb. 3, 1932] did not bore and repel them,

Babbitt and Anglicanism

1933, in Stockholm's *Nya Dagligt Allehanda*, exhibits *À la Recherche du Temps Perdu* as "a criticism of life as didactic as any that Matthew Arnold would demand, though a criticism pointing in a very different direction."[40] "Debarred by his naturalistic limitations from finding anything real in the ethical sanctions of love," Proust "is driven in his search for reality down through the superimposed layers of sentiment to the basic fact of animal desire."[41] And More traces his descent step by step from the world of moral obligation to "the last possibility of physical sensation in the masochistic union of pleasure with pain. So we reach the rock bottom of 'nature,' the end of the way which is not that of the humanist."[42]

In order to complete his selections from seventeenth-century religious literature for the Anglican anthology, More sailed April 7, 1933, on the *Westernland* from New York to Southampton. Running across Professor and Mrs. Frank H. Constant, of Princeton, on board and sitting at table with them, he "came to admire the perfect sweetness and goodness of their characters. . . . Their conversation . . . was easy, and I felt very much at home. . . . There was not a single table of bridge during the voyage, though I did play knock once or twice with a rather pretty girl from Washington state. A buxom widow tried to

---

their appreciation of art and life was immature—which only convinced them that he was too small to see Proust's greatness. Not quite jokingly he explained to Louis T. More in a letter of January 6, 1932, that Proust's "attraction is chiefly for callow youths who think they belong to the Intelligentsia and have no principles, for men who have great curiosity but an atrophied faculty of indignation, and for women from California." A month later he was still driving himself through Proust's writings with the same determination that had carried him through *The Brothers Karamazov*. "These Russians depress me. I don't understand them. Their characters act from motives which I can't penetrate and their ethics throw all the values of life into such confusion that I am just bewildered. Some people seem to enjoy such books for this very strangeness and exoticism. I confess that when it comes to fiction I do not care much to read about people who would bore or disgust or confound me in real life." [To Alice More, Jan. 4, 1924.]

[40] *OBH*, 59.   [41] *OBH*, 62.   [42] *OBH*, 64.

annex me, and almost succeeded. I had to shake her off rather
brusquely. Then there was a young French woman, travelling
with her fiancé, the world's champion indoor tennis player, who
flirted with me outrageously—very funny."[43]

Oxford "has lost its romantic charm for me, and I do not put
myself out to meet men and forgather with them at dinner and
at that mausoleum of old social urbanities, the Common Room.
However I have dined several times at Magdalen, with old J. A.
[Smith], and more recently with a Fellow and Tutor of English
named Lewis, who interested me more than any other Oxonian
I have met for a long time. You will smile when I tell you that
this is partly, not wholly, because he has gone through a deep
and today unusual religious experience; this he has written out
in a book,[44] in more or less disguised form I presume, which is
to appear shortly and a copy of which he promises to send me."[45]

"My mornings I spend with Cross[46] in the Bodleian or Pusey
House going through masses of bulky volumes, some of which,
as shown by uncut leaves, have never been read here before. It
is pretty frightful; but in their own way some of these old boys
were wonders. Their erudition is simply appalling. A book by
Barrow for instance on the Papacy makes the modern attacks,
even Coulton's, seem like the work of school children in comparison. Fortunately Cross and I get on admirably together, and
occasionally I relieve the monotony of the job by telling him
ribald tales of the clergy, which he apparently enjoys. For relaxation I get through five or six detective stories a week. . . .

"No doubt you have seen the first issue of Collins's new

[43] To Louis T. More, April 24, 1933.
[44] ". . . *The Pilgrim's Regress*, by C. S. Lewis . . . is an allegory auto-
biographical in a manner, relating the author's return to 'Mother Kirk,'
and by the way satirizing the intellectual fads of the modern world in a
style that will make you chuckle with joy." [To Prosser Hall Frye, Sept.
16, 1933. Cf. *OBH*, 111-12.]
[45] To Christian Gauss, May 11, 1933.
[46] Cross had worked with More on the Anglican anthology in Princeton "for fifteen or twenty days" at the end of March and the beginning
of April 1932. [To Louis T. More, April 15, 1932.]

venture.[47] I like the simplicity of the format and the lack of advertisements. And his programme is interesting, though it seems to me that Belloc and his henchman Chesterton in their scheme of 'distributism' do not reckon with the necessary economic changes since the Renaissance and with the fact that machinery and mass production render any return to the old system practically impossible."[48]

"The Shafers were here over the last week-end and broke the monotony of my life. . . . Shafer's manuscript on P. E. M. is even yet far from finished, but I read through what he has done. It impressed me as fairly, but not strikingly good."[49] ". . . the book is a good deal concerned with his own philosophy, which leaves me out and I rather fear will leave out some of his readers."[50]

"According to what Esther[51] has told the Shafers, I. B. gets no better at all. He is still in bed and has a trained nurse. He does get up to shave, but even that slight exertion raises his temperature."[52]

More left Oxford on May 30th for Edinburgh, where Gilbert Dymond then taught at the university, to spend most of June with Alice and his new granddaughter, Darragh Clare. On June 27th he accompanied his family "to the home of the Dymonds to be present at the christening of the baby"[53] in Hereford cathedral on the 28th.

The next day he moved to "the Kingsley Hotel, in Bloomsbury, partly because it is cheap, and partly to be near the Shafers who had an apartment of two floors near the Museum. Every evening we went out somewhere together for dinner, and then passed the evening in their rooms, talking, playing Russian

---

[47] *The American Review.*
[48] To Irving Babbitt, May 14, 1933.
[49] To Louis T. More, May 26, 1933.
[50] To Prosser Hall Frye, Sept. 16, 1933.
[51] Mrs. George Howe, daughter of Irving Babbitt.
[52] To Louis T. More, May 26, 1933.
[53] To Robert Shafer, June 19, 1933.

Bank, and enjoying ourselves as we could. It was a merry fortnight, though I did practically nothing in the way of seeing
people and sights."[54]

"I did not see Esther," More informed her father, "as she
sailed the day after I reached London, but George Howe tells
me today that he has received rather distressing news of your
condition. The doctors and the hospitals seem to have accomplished nothing for you. The news, I say, is most distressing to
me. I still hope that you will pull through and take up your
work, which, with all you have done, is still unfinished. Your
book on humanism and education promised to add the capstone
and to bind your theory to your first book on the American
college; and now you are lying in bed, and the doctors look
wise, no doubt, but bring no help. There are many besides myself who are hanging on the bulletin of your health, but none I
am sure so anxiously as myself. My Lowell Lectures are scheduled for February; it will be a sad occasion for me if you have
not made a turn for the better by then."[55]

"I have just written to Irving," he assured Mrs. Babbitt,
"moved by the distressing news George Howe has given of his
condition. I could not say all I felt, and so am adding a word
to you. I just cannot reconcile myself to the thought of Irving
lying weak and prostrate, and as it seems in real danger of his
life. It seems impossible to realize that one so strong as he has
been should be broken. I still hope, but meanwhile I want you
to know that my heart is with you."[56]

> "The Isis Private Hotel,
> Iffley Road, Oxford,
> July 17, 1933.

"My dear Dora,

"Your letter of the 4th came just after I had written to Irving
and to you. Then this morning came a note from George Howe

[54] To Prosser Hall Frye, Sept. 16, 1933.
[55] To Irving Babbitt, July 10, 1933.
[56] To Mrs. Irving Babbitt, July 10, 1933.

announcing the end. I cannot say that Irving's death was a shock to me in the sense that it took me by surprise. Ever since I saw him last November I have felt that something was radically wrong, that something had snapped. If I did not express my full anxiety in my letters you will understand the reason.

"I do not know what to say now. It is easy to write or telegraph 'sympathy,' but the word sounds terribly inadequate. For me it is the breaking of the closest friendship of my life. And though in these latter years we did not often see each other or correspond frequently, he was always as it were the background of all my thinking. My own movement back to Christianity was never a real interruption.[57]

"I do hope that Roy Elliott or some other one of Irving's followers will be able to tell the world what it has lost. I say 'lost,' but I do not for a moment believe his work and ideas will be forgotten. I think he will be remembered as probably the greatest teacher this country has ever produced.

Sincerely and affectionately yours,

Paul E. More."[58]

Towards the end of July, since Cross was "collating the texts, reading proof, and attending to the notes," More's part in the (for him) expensive and "horrid job" of the "disembowelling of the Bodleian"[59] neared its end. His "dull and dumpy"[60] days were pleasantly interrupted when P. S. Richards motored from Portsmouth to Oxford. On July 16th he took More to breakfast at Corpus; drove him to see the little church at Shilton, where More astonished him by remarking that had he been brought up amid such associations he might have had, "what

[57] ". . . for all our long and close friendship we never addressed each other except by our last names. . . . though he fought with me pertinaciously over my defection, as he thought it, yet he continued always to recommend my books to his classes. That was his magnanimity." [To Mrs. Irving Babbitt, March 10, 1934.]

[58] More had returned from London to "The Isis" on July 12th.

[59] To Percy H. Houston, July 22, 1933.

[60] To Robert Shafer, July 23, 1933.

he confessed he had never known, a direct 'experience' of religion"; and got him back to Oxford in time to lunch with the Dominican fathers at Blackfriars.

By Stanley Romaine Hopper, once a pupil of Lynn Harold Hough's[61] at Drew Theological Seminary, More's "presence in Oxford was made known to a student[62] at Mansfield, who called on me at the Isis. Through him the Principal (or Warden? I never can remember these titles) got to know of me, and invited me to dinner at the College. In the Common Room he seated me on the sofa at one end of the half inch, and said: Now I have two questions to ask Mr. More about matters in his books, etc. One of the questions was on sacramentalism. I answered to the best of my ability, and then the conversation became general. All the faculty, I believe, were present, besides two or three theological scholars as guests. The comments from man to man interested me deeply; they were so evidently sincere and so intelligent. One thing came out: they were all more or less consciously on the defensive, and I could see that they were all thinking seriously about the question of sacramentalism. And I felt, whether wrongly or rightly, that all—except perhaps one old man and one pure philologian—were perplexed and uneasy, acknowledging in their hearts that the difficulties of finding anything to take the place of sacramentalism were practically insuperable yet that without some such substitute organized institutional religion was highly precarious. I remember one quite young fellow, a scholar I judged and certainly an enthusiast, asking me whether I had not omitted from my theory the sacrament of the word. He had, he said, heard Alexander Whyte preach in Edinburgh; and if that sermon, he cried out, was not a sacrament, then what can a sacrament be?—But granted, I replied; and how many Alexander Whytes have you? —Ah, he whispered, that's it.—And for a while there was a

---

[61] Among Hough's books referring to More might be mentioned *Great Humanists*, New York (Abingdon-Cokesbury Press), 1952, pp. 171-213.
[62] Hubert Cunliffe-Jones.

deep silence.—It was an inspiring evening to me, one of the most interesting I have ever passed in Oxford. It seemed to me that these men were thinking as not many of the Anglican clergy were; and yet, this thinking was to them a tragedy, and not peace."[63]

The "renegade Presbyterian," as More had termed himself when he recounted to Cunliffe-Jones the perturbations of an American Ethical Society over his doubts about the non-existence of God, welcomed Eliot, who had lectured in Oxford on July 24th, for two days afterwards at The Isis. "One day I was having luncheon with T. S. Eliot (who was visiting me) in the rooms of a certain Wolfenden, a young tutor in philosophy who took my course in Aristotle several years ago at Princeton."[64] ". . . I asked him about Lewis, what the story of his experience was and whether he had become a Roman Catholic, and what was meant by 'Mother Kirk' to which his Pilgrim returns. Wolfenden said he didn't know much about it all, but was sure Lewis had not become an R. C. And then he added this tale. He, Wolfenden, and several other Fellows were talking together one day, when a friend came into the room in a state of high excitement. I say, said the newcomer, do you know what's going on with Lewis? So and so tells me he happened to see Lewis in the college chapel the other day, and, being amazed and making inquiries, discovered that he has been going there for weeks without anyone's knowing anything about it.

"This brought out one of Eliot's sly little sarcastic digs: It's quite apparent that if anybody in an Oxford college wishes to escape detection, the one place for him to go to is the chapel!"[65]

Sailing August 4th from Liverpool to Montreal More wrote to Shafer from the Canadian Pacific steamship *Duchess of Atholl*: "Martha[66] tells me—and I am grateful for her letter—

[63] To Lynn Harold Hough, Oct. 10, 1933.
[64] To Prosser Hall Frye, Sept. 16, 1933.
[65] To A. H. Dakin, Jr., Dec. 7, 1933.
[66] Mrs. Robert Shafer.

that P. E. M. in his *Greek Tradition* is causing you no end of trouble. In a way the line there is clear enough—from Hinduism to Platonism and from this to Christianity. Only in the last step there are two things to note: the feeling that Platonism points to, and has its almost inevitable complement in, Christianity, and the associated feeling that only by the retention of the true and final aspect of Platonism can Christianity develop a philosophy while remaining consistent with itself. Christianity begins with a fact, not a theory, at least what is given as a fact and must be so accepted if there is to be such a religion—the historic fact of the Incarnation. All dogma and all sacrament are simply involved in this or evolved out of this, and have their criterion of truth in that involution or evolution. Platonism is theory derived from speculation upon man's deepest experience of himself. The question is how and how far do the fact of Christianity and the inner experience beneath Platonism correspond. Christian theology has in my judgement gone into blind ways by forgetting this and attempting to assimilate the utterly different metaphysic of Aristotle and Plotinus. If I have anything to say to the world, now, it is the vital necessity of renewing the association between the fact of Christianity and the theory of Plato."[67]

From Montreal More reached Essex on August 12th. Harry Fine played quoits with him there but, being "very anxious over the state of the school,"[68] had to return to Princeton, whither Darrah followed him about the middle of September, leaving her father a short while longer in Essex with her children and two maids. Before she left, Miss McLinn and Cowardin visited them for a week-end of music. Louis and Catherine and their guests at "Camp Barberry," Professor and Mrs. Howard D. Roelofs, of the University of Cincinnati, frequently joined the

---

[67] To Robert Shafer, Aug. 9, 1933.

[68] To Prosser Hall Frye, Sept. 16, 1933. "When I read the paper it seems to me as if a thousand madhouses had let loose their inmates upon us. I am bewildered and ask myself where I shall be next year, hanged on a lamp-post or hoeing the garden of a poorhouse." [*Ibid.*]

Babbitt and Anglicanism

occupants of "The Cedars" for talk, music (Louis at the piano, Paul at the flute), tea, and bridge. Roelofs, a young teacher of the history of philosophy, defended Aristotle in long arguments with More, who ordinarily sided with Plato. The "pigmy," as Roelofs called himself, marvelled at the "giant's" generosity in sharing his immense knowledge and at his zeal for learning more. The eagerness of both disputants to agree as well as they could, possibly led one to read into Plato theories better developed by Aristotle, "thus increasing the superiority of Plato," and the other to borrow from Plato rays with which to heighten the brilliance of Aristotle.

A similar flexibility of system More advocated for bridge. He and Louis usually opposed their seasoned skill against the ingenious improvisations of Darrah and Roelofs. Once when only a large bid could prevent the younger generation from winning game and rubber, Paul More, with a groaning sigh, passed. Louis meditated over his bid at tiresome length. "Pop a button, Lou! Pop a button!" Paul exclaimed. And when Louis also passed, Paul shook his head, saying: "If a system can't pop a button, what good is it?"

In odd moments at Essex More toiled over his introduction to the Anglican anthology, a volume of more than eight hundred royal octavo pages—unindexed like his *Shelburne Essays* (which has nothing but an occasional list of chapter headings) and his *Greek Tradition.* "My fear is that when it is done it will suit nobody—that seems to be my mission in life, to suit nobody."[69] "I did not finish this up there, but have completed the third, but still rough, draught since my return to Princeton. Monday evening I read it to Bob Root, Jack Crocker, and Bill Edgar,[70] with the understanding that they were to criticise freely. They made some suggestions which I shall adopt for the final revision, but as a whole they seemed to feel that my view of Anglicanism

[69] To Prosser Hall Frye, Sept. 16, 1933, who died in 1934.
[70] William John Brown Edgar, an instructor in the philosophy and the history of Christianity at Princeton University.

was correct and enlightening. This, as far as it goes, is encouraging, since the work has cost infinite pains and even so has left me very anxious. You can imagine the difficulties I had to encounter."[71]

"The course of Anglicanism," according to More's introduction, "was peculiar in this, that deliberately and courageously they clung to the principle of mediation in regions of doctrine and discipline, where, as they contended, the Romanist and the radical Protestant did in fact stray aside into vicious extremes of exclusion. . . ."[72] The true thread of continuity, the Anglicans held, was broken either by superimposing new and disputable dogmas upon the divine revelation after the manner of Rome, or by disallowing due weight in the practical sphere of religion to the wisdom of accumulated human experience after the manner of Geneva.[73]

". . . if we are looking for a single term to denote the ultimate law of Anglicanism, I do not see that we can do better than adopt . . . the title 'pragmatism.' The self-styled 'pragmatist' of to-day is commonly one who, pretending to eschew what he regards as unverifiable theory, limits his assent to 'facts,' and whose criterion of fact is 'that which works'—works, that is, by the test of *physical* experience. But etymologically there is no reason why the word 'pragmatism' should be so narrowed in its meaning as to include only one half of human experience. . . ."[74]

"When Jesus thought and spoke of Himself as the Messiah, the son of God, was He what He proclaimed Himself to be or was He suffering a delusion? This . . . comes down to a simple question of fact, *pragma*, as do finally all questions of truth; but quite obviously the answer is to be sought otherwise than in the mere weighing of documentary evidence. We have passed from the province of history to that of philosophy and religion. All Christians of course believe in the actuality of this fact. If

---

[71] To T. S. Eliot, Sept. 27, 1933.
[72] *A*, xxiv.   [73] *A*, xxvii.   [74] *A*, xxxii.

the Anglican differs from the Romanist or the radical Protestant, it is because more definitely and consciously than either he justifies his belief by the pragmatic test of experience, namely: 'Does it work?' It is not that he rejects authority for an unchecked individualism; he sees that his personal experience is no more than a fragment of the larger experience of mankind, and must be controlled at every step by that accumulated wisdom which is the voice of the Church. What he rejects is the Absolute of authority based on *a priori* theories of infallibility. Rather, looking within and without, he asks the consequences of believing or not believing. How does acceptance of the dogma of the Incarnation work out in practice? Does faith bring with it any proof of its objective validity?"[75]

Then, forgetting the notion of "objective validity," More turns instead to the feeling of certainty. ". . . the experiment of believing may pass into experience, and the result of experience may be of such a kind as to bring the believer, however incapable he may be of convincing others, to a sure conviction that he has chosen the right way."[76]

". . . the pragmatic argument from effect to cause . . . permeates the theology of Anglicanism. Not only in the seventeenth century but from the time of Henry VIII to the present day, if there is any outstanding note of the English temper it is a humility of awe before the divine mysteries of faith and a recognition of the incompetence of language to define the ultimate paradox of experience."[77]

To an avowal from Louis, who then received no solace from attending church, but only sadness on account of its former association with his beloved wife, Paul replied: "I was impressed by what you wrote in your last letter about your hesitation over church-going, particularly impressed because your experience coincides so largely with my own. I too have some of the same difficulties to encounter; it is only by an exercise of the will that Sunday by Sunday I do not leave Trinity with less of religion

[75] *A*, xxxiii.   [76] *A*, xxxiv.   [77] *A*, xxxvii.

than I brought with me. . . . it requires some vigilance of mind
to remember always that . . . exasperating traits [of a priest]
are peculiar to the man, accidents so to speak, which may conceal but cannot annul the essential service which the Church
performs. After all it does not demand a very exacting or even
a very definite faith to join in the public exercise of adoration and
praise and prayer which is the substance of religion; and year
by year I find the *Book of [Common] Prayer* a more perfect,
miraculously perfect, guide in that great act. Personally I find
it quite possible to join in saying the Creed, though I have my
private reservations in regard to the literal interpretation of
some of the articles. And the eucharistic rite acquires a deeper
and deeper meaning by repetition. The point is that, despite the
errors of the Church and the failure of this or that priest to
maintain its larger spiritual function, it has stood through the
ages, unshakably and magnificently, for a fundamental truth
which, I believe, can meet the pragmatic test more completely
and finally than can the theories of science. *Experientia docet.*
And I find there is profit in attending the services of the Church,
even where these are unsatisfactorily conducted, which goes beyond what one can gain by reflection and meditation at home.
Perhaps that profit can be best expressed, though not completely
conveyed, by the word 'humility.' And humility, you will see at
once, is something quite different from humiliation. The latter is
a feeling that comes to one with a sense that all his efforts to accomplish some outstanding work may be futile; it is a feeling
which, when analysed, will be found to belong to personal
vanity, and its effect is to paralyse the will and to bring us to a
state of emotional despondency. Humility is on the contrary of
exactly the opposite quality and effect. It is a losing of one's self
in the mass, a feeling of solidarity with men in that which is
highest and least personal in their nature. It confirms the will
in its determination to do that which within one lies unhampered
by the fluctuating emotions of personal vanity; it brings strength
and courage and a kind of peace, if not happiness. I do not know

whether I make myself clear, but I mean something very definite and something easily verifiable by trial. As for the loneliness of which you speak and the broken associations, I know of these well enough. I can only say, or will only say, that in the community of worship which comes with the true spirit of humility, one may grasp a little of what is meant by the communion of saints, a feeling of union, which may be mystical and intangible and even vague, but which does yet mitigate the loneliness of separation. I am willing to approach these matters in the spirit of a child. What do we know, after all? In those unanalysable but profound and universal feelings we may be, I am sure we are, in touch with a reality more stable and tenable and more ultimate than anything that reason can grasp."[78]

In the autumn of 1933 the Oxford University Press published a study of the thought of Babbitt, More, and Seillière—*The Challenge of Humanism*, by Louis J. A. Mercier. "His analysis of my own approach to religion is extremely subtle, but does not touch on certain fundamental motives apart from those of an intellectual sort. His exposition of scholasticism is really masterly, but leaves me still convinced that the attempt to assimilate Aristotle and Christian theology introduced an intellectualist, and indeed rationalistic, element into religion for which we are still suffering heavily."[79] ". . . it is a little hard for me to understand the frame of mind which accepts Babbitt, who as a matter of fact was radically hostile to any form of revealed religion, and rejects one who argues for Catholicism even though repudiating the claims of Rome to infallibility. It only confirms my view that the outstanding question of religion today is Rome, and strengthens my conviction that the greatest mistake threatening the Anglican Church is the possibility of her being led astray by the overt or disguised Romanizers within her body."[80]

[78] To Louis T. More, Oct. 18, 1933. Cf. *CF*, 95-100.
[79] To Robert Shafer, Oct. 22, 1933.
[80] To Bernard Iddings Bell, Jan. 2, 1934.

1932-1934

Though busy corresponding with friends,[81] reviewing for *The Criterion*,[82] preparing for *The University of Toronto Quarterly*

[81] On T. S. Eliot's *The Use of Poetry and the Use of Criticism* More commented: "One or two matters puzzle me, or even displease me. I cannot feel your antipathy to Addison, and cannot believe you ought to feel it. He may be negligible as a poet and not profound as a critic. But he could write the English language, as old S. J. knew; and his satire is often delicious. I don't agree with you about Saintsbury. The old boy had taste; he could quote to perfection and he could write introductions to Thackeray that add something to one's joy of reading the novels. But in his history of criticism it seems to me that in dealing with the greater names he has almost a genius for missing the point. I relish him hugely when he discourses on his wine cellar; I am irritated when he professes to understand Aristotle or Boileau. I think your praise of Matthew Arnold is a little too grudging; and your manner of disagreeing with I. A. Richards at almost every point while eulogising him in general as a profound and important writer amuses me at times—and at times does not. That man is a second-rate psychologist and a third-rate literary critic. . . . I am looking forward to your next volume with keen expectation. . . . No doubt I shall agree with what you say about I. B.'s dabbling in Confucianism. But after all, you stand vastly closer to Babbitt than you do to Richards and it strikes me as a bit paradoxical that you should be grudging in your praise of the former and grudging in your dispraise of the latter. . . .

"It is easy to be detailed in adverse comments, but our commendation we have to sum up in a lump. The book was exhilarating to me. When I read your printed page I seem to hear you talking, and by that I mean very high praise indeed. And on some important points I seem to hear you searching your way towards a final judgement in a manner which for one who has followed your work from year to year is quite exciting. Particularly what you say on the problem of Belief in the enjoyment of poetry (pp. 90 ff.) interests me, partly because what you say is so sound, and partly because I see, or fancy I see, a real development and change from the opinion you once held. And your criticism of Shelley simply filled me with pure delight." [To T. S. Eliot, Nov. 17, 1933.]

Babbitt's "individualism seems to me to be not quite in accord with his general insistence on standards, and on tradition rightly understood. It is, you see, a question of the Church. A certain final lack of humility I must find in Babbitt's attempt to cut out for himself an individual path in religion, rather than submit to the great institutional experience of the race. . . . It will explain T. S. Eliot's veiled hostility amidst his commendation of Babbitt in other fields." [To S. E. Dubbel, Sept. 29, 1934.]

[82] More reviewed Paul Shorey's *What Plato Said* and Francis Macdonald Cornford's *Before and After Socrates* in *The Criterion*, April 1934, vol. 13, pp. 472-78. He criticized Shorey for not seeing "how the *Gorgias*, the *Republic*, the *Timaeus*, and the tenth book of the *Laws* fall into a group explicitly bound together by the author so as to stand out from the rest of the dialogues, and how from one to the other he de-

Babbitt and Anglicanism

an article about Babbitt,[83] and writhing over his Lowell Lectures, "trying desperately hard to avoid pedantry and to appear as human as possible,"[84] More managed "every Monday"[85] to play his flute in little concerts at 59 Battle Road with Mary Crocker and Darrah. He managed also to give, every other Sunday that winter, to the students of the Princeton Preparatory School a series of lectures on religion, drawn from his former university course on the origins of Christianity. In December his granddaughter, Molly, as a refreshing change for them both, visited him a few days. "I am mighty fond of the little thing, but I don't exactly know what I am to do to keep her amused. However, Mary will help, and Darrah will be here off and on."[86] The night of December 30th he regaled the Fines with "clam soup, a fat tender goose, a plum pudding sent over by Alice garnished with ice cream, . . . and after the meal we had games, ending with dumb crambo with extraordinary attempts at rhyming."[87] On New Year's eve "Darrah and Harry came in . . . and we celebrated the occasion by drinking from a bottle of legitimate Black and White. The whiskey was good enough, but I just cannot acquire a taste for the stuff. Prohibition did me no harm, except in so far as it curtailed my hospitality and dampened such social gatherings."[88] Early in February he stopped at "Great Hill," Brookes More's estate in Hingham, Massachusetts, on his way to Boston for his Lowell Lectures.

---

velops and in a measure corrects his conception of the place and function of Ideas." More then outlines this development and correction, which culminated in the thesis "that the doctrine of Ideas, though essential to sound philosophy and indeed to religion, must be subordinated to theology." [Cf. *SAR*, 68 ff.]

[83] "I sometimes think that he was greater as a teacher than a writer, and greater as a talker, particularly in his earlier years, than a teacher." [To Mrs. Irving Babbitt, Nov. 4, 1933.]

[84] To Louis T. More, Jan. 1, 1934.

[85] To Samuel Pendleton Cowardin, Jr., Oct. 26, 1933.

[86] To Louis T. More, Dec. 10, 1933.

[87] To the same, Jan. 1, 1934.

[88] *Ibid.*

17

SCEPTICAL APPROACH TO RELIGION
(1934)

WHILE he delivered his sparsely attended Lowell Lectures on the Mondays and the Wednesdays of February 1934, More (when he did not return to Princeton) stayed in Boston at the St. Botolph Club, going out to "I can't remember how many luncheons and evening entertainments. . . . To be sociable is more exhausting than to read Hebrew."[1]

Mercier, believing that More's essay in *The University of Toronto Quarterly* had failed to do justice to Babbitt's attitude towards revealed religion, presented his own view in an article called "The Legacy of Irving Babbitt" in *The Harvard Graduates' Magazine*.[2] Asked by the editor to reply to the article, More declined, not wishing to set his life-long intimacy with Babbitt against Mercier's slighter acquaintance. "As for the question of theism (over which I have just been talking with Mercier), Babbitt had grown tolerant of other men's beliefs, if they did not clash with his ethical principles, but—I speak from certain knowledge—there was no room for a God, in any proper sense of the word, or for Grace in his own philosophy.[3] So far as his religion could be related to anything Christian, it was in his sympathy with a mysticism of the kind professed by an Eckhart, where the conception of 'Godhead' passes beyond a 'God' or anything we understand as personality."[4]

Cowardin with his violin visited More in Princeton on March 23rd. They had a concert of Haydn, Mozart, and Schubert—

[1] To Edward DeLos Myers, Feb. 22, 1934.

[2] Vol. 42, pp. 327-42, June 1934.

[3] "Babbitt had a complete disbelief in Grace, though he would admit that the Christian doctrine of Grace by its illusion produced results comparable to those of the higher Buddhistic will." [To Folke Leander, Nov. 16, 1935.]

[4] To George Roy Elliott, Feb. 22, 1934.

Mary Crocker playing second violin, Darrah the piano, More the flute, and W. Frederick Stohlman[5] the cello.

An April repetition in Cincinnati of his Lowell Lectures "went off really with first rate success, better than in Boston. I am now doing a little final revision, and shall have them ready for the press in a few days. The social side of my life in Cincinnati, owing largely to my brother's popularity, was rather amazing. We dined [out] about four evenings a week, and for one night there were actually four invitations. . . . Unfortunately we had little time for music, so that my flute lay idle."[6]

"Several days ago I was walking down Mercer Street at a swinging gait. Three young girls were sporting a camera at one of the houses. I turned to watch them as I passed, tripped on an uneven flagstone, and pitched forward on my face as if shot from a catapult. Fortunately I threw out my arms, and threw my head sidewise; but even so my face struck the sidewalk with tremendous force. No bones were broken and no permanent injury done, but the skin was abraded in several places and my upper lip cut so badly that it required four stitches. The sensation was curious. I was stunned for a second or two, then lay for a moment wondering where I was hurt and what was broken, and then got up and stood looking about me dizzily. Mrs. Sinclair was driving by . . . saw me fall, and carried me straight to the hospital. Oddly enough I did not feel the shock that evening; but the next day I was a bit sore all over, and then for a couple of days felt nervously shattered. All that is gone today. The stitches have been taken out, my back no longer aches, and my nerves are almost normal. On the whole, I had a most lucky escape."[7]

At the General Theological Seminary in New York on May 23rd in the course of a commencement address on "Church and

[5] An associate professor of art and archaeology at Princeton University.
[6] To Samuel Pendleton Cowardin, Jr., May 8, 1934.
[7] To Louis T. More, May 13, 1934.

Politics" More reminded his audience that the "sentimental socialism" with which the clergy seemed to be flirting was not the
peculiarly Christian way of meeting the "unrest and fear and
cruel unemployment"[8] throughout the land. "I remember the
righteous indignation with which a young priest once turned
upon me with the question, for him a very practical problem,
how he could bring any thought of religion to a man distracted
with the anxieties of unemployment, or how he could talk to a
man of his soul's welfare while the body was unfed. Well, is it
impertinent to quote the words of Christ in the wilderness after
he had fasted forty days and the devil bade him turn the stones
into bread? Certainly Christ did not confuse religion with food
or think it should be deferred until the hunger of the body was
satisfied. Hunger is an evil, no doubt; it should be alleviated.
But hunger is not the only evil of life, or the most devastating.
There are pains of the flesh more agonizing than starvation;
there are calamities more terrible than social injustice. And what
is your religion worth unless it can bring healing to the broken-
hearted and to the downtrodden a hope not of this world? What
a mockery is made of the gospel if it cannot be preached to a
man until the iniquities of society have been set right. Is that
the spirit of the beatitudes? The call of religion is first of all
and last of all to a soul conscious of its own guilt, the function
of religion is first of all and last of all to offer to a soul despair-
ing of this world's peace the promise of eternal life. When under
the shadow of an atrocious death Christ said to his disciples:
'These things I have spoken unto you, that in me ye might have
peace: in the world ye shall have tribulation; but be of good
cheer, I have overcome the world,'—when he uttered these
words, perhaps of all the words that fell from his lips the most
wonderful, he was not announcing a gospel of economic re-
generation or postponing the hope of peace until the wrongs of
capitalism should be overcome, nor was he identifying the moral
obligations of the individual soul with a sentimental socialism."[9]

[8] *OBH*, 146.   [9] *OBH*, 152-53.

Sceptical Approach to Religion

For the month of August Darrah and her children and, when his school's business allowed it, her husband joined her father in Essex, where he had gone early in July to correct the proofs of his Lowell Lectures; to read *Vanity Fair* in order to prepare, at Shafer's request, an introduction[10] for a new edition planned by Doubleday, Doran and Company; and to go through "Lou's *Newton*. The book has many good qualities, but there is unquestionably an excess of unnecessary repetitions. I hope, and rather believe, it will have a good 'press.' The chapter on the *Principia* is masterly in its way."[11]

"I appreciate your congratulations over the splurge I am making round about my seventieth birthday," More thanked P. S. Richards, who had commended his literary activity. ". . . But you need not envy me. It may be the last crackle before the fire goes out. And, at the best, the deepest feeling I have is one of a sort of futility in all I have done or can do. In my more sanguine moments I say to myself that such a feeling is unreasonable. But it will not away, and would not away though sudden popularity should come upon me—as it never will. The cause lies much deeper than lack of popularity. It is partly due to the terrible crushing sense of mâyâ, the Oriental belief, born in me but fostered by my studies, that nothing in life is worth while, and partly it springs from the wandering drifting unanchored course of my own particular life. Impatience is my vice, and boredom my punishment."[12]

The Sceptical Approach to Religion, published in October, defended theism as an inference against the rationalizing sceptic, not because such a position entirely satisfied More but because he supposed it might be an acceptable starting point for discussion with sceptics and rationalists. Those who say "that I

---

[10] ". . . the result was not too good. I had only one original remark, and that was to ask what would have happened if Dobbin had married Becky instead of Amelia. I do believe it would have been a happy and successful mating; do you?" [To Philip S. Richards, Jan. 6, 1935.]

[11] To Robert Shafer, July 14, 1934.

[12] To Philip S. Richards, Sept. 19, 1934.

make God only an inference" are "wrong," he asserted. "My thesis is that for the rationalizing sceptic he may be that. But the determinism of the rationalist is certainly an inference, and, taking both as inferences, the theist is right in averring that his is the more reasonable. . . . faith appeals in the last resort to experience. So much ought to be clear from the last pages of the book."[13]

Numerous qualifying phrases, not to mention the variety of sources that he recognizes as contributing to faith, indicate his awareness of the limitations of the position he had assumed for polemical purposes. His procedure, he observes, involves no lack of sympathy with believers and no denial that belief in God may be attained, for example, "by an act of divine grace"[14] and "not so much by inference or rational demonstration as by clarifying and strengthening an immediate affection just as is our belief in an outer world of phenomena."[15] He had in mind Baron Friedrich von Hügel's "critical realism,"[16] which apart from "a foreign intrusion from the rationalizing metaphysics of Aristotle and St. Thomas Aquinas[17] and Kant, and to a lesser

[13] To A. H. Dakin, Jr., Jan. 13, 1935.
[14] *SAR*, 19.   [15] *SAR*, 3.
[16] "I am not sure that I can go with you entirely in your praise of Newman's *Grammar of Assent*. I must doubt whether certainty is ever attained on such matters through the reason or through the illative sense dealing with probabilities. Such a process of the mind may lead to a favourable attitude towards theism, but I believe the certainty of religion comes more by the method of von Hügel than of Newman. But here I am open to conviction. You will note that my *Sceptical Approach* really moves about this thesis." [To Philip S. Richards, Feb. 24, 1935.]
[17] "The ontological God of St. Thomas is not the rational demonstration of something which prepares the way for superrational revelation, but an abstraction out of which all religious experience has been pumped and which, consistently taken, would leave religion to gasp and perish *in vacuo*." [To James L. Hagerty, July 9, 1932.]
"You say: 'In philosophy he (the sensible scholastic theologian) proves from natural reason the existence of God.' My contention would be that he does no such thing, and that natural reason is incapable of doing such a thing. What the scholastic does, following Aristotle, is to show that reason (by its own law of procedure and from no fact of observation or intuition) demands an abstract Absolute, whether in the

degree of Plotinus and Spinoza," he described as "in line with the humanistic approach to the mysteries of religion."[18]

The Sceptical Approach to Religion is "in one sense . . . from beginning to end an exercise in epistemology, and might be characterized as an essay in 'critical realism.' It is non-epistemological in so far as it admits that the rational analysis of the process of knowing leads to a blank—as I think Descartes saw pretty clearly. The book might be called metaphysical in so far as it deals with that which is beyond nature. It is non- or anti-metaphysical in that it rejects the absolutes which the professional metaphysicians take as realities. In other words, it is epistemological and metaphysical as limited by the sceptical conclusion that reason does not give us any ultimate facts, but is the instrument which, by association and dissociation, by the perception of likeness and difference, manipulates the data of experience and intuition for practical purposes. I see, for instance, in St. Thomas Aquinas and others of his kind two disparate procedures: (1) a rational analysis and construction of the facts of religious experience, and (2) an hypostatizing of the mechanisms of reason as absolutes which, so far as they prevail,

---

field of causation or ontology. But this Absolute has no relation whatsoever to the God of faith. By assimilating to this the God of faith, in so far as he does make this assimilation, he introduces into religion a disturbing element and far reaching perversion (papal infallibility is the latest and most devastating result of this iniquitous conflation). Reason cannot demonstrate the existence of anything, let alone the being of God; reason is the supreme and indispensable faculty by which we make use of what is given to us otherwise. Besides the false rationalism of scholastic theology there was another element in medieval religion, a profound and vital faith, which depends not at all upon reason for its origin and loses its reality in so far as it believes itself dependent upon reason. Unfortunately, as it seems to me, along with the profound vitality of this faith there were certain baser elements of superstition which were carried over from the Dark Ages, and were fixed upon Rome by a false conception of development.

"Scholasticism I would maintain, at its centre and in essence, was not in possession of the perennial truths bequeathed by Socrates and Plato, but in its main thesis derives from Aristotle and Plotinus who, in their rationalistic conception of the first Cause, turned Plato upside down." [To George E. Ganss, Dec. 2, 1932.]

[18] *OBH*, 170.

are contrary to the facts. It is in this second sense that they are properly and technically metaphysicians as I use the word."[19]

A disadvantage of begging the question by "an immediate affection" is that "however imperative the immediate intuition of God may be for those who trust in it, there is no means by which its acceptance can be forced upon those—and they today at least would be the majority—who assert that they are unaware of any such experience."[20] Whether those to be "forced" are shallow, distracted, or correct, "if in our apology for religion we are to meet the intellectual unbeliever on his own grounds, we must fall back for our starting point upon some element of consciousness which is universal to all men and cannot be honestly disputed."[21]

Such an element, More claims, "can be found, if anywhere, in the sense of self-approval or disapproval which makes itself felt in the mind as a man acts in one way or another."[22] This moral sense or conscience "is an integral part" of a human being. ". . . in so far as it embraces not only a present feeling but an intention for the future, it is teleological."[23] "Now it is

[19] To Lynn Harold Hough, Oct. 16, 1934.
"I should like to add this as a postscript to the letter just finished and sealed. You say: 'If this gives one the sense that the book is written outside the Christian religion, in one way that adds to the power of its impact.' Those words are very comforting to me, when I need comfort. I am keenly, sometimes painfully, aware of my imperfections as a Christian. It is a truth that I can feel a whole-hearted sympathy with Platonism as I cannot with Christianity; yet my strongest desire is to write in a way to further the aims and truth of the Christian faith. Often I have the discouraged feeling that my efforts must be inefficient owing to the fact that they are made, in some measure, from the outside, and I ask myself whether I am not putting myself in a false position. At other times I bolster myself up by hoping that perhaps this very attempt to give support from the outside (at least not unreservedly from the inside), though it must be restricted in efficiency (it is the great believers who do the big things), yet may have its justification and its measure of genuine value." [To Lynn Harold Hough, Oct. 16, 1934.] Of SAR, "I believe, at least I hope, that nothing in my argument is contrary to the teaching of Jesus as we get this in the Gospels." [To William Lyon Phelps, Oct. 16, 1934.]
[20] SAR, 3.   [21] SAR, 4.   [22] Ibid.
[23] Ibid.

to be noted," More sweepingly declares, "that this moral sense comes . . . not at all by inference or reasoning."[24] It is, he avers, "a direct perception" or "an immediate affection; and as the perception of an inner state it may be called intuition, an ultimate fact of our conscious experience. As such, and so far, it is a matter of incontrovertible knowledge."[25] Moreover, as far as we know and despite its diversity of form and quality, "the teleology of conscience is universal."[26]

"Because at any moment I have a feeling of self-approval or disapproval, it does not follow that this judgement must correspond with what I should feel with larger experience of life or with clearer scrutiny of myself. In fact such feelings, if allowed to influence us unchecked and unexamined, may prove in the test to be very fallible guides to action. Nevertheless they are there, unfailingly with us; and they do involve the constant sense of responsibility and freedom and purpose. Furthermore, any attempt to get behind the bare working of conscience as a law of man's inner being, with whatever may be implied by the word law, any attempt to determine *how* or *why* it is there, or to prove from it the existence of a lawgiver who governs the world in which man's life is staged,—any such endeavour carries us forthwith out of the range of knowledge into the probabilities of inference and theory."[27]

Besides intuition, or "looking in at ourselves," we have observation, or "looking out at things set over against us."[28] "And the troublesome business for our thinking is that through observation we seem to be in contact with a set of facts not only different from, but contrary to, the facts of intuition. All that I immediately *observe* of the natural world and of man as a part of nature appears as mechanically shifting patterns or as a series of mechanical actions and reactions. There are no *visible* signs of voluntary choice controlling what we see happening about us, no direct indications to the eye of purpose."[29]

[24] *Ibid.*   [25] *SAR*, 5.   [26] *Ibid.*
[27] *SAR*, 5-6.   [28] *SAR*, 6.   [29] *Ibid.*

[348]

More realized that here his thought, or at any rate his language, ranging between that of the unconcerned and that of the specialist, moved on the bluff level of daily life.[30] But on that level and according to a mode of viewing things predominant in the occident, "to intuition I and all men are conscious of freedom and responsibility and purpose; to observation I and all men, like the mechanisms amidst which we move, appear to be not free and not responsible and to have no purpose. Is the human world, then, at once both teleological and non-teleological?"[31]

"True sceptics," holding their judgement in suspense, "deliberately refuse to let their minds play upon" this "paradox at all."[32] But "those who resolutely stop here and refuse to draw any inference from the facts of experience, are extremely rare. . . . the thinking man is drawn almost irresistibly by the needs of life and the tyranny of temperament to yield to the temptation of theorizing about what he sees and feels."[33] Influenced by science and accepting "the data of observation as true," he is likely "by explicit or covert inference" to "reject the contrary data of intuition as illusory."[34] In contrast to such a rationalist stands the man of faith who, influenced by other interests, like those of ethics and religion, and "accepting the content of intuition as valid," rejects "if not the data of observation, at least the dogmatic inferences therefrom, as illusory."[35] "Faith may then be defined as the faculty that urges us to carry over the immediate sense of personal freedom and responsibility and purpose into our interpretation of the world at large, in defiance, if need be, of that more self-assertive display of reason which we call rationalism. To faith the whole world thus becomes teleological just as the individual is conscious of being teleo-

[30] In a letter to More of Feb. 26, 1935, Norman Kemp Smith intimated, but more politely, that "purpose," "freedom," "responsibility," "common sense," "spirit," and "matter," as used in these lectures, rumble past like closed freight cars containing who knows what.
[31] *SAR*, 7.   [32] *SAR*, 8.   [33] *Ibid.*
[34] *Ibid.*   [35] *SAR*, 11.

logical; and religion is an attempt to live in harmony with a world so conceived."[36]

Having defined faith in this way, More then narrows attention "to consider briefly some of the inevitable corollaries of faith so defined, and to examine its warrant for acceptance."[37]

"First of all we must keep clearly before us the fact that the faith of religion, as we are considering it, is not knowledge but inference. . . . But if faith stands thus on the same basis with rationalism, as one alternative of two possible attitudes towards the paradox of experience, yet its procedure is not quite the same as that of the other alternative. In a sense the religious man's inference from intuition rejects the result of observation as an illusion, just as the rationalist's inference from observation rejects the results of intuition as an illusion. But the parallel is not exact. The inference of rationalism is by its nature all-embracing and fanatically dogmatic; it simply sweeps away the possibility of freedom and responsibility anywhere and everywhere; it tells me categorically that my intuition is a pure illusion having no correspondence with the facts of existence, and that if I think of myself as free and responsible I am merely a victim of self-deception. Theoretically, if I accept the contention of rationalism, I may seem to have reached a logical solution of the dilemma of experience, and I may thus bring a certain ease to my mind; but the simple truth must not be shuffled out of sight that I have accomplished this by means of pure inference, and that the consciousness of myself as a responsible being capable of purpose remains uneliminated and unaltered. I may by inference remove the immediate affection of freedom from my theory of life; I shall continue to live nevertheless precisely as if I had no such theory.

"In contrast with this procedure the inference of faith is more modest and consistent; it is thus, in the proper use of the word, more reasonable than rationalism, as it is far less subject to the corrosive acid of scepticism. It does not, at least it need

[36] *SAR*, 11-12.   [37] *SAR*, 12.

not, so much reject as transcend the immediate data of observation.[38] It may, without betraying its own demands, admit that the acorn, so far as we can see, develops into an oak by a law which leaves to the acorn itself no freedom of action and no responsibility for its growth; it may with perfect consistency admit, indeed in loyalty to itself is rather bound to believe, that the cosmic evolution has left no visible material records of a conscious purposive mind at work in the cosmos itself. In other words, faith normally does not transfer our consciousness of freedom and responsibility and purpose to, or into, the observed phenomena of the objective universe, but rather infers the existence of a free and responsible agent, whose purpose is operative in the world while He Himself is transcendent to the world. The content of faith is thus theistic rather than pantheistic or deistic. To sum up the argument in more technical language: the inference from observation is in the direction of a materialistic or pseudo-spiritual monism, whereas the proper inference from intuition leads to a dualism of spirit and matter. This is the true meaning of cosmic teleology as different from immanent law. . . ."[39]

Faith of this sort leads the believer to conform his free will to God's will, to find in his sense of responsibility an obligation "to a supreme Ruler and Judge. The morality of self-satisfaction is thus transformed into the morality of duty. And with the recognition of duty there enters a new hope. The sense of purpose is caught up into, and justified by a vaster teleology. The God of purpose, we trust, will not leave our deepest desires frustrate. In particular the instinctive belief in immortality, whether it comes to the primitive man by inference from the immediate consciousness of life or as a defensive reaction against the fear of death, acquires a new assurance from faith in an eternal and benevolent Lord of life."[40]

As faith "starts from, and receives at least its initial content from, man's immediate intuition of freedom and responsibility

---

[38] Cf. *OBH*, 136-37.   [39] *SAR*, 12-14.   [40] *SAR*, 14-15.

and purpose,"[41] More argues that "if cosmic teleology is an inference from the teleological knowledge of myself, if faith is a transference of this triple form of consciousness to a Being who transcends the world, then we are bound by our faith to a corresponding conception of the nature and operation of such a Being. . . . Growth in religion is thus in the direction of a deeper and broader anthropomorphism; *but not away from anthropomorphism.* . . . So long as God remains a purposeful Being—and to faith He can be only that—He must be imagined as working out a design, just as man is conscious of doing, through some sort of obstacle or hindrance and by the lingering processes of time. There can in fact be no conception of purpose without such limitation, though with deepening self-consciousness the inference of limitation may change in character. Similarly He must be held, like man, responsible to the moral law, though again the nature of the moral law will purify itself and deepen as human experience grows larger. And so God's freedom will correspond to man's liberty of choice, developed to that self-determination to choose only good which man sees as the far-off goal of his own endeavour."[42]

"Whatever others may have said of mystical visions, whatever tales there may be of violent irruptions from the supernatural world, I can only report that for myself I can see no sure warrant for the beginning of religion except in faith, and no warrant for rejecting the . . . identification of faith with desire."[43] ". . . this . . . is no more than a corollary of the sceptic's statement that knowledge, demonstrable knowledge at least, is limited to our immediate affections, and that faith is therefore not knowledge but undemonstrable inference. Nor has reason any power to demonstrate that the inferred existence of God is necessarily true. . . . we believe because we wish to believe, because we are afraid not to believe."[44]

[41] *SAR*, 15.   [42] *SAR*, 16-17.   [43] *SAR*, 20.
[44] *SAR*, 21. "You express surprise over my pessimistic sense of illusion. . . . Indeed, I have tried to keep it out of my books, at least the later ones. But from childhood the one haunting terror of my life has been

"I must either believe or disbelieve that there is within the world, or, rather, beyond the world, that which corresponds to my intuition of freedom and responsibility; I must either regard the universe as teleological, with all which this implies, or I must regard it as without purpose. There is for the honest and serious mind, for the practical rule of life, no middle ground. And faced with the compulsion of choosing between such alternatives I say to you, the champion of what you call facts, that your view is simply incredible. You ask me to believe that nature has planted in me, and not in me alone but in all men, desires which I must eradicate as pure deceptions, that I am the victim of a cosmic jest, only the more cruel if unintended, that the ultimate fact of existence is a malignant mockery."[45]

"I am not retracting the admission that faith, initially at least, is inference and not knowledge, or that a man believes because he wishes to believe; I am only saying that, all things considered, the so-called disbelief of the infidel is an inference which, if honestly examined, demands an act of almost impossible credulity. . . .

"It is hard to believe, harder not to believe."[46]

The second Lowell Lecture describes the development by Socrates and Plato of "the three factors of intuition"[47]—freedom, responsibility, and purpose—which together make up More's concept of teleology. In his third and fourth lectures he shows, as he had done in *The Greek Tradition*, how Plato "reached a completely teleological philosophy[48] by developing on parallel lines the doctrine of Ideas and the belief in God as the two co-

---

the unreality of the world. That was what carried me into Hinduism, the fact that the Hindus seemed somehow to snatch a sort of strength and peace out of the recognition of Mâyâ. Plato half saved me from that. And you will see in *The Sceptical Approach* that all my brave insistence on teleology is an effort to escape the pit." [To Philip S. Richards, Jan. 6, 1934 (an error for 1935). Cf. *OBH*, 93 ff.]

[45] *SAR*, 24-25. Cf. *ibid.*, p. 154.
[46] *SAR*, 25-26.   [47] *SAR*, 29.
[48] ". . . a teleology which might be taken as a secular confirmation of the divine purpose revealing itself in the Word made flesh." [*SAR*, 176.]

operative causes of order in the phenomenal world of our observation. . . ."[49] Spinoza and Kant hold More's attention in the fifth lecture, because one "reaches his substitute for faith by what he regards as the indisputable conclusions of reason from the data of observation, while the other reasons ostensibly from the data of intuition. Between them they thus cover pretty well the possibilities of quasi-religious rationalism."[50]

Spinoza's error, More believed, "can be traced back to the initial disregard of the prime lesson of experience, that we are intellectually impotent[51] and morally responsible.[52] In the case of Spinoza it is quite clear that he not only disregards but reverses these terms. Instead he will insist on intellectual responsibility and moral impotence. From the intuition of conscience we can draw no inference whatsoever; our only responsibility is to follow the headlong flight of reason which, leaping from the ground of physical observation, soars into the empyrean where all discriminations of good and evil vanish in the Infinite Indifference.

"Against this attempt to manufacture a religion out of pure logic arose the doughtiest of agnostics, David Hume, who will be sceptical and rationalistic in one and the same breath, and who leaves us in the end with the intellect and the moral sense both impotent.

". . . the aim of Kant was to find an escape from the double-barrelled agnosticism of Hume, and to establish religion on a thoroughly critical basis."[53]

". . . Kant, like Spinoza, had in mind what he regarded as the interest of pure religion when he set out on the tortuous path of metaphysics; but it is . . . certain that the elements of religion—the moral sense, freedom, responsibility, immortality, and God

---

[49] *SAR*, 39.   [50] *SAR*, 100.
[51] Should an "intellectually impotent" author have recourse to "a thoroughgoing use of reason"? [*SAR*, 1.] As Norman Kemp Smith asked More in a letter of Feb. 26, 1935, would not "intellectually fallible" be closer the mark?
[52] Cf. *HP*, 257, 385.   [53] *SAR*, 106-07.

—when passed through the alembic of his critical method come out as ghastly shadows of the realities of intuition and faith."[54] Who "can really believe in" Kant's "fantastic mummery? Indeed, scarcely the metaphysician himself. We do not know that we are free and responsible, but we must act as if we so believed. We do not know our immortality or the existence of God, but we must live as if we believed. It is all a ghastly mockery of the faith that begins in dim surmising at the mystery of the unseen, and by long experience takes on the body and assurance of conviction."[55]

"If any one lesson can be surely learnt from Kant as well as from Spinoza, it is that the endeavor to escape the human condition of intellectual impotence ends invariably in a denial of human responsibility."[56]

To temperament, instinct, will, fear, dim surmising, and desire, which More recognized as contributing, with inference from ethical intuition, to religious faith, he added in his sixth lecture mana and taboo as sources of otherworldliness and morality, "the two prime constituents of religion." "But when we pass from God and the moral code to the notion of redemption, we touch upon a phase of religion that belongs in unique fashion to the Jewish people. It is true that redemption can be in a general way connected with the confidence felt when mana is favourable and the laws of taboo have been properly observed, and in this sense it can be found among other peoples—which is no more than to say that the idea is essentially religious. But it is peculiar to the Jews by association with a particular event which occurred at the outset of their national life"[57]—their escape from the Egyptians at the Red Sea. "Now the influence and

[54] *SAR*, 113.
[55] *SAR*, 114. Writing to More on Dec. 1, 1934, Clement C. J. Webb objected to this interpretation of Kant, maintaining that Kant, like More, believed the demands of faith echoed "that within himself which is deeper than reason and more fundamental to his nature as man." [*SAR*, 181.] Kant, the intuitionist, More contended (in his reply of Dec. 15, 1934, to Webb), did not prevail over Kant, the metaphysician.
[56] *SAR*, 116.   [57] *SAR*, 130, 132-33.

importance of this event, however it occurred, can scarcely be exaggerated. Its result was *the bringing together of religion and history*, the associating of the will of God with the destinies of a chosen race, to a degree and in a manner absolutely unique."[58] ". . . from the historic fact of Israel's deliverance springs the teleological conception of a divine Providence working through the events of history, a conception of which one may find shadowy hints in other religions and for which Plato was reaching out in his philosophy, but which in its developed form belongs preeminently to the Hebrews."[59]

For his disciples in the coming of Jesus "the whole cycle of religious ideas had attained its realization, its climax, its *telos*. . . . These primitive Christians unquestionably believed that the God who had set apart the Jewish people and had spoken through the prophets, had at the last revealed Himself face to face in one whom they had known and handled and heard."[60]

"Today for any open-minded reader of the New Testament the issue is clear-cut and not honourably to be evaded. . . . We may believe that Jesus was a hypocrite or a self-deluded fanatic; in which case there is no Christianity. Or we may believe that he was in truth what he alleged himself to be; in which case it is hard to see how we can avoid identifying ultimately Christianity with the Catholic dogma of the Incarnation and with the Catholic sacrament of the Eucharist. To one who approaches the subject from a critical study of the Old Testament the same question may present itself philosophically in slightly different form: has the historic evolution of Hebraic religion a true *telos* in the coming of the Son of man, or is that evolution part of the grand illusion of creatures doomed to live in a world devoid of purpose and without meaning?"[61]

More's "rapid survey of the growth of religion among the Jews" aimed to supply evidence for "the thesis that, as Platonism is the only philosophy which independently developed a high

58 *SAR*, 133.   59 *SAR*, 135.
60 *SAR*, 139.   61 *SAR*, 144.

form of teleology, so Christianity is the only completely teleological religion of the world."[62] By teleology, he explained in
his seventh lecture, he meant not merely evolution but "purposive evolution."[63] ". . . from the purely evolutionary point
of view, the genuine *telos* of Judaism must be sought in Christianity."[64] But this "brings us . . . to the problem of teleology in
the higher and special sense of the word: was the *telos* of Christianity something more than the mere conclusion of an historic
process? does it indicate a purpose behind the development of
religious ideas, a conscious planning agent who foresaw the end
from the beginning and guided Israel step by step until its task
was finished? was there indeed a Jehovah speaking through the
prophets as they themselves proclaimed, or was their faith a
pure illusion? was he who, at the conclusion of that process,
assumed more than prophetic authority a deluded fanatic, or
did he in truth speak as no man ever yet had spoken? in a
word, does this evolution imply revelation?"[65]

These questions, More believed, cannot be answered by "the
probabilities of reason. But there is this fact also to consider,
that he who makes the venture of faith and endeavours so to
live as to conform his will to what he believes is the will of God
—that he who practises religion, with courage and in humility,
becomes more and more convinced of some voice out of the
infinite silence answering to the plea of his own heart. Faith appears to him less and less a bare conjecture from his own longing desire, a will to believe, more and more the response to a
summons of compelling power.[66] To this conviction the honest
sceptic can only say, you may be right, but I know nothing
about it."[67]

Though More admitted, "I for one simply cannot conceive a
further step in the scale of revelation beyond the historic event
of the Word made flesh,"[68] he acknowledged that "when we turn

[62] *SAR*, 145.   [63] *SAR*, 146.   [64] *SAR*, 151.
[65] *Ibid*.   [66] Cf. *RP*, 62, 64-65.
[67] *SAR*, 152.   [68] *SAR*, 167.

to the subjective side of religion, there is a different story to tell. There is no reason to suppose that faith may not grow from strength to strength, or that knowledge may not deepen from age to age. The fact of revelation is there, unchanged, final, complete; but this does not preclude the possibility, even the probability, of an ever clearer perception of the meaning of the Incarnation, of an ever wider and truer application of the moral law to the relations of man to man and of man to God, in purity and humility and love, of an ever deeper penetration into the end of redemption, of an ever fuller participation in the mystery of worship and sacrifice. Here would enter the function of the Church. As the Incarnation came in response to the faith of a separate nation, so we may suppose the Parousia and the realization of the Messianic Kingdom to depend on the fidelity of the Church as a separate people within the world."[69]

Of all More's books this evoked the most thoughtful response from his friends. Beneath the academic conventions of lectures of this kind and occasional bits of pulpit rhetoric they admired his honesty and realism, his reach if not his grasp, his independence and integrity. Nor were they unaware of the questionable theories lurking in his "indisputable facts" or of his error (in procedure if not in substance) in seeking to derive theism from sceptical premises.

"As for what you say about God as *purus actus*, as the Absolute, there," More admitted to C. S. Lewis, "you have put your finger unerringly on the most disputable and in a way the weakest point of my whole argument. Yet, in saying that, I do not mean to abandon my position: I do not see how I can accept the Absolute without rejecting the sort of teleology on which I base my faith and on which, as it seems to me, the *faith* of the Church, not her metaphysical theology, is based. As for my teleology, it does imply some sort of limitation to the Agent's will, something outside Himself which has some power of resistance: without that I do not see how we can have anything

[69] *SAR*, 168-69.

but a static a-cosmos. It does not involve that He may fail. . . .
Faith is belief in the ultimate victory of the good. . . .

"I quite understand why you demand the Absolute, and why
the Church has made belief in the Absolute the orthodox creed
(Credo in Deum impassibilem). We crave something fixed,
final, immovable amidst the everlasting, unceasing flux about us.
That craving is indeed an essential factor of faith. The point is
made forcibly by Ronald Knox to Arnold Lunn in one of the
letters of *Difficulties*:[70] 'You (Lunn) will not go with me to
worship a God who is limited by nothing outside himself, because you do not think that he exists. And I will not go with
you to worship a God who is limited by anything outside himself, because I do not care a rap whether he exists or not.'

"But isn't there some confusion in all this? To use a term of
Webb's (though he does not develop the idea) isn't that which
we really crave and need an Ultimate rather than an Absolute?
I have been brought to consider this by reading von Hügel's
essay on *Suffering and God*. The Baron takes the orthodox view
and rejects Patripassianism outright. But then he is faced by
the fact of the crucifixion. What is to be done? He calls in the
Definition of Chalcedon and the two natures. It is the manhood
of Christ that suffers, while the Godhead is impassive. But that
is to forget the terms of the Definition which writes the two
natures indissolubly into one person, and to fall into pure Nes-
torianism. Worse than that, it makes nonsense of the whole Incarnation, if it does not reduce it to pure Docetism. It is to turn
the great text: God so loved the world, etc., into blasphemy.
And who can love a father who gives his son to suffering, without a pang! . . .

"But to go back to the question of ultimate or absolute. I
look at it this way. Take a strong man: suppose him to undergo
a great loss. He will suffer, even suffer in proportion to his

[70] More reviewed *Difficulties, Being a Correspondence about the Catholic Religion between Ronald Knox and Arnold Lunn*, in *The Criterion*,
July 1932, vol. 11, pp. 739-44.

strength. Yet all the while there is that in him which stands apart from his suffering, which submits not, which in the end even wins grace and peace out of his suffering,—the thing Milton had in mind:

And what is else not to be overcome.

"We all in our measure have this experience, the stronger more than the weak. Now what theology does is to take this unsuffering factor of our being out, abstract it from the suffering element, and set it up as an Absolute. But the moment this is done, you have something monstrous, dead, and for us perfectly unmeaning. What we need, what we are really thinking of, is an Ultimate, a Being in whom the unsuffering element is absolutely in command, unshakable, final, with no shadow of turning. This is not human, it is infinitely beyond man: but it is anthropomorphic."[71]

Though some of his friends believed that from their acquaintance with his tastes and ideas they could predict his choices and answers, and though when he was ill, irked, careless, making fun of himself, or arousing a hearer, he expressed his patterns of thought dogmatically, almost automatically—at his best More recognized his opinions as tendencies subject to improvement rather than as irrevocable conclusions. He held his positions tenaciously in so far as he knew no better, but, aside from that, he no more "held a position" than does a walker who climbs hill after hill for wider views. Convinced of the necessity of a "constant exercise of our will and intelligence in making an adjustment never quite final,"[72] of the continual dependence of knowledge upon "larger experience of life" and "clearer scrutiny" of self,[73] and suspicious of "premature fixation,"[74] he considered philosophy as an attitude, a living growth, a process— "a search and not a thing found . . . fluid and not crystallized, kinetic and not static."[75]

[71] To Clive Staples Lewis, Nov. 29, 1934.
[72] P. 306 above.   [73] P. 348 above.   [74] *A*, xxi.
[75] So More described Plato's philosophy, on a blank page in the front

His attitude towards religion he summed up in two words: humility and honesty.

"Humility.

"(1) Recognition of limits of reason.

This is not a denial of reason, not anti-intellectualism in any absolute sense of word.

All the order and comeliness and health of life depend on rational analysis and comprehension of what actually comes to us by perception, intuition, experience.

It rejects the conversion of these data into the absolutes of reason. E. g. it denies any such statement as this canon of the Vatican Council: 'Si quis dixerit, Deum unum et verum, Creatorem et Dominum nostrum, per ea, quae factae sunt, naturali rationis humanae lumine *certo cognosci* non posse; anathema sit.' This is a contradiction of position of early church and by its *certo* leads to the definition of God in terms of pure metaphysical abstractions, as in the famous decree of the same Council. . . .

"(2) Recognition of limits of emotions.

This is not a denial of validity of emotions.

It makes much of the value of human affections and of beauty.

In worship it admits importance of aesthetic and personal emotions.

It counsels a very childlike and (to a point) uncritical submission to such appeals.

But it recognizes also the fact that such emotions, if over-indulged, may run off [into] vague pantheism and enfeebling revery if allowed free sway apart from reason and will; or

---

of his interleaved copy of *Platos Ausgewählte Dialoge*, erklärt von C. Schmelzer, Bd. VII, *Der Staat*, Berlin (Weidmannsche Buchhandlung), 1884. ". . . real Platonism . . . is not a dogmatic statement of the truth, but a continuous approximation thereto, which, for us as we are constituted, is more veracious than truth; it is not a metaphysic but a discipline . . ." [*SE* VI, 346.]

may run into fanaticism if allowed to dominate reason and will.

"(3) Recognition of limits of will.

Not rejection of will.

Our happiness and health depend on exercise of will.

But it sees the danger of forgetting that will may be governed by imperfect knowledge and by personal emotion taken as absolute knowledge and absolute law.

"Honesty.

"In a sense this is merely another phase of humility. It is an honest response to, and use of, limits of reason, emotions, will. More specifically it is a recognition that all we know must come to us in form of anthropomorphism, and that, equally, there may be a vast reach of truth beyond anthropomorphism. God, we say, is good. That is anthropomorphic, taken from human sense of values. It is dishonest to accept such a dictum of faith, and then to define goodness so that it retains no relation to what goodness means in human experience. E. g. Calvin defines God as good, and then declares that He for His own good pleasure caused the fall of man and the damnation of the major part of humanity.—Spinoza and von Hügel raise (reduce?) God's love to infinite and self-sufficient love of Himself.—To accept the Incarnation as act of love and then to define God as incapable of suffering [is dishonest].[76]

"What, if anything, lies beyond the humane attributes of goodness and love belongs to the mystery of the Unknowable; at least it cannot be defined in humane terms. That is the final dishonesty.

———

"Vaughan:

The world
Is full of voices; man is call'd, and hurl'd
By each.

[76] The interpolated words come from a similar draft of these notes, which More retained among his papers.

1934

"The truths of religion are scattered everywhere, but broken, and unauthoritative, and entangled in error. What to do? Personally, I find three supreme teachers: Buddha, Plato, Jesus.

"*Buddha.*

The truth of Karma. Our good and evil deeds follow us beyond this life, and their effects are inescapable.

The truth of the Higher Will. Man must work out his own salvation.

His *anatta* doctrine (there is no permanent soul) is theoretically false, contradicts the law of personal responsibility involved in Karma. But practically Buddha does not permit it to lessen personal responsibility.

The serious errors are the omission of God and cosmic teleology. The human will (the Higher Will) is not sufficient. Man is weak and needs the support of God's grace.

The Higher Will is ultimately regarded as an abstraction which rejects all human emotions and reason. Nirvana an escape from human affections, not a spiritualization of them; an escape from the implications of beauty. It leaves no place for cosmic teleology, for spiritual meaning in phenomena. For myself, I cannot, or will not, believe that the great spectacle of earthly beauty is without ultimate meaning, or will not somehow be carried on into eternity. So of the pure human affections.

"*Plato.*

His ethics correspond to Buddhist Karma.

His psychology includes Buddhist Higher Will.

He has cosmic teleology, involved in God, Ideas, ἄτακτος κίνησις.

He has the truth of Buddhism and fills in the omissions.

Errors, or weakness: his θεός and his θεία μοῖρα (Grace) remain shadowy, never get out of the penumbra of philosophic hints. His doctrine of Ideas, as giving objectivity to the moral law (it is Karma passed through a great poetic imagination), is the *sine qua non* of any ethics. But he does

[363]

not see that Ideas only become ethical when connected with, taken into, personality. The mysterious relationship between objective law of right and subjective motivation; between Ideas as entities and the *a priori* intuition of values;—that goes beyond comprehension; Plato apparently did not feel it (yet, I do not know; perhaps his confused debate over the teachability or not of virtue involves the mystery).

"*Christianity.*

Contains the good of Buddhism and Platonism.

Balances human will and Grace, Karma and forgiveness.

It is the ultimate teleology. (As I have tried to show in *The Sceptical Approach.*)

Why then not be satisfied with Christianity? Why cling to Buddha and Plato? Apart from secondary reasons, my answer would be as follows. Theology has tended persistently to develop Grace at the expense of the human will. Catholicism theoretically preserves the truth, but in practice even Rome lowers function of human will and freedom almost to the vanishing point; and Protestantism (Luther, Calvin, Barth, Nygren) unite theory and practice in complete denial of human will. Hence the corrective value of Buddhism.

Christianity is essentially sound in ethics, preserving the truth of Karma and Ideas, and supplementing it [with] clearer theism. In the Logos made man, in the intrinsic meaning of the Logos apart from the Incarnation, Christianity has mythically (a true myth, we will say) brought together the objectivity of the ethical law and the subjectivity of personal morality. But the theologians have tended to regard morality as purely subjective, as the bare will of God. There is real danger in this excess of subjectivity, which really reduces the moral law to arbitrary whim, voluntarism. The Platonic doctrine of Ideas, held by the early Christians but swept away in the tide of metaphysics, is a needed corrective, not of Christianity, but of rationalized theology."[77]

[77] To A. H. Dakin, Jr., Jan. 13, 1935.

18

THE LONG HOPE (1934-1937)

FOR several years as daily exercise More had walked with brisk step, head high, and twirling cane, the mile or so from his house to the university library and back. After Mary's illness late in 1931 and during her long convalescence at 59 Battle Road in 1932, he occasionally crowned his walk with tea and a chocolate éclair at the Baltimore Dairy Lunch, a Nassau Street restaurant opposite the campus, with white tile walls and small round tables, where amid the crowd of students he might find Oates, Hinds, Greene, Mather, Godolphin, or someone else to talk to. These casual conversations became so valuable to him and to his most frequent associates that by 1934 they found themselves going to the "Balt" as an afternoon habit.

Although some of the "Baltimoreans" took to More easily, feeling in his presence (as an English friend of his put it) "that sense of comfort and security and well-being which a child has" with "grown up relatives whom it likes" and in his conversation (as one of his students recalled) "a compound (in exactly the right proportions) of directness, humor, dry wit, and warmth, all of it flowing as smoothly and urbanely as he wrote," a certain professor among them suffered a few years as a victim of the Platonist's first impressions, often harshly unfavorable; of his scathing tongue ("I have been scandalously outspoken and censorious." "Nothing counts so much as simple kindness."[1]); and of his aloof air, dogmatic manner, and redoubtable erudition. The professor was nonplussed by such a prodigy: one who could not be ignored in literature, philosophy, and theology; a believer and a sceptic; in some respects a radical ahead of his

[1] These two and subsequent sentences quoted in this and the three following paragraphs, without other indication of source, are More's words as remembered by a "Baltimorean." Also quoted are some passages from More's letters approximating what he said in conversation at the "Balt."

time,[2] in others a conservative out of the past;[3] solitary, intellectual, aristocratic—sociable, earthly, middle class; susceptible to the attractions of the world and the senses, emotional, romantic, yet sound, sober, practical; proud, egotistic—diffident and considerate; serious and contemplative—gay, humorous, revelling in mischievous[4] and indiscreet remarks. "I can afford to say these things, but you are not yet established."

One afternoon in the "Balt" the professor found himself alone at a table with More. After some embarrassment and small talk he bravely mentioned a problem that perplexed him. More, instead of thundering from Olympus, entered at once into a genuine concern of a soul. Having hurdled their surface selves, from then on, notwithstanding disagreements, they became friends.

Beyond his hearing some of the "Balts" called him "The Mahatma." Oates referred to him as the Demon of the Absolute. "Yes, there's more in that than people think," More, when told of it, replied. But apparently he scarcely suspected that anyone could find him rebuffing. He often began to talk with an extreme stand, as though to say: "Bring on your bantering opposition, than which, as a matter of curious fact, there's nothing I delight in more." "My words are often extravagant and as a consequence not to be taken too seriously, or, shall I

[2] "At Princeton the establishment of the Division of the Humanities, paralleling similar movements in other universities, was largely due to the initiative of a group of younger scholars who had been stimulated by his [More's] lectures, books, and conversation." ["Conversations with Paul Elmer More," by J. Duncan Spaeth, *The Sewanee Review*, Oct.-Dec. 1943, vol. LI, no. 4, p. 534.]

[3] "More was critical of the vague and 'expansive' humanitarianism of the New Deal, not because he was insensitive to the plight of the impoverished or blind to the struggles of the underprivileged, but because he was suspicious of a democracy of the Heart that repudiated the aristocracy of the Intellect and while remembering the forgotten man, forgot the memorable man." [*Ibid.*, p. 541.]

[4] John Erskine spoke at the Princeton Graduate School on contemporary French opinion of American authors. More, who had listened rather fretfully, in the question period after the lecture asked: "What is the contemporary French opinion of Henry van Dyke?"

say? literally."[5] But if intelligently opposed, if convinced of error, he gratefully qualified his position. "You know," he reminded Myers, in criticizing an article, "how one sets a comment down in harsh terms which would be much modified in conversation."[6]

With the "Balts" it was a continuous give and take of metaphysics, science, religion, education, literature, politics, ethics, and humanism. About the humanistic furore: "I felt they were whispering behind my back and disdaining me in Princeton when I walked about." It is "a desperately hard thing to go all one's life against the current of one's age." "We are, it must just be said, in the main a frightfully uneducated and intellectually flabby people, except in matters of economics and science."[7] "I am no individualist by choice or principle. But in the world at large anyone who adheres to tradition and to the institutional Church as a (partial) supporter of that tradition must appear more or less in isolation."[8] And yet besides detective stories and the ghost stories of Montague Rhodes James, life had its "bright spots,"[9] especially in England. "More and more, year by year, the regret grows on me that, when I gave up my office work in New York, I did not transplant myself to England."[10] And as he walked home from the "Balt" along Mercer Street while the sun set behind the ancient trees on the Marquands' pastoral grounds ("very English in its lawns and simplicity"[11]), he bethought himself to reconsider Wordsworth.

Though tired and unwell ever since he left Essex for Princeton in September, during the winter of 1934 More aided Cowardin with his textbook, *The Study of English Literature.* "I . . . offered to read the manuscript as he turned it off. (I

[5] To Austin Warren, March 10, 1932.
[6] To Edward DeLos Myers, Oct. 23, 1932.
[7] To Philip S. Richards, Aug. 17, 1932.
[8] To Cyril N. McKinnon, Nov. 5, 1932.
[9] To Louis T. More, Oct. 6, 1934.
[10] To Philip S. Richards, Feb. 24, 1935.
[11] To Alice More, Oct. 29, 1913.

The Long Hope

should explain that he is an excellent violinist, and his wife a good pianist, and that Darrah and I used to go to their house every Monday for music; hence our friendship.) I got interested in the work, and in the end became what you might call a collaborator. The plan is his, and is based on his experience in preparing boys for the College Board general examination in English. Almost all the writing is primarily his. But he wrote and rewrote in response to my criticism. Some of the chapters I sketched out for the ideas, and he then worked them up and over. My notion was that his name alone should appear on the title-page, and that he should give me due credit in the preface. But in the end he insisted on my name appearing on the title-page, and I acceded. Though in one sense the heavy labour is all his, and the plan too as well as all the textbook features; still the thing could never have been written without my assistance. It cost me time and labour."[12]

Besides seeking Shafer's help to interest a publisher in the textbook, More recommended the printing of the manuscript of Babbitt's *Dhammapada*, about which the Oxford University Press asked his advice. He could not, however, second Mrs. Babbitt's proposal for the publication of a volume of her husband's letters. ". . . my decision is formed from his letters to me, and only from these. As you know, we corresponded very infrequently and only on some special point of business or criticism. His letters are fine of their sort, expressed with a telling straightforwardness, but they are brief, not at all discursive, and the personal note is very rare. They were perfect for their purpose, but not the sort of writing that would make an interesting book."[13]

Early in December he was preparing an essay on von Hügel.[14] "In the most general terms" he aimed "to show first the depth and strength and reality" of von Hügel's "religious ex-

12 To Robert Shafer, Feb. 4, 1935.
13 To Mrs. Irving Babbitt, March 31, 1935.
14 Cf. *OBH*, 160-83.

perience. This is indicated by the 'tensions' on which he is continually insisting. The point is that in him these tensions are genuine and powerful—he *was* living in two worlds." Secondly More tried to show that von Hügel's "metaphysical conception of God as the timeless, impassive, unrelated Absolute (borrowed ultimately from Aristotle but induced in von Hügel chiefly by immersion in German and scholastic philosophy) introduces an element of strain into these tensions which is not necessary to, indeed is hostile to, the peace of religion. . . .

"God conceived in the Aristotelian and scholastic manner (which is not at all the Gospel and early patristic conception) ought to result, and in the stronger souls, has resulted, in an ideal of absolute mysticism and of radically ascetic escape from the world. Von Hügel is drawn in this direction, though he fights against it. On the other hand his native bent is towards a broad sacramental view of the world, in accordance with which the other great fields of experience (science, art, etc.) are not to be evaded but combined with the religious. The true 'tensions' of religion, between the two fields, which aims not at severing them but at uniting them teleologically, is thus changed in him to a tension between two aims, the ascetic-mystical and the teleological. The result can be seen in the anxiety imprinted on his face (as with Newman and others who have been too religious for their peace)."[15]

After church on Christmas morning "Harry and Darrah brought the children. We opened some presents, and then had a nice turkey dinner. In the evening I went to the Fines' for supper, after which . . . we played 'ghosts' and other wit-sharpening games. Tomorrow afternoon I am going to the Geroulds' for egg-nog (is that the way you spell the thing?) and any other intoxicant desired. All very well, but I shall be glad when these *dies nefasti* are ended, and the postman makes his regular two calls a day, and carries something else in his pack besides

[15] To A. H. Dakin, Jr., Nov. 26, 1934. The strain More believed he found in von Hügel's face may possibly be explained by physical causes.

Christmas cards."[16] "Christmas is no longer a merry season for me . . . and the new years no longer hold out any promise. But that is to be expected, and accepted."[17]

Early in 1935, when Louis, whose *"Newton* is proving a notable success with the press and, I believe, in sales,"[18] visited him for two weeks, More considered writing for *The American Review*, despite its editor's unpredictable conduct towards him, an article explaining "by what experience of life and by what theories of art a man capable, when barely more than a youth, of writing the last scene of *The Dead*, should have been brought to wallow in the moral slough of *Ulysses* and to posture through the linguistic impertinences of *Work in Progress*."[19] "The Oxford University Press has proposed to bring out a volume of *Selected Shelburne Essays* this spring," More wrote to Collins in connection with his projected article on Joyce; "and the *opus* 'Anglicanism' will soon appear heralded with recommendations by the Archbishops of Canterbury and York and by T. S. Eliot. There are other indications that I shall soon be more at home in England than in America. I do not write this in a spirit of boasting or of egotism, but rather of sadness. My only really sympathetic editor in this country, by his obstinate silences and irresponsibility, forces me to look abroad. I will not conceal the truth that the discord between his protests and his acts does cut me to the quick."[20]

On February 21st he signed what proved to be his last will. After providing bequests for his sons-in-law and, if they were employed by him at the time of his death, for William and Mary, he left the bulk of his property to be divided equally between his daughters.

Most of that month and March he suffered from haemorrhoids. In April "three doctors and the X-ray photographer" gave him "a pretty clean bill of health, and . . . failed utterly to discover any symptom of a malignant growth which they feared

[16] To Louis T. More, Dec. 31, 1934.
[17] To Robert Shafer, Dec. 30, 1934.
[18] To Samuel Pendleton Cowardin, Jr., Jan. 26, 1935.
[19] *OBH*, 70.   [20] To Seward B. Collins, Jan. 20, 1935.

—or hoped. But weeks of pain and sleeplessness have left me rather nervous, and I still lie down a good part of the day. Added to this I have taken on engagements for essays[21] and reviews and lectures that call for all my energy."[22]

As the simplified version of his university lectures on the "Origins of Christianity" that More had delivered in the winter of 1933-34 at the Princeton Preparatory School had been over the boys' heads, in the spring of 1935 Harry Fine spoke to them in his study on Sunday evenings about religion in such a way as to elicit their queries, which More, who attended the series of discussions, answered patiently and sometimes with amusement. When the headmaster expressed to his father-in-law his disappointment that one of the boys, who on those Sunday evenings had listened intently without saying a word, was too poor to enter Princeton, More sent the youngster funds that started him on a successful university career.

". . . I have been reading over, or running through, eleven volumes of my own essays to make a selection for the book the Oxford University Press is to bring out in their World's Classics. The result of that search has been on me just depressing. So much of the work seems unsatisfactory after the lapse of years, and the whole of it gives me the impression of a mind groping about and not knowing whither it is bound. The field is too wide and the effect scattered. I seem not to be one intelligence but an unassimilated bundle of impulses and curiosities."[23]

In the middle of April, with Miss McLinn at the piano, More and some other friends of his "gave a really spirited rendering

[21] In "The Modernism of French Poetry" (*OBH*, 97-116), an essay apparently written about this time and published in *The American Review* in June 1935 More approached his topic in the same way as he had approached Proust and Joyce. Beneath the aesthetic aspects of the subject, so closely do life and art interpenetrate, lies the vital struggle, the eternal choice of direction: either humanism and classicism and full use of the highest spiritual traditions and institutions, leading towards order, theism, life, and God; or naturalism, romanticism, and egoism, overwhelmed by the subconscious, ending in chaos, atheism, death, and the devil.

[22] To Louis T. More, April 7, 1935.

[23] To Erna Obermeier, April 11, 1935.

of Haydn's Second Symphony."[24] And on a walk about ten days later he exulted in Princeton's assumption of "its robes of glory." "The loveliness of this annual outburst of beauty affects me more and more as I grow older with an intensity that is almost painful."[25]

On May 17th at the Presbyterian Hospital in New York he was operated on for carcinoma of prostate, although he had been told only that he had a fibroid tumor. The next two weeks he barely survived. Early in June, however, he improved. Whenever the doctors allowed it, Darrah visited him. Myers called on him as devotedly as a son. Oates, Godolphin, and Hoffman Nickerson admired the calmness of his spirit. By the end of the month he returned to 59 Battle Road to "lie doggo"[26] and under the affectionate care of his daughters (for Alice returned that summer) to recover his strength.

Turning over his house in Princeton to Myers, about the middle of July he went to "The Cedars." While his brain "was completely fagged and sapped,"[27] he composed his slight introduction to the *Selected Shelburne Essays*, for which Myers sent him such information as he needed from his library in Battle Road. At Essex things went "on as usual. We play bridge every evening, and so far I have had a run of extraordinary luck. . . . My strength comes back steadily but slowly."[28]

"Every year I feel more keenly the hardship of our separation," nearly two months after his return to Princeton he wrote to Louis, for whose son, John, he wished "a happy marriage, than which this world has nothing better to offer"; "for we understand each other as brothers do not commonly do; and our depressions cancel out, so to speak. Though, as a matter of fact, despite my pain and weakness, I have not felt much de-

[24] To Samuel Pendleton Cowardin, Jr., April 18, 1935.
[25] To Louis T. More, April 26, 1935.
[26] To A. H. Dakin, Jr., July 4, 1935.
[27] To Oxford University Press (Mr. H. V. Clulow), Oct. 20, 1935.
[28] To Mrs. Harry B. Fine, July 20, 1935.

pression—perhaps the good God is teaching me patience and humility; if he is trying that, he is succeeding."[29]

"Darrah comes every day, sometimes two or three times a day, and we talk and read aloud."[30] "We are now just finishing *Pendennis*, which reads aloud wonderfully—when the pathos does not choke our voices. Harry drops in almost every evening to take Darrah home, and we (Harry and I) have really good talks together."[31] "And friends[32] are amazingly good. Scarcely a day passes but one or two [or] three men call in. I particularly enjoy the visits of the 'Baltimoreans,' who bring in fresh life and new ideas. Besides other visits, the four[33] of them come in every Friday afternoon for tea and talk. If I could only get back my strength!"[34] "Meanwhile my infirmities have drawn us all closer together in a manner I can hardly think about without tears."[35]

Except to complain of the surgeon's fee and of his inability to tackle the program of writing that he had laid out for himself, More grumbled little, never invited pity, referred to his physical condition only when directly questioned about it, and bore his ordeal with cheerful courage. He took such an interest in his friends' doings and talked so much in his exhilarating way that they argued with him and with one another as though they were in the presence of a well man. And his old crony, Mather, who scarcely agreed with More on anything, would ramble on interminably, stopping merely to return in kind his host's petulant objections or humorous insults. "Poor Mather," More sighed, "has gone all to words, like a dandelion to seeds."

"You will be glad to know that I did actually begin work the

---

[29] To Louis T. More, Nov. 11, 1935.
[30] To the same, Nov. 24, 1935. [31] To the same, Nov. 11, 1935.
[32] Among his faithful visitors were the two women in Princeton whose conversation he found the most intelligent and refreshing, Mrs. Henry Post Mitchell and Miss Henrietta Ricketts, and his neighbors on Battle Road, Professors Frank H. Constant and Charles F. W. McClure.
[33] Oates, Hinds, Greene, and Godolphin.
[34] To Louis T. More, Nov. 24, 1935.
[35] To the same, Dec. 31, 1935.

day after my birthday. But from that date until today I have done nothing—today I put in a good morning. The interruption was caused by streams of visitors, culminating Saturday morning when Bishop Matthews brought the Archbishop of York to visit me. The latter had received an honorary degree the day before, and had, so it was repeated to me, made a capital address. . . . Bow your head when you think of me chatting with an Archbishop here in my own study. I hold my leather chair sanctified, though while he was sitting in it I was more afraid it would be shattered to bits—for he is a great man in more senses of the word than one."[36]

". . . I am hoping that, when spring has come in sufficiently to enable me to get out of doors, my strength will come back with a rush—I am hoping. Meanwhile at least my brain has got back almost to normal condition: I can read solid books with gusto and even have ideas floating about in my head. I have not yet started actually to write; but have my notes ready for a light essay on John Bailey's *Letters*[37] (a delightful book), and was just on the point of writing when the proof of Cowardin's (and my) venture began to come in in floods.[38] Having so secondary a part in that performance, I can say, with no breach of modesty, that it impressed me as a mighty good piece of work."[39]

"Presumably Asher Hinds is behind the movement," Paul wrote to Louis on sending him a bookplate for volumes bought for the Princeton University Library from a fund named in honor of Paul Elmer More; "but however that may be, he and

[36] To Louis T. More, Dec. 18, 1935.

[37] *John Bailey, 1864-1931, Letters and Diaries*. More's essay on this irradiator of the humanities appeared in *The American Review*, April 1936.

[38] On Sept. 12, 1935, More signed with Henry Holt and Company a contract for the publication of *The Study of English Literature*, the first edition of which came out in May 1936.

[39] To Robert Shafer, Jan. 20, 1936. "I am sorry to say it, but the poorest paragraphs of the work are those to which I contributed the most. Sometimes I wonder whether the book would not have been clearer and better if I had had nothing to do with it." [To Samuel Pendleton Cowardin, Jr., Feb. 29, 1936.]

a group of other men have started this memorial library, which is to say the least very flattering. Whatever has come over the world I don't know, but there has been some sort of conspiracy now for eighteen months or so to deprive me of the glory of martyrdom. If they could only give me a bit of popularity in its place! As it is I almost resent their kindness."[40]

Except for certain mechanical devices prescribed by his doctor to keep him ambulatory and for a minimum of drugs to numb his occasionally acute pain, More's medical treatment from the end of March onwards was imperceptible starvation. Dr. Joseph S. Vanneman, of Princeton, believed his "most wonderful patient" knew he had a malignancy but refrained from asking about the cause of his declining health because he did not want to embarrass his physician. Others about him also suspected he knew he was dying, though they seem never to have mentioned the subject to him and he seems to have referred to it but once, inadvertently. When Roger Bruce Cash Johnson, a retired Princeton professor of philosophy, came to see him, More offered him a cigar and proposed to have one himself. Johnson's attempt to refuse, on the ground that it would be harmful to More, caused the latter to retort: "Come on, Johnson, this is the last cigar we shall ever smoke together."

"I was of course rather surprised to hear of your sudden resolution to go over to England," Paul More informed Louis, "but I can only congratulate you at the chance and wish that such a lot had fallen to me too. How often I ask myself now whether I shall ever see the dear land again. And more and more I feel that in many respects my life would have been richer and fuller if, when I tore up stakes in 1914, I had gone with my family and settled down in some town of Sussex or Somerset. But I have to take into account also the fact that I should be separated from Darrah and her family and that the regularity of our fraternal joys would have been broken. On the other side you might have been persuaded to pass most of your summers in England. However that is all a dream; I did not

[40] To Louis T. More, Feb. 14, 1936.

go. . . . my *Sceptical Approach* . . . is still a best-seller—I mean of course in the non-fiction class. A few days ago I sent Tomlinson[41] the manuscript for a third volume of New Shelburne Essays, to be entitled *On Being Human.*[42] Tomlinson's note of acknowledgement amused me. Our relations have always been cordial, but there was a certain tone in this letter which showed that I was regarded as a commercial asset. What it must be to have a publisher on his knees before you as a *real* best-seller!—a joy neither of us I fear shall ever experience."[43]

In May *The American Review* published More's essay on "How to Read *Lycidas*," which he had let the "Baltimoreans" criticize when they came to see him. "After passing, as I might say, through the valley of the shadow of death, after months of physical prostration when reading of any sort was beyond the strength of a depleted brain, the poet to whom I turned instinctively with the first renewal of health was Milton. And so I have been reading Milton again and books about him, with the old zest I had as a boy, and with an added joy of almost tremulous excitement such as a miser might feel at the rediscovery of a treasure of gold stolen from him and long buried out of sight. But with this delight have been mingled certain scruples which vexed me a little more than they did in the old days."[44]

His difficulty was how to combine the dislike that he and Samuel Johnson had of certain faults of Milton as a man with the conviction that More held, in defiance of Johnson but in common with Tennyson, that *Lycidas* is "the greatest short poem of any author in English, the very criterion and touchstone of poetical taste."[45] His solution came from a sentence in one of Eliot's *Essays Ancient and Modern*: "The 'greatness' of literature cannot be determined solely by literary standards;

[41] Paul G. Tomlinson, director of the Princeton University Press.

[42] The book contained "A Revival of Humanism," "Irving Babbitt," "Proust: The Two Ways," "James Joyce," "The Modernism of French Poetry," "Religion and Social Discontent," "Church and Politics," "A Scholar-Saint," and "How to Read *Lycidas*."

[43] To Louis T. More, April 11, 1936.

[44] *OBH*, 184.   [45] *OBH*, 190.

though one must remember that whether it is literature or not can be determined only by literary standards."[46] "That *Lycidas*," More concluded, "is literature, poetry and not mere verse, depends on the language, the images, the form, on that mysterious working of the imagination which we can feel but cannot ultimately analyse or adequately describe; that it is great literature must depend on the junction of such qualities with nobility of content. And such nobility is there, in full measure."[47]

His evidence for his statement is too subtle to be summarized, appealing as it does to passages from *Lycidas* that speak for themselves to those "equally sensitive to the delicacy of its art and to the sublimity of its ideas."[48] "I do not know how others are affected, but I can never peruse the climax of the poem without a thrill such as scarcely any other verses of the language excite.

> Weep no more, woful Shepherds weep no more,
> For *Lycidas* your sorrow is not dead,
> Sunk though he be beneath the watry floar,
> So sinks the day-star in the Ocean bed,
> And yet anon repairs his drooping head,
> And tricks his beams, and with new spangled Ore,
> Flames in the forehead of the morning sky:
> So *Lycidas* sunk low, but mounted high,
> Through the dear might of him that walk'd the waves
> Where other groves, and other streams along,
> With *Nectar* pure his oozy Lock's he laves,
> And hears the unexpressive nuptiall Song,
> In the blest Kingdoms meek of joy and love.
> There entertain him all the Saints above,
> In solemn troops, and sweet Societies
> That sing, and singing in their glory move,
> And wipe the tears for ever from his eyes."[49]

The sweltering summer days he often lay, covered only by a

46 As quoted in *OBH*, 195.   47 *OBH*, 195.
48 *OBH*, 201.   49 *OBH*, 199.

sheet, on the sofa in his study. The lamp shone on his white hair and frail, fine, ivory face as with beautiful enunciation he read *Orley Farm* aloud to his daughters[50] in his yet resonant voice, chuckling and laughing as though in perfect health. He corrected the proofs of *On Being Human*, which was published in September, and dictated to Darrah "a series of short sketches or essays on any and every subject, to be called 'Marginalia.' "[51] After Alice left for England, Darrah and her children stayed with her father at 59 Battle Road, where Harry, who had closed his school and now taught Latin at the Lawrence School in Hewlett, Long Island, returned to them every week-end. T. S. Eliot came to see the invalid, and Louis visited him in August and November and at the beginning of the next year. Molly, "the perfect little lady" as her grandfather called her, passed much time playing "old maid" with him. He read aloud to her and her younger brother, Johnny; told them stories on the spur of the moment; and after supper welcomed them in his bedroom to listen to "Lum and Abner" over a radio given him by his cousin, John N. Brooks.

"Two foreign students recently, one from Switzerland, the other from Sweden,[52] have consulted me about my philosophical theories, which they are studying for the doctor's degree in their respective universities. To both of them the dualistic thesis stood out as the binding thread running through all my work. This is an obvious view, which has been accepted by every critic, so far as I know, who has written on the subject. But it is as true as it is obvious that dualism may vary widely in its

[50] Mrs. Dymond went to Princeton for the summer.

[51] Mrs. Harry B. Fine to Erna Obermeier, undated. More never completed for publication the marginalia he had planned on "Great and Perfect Art," "Technique and Arts," "Dom John Chapman's *Spiritual Letters*," "Hardy," "La Harpe," "Greek Tradition," "James Bowling Mozley," "Newman," "Plato's Idea of Beauty," "Shelburne Essays," "Ste. Thérèse of Lisieux," "Symbols," and "Mercer St.—sunset."

[52] The Swedish visitor was Folke Leander, author of *Humanism and Naturalism, A Comparative Study of Ernest Seillière, Irving Babbitt, and Paul Elmer More*, Göteborgs Högskolas Årsskrift XLIII, 1937:1, Göteborg (Wettergren & Kerbers).

connotation, and my own use of the term has perhaps a certain peculiarity which needs to be noted. Emphatically I have not meant by it to set up an ironclad rival to the various metaphysics of the One. My intention has been much less ambitious than that, and implies no more than this, that in every field of experience, if I push my analysis to the end of my resources, I find myself brought up against a pair of irreconcilable, yet interrelated and interacting, contraries, such as 'good' and 'bad,' 'mind' and 'body,' the 'One' and the 'Many,' 'rest' and 'motion.' The dualist is one who modestly submits to this bifurcation as the ultimate point where clarity of definition obtains. Beyond this he refuses to follow reason in its frantic endeavor to reconcile these opposites by any logical legerdemain in which one of the controlling factors of consciousness is brought out as an Absolute while the other disappears in the conjuror's hat. The dualist, in other words, though he may do homage to the reasoning faculty as the governor of practical conduct, yet balks at its pretension to discover in its own mechanism the ultimate source and nature of Being. He remains half-brother to the sceptic, whereas the monist is a metaphysical dogmatist.

"I have said that it is the function of reason to deal with the contraries of experience in the field of 'practical conduct.' But this, it may be said, is only the superficial aspect of dualism; for the root of the matter, it should seem that we must look not to the logical faculty at all, but must penetrate to some deep substratum of the temperament or the emotions, to some obscure region of the soul itself, out of which spring the conflicting impulses to the religious and the worldly life. There, in that darkness where definitions fail us, lies the origin of the apparent and definable bifurcations. It is a division of what finally interests, and the nature of the dividing force, in so far at least as it touches religion, can be studied better in Newman perhaps than in any other English writer. . . .

"[Newman's] imagination is haunted by that invisible realm beyond or outside of the range of the senses, which was called

The Long Hope

Ideal by Plato as constructed of Forms, or Ideas, seen by the eye of the soul, or Noetic by the later Platonists as grasped by the *nous*, or Spiritual by St. Paul. This to Newman, as I take it, even more than the being of a personal God, was the one thing important, the one thing he must make real to his soul against all the distractions of the world. For the mystery of this sense of the Otherworld is that, though never an illusion, it is strangely elusive. . . . It is never an illusion, I say; never a power that deceives or allures into evil and error; but it is elusive, impalpable, slipping from our grasp when we think we have it most firmly fixed, and hard to make concrete to the imagination and to impose on the will; lying like the shadowed reflections of the sky on the surface of a quiet pool but vanishing away when a breeze ruffles the mirror. . . .

"But beside this realm of the Spirit lies another kingdom, that of nature, as we call it, which is not at all retiring or evasive. Rather it is visible, palpable, insistent, ever clamorous of attention. It is not elusive, but by a strange paradox illusory, the very heart and fountain of illusion. That is to say its real substance is less than its apparent substance, and its promises end in deception, disappointment, sometimes even in despair. But of the noetic world the truth and substance become more real by testing, and its promises are more than fulfilled if you grasp it tightly, cling to it, and obey its laws. . . .

"Its reality, its substantiality, was there, in itself, was its very being; this you knew always; yet somehow, in its relation to you, this substantial reality seemed dependent on your own endeavor and constancy, as if created by you. It is scarcely too much to say that the development of my noetic life, the history of the altering attitude towards certain fundamental articles of belief from book to book as these were written, has been governed by the intermittent endeavor, from varying angles of approach, to discover some instrument, some formula of thought, which would give a fixed solidity to the tenuity of a vision always present, always inviting, yet always threatening to vanish away—this rather than any transaction with a logical rationalization of dualism."[53]

"A lovelier ode to spring was never indited than Horace's *Solvitur acris hiems*. . . . This is not the only ode in which Horace bids us forgo the long hope—*spem longam resces*; such a deprivation is the very root of his philosophy, *carpe diem*, snatch the day and be not credulous of any tomorrow. . . .

"And then I turn to the most fragrant of the Christian poets:

> How fresh, O Lord, how sweet and clean
> Are thy returns! Ev'n as the flowers in spring. . . .
> > Grief melts away
> > Like snow in May,
> As if there were no such cold thing.

No one can read Horace and George Herbert together without feeling that a whole world of emotion has slipped in between them; for the very gist of Herbert's song, in the lines that follow, is hope, the long hope, that the returning spring bade the ancient poets cut away. We do not often, I think, pause to consider the change that came into the world with the advent of this new hope. Christianity may seem to have failed in so many ways; it has done so little for the morals and intelligence of civilization, so little to mitigate the evils of social and international injustice, so little to impose restraint on the insurgent passions of mankind; but this one thing it has effected, the offering of hope, the long hope, to the souls of individual men.[54] You cannot forget it, cannot hide away the fact.

'Une immense espérance a traversé la terre.' . . .

"I like to think historically of the advent of this hope as indicated by three quotations from the Greek. The first is from the great chorus of the *Agamemnon* of Aeschylus: 'Sing woe! Sing woe! but let the good overcome.' It is, as it were, a desire, not a hope, but a desire prophetic of fulfillment.

---

[53] *M*, 17-23.   [54] Cf. *SAR*, 183 ff.

The Long Hope

"The second is from the *Phaedo* of Plato, giving Socrates' intimations of immortality to his circle of timid friends on that last day of seeming defeat: 'Fair is the prize [of immortality],[55] and the hope great.'

"And the third was the utterance of another, also on the day of seeming defeat: 'In the world ye shall have tribulation; but be of good cheer, I have overcome the world.' "[56]

So emaciated was More that on Thanksgiving Day a practical nurse, Mary E. McCormick, arrived to help his daughter take care of him. His brass bed was moved into his study, where he remained for the rest of his life. Since he could no longer read or write more than a few minutes at a time, Darrah read aloud to him, now and then until three in the morning, or he listened on his radio to music or "eagerly to all the news from England."[57]

Most of December he was desperately ill. As his mind raced about with obsessive force, sometimes in incoherent, almost inarticulate, moments he would want to dictate notes to Darrah. The earnestness and devotion of Crocker, who called on him almost every morning, did much to sustain him. Shortly before Christmas More invited the "Baltimoreans" to hear the chaplain say some collects for him in his study, a service that soon became for them a daily noon custom. The proceedings were simple, almost conversational in tone, lasting about five minutes: between some brief introductory and closing remarks, a short passage of Scripture and a few prayers, not all of them specifically for the invalid.

"Wonderful phrase! Wonderful phrase!" he would repeat of the words, "means of grace and hope of glory." He particularly liked Newman's: "O Lord, support us all the day long, until the shadows lengthen and the evening comes, and the busy world is hushed, and the fever of life is over, and our work is done. Then in thy mercy grant us a safe lodging, and a holy

---

[55] The interpolation is More's.   [56] *M*, 27-30.
[57] Mrs. Harry B. Fine to Erna Obermeier, Dec. 10, 1936.

rest, and peace at the last." And whenever some of Dr. Johnson's prayers were used, More "spotted" them with glee.

In Crocker's rare absences one of the "Baltimoreans" would read the prayers instead. They all tried to attend the noon service and at least one of them arranged to call again in the afternoon. Over the tea-table they perceived More's interest in the Gifford Lectures,[58] for which (though he was never invited to give them) he hoped his proposed book on Aristotle would serve; his pleasure in being thought of in Sweden as a figure of consequence; his desire to take the "Baltimoreans," none of whom was then an Episcopalian, "by the scruff of the neck to Trinity church to join up," after which he jocosely but seriously apologized for any effort to sway them in such a matter; his own elaborate reasons for not "joining" the Episcopal Church; his avidness for appreciation and yet his suspicion of flattery when the "Baltimoreans" told him his ideas were being better received; his notion that in a world so hard to dent, Christ's influence might be an argument for his divinity; his chagrin at the way critics had distorted his position that a certain amount of private property is essential to individual liberty into the thesis that the dollar is more important than the man; his disgust with the arrogance sometimes evoked by great wealth; his realization of the fugitiveness of the *Shelburne Essays* and of literary criticism in general; his susceptibility to sensual temptation and his corresponding conviction that a Puritan is "a good thing to be"; his view of life as a battle of ideas and principles, which, with his sensitiveness and a feeling of uncertainty about his own judgement, may have accounted for some of his asperity and tactlessness; his suffering like a drug fiend without his "dope" when he could get no new detective story; his simplicity of taste and habit; his awareness that throughout much of their lives Louis and he "were like a couple of chickens tied together

[58] On Oct. 5, 1935, Norman Kemp Smith advised Robert Shafer that he would be glad to propose More's name to the Gifford Committee but that nothing could be done about it soon, since appointments for the Gifford Lectures had already been made for the next three years.

and strung over the same wire—we can't help fighting"; his fearfulness of committing great indiscretions and his defensiveness towards new writers; his belief (perhaps heightened by the shock to his religious faith when he could not assimilate the flood of new ideas that overwhelmed him in his college days) that undergraduates should be taught the "right" things (for example, humanism) in philosophy before being exposed indiscriminately to all schools of thought; and his paternal gratitude—"there is nothing in life like the voluntary devotion of my two daughters."

As the Episcopal Church provides that those in danger of death may, though unconfirmed, receive the Holy Communion, Bishop Matthews and the student chaplain brought the sacrament several times to Mr. More, until he decided that the short noon service sufficed him. Both bishop and priest, wanting him to have every benefit the Church could give, hoped More would ask of his own accord to be confirmed. Early in February 1937 the bishop felt in duty bound to broach the matter to him, which he did, rather hesitantly, in the presence of Hinds and Oates. More answered calmly that he would think it over.

For a few days he was greatly disturbed, torn between his respect for tradition, of which the Church seemed to him to be one of the nobler strands, and between his individualistic and Protestant tendencies, his suspicion of deathbed conversions, and his desire to remain true to his own best light. Complicating the matter may have been the laceration of soul, apparently still keenly felt, when he gave up receiving communion in his young manhood. A certain loneliness also restrained him. "If one of you," he told the "Baltimoreans," "will join the Church with me, I will take the step." In the end he decided that he had "made his bed and ought to lie on it"; so he dictated to Darrah a brief note to that effect to Bishop Matthews.

The Princeton Alumni Weekly on February 5th printed an article, "Paul Elmer More," by T. S. Eliot, which Darrah read several times to her delighted father. It was, Eliot admitted privately to Professor Thorp, of Princeton, "a eulogy and a 'demonstration.' I think that in some ways More's theology is rather narrow and defective; that he tends to emphasize those things in Anglicanism which were absent from the doctrine of his childhood, and to ignore those things which the two have in common. I think he remains a little sectarian, and not wholly orthodox. But this is not the place, nor am I quite the person, to sift his work in this way. Then he is 'anglophile,' in that he sees the excellence of English institutions where a person resident here is more likely to see their shortcomings and corruptions. And I suspect that in some of his views on contemporary political affairs he was a somewhat conventional conservative; but I am not sure."[59]

"I . . . consider *The Greek Tradition*," Eliot wrote in his article, "More's greatest work. . . . And what will keep the work permanently alive . . . is that nowhere is it a mere exercise of intellect, intelligence, and erudition, or the mere demonstration of a thesis held by the mind. . . . More's works are, in the deepest sense, his autobiography. One is always aware of the sincerity, and in the later works the Christian humility . . . of the concentrated mind seeking God; still with restless curiosity analyzing the disease and the aberrations of humanity. . . .

"In his treatment of Christian Mysticism (in *The Catholic Faith*) he seems to me to fail to appreciate the greatness of St. John of the Cross. And in his introduction to *Anglicanism* . . . he fails . . . to emphasize the continuity of the Church; one might think that it was the invention of Hooker. He does not give recognition to the probable importance of the mystics of the fourteenth century—of Richard Rolle and Juliana of Norwich for instance—as late as the time of Lancelot Andrewes and George Herbert. But his understanding of the spirit of Anglicanism is remarkable. . . ."

[59] T. S. Eliot to Willard Thorp, Jan. 14, 1937.

The Long Hope

And Eliot concluded of More and Babbitt: ". . . these seem to me the two *wisest* men that I have known."[60]

Early in February More asked his daughter to look through his desk and dispose of his papers. She found in it outlines of lectures, his translation (begun in Shelburne in 1899) of the first four hundred and seventy lines of *Oedipus Rex*, rough notes for his book on Aristotle, which she gave to Oates to use at his discretion, and the *Pages from an Oxford Diary*. "Darrah has discovered this manuscript which I wrote in 1925 in Oxford," More explained to Oates a few days later, after the midday prayers, giving him the pages to look over. Having read them in an hour and a half, Oates returned that afternoon to urge their publication. "All right, you get it published," said More. Oates showed it at once to Tomlinson, assuring him that More could revise it swiftly. Aided by Darrah, Greene, and Hinds, Oates read most of the manuscript aloud to its author. More suggested corrections and deletions, and composed additional passages without making any essential change in tone or substance. On February 23rd he dictated to Darrah the short preface. A few days later Oates took the manuscript to the Princeton University Press and, with Godolphin's help on the proofs, saw it through.

During this work More remained equable and amiable, though his body had wasted away to a skeleton of about seventy-five pounds. Late in February he talked well for two hours when Oates called on him one evening. Soon, however, his legs began to swell most uncomfortably. A friend then allowed to see him a few moments found him bloodlessly white, propped up on masses of pillows, with a Greek text of *The Odyssey* in one hand and a French translation of it in the other. He smiled as his visitor entered but could barely whisper an affectionate greeting. On the night of March 8th, with Mrs. McCormick and Crocker, Mrs. Fine sat by her father, then in a coma, until at nine o'clock the next morning he died.

[60] *Princeton Alumni Weekly*, Feb. 5, 1937, vol. xxxvii, no. 17, pp. 373-74.

Thursday, the 11th, Bishop Matthews, Crocker, and the "Balts," whose flowers Mrs. Fine and Mrs. McCormick had arranged on Mr. More's empty bed, went for the last time to pray in his study. Burial next to Mrs. More's grave followed the funeral that afternoon in Trinity Church, where a hymn of his choice was sung:

> Dear Lord and Father of mankind,
>> Forgive our foolish ways!
> Re-clothe us in our rightful mind,
> In purer lives thy service find,
>> In deeper reverence praise.

BIBLIOGRAPHICAL NOTE

NO bibliography, in the strict sense, yet exists for More. As indicated in the preface and the footnotes, many individuals and several institutions possess manuscript sources of information about him, of which only an infinitesimal fraction has here been reproduced. Although so much of his journalism was printed unsigned and without adequate external means of identification that a complete inventory of his writings is apparently impossible, some publications by and about him are listed in *Paul Elmer More: A Bibliography*, by Malcolm Young, Princeton (Princeton University Press), 1941, and in *A Paul Elmer More Miscellany* published by the Anthoensen Press, of Portland, Maine, in 1950. To the nearly six hundred anonymous items by More noted in the latter might be added these reviews from *The Independent* (New York): "A Novel by Zola" [*Travail*, by Émile Zola], May 30, 1901, vol. LIII, no. 2739, pp. 1256-57;[1] "The Roadmender" [*The Roadmender*, by Michael Fairless], April 2, 1903, vol. LV, no. 2835, pp. 796-97;[2] "American Literature" [*A History of American Literature*, by William P. Trent], July 16, 1903, vol. LV, no. 2850, pp. 1687-88;[3] and these anonymous editorials designated as written by More in William Hayes Ward's file of *The Independent* (vol. LIII) at Rollins College, thoughtfully reported by Mr. Warren F. Kuehl: "The Gospel of Wealth," May 30, 1901, pp. 1263-64; "The Literary Editor,"[4] June 13, 1901, pp. 1386-88; "John Fiske," July 11, 1901, pp. 1631-32; "The Historical Novel," September 5, 1901, pp. 2127-28; "System in Reading," September 26, 1901, pp. 2311-12; and "Keats and Browne," November 14, 1901, p. 2728.

[1] Cf. Mrs. Lundy Howard Harris to P. E. More, May 30, 1901.
[2] Cf. same to same, April 9, 1903.
[3] Cf. to Prosser Hall Frye, July 2, 1903.
[4] Cf. Mrs. Lundy Howard Harris to P. E. More, June 17, 1901.

INDEX

Index

"Art and Decision," 136n
Arvin, Newton, 277n
asceticism, 69, 153, 206, 369
Ashurst, 300n
"Aspects of Reaction," 142
Asquith, H. H., 1st Earl of Oxford
and Asquith, 133
Athanasius, St., 244
Athenaeum Club, 134, 262
Athens, 47, 230
The Atlantic Monthly (Boston),
96n, 101, 159n, 301n; More's
contributions to, 59, 63f, 74, 76,
95f
Atwood, Albert W., 204
Augustine, St., 44, 79, 108n
Aurora, N.Y., 208
authority, 118f, 156, 183, 199, 244,
282, 306, 336, 357
Authors' Club, 163
Axel's Castle, 277n
Aylmer, John, 3

Babbitt, Irving, 48, 68, 70f, 76f,
81f, 106, 111n, 120, 180, 191f,
226, 234f, 242f, 249, 258n, 260,
270f, 276, 277n, 328n, 338-40,
368, 378n, 385; visits to or by
More, 49, 57, 64, 71f, 82, 93,
101, 107, 111f, 113n, 140, 148n,
160, 162, 169, 182, 191, 197,
204, 221f, 241f, 247, 277, 317,
319, 323; characteristics of, 78n,
93, 101, 105n, 107, 204, 241f,
267, 317, 319f, 323f, 340n; submits his proofs to More, 105,
140, 170n, 182, 213, 253; reads
More's proofs, 63, 140, 160,
170, 197, 218, 247, 302; fur-
thered by More, 113, 162n, 197,
223; seconds More, 295n; influences More, 64, 234, 237, 249,
323, 330; differences with More,
221f, 273, 282ff, 310-13, 317ff,
338, 341; last illness, 328ff. *See
also* letters from P. E. More to
Babbitt, Mrs. Irving, 82, 93, 111,
148n, 169, 191, 240, 247, 260,
273, 329, 368. *See also* letters
from P. E. More to

Babbitt, Katharine, 106, 235, 241
Bach, Johann Sebastian, 134n,
297
Baden-Baden, 23
Bailey, John, 374
Balfour, A. J., 1st Earl of Balfour,
166
Balliol College, 225, 231
Baltimore, 161
Balzac, Honoré de, 105, 169n
Barber, Margaret Fairless, 300n
Bard College, 292
Barrow, Isaac, 327
Barth, Karl, 364
Basil the Great, 190
Bath, 135, 261, 300
Baum, Maurice, 215. *See also* let-
ters from P. E. More to
Baur, F. C., 44, 314
Baxter, Richard, 209
Bayport, N.Y., 75
Beaumont, Francis, 186
beauty, 31, 36ff, 40, 42f, 46, 100,
115, 117, 215, 229f, 235, 244,
288, 309f, 361, 363, 372, 378n
Beck, Henrietta, 10, 23ff, 45, 52,
55, 61, 71, 72, 75ff, 79-82, 257.
See also letters from Henrietta
Beck *and* More, Mrs. P. E.
Beck, Mrs. John, 10, 81, 110, 111n,
113, 138n, 175, 177
Beckford, William, 114, 139
Beckley, Quitman F., 297
Beethoven, L. van, 28, 297
Before and After Socrates, 339n
Behn, Aphra, 186
Belgium, 149, 160
Bell, Bernard Iddings, *see* letters
from P. E. More to
Belloc, J. H. P., 280n, 328
Bemerton, 130
Benjamin Franklin, 74n, 81, 84f
Benson, Robert Hugh, 268
*Berengar and the Reform of Sac-
ramental Doctrine*, 294
Berenson, Bernard, 229
Bergson, Henri, 123
Berkeley, Calif., 274, 279, 281,
287f, 319

Index

Index

California, University of, 274n, 279f, 287f
Calvinism, 4, 17f, 44, 290, 362, 364
Cambridge, England, 137, 184, 250, 260f, 265, 299, 301
Cambridge, Mass., 44, 51, 60, 64, 71, 74, 76, 93, 111, 113n, 125, 140, 148, 169, 204, 226, 240f, 243, 247
"Camp Barberry," 111n, 320, 333
Campion Hall, 263
Capps, Edward, 155, 177, 236
Carlyle, Thomas, 78n, 95
The Case for Conservatism, 159n
Cassady, Edward E., 287
The Catholic Faith, 218n, 257, 296, 299, 302, 307, 309f, 315, 319n, 385; cited, 169n, 206-07n, 218n, 227n, 229n, 245-46n, 260n, 262n, 279n, 302-11n, 338n
Cato, 137
Catullus, 52
Cayuga, Lake, 80
"The Cedars," 111n, 143, 162, 182, 214, 251, 310, 320, 334, 372
Cedarville, N.J., 3
"Celebrating Milton and Reading Him," 124n
"The Centenary of Longfellow," 103
The Century Association, 107, 126, 135, 143, 163, 188, 204
A Century of Indian Epigrams, Chiefly from the Sanskrit of Bhartrihari, 51n, 59, 68-71, 314
Chalcedon, Council of, 218, 244, 246, 286f, 304, 322, 359
"The Challenge of Humanism," 338
"The Challenge of Paul Elmer More," 249n
Champaign, Ill., 114
Champlain, Lake, 106, 143, 149, 182
Chapman, Henry Otis, 26, 28-31
Chapman, John, 378n
Chapman, John Jay, 125
Chapman, Percy Addison, 252
Chepstow, 261

Chesham, N.H., 191
Chester, 224, 300n
Chesterfield, Philip Dormer Stanhope, 4th Earl of, 106, 121n
Chesterton, G. K., 211, 328
Chevrillon, André, 205
Chicago, 179, 181, 189
Chicago Record, 75
Chicago Tribune, 181
Chicago, University of, 169
The Children of Light, 66n
"Children's Books," 21n
Children's Island Sanitorium, 247
Chilton, Carroll Brent, 134
China, 163, 167, 229
Chopin, F. F., 297
The Christ of the New Testament, 210, 218, 221, 234, 247, 249n, 299n, 321; cited, 183n, 208n, 218-21n, 308-09n
Christ the Word, 218n, 234, 243, 253, 287, 322; cited, 189n, 203n, 206n, 219n, 237-38n, 242n, 244-46n, 309n
Christian Science, 72, 90
"Christian Science Triumphant," 72n
Christianity, 62, 84, 140, 201, 210, 229, 235, 238, 242, 246, 260, 284, 286, 308n, 318, 322, 335, 341, 343, 356ff, 381; More's early attitude towards, 6f, 17ff, 29, 39f, 42, 67f, 72, 116, 118f; More's return to, 242, 263, 284, 290, 307, 315f, 330, 333, 347n, 364, 385; and Babbitt, 341n; and Platonism, 117n, 198, 218, 220f, 227, 244f, 305n, 315, 333, 356f, 364; and Buddhism, 303ff, 364; its metaphysical theology, 206n, 210n, 307, 338, 364. *See also* "The Origins of Christianity"
Chrysostom, St., 178, 182
church, 115ff, 183f, 220, 245f, 269f, 284, 286, 305f, 308f, 311, 336ff, 339n, 358f, 367, 383ff
"Church and Politics," 342f, 376n
Cicero, 52, 97, 201, 251
Cincinnati, 93n, 151, 196, 288, 320, 342

Index

Index

Index

Index

Index

Index

Index

Horace, 49, 52, 111, 126, 263, 313, 323, 381
Hoskyns, Sir Edwyn, 322n
Hough, Lynn Harold, 331. *See also* letters from P. E. More to
Houghton Mifflin Company, 59, 63f, 74n, 85, 95n, 120n, 139, 160
The Hound and Horn (Cambridge, Mass.), 323
The House of the Whispering Pines, 158n
Houston, Percy H., *see* letters from P. E. More to
"How to Read *Lycidas*," 376
Howe, George, 329
Howe, Mrs. George, 328n, 329
Hügel, Baron Friedrich von, 206n, 345, 359, 362, 368f
Hughes, Charles E., 157
humanism, 90, 142, 185, 222n, 242, 249, 264, 270-73, 276ff, 280-85, 287, 311f, 317, 323, 326, 329, 346, 367, 371n
"Humanism," 131n
Humanism and America, 270-74, 277, 281ff, 285n
Humanism and Imagination, 321n
Humanism and Naturalism, A Comparative Study of Ernest Seillière, Irving Babbitt, and Paul Elmer More, 378n
"Humanism and Religion," 273n
The Humanism of Paul Elmer More, 270n
humanitarianism, 67f, 89f, 95, 140, 144, 151, 161, 167n, 181, 194n, 220, 242, 366n
Hume, David, 17, 354
humility, 336-39, 357f, 361f, 385
"The Humility of Common Sense," 277
Hurricane, N.Y., 215
Hutchinson, Anne, 195
Hutchinson, Cary T., 10, 80, 86
Huxley, Thomas Henry, 127n, 139, 207

Ideas, Platonic, 41, 83n, 118, 171, 173ff, 183, 194n, 207n, 215,

220f, 227, 239, 244f, 255, 283n, 300n, 309f, 314, 318, 340n, 353, 363f, 378n, 380. *See also* Plato *and* Platonism *and* More, P. E., his Platonism
The Iliad, 143n
Illinois, University of, 113f, 259; acknowledgements, 96n, 112n, 114-15n, 122n, 124n, 142n, 145n, 149n, 152n, 154n, 161n, 163n, 178n, 180n, 182n, 189n, 194n
illusion, 41f, 68, 70, 118f, 168, 175, 182f, 227, 235, 283, 286f, 300n, 314, 318, 344, 350, 352n, 356f, 380
imagination, 17, 24n, 82, 84, 116, 154, 159, 171, 173ff, 188n, 200n, 204, 222n, 226, 228, 318, 377, 379
Immaculate Conception, 262
immortality, 187n, 282, 291, 351, 354, 382
"In Memory of an Autumn Day," 11, 36n
Incarnation, 118, 197n, 198, 218ff, 228, 244, 246, 286f, 305, 308, 321f, 333, 336, 353n, 356-59, 364
The Independent (New York), 86, 87f, 90, 94, 187n; More's contributions to, 72n, 87, 88-90n, 95, 113n, 388
The Independent and The Weekly Review (New York), 180, 195n
India, 45, 108n. *See also* Hinduism
Indiana, University of, 159
individualism, 241, 272, 306, 336, 339n
"The Influence of New York," 161n
"The Influences of Hindu Thought on Manichaeism," 44
Inge, W. R., 198n, 211, 238
inner check, 172, 237, 319n
International Congress of Philosophy, 247
The International Quarterly (New York), 95
Interpretations of Poetry and Religion, 83

Index

Index

Index

Index

Index

McCormick, Mary E., 382, 386
McKenzie, Kenneth, 240
McKinnon, Cyril N., *see* letters from P. E. More to
McLinn, Ruth, 156, 297, 333, 371
Mead, W. R., 202
measure, 61, 200, 303
Meadville, Pa., 185
mediation, 200, 311f, 335
The Mediaeval Mind, 126
medievalism, 40, 62, 289f, 314, 346n
Mees, Graham C., 298
Mencken, H. L., 181, 191f, 193, 211, 278
Mercier, Louis J. A., 249f, 338, 341
Meredith, George, 64, 74n, 79, 95, 158
metaphysics, 206, 231f, 237f, 246, 333, 345ff, 354f, 358, 361, 364
Meynell, Alice, 134
Meynell, Wilfrid, 134
Michigan, University of, 140
Middlesex Women's Club, 169
Mills Foundation, 274n
Milton, John, 6, 112, 124, 154, 155n, 217, 263, 269, 272, 360, 376
Milwaukee, 114
Mind (London), 239n
Mind Association, 231
Minehead, 135
Minneapolis, 84n
Minnetonka, Lake, 84n
miracle, 171, 308, 322
"The Miracle of the Stone and of the Mountain," 72n
"Mr. More Moralizes," 196n
"Mr. P. E. More and The Wits," 108n, 168n, 186-88n, 271n
Mitchell, Donald G., 106
Mitchell, Mrs. Henry Post, 373
"Modern Currents in American Literature," 249n, 258, 298n
"The Modern Movement," 161n
"The Modern Tendency in Poetry," 161n
modernism, 308n

"The Modernism of French Poetry," 371n, 376n
Mohonk Lake, N.Y., 141
Molière, 112, 204
"A Moment of Tragic Purgation," 160
monism, 69, 238n, 290f, 319n, 351
Montagu, Lady Mary Wortley, 186
Montaigne, M. E. de, 276
Montreal, 332f
Moody, William Vaughn, Lectures, 169
Moore, Clifford, 226
Moore, Enoch, 4
Moore, George Foot, 243
More, Alice (daughter of P. E. More), 99, 104, 106f, 114f, 124f, 131f, 141, 143, 149, 151n, 156, 177, 191, 202, 215, 223f, 229ff, 246, 250-53. *See also* Dymond, Mrs. Edmund Gilbert
More, Alice (sister of P. E. More), 6, 8, 13ff, 18, 28, 31, 35, 46, 52, 57, 60, 61n, 73n, 74, 76, 79, 81f, 87, 92f, 98f, 105n, 106, 109f, 115n, 124, 135, 138, 144, 152f, 161n, 162f, 177, 184, 191, 200, 214, 255, 265, 278, 292ff. *See also* letters from *and* letters from P. E. More to
More, Brookes, *see* More, James Brookes
More, Caroline Hoff, 177n
More, Catherine Elmer, 223f, 229f, 300, 320, 333
More, Edward Anson, 12n, 82, 93, 201
More, Mrs. Edward Anson, 12n, 76, 82, 93, 153n, 177n, 214, 292ff. *See also* letters from P. E. More to *and* More, Mary Caroline
More, Enoch Anson, 3-7, 12f, 18, 29n, 46, 55, 60, 71, 83n. *See also* letters from P. E. More to
More, Mrs. Enoch Anson, 3-6, 8, 11, 18, 29, 33, 46, 55, 72f, 78-82, 87, 92f, 98n, 106, 109f, 115n, 148. *See also* letters from P. E. More to

Index

Index

his friendships, 10, 29ff, 80, 88n, 93, 107, 149f, 223, 255f, 262, 284, 295, 324, 330, 339, 366, 373

his generosity, 93n, 107, 162, 177n, 179, 188n, 213, 215, 310n, 371

his health, 4, 7, 13, 25f, 60, 114, 127, 144f, 152, 175, 218, 221, 256, 268, 293, 342, 367, 370, 372f, 376, 382, 386

his homes, 4f, 12, 29n, 44, 57, 74, 77f, 81, 105, 114f, 149, 150n, 251, 274, 278, 293. See also "The Cedars"

his honorary degrees, 106, 142, 169, 186, 300

his hospitality, 66, 81f, 143, 148, 150f, 156, 157n, 163, 179, 182, 192, 212, 246, 248n, 269, 296ff, 325, 332, 340

his humor, 88, 150f, 195, 212, 365

literary critic, 14, 50, 79, 83n, 85f, 88n, 90, 95-98, 101f, 105f, 108, 111, 119n, 153f, 160, 170n, 195f, 200n, 213, 217, 258f, 263, 269n, 273, 310-13, 339n, 368

his loneliness, 22f, 39, 47, 60, 74, 96n, 101, 112, 132, 243n, 261, 273, 280, 287, 321, 338, 384

his otherworldliness, 31, 34, 41, 43, 46, 55, 62, 182, 194, 255. See also otherworldliness

photographs of, 7n, 182n, 297n

his physical characteristics, 4, 7, 10, 26, 59, 67, 78, 164, 211, 263, 378

his Platonism, 171-75, 197ff, 236-40, 315, 347n, 353n. See also Ideas, Platonic and Plato and Platonism

his poetry, 11-17, 20, 23, 25, 27, 35f, 43, 143, 288

public speaker, 9, 20, 55, 79, 103, 106f, 111, 114, 119, 127, 139f, 142, 151n, 158f, 161, 167, 169f, 185, 196, 200, 204, 210f,

214, 217, 231f, 241f, 272f, 281, 292, 295, 301n, 322, 325, 340-43, 371

reader, 6, 51, 66, 71, 77f, 93, 99, 107, 128, 152, 160, 167, 169, 200, 206, 209, 225, 251, 256, 274, 278f, 289, 320, 373, 378

his recreations: bridge, 107, 124f, 129, 143, 148, 150f, 156, 160, 169, 252, 298, 324, 334, 372; detective stories, 157f, 263, 278f, 287, 317, 327, 367, 383; gardening, 154, 155n, 205; golf, 93, 150, 215, 320; music, 13, 23, 25, 27f, 156, 251, 253, 279, 297, 334, 340ff, 368, 371f, 382; skating, 10, 60; smoking, 43, 54, 58, 152, 156, 163, 167, 209, 263, 278, 287, 293, 375; swimming, 11, 45, 149; tennis, 11, 13, 45, 93, 186; walking, 13, 23, 25, 45, 49, 58, 60, 65, 76, 107, 112, 135, 155, 225, 262, 265, 294, 365

his religion, 4, 6f, 15, 17ff, 23, 27, 29, 32, 39ff, 44, 47, 55, 67f, 83n, 92, 115, 118f, 208, 226-29, 242, 249, 251, 259f, 274, 276, 291, 300n, 313-16, 331, 333, 336ff, 347n, 359-64, 382, 384. See also Christianity

his romanticism, 11, 16, 19, 22, 25, 38, 40, 49, 61, 63f, 112, 140, 226, 294, 313f, 366. See also romanticism

scholar, 48, 51, 144, 192n, 209

story-teller, 8, 24, 99, 378

talker, 4, 11, 112, 126, 150, 252, 265, 267, 287, 365ff, 373

teacher, 78, 295; at Smith Academy, 21, 36; at Harvard, 51, 226, 241f; at Bryn Mawr, 51-56, 73; at Princeton, 177ff, 183, 190, 192, 211ff, 218, 226, 236, 240, 274f, 294, 296, 310, 321; at Radcliffe, 241; at University of California, 274, 279, 287f

translator, 50, 64f, 67, 70, 73, 76, 79, 83, 108n, 257

Index

trustee, 294n, 295
various traits of personality, 4,
9f, 14, 20, 27, 54f, 59, 73, 78,
88, 106, 110, 126f, 146, 150n,
179, 187n, 191, 240, 344, 358,
365ff, 373, 382, 383, 385f
More, Mrs. Paul Elmer, 80-83,
92f, 99, 104ff, 110, 113ff, 125,
127f, 132n, 136f, 138, 140f, 143,
145, 149-52, 155ff, 177, 191,
192n, 202, 204, 214ff, 218, 223f,
229ff, 235, 246n, 249, 251f, 254,
263, 321, 338, 387. *See also*
Beck, Henrietta *and* letters from
Henrietta Beck *and* letters from
P. E. More to
"More's Shelburne Essays," 96n
Moriah, Mt., 51, 57
Morley, John, Viscount Morley of
Blackburn, 159n, 184
Morris, William, 111n
Morton, Hugh Harold Franklin
Ogden, 254. *See also* letters
from P. E. More to
Moses, Montrose J., 150
Mount Holyoke College, 185
*Le Mouvement Humaniste aux
États-Unis,* 249n
Mozart, W. A., 28, 297, 341
Mozley, James Bowling, 378n
Mozley, Thomas, 135
Munich, 24f
Munson, Gorham B., 271
Murphy, Harriet, 26
Murray Bay, 292
Musset, Alfred de, 381
Mussey, Henry Raymond, 179
Myers, Edward DeLos, 298, 324,
367, 372. *See also* letters from
P. E. More to
Myers, Gustavus, 88
Mystical Crucifixion, 230, 279
mysticism, 42, 206f, 221, 237, 292,
303f, 309, 311, 314, 341, 369,
385
mythology, 119, 154n, 197ff, 218,
221, 244, 284, 286, 314, 364

Nassau Club, 158
The Nation (London), 180

The Nation (New York), 82, 86n,
94, 98, 103, 107ff, 111, 144-47,
150f, 167, 179, 193, 224, 237n;
More's contributions to, 21n,
77n, 83n, 91n, 101, 112n, 119,
131n, 145n, 148, 151, 155n, 157-
58n, 257. *See also* More, P. E.,
edits *The Nation*
National Institute of Arts and Letters, 106, 162n, 196n, 259n
"Natural Aristocracy," 160n, 184
naturalism, 139n, 181, 242, 276,
281, 283, 326, 371n
nature, human, 88n, 93, 104, 122f,
159, 172, 189, 256n, 326, 337,
355n
Nebraska, University of, 60, 72,
94n
Nemesis, 60f, 95
Neoplatonism, 210n
Nevill, Ralph, 191n
Nevins, Allan, 85n
New England, 3, 77, 146, 153n,
161n, 241, 272n, 293
A New England Group and Others,
193ff, 196n, 277n; cited, 16n,
91n, 112n, 152n, 159n, 179n,
184n
New England Saints, 49n
New Haven, Conn., 111
"A New Intrusion of Pedantry,"
91n
New Jersey, 3f
The New Laokoon, 111
New Lebanon, N.Y., 325
"The New Morality," 160n
The New Republic (New York),
136n, 157, 193, 195f, 277n
New Thought, 72
The New World (Boston and New
York), 59, 61, 95
New York, 72, 81, 86, 88, 94,
104f, 107, 114f, 124-27, 129,
134, 138f, 148, 150n, 161n,
162f, 165ff, 201f, 214, 223, 260,
277n, 292, 326, 342, 367, 372
New York Herald Tribune, 239n
New York Times, 85n, 144, 292n
Newell, William Wells, 59n
Newman, John Henry, 114f, 118f,

Index

Index

Index

Index

Index

Index

Index

Street, Julian, 252
Strunsky, Simeon, 144, 146
Stuart, Duane R., 204, 252
Student Life (Washington University, St. Louis, Mo.), 15, 16-17n, 18, 20n, 36
Studies in Philology (University of North Carolina), 257
The Study of English Literature, 367f, 374
Stuttgart, 25
style, 121
"Suffering and God," 359
supernatural, 219, 283, 308, 317ff
Sussex, 300, 375
Swartz, Roberta, 242, 263
Sweden, 61n, 298f, 378, 383
Swift, Jonathan, 186, 189
Swinburne, A. C., 96
Switzerland, 23f, 378
symbolism, 39, 83n, 116, 119, 197, 227, 246, 286, 307, 308-09n, 378n
Symons, Arthur, 95, 101n, 148
Synesius, 190
"System in Reading," 388

Tabb, J. B., 179
Taft, William Howard, 93n, 132
Tate, Allen, 276f, 282
Taughannock Falls, N.Y., 79f
Taunton, 300
Tavistock, 129
Tawney, R. H., 298
Taylor, A. E., 236, 238, 239n, 301
Taylor, Henry Osborn, 126
Taylor, Hugh S., 297
"The Teaching of the Classics," 91n, 113n
teleology, 215, 227f, 235, 253n, 281f, 288, 291, 303, 309, 311f, 320n, 347-53, 356ff, 363f, 369
Temple, William, 238, 370, 374
Tennyson, Alfred, 1st Baron Tennyson, 107, 111n, 376
Texas University, 136
Thacher, Clara, 26, 28
Thackeray, W. M., 112, 133, 339n
Thayer, William Roscoe, 85f, 96,

119, 120n, 121. *See also* letters from P. E. More to
theism, 17, 227f, 238n, 243, 284f, 322, 341, 344, 345n, 351f, 358, 364, 371n
"Theodore Dreiser, Philosopher," 181n, 211n
theology, 197ff, 220f, 228, 245f, 292, 299, 338, 340n, 358, 360, 364
Theology (London), 322n
Therapeia, Plato's Conception of Philosophy, 232n
Thérèse de Lisieux, St., 378n
"They are all gone into the world of light!" 263
Thomas, Augustus, 205
Thomas, John Martin, 92n
Thomas, Martha Carey, 51, 53, 56, 103
Thomas à Kempis, 287n
Thompson, Alan Reynolds, 285; *see* letters from P. E. More to
Thompson, Francis, 111n, 134
Thomson, James, 36n, 103n, 106
Thoreau, H. D., 66, 83, 95, 101, 106
"Thoreau and German Romanticism," 101
Thorp, Willard, 297n, 384
Three Fates, 131, 279
Three Philosophical Poets: Lucretius, Dante, and Goethe, 83n
"Three Poets of the South," 161n
Tibullus, 112
Tieck, Ludwig, 20
Timaeus, 238n, 309, 339n
The Times Literary Supplement (London), 157, 195, 236n, 250
Tintagel, 300
Tintern, 261
Tolstoy, Count Lev Nikolaevich, 95
Tomlinson, Paul G., 376, 386
tradition, 55, 92, 135, 171, 183, 258n, 272, 283n, 306, 339n, 367, 371n, 384
Traherne, Thomas, 107
Travail, 388

Index

A *Treasury of Irish Poetry*, 87n
Trent, William Peterfield, 126, 132, 134ff, 149, 163n, 388. *See also* letters from P. E. More to
trinitarianism, 67, 210-11n, 245, 307
Trinity Church, Princeton, 254, 296, 336, 383, 387
Trinity College, Cambridge, 265
Trinity College, Durham, N.C., 167
The Triple Thinkers, 279n
Trollope, Anthony, 105, 124, 169, 200, 251, 256, 275
Trowbridge, Augustus, 165n
Turnbull, Percy, Memorial Lectures, 161
Twentieth Century Club, 217
"Two Famous Maxims of Greece," 59n, 61, 95f
Tyrrell, George, 300

ultimate, 359f
Ulysses, 370
Unitarianism, 195, 286f
University Club, 163
University of Toronto Quarterly, 339, 341
The Unpartizan Review (New York), 151, 188, 191n
The Unpopular Review (New York), 151
Upanishads, 49, 70, 314, 319n
Urbana, Ill., 113f, 163
The Use of Poetry and the Use of Criticism, 339n
Usk, 135, 257

Vaka, Paul F., 297. *See also* letters from P. E. More to
Valera, Juan, 78n
"The Value of Academic Degrees," 91n
van Dyke, Henry, 96, 366n
Vanity Fair, 344
Vanneman, Joseph S., 375
Vanuxem Lectures, 170, 177, 224n
Vassar College, 185, 214
Vatican Council, 361

Vaughan, Henry, 135, 200, 257, 263, 362
Vedanta, 41, 44, 49, 69
Venice, 230
Vermont, University of, 143
La Vida es Sueño, 71
La Vie de Jésus, 32
The Villager (Katonah, N.Y.), 180, 187-88n, 190, 198n, 243n
Villard, Oswald Garrison, 114, 144-47, 179
Vinci, Leonardo da, 31, 229
Virgil, 52, 111, 272, 289
Visions and Chimeras, 269n
A Vision of Empire, 160
Viviani, R. R., 166

Wagner, W. R., 297f
Walden, 66
Wale, 133
Walk, C. E., 158n
Walker, Luke, 263f
Walpole, Horace, 101n, 167
Walpole, Sir Robert, 166
Ward, Mrs. Humphrey, 195
Ward, Wilfrid, 183
Ward, William Hayes, 86, 88, 92n, 388
Warner, Charles Dudley, 63
Warren, Austin, 49n. *See also* letters from P. E. More to
Washington, D.C., 292, 301
Washington, George, 85
Washington University, 13, 15, 19ff, 27, 31, 33, 73, 142
The Waste Land, 269
"Wealth and Culture," 89n
Webb, Clement C. J., 355n, 359
Weber, Shirley Howard, 210
Wednesday Club, 103
The Weekly Review (New York), 180, 211n
Wellesley College, 185
Wells, 135
Wells College, 148, 208
Wendell, Barrett, 85f, 96
Went, James, 224, 231, 260
Went, Stanley, 125f, 150f, 224, 260
Das Wesen des Christentums, 322
West, Andrew Fleming, 184, 240

Index